THE ARCHITECTURE OF CHACO CANYON

Frontispiece: Aerial view of central area of Chaco Canyon, looking north. (Photograph by Adriel Heisey, © 1995 by Adriel Heisey)

The Architecture of Chaco Canyon, New Mexico

EDITED BY

STEPHEN H. LEKSON

THE UNIVERSITY OF UTAH PRESS

Salt Lake City

The Defiance House Man colophon is a registered trademark of the
University of Utah Press. It is based upon a four-foot-tall, ancient
Puebloan pictograph (late P III) near Glen Canyon, Utah.

LIBRARY OF CONGRESS CATALOGING-IN-PUBLICATION DATA

The architecture of Chaco Canyon, New Mexico / edited by Stephen H.
Lekson.
        p. cm.
    Based on a conference held Sept. 28–Oct. 3, 2000 at University of
New Mexico, Albuquerque and at Chaco Cannyon.
    ISBN-13: 978-0-87480-846-4 (cloth : alk. paper)
    ISBN-10: 0-87480-846-4 (cloth : alk. paper) 1. Chaco Culture
National Historical Park (N.M.) 2. Chaco culture—New Mexico—Chaco
Canyon (N.M.)—Antiquities. I. Lekson, Stephen H.
    E99.C37A74 2007
    720.89'9740978982—dc 22
                                                           2007005071

11 10 09 08 07   1 2 3 4 5

Cover photo © 1995 by Adriel Heisey

www.uofupress.com

CONTENTS

ILLUSTRATIONS

viii

Illustrations

ix

x

TABLES

THE ARCHITECTURE OF CHACO CANYON

1

Introduction

Stephen H. Lekson

CHACO CANYON WAS THE CENTER of the Pueblo Southwest during the eleventh and early twelfth centuries AD. Today it is a National Historic Park. Its ancient buildings evoke a remarkable range of responses from Pueblo and other Native peoples; from architects and artists and poets; from New Age spiritualists; from archaeologists; and from the eighty thousand visitors who brave seemingly endless bumpy roads each year to see its ruins. Architecture is Chaco's central matter: a dozen "great houses," including such famous sites as Pueblo Bonito and Chetro Ketl. Great houses were the reason Chaco was named a national monument in 1907, promoted to national park status in 1980, certified as a cosmic vortex by the harmonic convergence of 1987, and elevated to the Earth's cultural patrimony that same year when Chaco was listed as a UNESCO World Heritage site.

Chaco is also a key place, or site, or phenomenon for archaeology. Archaeologists have explored its ruins and pondered its prehistory since the mid-nineteenth century (Lister and Lister 1981). (Good recent summaries of Chaco archaeology include Frazier 2005; Mills 2002; Noble 2004; Reed 2004; Stuart 2000; Vivian 1990; and Vivian and Hilpert 2002.) What was Chaco? Opinions vary widely, perhaps wildly. Interpretations range from a valley of peaceful farming villages to the monumental capital of an empire. Great houses themselves have been interpreted as Puebloan towns (Vivian 1990), elite residences (Neitzel 2003), "monumental expressions of Chacoan ritual" (Judge 2004:4), and "occult engine[s] powered by the cycles of the cosmos" (Stein, Ford, and Friedman 2003:59)—among other things. The authors of the

chapters that follow reflect this range of ideas and interpretations.

The largest great houses at Chaco define the architectural tradition and the archaeological phenomenon (Frontispiece, Figure 1.1). The first great houses rose in the late ninth and early tenth centuries (all dates in this book are AD or CE); then followed a hiatus of almost a century, and an explosion of construction between about 1020 and 1125. The period of great house construction is called the Bonito phase (850–1150), named for Pueblo Bonito, the largest of all great houses. There are hundreds of anonymous smaller structures ("small sites") and only a dozen named great houses, but in this volume "Chaco Architecture" refers solely to those few, proud, remarkable buildings. Architecture of small sites has been ably described by McKenna and Truell (1986) and summarized by Vivian (1990) and Mathien (2005).

Formal field research at Pueblo Bonito, sponsored by the American Museum of Natural History, began in 1896. There were a few short hiatuses, but archaeologists from the Smithsonian Institution, the University of New Mexico, and a dozen other institutions have infested Chaco more or less continuously ever since. The last major effort was the National Park Service's Chaco Project (1971–1986), which excavated many small sites and one great house, Pueblo Alto (and tested several others, particularly Una Vida). The history of the Chaco Project is well chronicled by Mathien (2005) and Frazier (2005).

Ten years after the end of the Chaco Project's fieldwork, the National Park Service and the University of Colorado jointly undertook a synthesis of

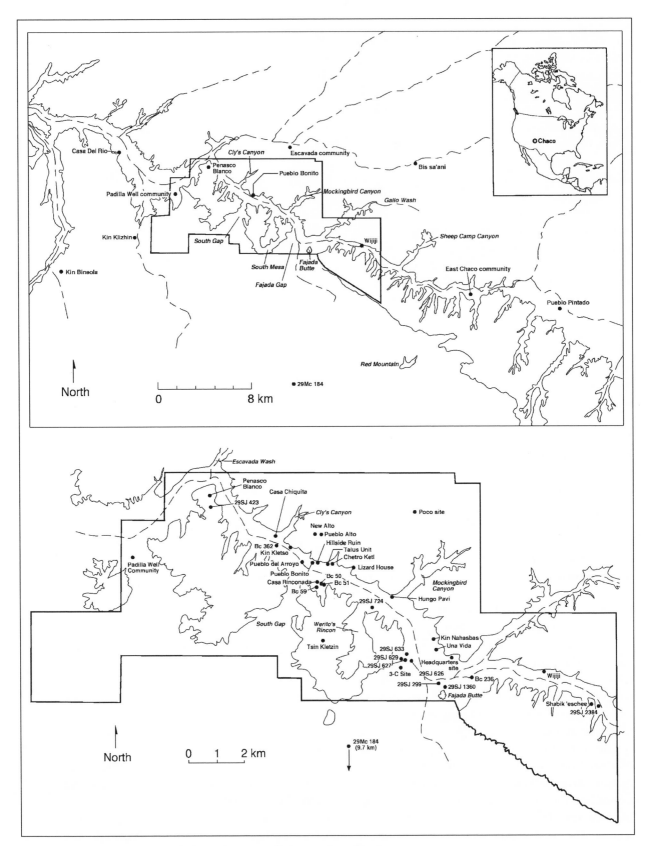

FIGURE 1.1. Location of Chaco Canyon and sites mentioned in the test.

Stephen H. Lekson

its results. That program was called, perhaps prosaically, "the Chaco Synthesis." I directed the Chaco Synthesis from 1997 to 2004. The synthesis was structured as a series of small, thematic conferences (Lekson 2000; Lekson and Burd 2000). It was not the intent of the project to synthesize everything known about Chaco, or even the vast data of the Chaco Project; rather, we hoped to bring a range of views—conventional, current, neoteric—to themes evident in those data. Small, working conferences covered Economy and Ecology, Society and Polity, Organization of Production, and the Chaco World.

One conference focused on great house architecture, and this book is a product of that meeting (Figure 1.2), which took place September 28 through October 3, 2000. On September 28–29 we met at the University of New Mexico in Albuquerque. On September 30 we traveled to Chaco, where we toured Pueblo Bonito and Chetro Ketl and organized our work. The park allowed us to use the "VIP" campground (which, unlike the public campground, has showers!). The morning of October 1, we hiked to Pueblo Alto; in the afternoon and evening we convened in the library of the Visitor's Center. That evening, we offered public presentations for park visitors and staff. October 2 we continued our meetings in the Visitor's Center; late in the afternoon we had a brief "recess" to enjoy the canyon (several participants took a quick tour of Pueblo del Arroyo). That evening, the NPS staff treated us to a traditional Navajo dinner. After a brief meeting on the morning of October 3, we headed to our various homes. Lekson, Tom Windes, and Peter McKenna subsequently wrote a chapter on Chaco Architecture for the volume reporting on all the synthesis efforts (Lekson 2006).

The plan for the Chaco synthesis called for each small, working conference to consist of two or three Chaco "insiders" and two or three "outsiders": respected scholars who would bring fresh insights and new "eyes" to Chaco. "Outsiders" at the architecture conference were Wendy Ashmore (University of California, Riverside), Patricia Fournier (Escuela Nacional de Antropológia e Historia), and Ben Nelson (Arizona State University), and they did an exemplary job of mastering the Chaco data and offering new ideas about the canyon and its architecture. They were greatly outnumbered by "insiders." From the old Chaco Project: Nancy Akins

(Museum of New Mexico), Joan Mathien (National Park Service), Bob Powers (National Park Service), John Schelberg (U.S. Army Corps of Engineers), Thomas Windes (National Park Service). From the Navajo Nation's Chaco Protection Sites Program: Taft Blackhorse, Richard Friedman, and John Stein. From the Solstice Project: Anna Sofaer and Phillip Tuwaletstiwa. Ruth Van Dyke (Colorado College) participated in both University of New Mexico and Chaco sessions; David Stuart joined us at the University of New Mexico. Chaco Culture National Historical Park was represented by Superintendent Butch Wilson, Supervisory Archaeologist Dabney Ford, Chief of Interpretation Russ Bodnar, and other staff when their duties permitted. In addition to their valuable archaeological insights, our NPS colleagues were magnificent hosts. We were joined by several graduate student observers: from the University of New Mexico, Marianne Tyndell and Elizabeth Bagwell; and from the University of Colorado, Gretchen Jordan, Christine Ward, Devin White, Michael Larkin, and Karin Burd (who was also the Chaco Synthesis Research Assistant at the University of Colorado, responsible for logistical arrangements). Our numbers varied, but the pack typically ran between 20 and 25, rather larger than the original target of four to six. There's a lot of interest in Chaco architecture.

We met at Chaco in 2000. The plan was to have this volume published by early 2004, but that didn't happen. (The final "capstone" volume, *The Archaeology of Chaco Canyon*, was published in 2006.) The convoluted story explaining the delay would be of interest only to the authors, editor, and publisher: I commend all concerned for their patience. When all the chapters were in, Catherine Cameron and Danielle Benden at CU were enormously helpful in pulling the book together. The final technical editing was ably undertaken by June-el Piper, with support from the Navajo Nation Chaco Protection Sites Program and the National Park Service, Chaco Culture National Historical Park, for which I tender Piper, John Stein, and Dabney Ford my very sincere thanks! June-el did a tremendous job getting a side-tracked project back on the right line, heading in the desired direction. Her contributions to this volume went far beyond any known definition of "technical editing," and I hope she is pleased with the result. I would also

3

FIGURE 1.2. Chaco Field Conference, September 28 to October 3, 2000. Left foreground: Mike Larkin's back; left rear row, left to right: Ben Nelson, Wendy Ashmore, Karin Burd (behind Larkin), Gretchen Jordan, Chris Ward, Dabney Ford (obscured behind Ward), Nancy Akins (obscured behind Tyndell), Marianne Tyndell, John Schelberg, Devin White, Tom Windes; right rear row, left to right: Ruth Van Dyke, Elizabeth Bagwell, Phillip Tuwaletstiwa; right foreground, left to right: John Stein, Anna Sofaer, Taft Blackhorse, Rich Friedman.

like to acknowledge the excellent work of David Underwood, of the University of Colorado, for drafting figures in my chapters.

The conference and this book focus on form: what Chaco looked like during the era of the great houses (formally, the Bonito phase). This is not to deny or diminish the interest in small sites at Chaco. But what made the canyon famous were the monumental great houses and the landscape to which they were central.

"Monumental" implies costly and laborious, and great houses were both. The technical and organizational aspects of Chacoan architecture are matters of great interest (e.g., as recently documented by Betancourt, Dean, and Hull 1986; Metcalf 2003; Wills 2000; among many others). This book is not about construction, but that subject was addressed in several chapters of the "capstone volume" from the Chaco Synthesis project (Lekson 2006).

This book does not intend to present a comprehensive account of Chaco architecture. I had the youthful temerity to attempt something like that during my tenure with the Chaco Project, in a volume titled *Great Pueblo Architecture of Chaco Canyon* (Lekson 1984). I am now acutely aware of that book's failures and limitations, and how much more could (and should) be said on the subject. Happily, much recent innovative work addresses Chacoan architecture (e.g., Bernardini 1999; Bustard 2003; Crown and Wills 2003; Marshall 2003; Metcalf 2003; Wills 2001; as well as new work reported in this volume). But a comprehensive, single-volume account of Chacoan building is simply not possible. Buildings are very complex artifacts: the National Park Service's "how to" manual for recording standing structures at Mesa Verde exceeds 160 pages (Nordby et al. 2002), and Chaco has many, very large standing structures. If each wall and each feature at every great house in Chaco Canyon were recorded to that degree of detail, the data would choke a supercomputer, and then someone would have to make sense of it all. That's just the buildings: landscapes and cityscapes are even more difficult to describe, analyze, interpret.

So, this book is not intended to be a guide to Chaco architecture. Rather, the chapters in this volume represent a sample of the current approaches to studying great houses and reprise a couple of older but still useful contributions. It begins with Chapter 2, "Great House Forms" (Lekson), a revised version of a chapter in the frequently cited, but long out-of-print, *Great Pueblo Architecture of Chaco Canyon*. Chapter 3, "Gearing Up and Piling On" (Windes), summarizes new research on the earliest stages of the great house tradition. Chapter 4, "Great Kivas in Time, Space, and Society" (Van Dyke), offers a comprehensive reinterpretation of those integral elements of Chacoan architecture (the last comparable review was published forty years ago: Vivian and Reiter 1965). Chapter 5, "Architectural Studies of Pueblo Bonito" (Neitzel), summarizes the very new ideas presented in Neitzel's (2003) edited volume *Pueblo Bonito: Center of the Chacoan World* and offers new ideas about that most important Chacoan building. Chapter 6, "The Changing Face of Chetro Ketl" (Lekson, Windes, and Fournier), complements the chapter on Pueblo Bonito with a consideration of Bonito's near neighbor (argued by its excavator, Edgar Hewett, to be the more handsome of the two), updating the 20-year-old report on that site (Lekson 1983) and offering new ideas on its monumentality and its reflection of Mexican architectural forms. Chapter 7, "Building Social History at Pueblo Bonito" (Ashmore), presents a methodologically innovative and compelling reading of Pueblo Bonito, with insights for the larger matter of Chacoan architecture. Chapter 8, "Revisiting Downtown Chaco" (Stein, Friedman, Blackhorse, and Loose), offers a very unconventional understanding of the heart of Chaco; Stein and his colleagues are remarkable interpreters of Chacoan landscapes, and their work deserves wide attention. Chapter 9, "The Primary Architecture of the Chacoan Culture" (Sofaer), reprints an unfairly undercited, pathbreaking argument that was ahead of its time. Published almost a decade ago (in Morrow and Price 1997), "Primary Architecture" could stand alongside many current, postprocessual, poststructural visions of ancient architectures.

Thematically, the chapters address the architectural origins of great houses (Chapter 3); summarize the two major Chacoan architectural forms (great houses, Chapter 2, and great kivas, Chapter 4); present new ideas about the two largest, archetypical great houses (Pueblo Bonito, Chapter 5; Chetro Ketl, Chapter 6); and offer innovative readings of Chaco Canyon and its architecture (Chapters 7, 8, and 9). These chapters offer a fair sample of archaeological thinking about Chacoan architecture since the end of the Chaco Project. A "fair sample" but, as with all samples, not fully representative. Several widely accepted interpretations are not here: most notably, Gwinn Vivian's cogent arguments for great houses as pueblos (i.e., towns; Vivian 1990, 1990) and Chip Wills's intriguing interpretations of great houses as ritual centers (Crown and Wills 2003; Wills 2000). Quod, I urge you, vide.

Many others study great houses to great effect (e.g., the younger scholars cited above). Chaco architecture is a rich field of study, deep and wide. Great houses and the canyon itself will continue to inspire fresh ideas and interpretations, and younger archaeologists and archaeologists yet-to-come will no doubt overturn current ideas. They will raze our old interpretive edifices, rickety and crumbling, and erect in their place new great houses of cards. To each age its own Chaco.

REFERENCES

Bernardini, Wesley
1999 Reassessing the Scale of Social Action at Pueblo Bonito, Chaco Canyon, New Mexico. *Kiva* 64:447–470.
Betancourt, Julio L., Jeffrey S. Dean, and Herbert M. Hull
1986 Prehistoric Long-Distance Transport of Construction Beams, Chaco Canyon, New Mexico. *American Antiquity* 51:370–375.
Bustard, Wendy
2003 Pueblo Bonito: When a House Is Not a Home. In *Pueblo Bonito: Center of the Chacoan World*, edited by Jill E. Neitzel, pp. 80–93. Smithsonian Books, Washington, DC.
Crown, Patricia L., and W. H. Wills
2003 Modifying Pottery and Kivas at Chaco: Pentimento, Restoration, or Renewal? *American Antiquity* 68:511–532.
Frazier, Kendrick
2005 *People of Chaco: A Canyon and Its Culture*, third ed. W. W. Norton, New York.

Judge, W. James
2004   Chaco's Golden Century. In *In Search of Chaco: New Approaches to an Archaeological Enigma*, edited by David Grant Noble, pp. 1–6. School of American Research Press, Santa Fe.

Lekson, Stephen H.
1984   *Great Pueblo Architecture of Chaco Canyon, New Mexico*. Publications in Archaeology 18B. National Park Service, Albuquerque.

Lekson, Stephen H., ed.
1983   *The Architecture and Dendrochronology of Cheto Ketl, Chaco Canyon, New Mexico*. Reports of the Chaco Center 6. National Park Service, Albuquerque.

2000   Ancient Chaco's New History. *Archaeology Southwest* 14(1): whole issue.

2006   *The Archaeology of Chaco Canyon, New Mexico*. School of American Research Press, Santa Fe.

Lekson, Stephen H., and Karin Burd
2000   A New Synthesis of Chaco Canyon Archaeology. *Anthropology News* 41(9): whole issue.

Lister, Robert H., and Florence C. Lister
1981   *Chaco Canyon: Archaeology and Archaeologists*. University of New Mexico Press, Albuquerque.

Marshall, Anne
2003   The Siting of Pueblo Bonito. In *Pueblo Bonito: Center of the Chacoan World*, edited by Jill E. Neitzel, pp. 10–13. Smithsonian Books, Washington, DC.

Mathien, F. Joan
2005   *Culture and Ecology of Chaco Canyon and the San Juan Basin*. Publications in Archeology 18H. National Park Service, Santa Fe.

McKenna, Peter J., and Marcia L. Truell
1986   *Small Site Architecture of Chaco Canyon, New Mexico*. Publications in Archeology 18D, Chaco Canyon Studies. National Park Service, Santa Fe.

Metcalf, Mary P.
2003   Construction Labor at Pueblo Bonito. In *Pueblo Bonito: Center of the Chacoan World*, edited by Jill E. Neitzel, pp. 72–79. Smithsonian Books, Washington, DC.

Mills, Barbara J.
2002   Recent Research on Chaco: Changing Views on Economy, Ritual, and Society. *Journal of Archaeological Research* 10:65–117.

Morrow, Baker H., and V. B. Price, eds.
1997   *Anasazi Architecture and American Design*. University of New Mexico Press, Albuquerque.

Neitzel, Jill E., ed.
2003   *Pueblo Bonito: Center of the Chacoan World*. Smithsonian Books, Washington, DC.

Noble, David Grant, ed.
2004   *In Search of Chaco: New Approaches to an Archaeological Enigma*. School of American Research Press, Santa Fe.

Nordby, Larry V., Todd Metzger, Cynthia L. Williams, and James D. Mayberry
2002   Standards for Field Data Collection and Documentation. Mesa Verde National Park Archaeological Site Conservation Program Guidelines, Vol 1. National Park Service, Mesa Verde.

Reed, Paul F.
2004   *The Puebloan Society of Chaco Canyon*. Greenwood Press, Westport, CT.

Stein, John R., Dabney Ford, and Richard Friedman
2003   Reconstructing Pueblo Bonito. In *Pueblo Bonito: Center of the Chacoan World*, edited by Jill E. Neitzel, pp. 33–60. Smithsonian Books, Washington, DC.

Stuart, David E.
2000   *Anasazi America*. University of New Mexico Press, Albuquerque.

Vivian, Gordon, and Paul Reiter
1965   *The Great Kivas of Chaco Canyon and Their Relationships*. School of American Research Monograph 22. Santa Fe.

Vivian, R. Gwinn
1990   *The Chacoan Prehistory of the San Juan Basin*. Academic Press, San Diego.

Vivian, R. Gwinn, and Bruce Hilpert
2002   *The Chaco Handbook: An Encyclopedic Guide*. University of Utah Press, Salt Lake City.

Wills, W. H.
2000   Political Leadership in Chaco Canyon, New Mexico, AD 1020–1140. In *Alternative Leadership Strategies in the Prehispanic Southwest*, edited by Barbara J. Mills, pp. 19–44. University of Arizona Press, Tucson.

2001   Ritual and Mound Formation during the Bonito Phase in Chaco Canyon. *American Antiquity* 66:433–451.

6

2

Great House Form

Stephen H. Lekson

THIS CHAPTER PRESENTS a revised version of an essay on "form" in Great Pueblo Architecture (Lekson 1984a: Chapter 3) as well as new material summarizing facts about great house form (Figure 2.1). The basic data on form, room sizes, ground plans, etc., have not changed much since 1984 (Figures 2.2 and 2.3), and this summary information still seems useful, if somewhat drier in presentation than if it were written today. Bare facts, numbers, statistics, graphs, and ground plans do not tell the story of Chacoan architecture. But they are the necessary foundation for more spirited readings of that remarkable tradition, which you will find in the chapters that follow.

Chacoan building is often described as "planned," which could be taken to mean that non-Chacoan Anasazi building traditions were not planned. Compared with most other Anasazi building, the design units of Chacoan building are much larger and the scale of construction more massive. It seems intuitively obvious that more thought, more preparation, more administrative coordination—in short, more planning—were required to build Pueblo Bonito than to construct the ubiquitous five-room, rubble masonry house (Figure 2.4). Although we may all agree that there must have been qualitative as well as quantitative differences in the planning processes at large and small sites, there is very real and in some respects fairly important disagreement as to how to conceptualize this difference. As a result, we have odd terms like "pre-planning" to describe Chacoan building. The five-room house was surely also the product of planning, for to suggest otherwise is to imply that the Anasazi built by reflex or instinct (Lekson 1981).

It is useful to consider architectural form as the product of three roles: designer, builder, and user. The designer determines the form with a plan, verbal or graphic. The builder translates this plan into a physical structure; the user has to live with the results. In our society, it is common for these three roles to be filled by three individuals: an architect, a contractor, and a client; in simpler societies, these roles are often synonymous. If the three roles are united, the fit of form and function over time should be close. If they are separate, the fit will be less close.

In the five-room small house, the designer, the builder, and the user could easily have been the same person. Although other residents may have influenced the design of the structure, for most small-site construction the three roles of designer, builder, and user were at least confined to the household, if not to one individual.

For the larger structures, this cannot have been the case. Typically, units of construction consisted of 20 or more rooms. Since complete sets of foundations were laid out and wall widths (and thus, the number of stories) were fixed prior to construction, we can be sure that the form of the structure did not somehow "evolve" during building. Someone had a plan rather firmly in mind before the first stone was laid. Since the scale of construction obviously exceeds the needs of a single household, that person assumed the role of designer for a group of users. It is in this way that the planning of Chacoan building differs most significantly from that at small sites.

FIGURE 2.1. Chetro Ketl, Kiva G complex, looking south. (Photograph by S. H. Lekson)

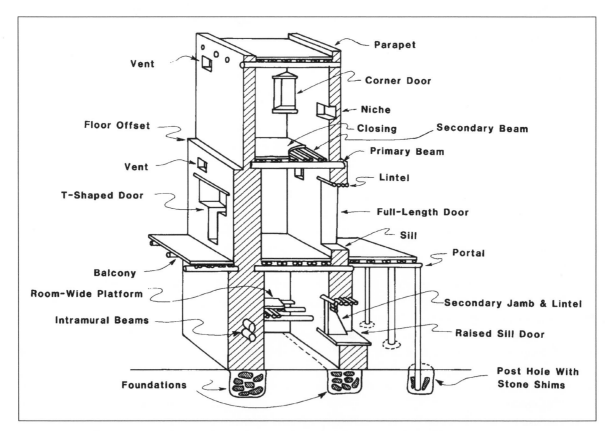

FIGURE 2.2. Schematic cross-section of great house construction features. (From Lekson 1984a:16, Figure 2.3)

Stephen H. Lekson

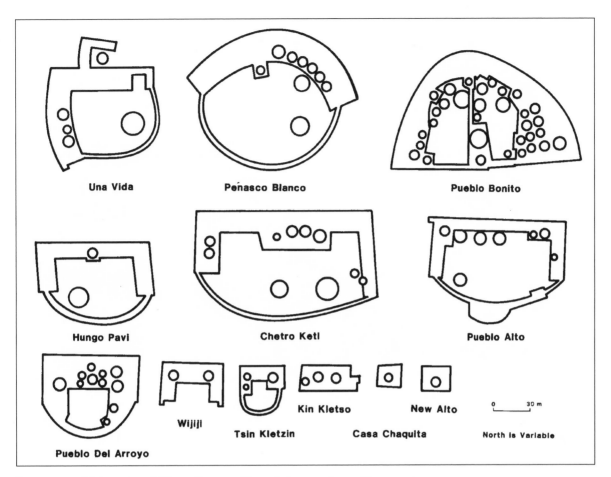

FIGURE 2.3. Major ruins of Chaco Canyon. (From Lekson 1984a:3, Figure 1.2)

The larger the building, the more the differentiation between the roles of designer and builder and user.

Add the element of permanence. At a small site, with a relatively plastic and mutable building technology, any change in perceived needs could be met almost immediately by modification of form. Need a larger room? Knock out a wall and rebuild, larger. The result is the repeated rebuilding and alterations that are a hallmark of small sites, particularly their pitstructures. In the massive Chacoan buildings, any but the most minor modification was a formidable task. Since several of these buildings were in use for perhaps 250 years, the original designs were imposed on several generations of users. A notable exception to this pattern was the frequent modification and rebuilding of "kivas" (Crown and Wills 2003).

To discuss form and design in Chacoan buildings, it is useful to recognize a series of forms:

Room: four walls and a roof
Suite/Module: patterned, interconnected rooms
Roomblock: a group of suites or rooms, built as a unit
Building: a freestanding structure composed of one
    or more conjoined roomblocks
Settlement: the community of buildings

ROOMS

A room is a small, roofed area in a building, separated from other areas by walls or partitions. A room is an area enclosed by walls and a roof. This definition includes (typically, but not invariably) four walls in aboveground rooms and circular walls for "kivas." In most Chacoan buildings, walls and evidence of roofing are usually quite apparent. In small sites and less-well-preserved Anasazi buildings, walls are sometimes difficult to define, and a roof is frequently a matter for demonstration rather than observation.

9

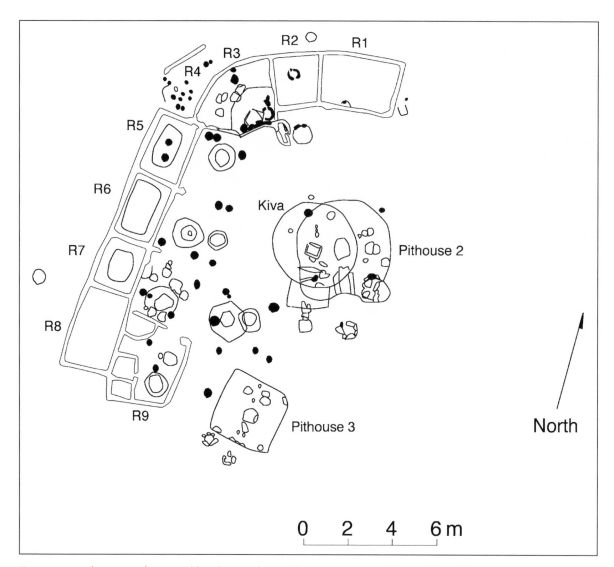

FIGURE 2.4. Plan view of unit pueblos (kiva and roomblock complex), 29SJ629. (After Windes 1993: Figure 1.3)

Even in Chacoan buildings, however, the subject of "rooms" is less simple than it might seem. Balconies and terraces are included in this section, even though they are not rooms by the above definition. Another point of possible confusion is use of the term "round room" for structures traditionally referred to as "kivas." I have abandoned the use of the term "kiva" except for highly specialized forms (tower kivas, great kivas)—where new terminology would be tedious (e.g., "great round room")—and in the case of specific named or numbered units, for example, Kiva G or the Court Kiva, both at Chetro Ketl. The argument for this usage is given below, in the section on round rooms.

Rectangular Rooms

Most rooms in Chaco buildings are aboveground and have four corners. Not all of these rooms are truly rectangular; for example, in buildings with curved plans, long walls in many rooms may be parallel arcs. In other cases, where construction events met at odd angles, corners are more or less than 90°. The three aspects of rectangular rooms—size, proportion, and function—will be discussed in this section.

ROOM SIZE
The mean size of 1,133 rooms at Chacoan buildings is 11.97 m² (s.d. = 8.03). This statistic masks a great deal of temporal variation and encompasses

Stephen H. Lekson

several distinct size classes. Rooms vary in size with their distance from the plaza; thus room size will be discussed in terms of front, intermediate, and rear rows of ground floor rooms in single construction programs. Ground floor lengths and widths, measurable when upper stories have vanished, were usually repeated in upper stories; that is, upper story rooms were not appreciably different in size and shape from those below. Floor offsets/setbacks cause room size to increase slightly from lower to upper floors, but this increase is slight and probably insignificant.

Using ground floor data, Figure 2.5 shows changes through time in the average floor areas of rear, intermediate, and front row rooms. The area of rear row rooms is much less variable than that of front row rooms. In fact, the former varies little from an average of about 12 m² through the entire two centuries of Chacoan building. Intermediate rows of rooms seem to repeat either front or rear row room areas up to about 1075; after 1075 the intermediate row rooms seem nearer in size to the rear than to the front rooms. Front row room areas vary greatly, from 45 m² in the early 900s to only 10 m² in the early 1100s. There is a strong suggestion of a steady decrease in front row room

size through time, particularly when the data noted as questionable or unique on Figure 2.5 are eliminated. It is also possible that beginning about 1060 there are two size classes of front row rooms: first, those tending toward floor areas identical to intermediate and rear row rooms, and second, those continuing the earlier distinction in size between front and rear rows.

Room area reflects only length and width; the third dimension of room size is height, the distance from floor to ceiling. The average room height is about 2.40 m (s.d. = 0.53, $N = 804$, with 90% of the sample from Pueblo Bonito and Pueblo del Arroyo), but heights up to 4.28 m are known (at Pueblo Alto) and heights of 3.0 m are common.

Variation in room height was examined along three dimensions: first, with respect to distance from the plaza (and thus, perhaps, reflecting room function); second, between stories (perhaps responding to structural requirements); and third, through time. There is a suggestion of slightly lower room height in rear row rooms in some construction programs at Pueblo Bonito relative to front row rooms; however, this difference is not statistically significant. There is no evidence elsewhere (Chetro Ketl, Pueblo del Arroyo, Pueblo

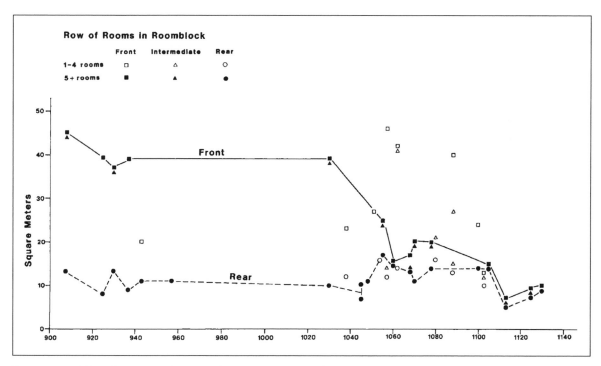

FIGURE 2.5. Mean floor area of rectangular rooms. (From Lekson 1984a:41, Figure 3.1)

Alto, Kin Kletso) of significant variation from front to rear rooms in individual construction programs. The variation in room height does not seem to correspond to room function, insofar as room function is reflected by distance from the plaza.

Average room heights by story at eight buildings are given in Table 2.1. Room height decreases from the second to the fourth story, but first-story heights are less than those of the second. It is important to note that the range and particularly the maximum heights of first-story rooms are larger than those of any upper story. Lower average first-story heights may be the result of multiple, superimposed ground floors.

Analysis of room heights through time is limited to samples from Pueblo Bonito and Pueblo del Arroyo. Mean values for room heights from a series of construction events at Pueblo Bonito and Pueblo del Arroyo, which approximate a temporal sequence, are given in Table 2.2. This table shows no clear trends through time, although the earliest figures are generally lower than later ones given for heights of each story. Since most of the early rooms are one story, the ground floor bias may affect these figures.

Room height does not appear to vary with distance from the plaza, nor does it appear to vary through time. Height does seem to vary in the upper stories, decreasing from the second (and perhaps the first) story up.

PROPORTIONS

In Chacoan building the long axis (length) of a room was almost always parallel to the plaza-facing wall of the roomblock. An index of proportion was calculated by dividing the width by the length. An index of 1.0 means the width equals the length, 0.50 means the width is one-half the length, etc. The mean index is 0.53 (s.d. = 0.25, N = 1,133). Table 2.3 shows this index for a series of selected plaza-to-rear-room suites. While rear rooms average about 0.50, with little variation, front rooms range from indexes of 0.30 to 0.40 in early building to almost 1.00 in later building. There is clearly a temporal trend toward squareness in front rooms, although the small front row rooms at early Pueblo Bonito complicate this picture since they too are almost square. One or two long, narrow rooms (with very low indexes of proportion) are found at almost every excavated Chacoan site. These are discussed below as a separate class of rooms.

ROOM TYPES

The function of a room refers to those activities that the room was designed to house. Defining functions of rooms in prehistoric buildings is an immensely difficult task. In Chacoan building the problem is complicated by the long life of the structures. Built over a period of two centuries, and occupied for at least a century after construction,

TABLE 2.1. Mean Room Height by Story at Eight Chaco Canyon Buildings

STORY	MEAN HEIGHT (m)	S.D.	N
1	2.33	0.67	345
2	2.53	0.67	277
3	2.33	0.21	130
4	2.17	0.26	23

Source: Lekson 1984:43, Table 3.1

TABLE 2.2. Mean Room Height (m) by Story and Temporal Sequence

STORY	PUEBLO BONITO I	PUEBLO BONITO II	LATE PUEBLO BONITO	PUEBLO DEL ARROYO
1	2.18	2.68	2.61	2.16
2	2.25	2.38	2.86	2.48
3	2.23	2.86	2.43	2.43

Source: Lekson 1984:43, Table 3.2

Stephen H. Lekson

TABLE 2.3. Index of Proportion (Width / Length) for Selected Suites

	REAR	INTERMEDIATE		FRONT
Pueblo Bonito I (920–935)	0.53	0.38		0.91
Pueblo Alto IA, IB (1020–1040)	0.29	0.30		0.31
Pueblo Alto III (1040–1060)	0.50	0.47		0.44
Pueblo Bonito IIIA (1050–1060)	0.56	—		0.51
Pueblo Bonito IVA (1060–1075)	0.45	0.48	0.52	0.75
Pueblo del Arroyo I (1065–1075)	0.66	0.77		0.78
Pueblo Bonito VIA (1075–1080)	0.50	0.69	0.75	0.87
Pueblo del Arroyo IIA (1095–1105)	0.60	0.57	0.68	0.96

For all suites, mean = 0.76, s.d. = 0.14, N = 52.
Source: Lekson 1984:43, Table 3.3

the original (designed) functions of the rooms may be entirely obscured by architectural modification required for later functions.

Archaeological approaches to room function usually involve the congruence of several lines of evidence, including artifacts, plant and animal remains, and the manner in which these were deposited in the rooms. This wide variety of information cannot be considered here. In the absence of these data, my discussion of rectangular room functions is limited to rather obvious classes of rooms with conspicuous fixed features: mealing bins, firepits, bins, etc.; rooms with combinations of these features; and rooms with no fixed features.

Featureless rooms (storage rooms). A room with no fixed features or furniture is often called a storage room—that is, a room designed for housing goods rather than activities. Featureless space in a room does not, of course, automatically indicate absence of activities in that space, but the equation of featureless space with storage is probably correct when applied to rooms at least one room removed from exterior access (i.e., interior rooms). With limited artificial lighting, interior rooms would probably not have been useful for many domestic activities. Interior rooms were no doubt used for sleeping, staying warm in the winter, and retreats (from domestic routines or for religious seclusion, or both); nonetheless, they probably generally functioned as storage facilities.

Storage is the shelter of materials over time, a definition that may include many potentially distinct functions. Domestic storage of food, either short- or long-term, is a function different from the storage

of religious paraphernalia, of craft materials/goods, or of building materials: all these can be documented in Chacoan storage rooms (e.g., at Pueblo Bonito: Judd 1959, 1964; see also Neitzel 2002). It is likely that a given room might be used for different storage functions at various times, yet the only positive architectural evidence for a storage function of any kind might be room-wide platforms (see "Rooms with room-wide platforms").

Rear rooms in Chacoan buildings have usually been considered storage rooms. In buildings of the tenth and early eleventh centuries, paired small rear rooms probably continued the formal storage function of earlier "tub" rooms of ninth-century small sites (Truell 1983). These rooms connect directly to the large rooms in front of them. This pattern of front-to-back connection continues even after the paired rear rooms give way to single or even irregularly spaced rear rooms in the middle and later 1000s. In the early 1000s, some rear rooms are added to existing structures (e.g., at Chetro Ketl and Pueblo Bonito) and designed to connect laterally, but not frontally—that is, rear rooms open into other rear rooms, not into the front row. These rows of rear rooms continue the cross-wall spacing of the older rear rooms they adjoin, and are almost identical in size.

Are they similar in function to the earlier rear rooms? Size and placement suggest that they are; however, at Pueblo Bonito and Chetro Ketl, the evidence informing our interpretation goes beyond size and location. At Pueblo Bonito, several (probably most) of the added rear rooms in the north-central part of the arc had single-pole racks or room-wide platform supports. The absence of this feature in the earlier rear rooms suggests different functions.

At Chetro Ketl, at least two of the added rear rooms have room-wide platforms, as do at least two in the original rear row. More indicative of other functions is the presence of an unusual feature in the Chetro Ketl row. Each of the rooms in the added row at Chetro Ketl has a very large niche centrally located in the south wall; these niches are unique to this row of rooms. Nothing comparable is known from the earlier rear row rooms at Chetro Ketl, or any other Chacoan building. Again, the presence of a unique feature suggests different functions.

Connections differ radically between the old and new rear rows. If domestic activities were oriented toward the plaza (centered in large, front row, rectangular rooms), patterns of access suggest that the old rear rooms were intended for shorter-term storage (more frequent introduction or extraction) and the newer rear rooms for longer-term storage (less frequent introduction or extraction). While the repetition of older cross-wall patterns in the newer rear rooms suggests an extension of the existing suite associations into this row, the later connection of those rooms also suggests a community-wide (supra-suite) function of the newer rooms. Room-wide platforms and niches suggest differing or added functions in newer rear rooms. Windes (1987:362–369) presents a strong case for road associations of long, internally connected rows of storage rooms on the exterior of many great houses. That is, these rear row additions to great houses played a role in the operation of roads which linked these sites.

These additions of multistoried rows of storage rooms underscores a prominent Chacoan design characteristic from the 1020s on—the addition of massed interior rooms with decreasing proportions of rooms adjacent to the exterior. The ratio of interior or rear row "storage" rooms to exterior, adjacent rooms in the 1020s–1050s building approaches 1:1, whereas from 1075 to 1105 that ratio is closer to 4:1.

After 1105, the ratio of rear and interior rooms to exterior adjacent rooms was about 2:1, a decrease from the 1075–1105 ratio. It is unlikely that the rooms with exterior access after 1105

were functionally similar to their counterparts in earlier periods—most importantly, the later rooms were considerably smaller (see the discussion of rectangular room size above).

The general pattern from 1075 on is one of greatly increased proportions of interior room space, presumably for storage. Unfortunately, we have almost no knowledge of what was stored in this added space. Pepper (1920) and Judd (1954) found perhaps half a dozen rooms at Pueblo Bonito that contained bulk materials, but probably 90% of the excavated "storage" rooms at Chaco were empty (see also Neitzel 2003). A few interior and rear rooms are equipped with room-wide platforms, but most are simply large, empty rooms. The generalized space created suggests that the goods stored varied from room to room and perhaps through time within individual rooms.

Long, narrow, featureless rooms. A number of rooms have very low indexes of proportion. Many are the result of partitioning a large square room for construction of a round room within it, and as such belong to the broad category of "incidental" rooms (discussed below). However, some long, narrow rooms were clearly designed as such. These include two rear row rooms (Pueblo del Arroyo Room 9-10-11 and Chetro Ketl Room 1-4); one intermediate row room (Pueblo Alto Room 105); and two plaza-facing rooms (Chetro Ketl Room 81-105-76-32 and Pueblo Alto Room 131-135-141-160). The two rear rooms were both long on the ground floor but were subdivided on the upper story, with cross-walls supported on beams. The ground floors of both were originally featureless; both apparently had direct access to the exterior. The only clue to the function of these rooms is from Room 1-4 at Chetro Ketl, which contained three or more extremely large timbers.

Timber storage could hardly have been the function of Room 105 at Pueblo Alto, an intermediate row room with no direct access to the exterior except through the roof. The room is unexcavated, and little more can be said about it.

The two remaining long, narrow rooms (the "gallery" or Room 131-135-141-143-160 at Pueblo Alto and the "colonnade" or Room 81-105-176-32 at Chetro Ketl) are both plaza-facing units but of greatly different age and detail. The Pueblo Alto room, which consists of an extremely narrow, long passage along the front of a row of very large rooms, dates to 1020–1040. The Chetro Ketl colonnade fronts a complex of elevated round rooms and a tower kiva, and postdates 1100. The gallery at Pueblo Alto had only a few doors, aligned with the doors of the larger rooms behind it, whereas the colonnade at Chetro Ketl consisted of a series of square piers or columns. The columns did not rise from the floor or plaza level; rather, they were set on a low wall. The colonnade did not exactly facilitate traffic; a step over the base wall was required for movement from the plaza to the area behind the columns.

Rooms with room-wide platforms. In many rooms, several small beams (10–15 cm diameter) ran across the short axis of the room about 1.40 m (s.d. = 0.27, N = 19) above the floor, midway between floor and ceiling. The line of beams extended, on average, about 1.40 m (s.d. = 1.39, N = 20) from the side wall toward the center of the room (Figure 2.6). Smaller, secondary beams were laid at right angles to the larger beams; over these were all the closing material, clay, etc., normally found in a regular roof or ceiling. Some rooms had

these constructions in both ends, extending from the side walls into the center of the rooms and narrowing the standing area to a walkway from the front to the rear door (e.g., Room 62, Pueblo Bonito; Room 92, Chetro Ketl; Room 145, Pueblo Alto).

Judd identified these features as shelves (1954:45, 1964:29); Di Peso (1974:238) suggested that they were sleeping platforms. Depending on which of these interpretations you wish to believe, rooms with platforms would have had either storage (shelves) or domestic (sleeping) functions. The only direct evidence came from Room 249 at Pueblo Bonito, where Judd (1964:107) found the remains of five macaws that had apparently occupied a platform in one end of the room. It would be wrong, of course, to infer that all platforms were parrot perches.

Room-wide platforms are not particularly common (fewer than 25 rooms in the canyon are known to have had them, although many more were undoubtedly present in both the unexcavated and excavated buildings), but their interpretation is fairly important. If they were in fact used for

FIGURE 2.6. Primary beams of a room-wide platform, Room 48, Chetro Ketl. (Reiter No. 1115.599, Chaco Culture National Historical Park, Chaco Archive No. 2176H; from Lekson 1984a:47, Figure 3.3)

storage, "such shelves would measurably increase the storage capacity of a given room" (Judd 1964:29), particularly for items that could not be stacked above about 1 m. In rooms with two very deep shelves, the storage area (not volume) of a room would be almost doubled. If, on the other hand, the platforms are for sleeping (and it must be noted that the reasons for this interpretation were never made clear by Di Peso), the design of both fixed furniture and specific rooms for this function is unique in the Anasazi record. Whatever their function, room-wide platforms seem to be a peculiarly Chacoan item in the Anasazi area.

Room-wide platforms are particularly evident at the Chacoan outlier at Aztec (Morris 1928). In the east and north wings at Aztec, platforms are found in several plaza-facing rooms (e.g., Rooms 50, 51). Room 66 at Aztec, a plaza-facing room in a five-room suite, had a pair of room-wide platforms and no other features; passing through Room 66, one reached two rooms with large firepits and mealing bins—features usually associated with domestic rooms; behind these were two more rooms totally devoid of furniture, both of which would usually be interpreted as storage rooms. Ceramics date these features to the Chacoan occupation of Aztec, rather than the Mesa Verde reoccupation. The room-wide platforms in Room 66, a plaza-facing room, seem oddly positioned for storage.

At Chaco, most platforms are in rear rooms. Room-wide platforms first appear at Chaco about 1040 in the rear rooms of three- or four-room-deep room suites (at Chetro Ketl). In later construction (at Chetro Ketl, Pueblo Bonito, and Peñasco Blanco, about 1050–1085), room-wide platforms are found mainly (but not exclusively) in rear row rooms. In the canyon, at least, room-wide platforms do not occur in post-1085 building.

The most notable exception to the rear row rule is a block at Pueblo Bonito of uniformly sized rooms, two rows deep and six rooms wide (built about 1050–1060 but subsequently heavily modified). In this roomblock, room-wide platforms occur in at least three (and probably more) rooms of both the front and rear rows. A few platforms in plaza-facing rooms were also found in rooms at Pueblo Bonito and Pueblo Alto.

There is one important similarity between the Aztec plaza-facing and Chaco Canyon rear-row room-wide platforms: in both cases, the platforms were in rooms that originally had direct exterior access. Even in the rear row, platforms were usually in upper story rooms. More than three-quarters of the room-wide platforms at Chaco were in rooms with direct access to the exterior, either through a door or through the roof.

It would be difficult to use exterior access to argue for exclusivity in either sleeping or storage functions, although an argument might be made against long-term storage. Exterior access at least implies frequent introduction and retrieval of whatever had been left on the platform (sleepers or goods). Evidence is either absent or ambiguous. The function of room-wide platforms is moot, but important.

Rooms with firepits. Firepits, presumably used for cooking, heating, and lighting, are conventionally cited as evidence of domestic activities. Firepits have often been equated with a minimal domestic unit or family, a relationship which may overlook the considerable variability in these features (they range from relatively small, shallow, hemispherical, unlined pits to very large, cylindrical or rectangular, deep, masonry-lined pits) and in their architectural contexts (firepits in large vs. small rectangular rooms; firepits in round rooms). However, since firepits have been considered indicative of a very broad class of domestic functions in the past, and since a detailed analysis of firepit form is beyond this study, all rectangular rooms with one or more firepits of any form or size are considered to be of a single class.

About 20% of the ground-floor rooms at Pueblo del Arroyo and Pueblo Bonito had firepits, but less than 10% of the ground floor rooms at Kin Kletso and the excavated portion of Chetro Ketl were so equipped. In many of these rooms, firepits were not the only floor features; for example, all but one of the half-dozen storage bins reported from Pueblo Bonito are located in rooms with firepits, and four of eight rooms with mealing bins (described below) also had a firepit. In several cases, rooms had more than one firepit or heating pit.

Ground floor firepits were located in rooms with direct access to the exterior—specifically, in plaza-facing rooms. At Pueblo Bonito, rooms with firepits are found mainly in two areas: first, in an almost continuous arc of plaza-facing (or originally

16

plaza-facing) rooms around the front of the older sections of the building; and second, in the rooms immediately surrounding Kiva B. Of the dozen firepits not included in these two areas, about half were located in exterior spaces (plazas, terraces, etc.); several others were in the lines of rooms enclosing and subdividing the plaza. Only three firepits were found in interior rooms.

Judd and many others have suggested that firepits were also located in upper story rooms with direct access to the exterior. Some second-story floors survived intact, and a few of these (two at Pueblo Bonito, two at Pueblo del Arroyo, and three at Aztec) had firepits (Judd 1959:9, 51, 1964:93; Morris 1928:361, 367). The vast majority of upper story floors are gone. This is cause for archaeological grief, since the presence or absence of firepits in upper story rooms would drastically affect the number of inferred domestic units and, hence, the population estimates for each building (Judd 1964:93; Morris 1928:361, 367; Windes 1984). Because of the importance of this problem, I will digress briefly and discuss various inconclusive attempts to determine if, in fact, upper story rooms had firepits.

It is not impossible to detect fragmented firepits in the debris of a fallen upper story; however, very few are reported from Chacoan sites. We might assume that earlier excavators, treating room fill as overburden, simply failed to observe the evidence. Some earlier workers, clearly aware of the possibility of upper story firepits, carefully monitored room fill for fragmentary features (Reiter 1933; Vivian and Mathews 1965). Subsequent, more tightly controlled work at multistoried Chacoan buildings has failed to define upper story firepits (Cynthia Irwin-Williams, personal communication 1978). There remain justifiable doubts concerning their recognition by earlier workers, and their absence in the published literature is probably not sufficient evidence to conclude that upper story firepits were not present.

A second line of evidence involves extrapolating from ground floor rooms with firepits to upper story rooms. Room size is measurable in both ground floor and upper story rooms. As noted above, intermediate and rear row rooms of all stories are, on the average, smaller than front row rooms, where most known firepits are located. It

might be reasonable to conclude that features in the larger front row rooms were not repeated in the smaller rooms to the rear, regardless of story. However, not all front row rooms have firepits, and some of those that do (at Pueblo Bonito and elsewhere) are rather unusual in size and shape. The mean size for all ground floor rooms with firepits at Pueblo Bonito is 11.98 m² (s.d. = 8.05, N = 72), which is very close to the mean size for rear row rooms of all periods at Chaco (see Figure 2.5). This suggests, of course, that there is no reason on the basis of size alone to exclude any upper story rooms from a list of those potentially having firepits.

Many of the rooms with firepits at Pueblo Bonito are "incidental" rooms (i.e., rooms built into the corners of the square enclosures around the elevated round rooms described below) and do not represent designed front row rooms. If "incidental" rooms are excluded, the average size of a room with a firepit at Pueblo Bonito increases to almost 17.66 m² (s.d. = 8.73, N = 22), a figure in general agreement with mean front-row room area from 1070 or 1075 on. Even with the elimination of "incidental" rooms with firepits, however, the picture is still unclear. Arguments could be made from the 17.66 m² figure both to support and to deny the presence of upper story intermediate and rear row firepits, since after 1070 rooms of all rows are very similar in floor area.

A third approach involves wall niches, which remain visible in standing walls regardless of floor preservation. Niches, like firepits, are clustered in plaza-facing ground story rooms at Pueblo Bonito. Twenty-nine plaza-facing rooms with niches lack firepits; 43 rooms with firepits lack niches. In 15 rooms they co-occur. Fifteen is about twice the number of rooms that would be expected to have both features if firepits and niches were randomly distributed with respect to each other in plaza-facing rooms. If the relationship observed in ground floor rooms holds for upper story rooms, there should be about four rooms with firepits for every three rooms with niches. At Pueblo Bonito, there are six upper story rooms with niches and, by extension, eight upper story rooms with firepits.

In summary, the evidence from published reports and that of the association of firepits with niches both suggest few upper story firepits, while the evidence of room size is ambiguous at best. I believe that some upper story rooms—particularly second story rooms opening onto plaza-facing terraces—might have had firepits, but that the majority of upper story rooms did not.

Rooms with mealing bins. Only eight rooms with mealing bins are known from excavations at Chaco (Pueblo del Arroyo, Rooms 41 and 55; Pueblo Bonito, Rooms 90, 222, and 291; Chetro Ketl, Room 35; Pueblo Alto, Rooms 103 and 110). The usual complement of bins in these rooms ranged from three to six, with Pueblo Bonito Room 90 being an exception with ten bins. Four of these rooms also had one or more fire or heating pits; four had none. One room, Room 35 at Chetro Ketl, may have had a room-wide platform at one end of the room, opposite four mealing bins. All but one of these rooms had evidence of direct access to the exterior, either through the wall or the roof, a fact which suggests that more mealing bins might have been located in upper story rooms of the middle and rear tiers of multistoried buildings. All these rooms probably postdate 1050, and several (at Chetro Ketl, Pueblo del Arroyo, and Pueblo Bonito) date as late as the 1100s.

Rooms with firepits, ventilators, and deflectors. These rooms are a subset of rectangular rooms with firepits, but some authors (notably Judd 1964) consider them entirely distinct, and probably ceremonial. Several rooms in the group are exceptional (e.g., Rooms 350 and 351 at Pueblo Bonito—a pair of odd, rectangular pitstructures with corner ventilator shafts). In general, ventilators in other rooms are obviously later modifications of partially buried earlier rooms, enabling their continued use (e.g., Rooms 71, 315, 316, and 328 at Pueblo Bonito). The rooms are remnants of earlier building, which continued in use even though the plaza level rose well above the original roof level. At least two other rooms at Pueblo Bonito (Rooms 3a and 309), three rooms at Una Vida (Rooms 23, 60, 63), and perhaps two at Chetro Ketl (Rooms 38, 87) were equipped with less easily explicable ventilators and occasionally with deflectors in front of their firepits. Are these rooms ceremonial chambers? This is possible, but I do not think it is a necessary explanation for the construction in later aboveground rooms of what, in earlier pithouses, was part of the essential furniture of domestic structures.

For example, Judd records Room 309 at Pueblo Bonito as an aboveground ceremonial chamber, with firepit, deflector, and ventilator, but a map of its features (Judd 1964: Figure 12) shows the floor littered with pits and bins, the very features most archaeologists believe are evidence of domestic use. Other rooms at Chetro Ketl and Una Vida also have the general appearance of domestic rooms with ventilators, perhaps without the plethora of bins and pits that characterized Room 309. If we ignore the ceremonial connotations of the ventilator and consider it as a functional construction, these rooms seem similar to other rooms with firepits, although the former have a more complex pattern of air flow. The system of ventilation serves much the same purpose in pithouse, kiva, or rectangular room. Rooms with firepits, ventilators, and deflectors fall in the same size range and are located in the same situations as other rectangular rooms with firepits only. In the absence of compelling evidence to the contrary, I consider these rooms architecturally the same as other rectangular rooms with firepits.

Round Rooms (Figure 2.7)

Round rooms at Chaco are usually called "kivas"—a term that refers to round or rectangular rooms used by male ceremonial associations in the modern pueblos. Archaeologists divide Chacoan kivas into three groups: great kivas, tower kivas, and small "clan kivas" (with some subdivision of this last, to be discussed below). My disagreement is with the usage of the designation "clan kivas," the term most often used to identify round rooms. To avoid tedious terminology, "clan kivas" will be referred to hereafter as "kivas." The following discussion does not apply to great kivas or tower kivas, which will be considered separately later in this section.

Kivas at Pueblo Bonito and at modern pueblos are seen as originating in form in the earliest Anasazi pithouses. It is widely assumed that pithouses became kivas. A long-standing question in Southwestern archaeology is, "When did pithouses become kivas?" The usual answer is sometime in the 700s or 800s. "There is an extremely well-defined developmental history in kiva architecture, with strong continuity in physical similarity from the earliest examples dated between AD 700 and

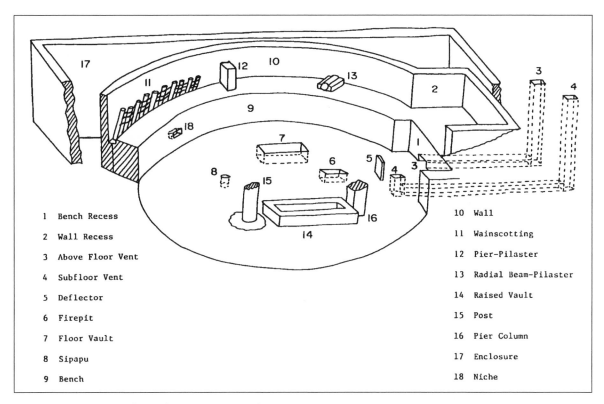

FIGURE 2.7. Features of round rooms. (From Lekson 1984a:53, Figure 3.4)

900 to those of the modern period" (Crown and Wills 2003:518).

A great many pages have been filled with discussions of the evolution or development of the Anasazi kiva (e.g., Adler 1993; Smith 1952), usually in terms of architectural form and detail, or analysis of activities taking place within the structure (e.g., Cater and Chenault 1988; Gillespie 1974). A third approach, also with a respectable history (e.g., Steward 1937; Lipe 1989), focuses less on architectural details and activities and more on the architectural context of the room. Ratios of households (or surrogate indices, such as rooms) to kivas are assumed to reflect the integrative function of kivas.

Modern kivas are used by male ceremonial associations, with members from numerous households and clans. Cross-kinship membership in ceremonial associations helps to integrate a village. Socially, that is one clear "function" of modern kivas, and for my purposes, a defining property. Pithouses are presumed to represent a single household; that is, a pithouse houses one household. Kivas, at modern New Mexico pueblos, are associated with many households. A simple index of the pithouse-to-kiva transition (if such a transition is definable as a boundary rather than a continuum) should then be found in the number of domestic groups per pithouse/kiva (Steward 1937; Lipe 1989). Archaeologically, we can (with caveats) substitute the number of aboveground rooms for the number of domestic groups in this ratio.

At Pueblo Bonito, with a total of about 530 rooms, about 30 of the smaller round rooms were built as part of the original structure (5–10 more were later built into existing square rooms). The ratio of kivas to rectangular rooms was about 1 to 18. However, not all rectangular rooms were habitations. As a general rule, we can assume that habitation was limited to the exterior rooms. Fewer than half of the rooms at Pueblo Bonito had direct access to the exterior. The ratio of kivas to those rooms is only 1 to 7.

As noted above, only a small number of exterior rooms actually contained firepits, so the ratio of kivas to conventionally defined habitations was probably closer to 1 to 3. With so few potential domestic units per "kiva," it is difficult to see what

19

is being integrated. Is a "clan kiva" a kiva, or is it simply a pithouse built in stone? I suggest that the latter is correct, and "clan kivas" are in fact domestic rooms. The absence of some pithouse floor features (removed to aboveground rooms) should not alarm us; obviously there were reorganizations of domestic architecture during the 900s and 1000s. Just as the aboveground component of an Anasazi house became more formal and elaborate, so too did the old pithouse: walled in stone, formalized in arrangement, etc.

The situation at Chaco is clarified by looking at kivas at slightly later sites in the Mesa Verde region. The Mesa Verde region in Pueblo II was clearly part of the Chacoan region; presumably Mesa Verde in Pueblo III informs, historically, on those earlier periods. "Kivas" at Mesa Verde sites are clearly associated with single households; the number of kivas has been used as a direct index of the number of households (Rohn 1983). At the largest Mesa Verde site, Yellow Jacket ruin, the ratio of rooms to kivas approached 3 to 1 (Kuckelman 2003); clearly, these round rooms were not the kivas we see at modern pueblos; in context, they much more closely recall Pueblo I pithouses. That is almost certainly what they were. If Pueblo III "kivas" were houses, why should we presume differently for Pueblo II round rooms at Chaco?

Many archaeologists, I think, are aware of the unlikely implications of a pithouse-kiva transition in the 700s, but our use of the term "kiva" leads to some amazing interpretations of Anasazi archaeology. One National Park Service sign suggests that the inhabitants of Pueblo Bonito were unusually religious (more so than their neighbors at Chetro Ketl) because they had so many kivas. I offer only this one example, but "kiva" nonsense pervades much of the archaeological, and especially the ethnohistorical, literature.

Small, round rooms at great houses probably represent units of domestic architecture organizationally similar to other functionally specific domestic spaces. For this reason, I do not refer to the small round rooms as "kivas," although I retain the terms great kiva and tower kiva. Hereafter, "clan kivas" rooms will be termed "round rooms"—an unfortunate loss in color, perhaps, but an overdue recovery of precision in the use of the word "kiva."

Great kivas and tower kivas will be described below, followed by more extensive discussion of two subdivisions of the former "clan kiva" group: Chacoan round rooms and small round rooms.

GREAT KIVAS

Great kivas are almost certainly multihousehold in association (Adler and Wilshusen 1990). Assuming that great kivas may have operated as village-integrating structures, it is useful to revisit room-kiva ratios. Great Kivas A and Q, the last in use at Pueblo Bonito, had a total room-to-great-kiva ratio of about 265 to 1. Correcting for probable habitation rooms, this ratio is more like 75 to 1. Great kivas may be more relevant to the historical development of the village-integrating kiva than are the more numerous, small round rooms at Chacoan sites (an interpretation shared by Adler 1993 and Crown and Wills 2003:518, among others).

At their peak (about 1120), Chacoan great kivas were very large, round, semisubterranean structures containing a set of highly formalized interior features and furniture: a low masonry bench around the base of the wall, four wooden posts or masonry piers to support a square room frame, raised floor vaults running north-south between the posts or piers, a raised firebox and deflector, an antechamber on the plaza level north of the subterranean structure, and, frequently, peripheral rooms on the plaza surface surrounding the great kiva (Marshall et al. 1979; Vivian and Reiter 1960). In the tenth to twelfth centuries, at least 12 of these structures were associated with great houses at Pueblo Bonito, Peñasco Blanco, Hungo Pavi, Una Vida, and Chetro Ketl, and there were also a number of "isolated" great kivas (such as Casa Rinconada) (Stein et al., Chapter 8, and Van Dyke, Chapter 4, this volume).

Great kivas in Chaco Canyon represent a local elaboration of a building type with a very long history and a very broad distribution. Most (but not all) great kivas are associated with, and in some sense central to, settlements. Great kivas at great houses have obvious associations, but so-called isolated great kivas at Chaco are in some sense a terminological fiction; they were not "isolated" from the dense settlement in the canyon.

Even at great houses, it is difficult to determine the association of a great kiva with specific building

20

programs; however, from an analysis of building events and great kivas at Pueblo Bonito, Chetro Ketl, Una Vida, Peñasco Blanco, and Hungo Pavi, it appears that a great kiva was constructed with each increment of about 150 rooms (mean = 147, s.d. = 27, N = 8). This suggests an integrative function geared to increments of population (or, at least, structure) rather than a simple "community house" not necessarily tied to village population levels. It is interesting that Pueblo Alto, with only 100 rooms in the original west, central, and east wings, definitely did not have a great kiva (Windes 1987).

Formalization of integrative functions in the great kiva may also be reflected in the impressive labor investments in their construction. Several details attest to heavy labor investment in these large structures: (1) up to 1,104 m³ (Judd 1964:141, 216) of fill was removed for a single great kiva at Pueblo Bonito; (2) the circular masonry walls built in the excavated pits were apparently faced on both sides, when only the interior actually required facing (Reiter 1946); (3) in several great kivas, the huge posts supporting the roofs were seated in faced masonry cylinders on a stack of several sandstone disks, with each disk exceeding 1 m in diameter and 15 cm thick and weighing more than 680 kg (Hewett 1936; Vivian and Reiter 1960); (4) the roofing of the relatively small great kiva at Aztec, when reconstructed by Morris (1921), required fifty 20–30 cm by 3.7 m and eight hundred 1.8 m by 8 cm timbers. Similar material requirements were projected for a never-completed reconstruction of Casa Rinconada (Vivian 1936).

Beyond these costs in materials and labor, additional wealth was expended on great kivas in the form of impressive deposits of beads sealed in "wall crypts" or niches (Hewett 1936); the addition of presumably high-value goods to the building fabric suggests a transfer of that high value to the great kiva structure itself, creating a value beyond that of a simple enclosure for community activities. The organization required for the prodigious labor investments in construction further implies that at least part of the structure's value reflected formalized integrative functions. In a limited sense, great kivas can be considered public monumental buildings.

TOWER KIVAS

Tower kivas are two- or three-story round rooms with rectangular enclosures. The two best-known tower kivas are outside Chaco Canyon: Kin Ya'a and Kin Klizhin (Marshall et al. 1979; Powers et al. 1983). Both of these structures consist of small roomblocks (10–30 ground-floor rooms) with several elevated circular rooms toward the front of the building, and near the center of the rear wall, a three-story tower kiva.

In the canyon, similar towers at Kin Kletso (Kiva A) and Chetro Ketl (Kiva N) stood at least two stories tall. Each had a T-shaped door on its lowest floor. (The tower at Kin Kletso was built over a large boulder, which raised the tower's lower story to the building's second-story level.) No floor features were found on the lower story of either tower. Neither had a bench on the first story, but a bench was evident on the second story of the Chetro Ketl tower. The heavily modified cylinder in and below Room 29-31 at Chetro Ketl may be the lower part of a third tower. Its interior diameter falls within the restricted span of 5.0 to 5.6 m of the Kin Ya'a, Kin Klizhin, Kin Kletso, and Chetro Ketl towers. All tower kivas appear to have been built after about 1110.

CHACOAN ROUND ROOMS

Thirty-five of 53 excavated small round rooms ("clan kivas"), neither tower nor great kivas, form a group long recognized as distinctively Chacoan:

> The majority are equipped with a central fireplace, an underfloor ventilating system, a subfloor vault to the west of the fireplace, and an enclosing bench having 6 to 10 low pilasters and a shallow recess at the south. These several features unite to distinguish what I have termed the "Chaco-type" kiva (Judd 1964:177).

Judd described an assemblage of features (Figure 2.8) that characterize the highly formalized Chacoan round rooms of the 1075–1130 period. To his list could be added the elevation of the round room in a square, aboveground enclosure, and a wattlework or board wainscoting (or bench backing) (Figure 2.9).

The archetype. Chacoan round rooms of the 1075–1130 period are so distinctive that the term

21

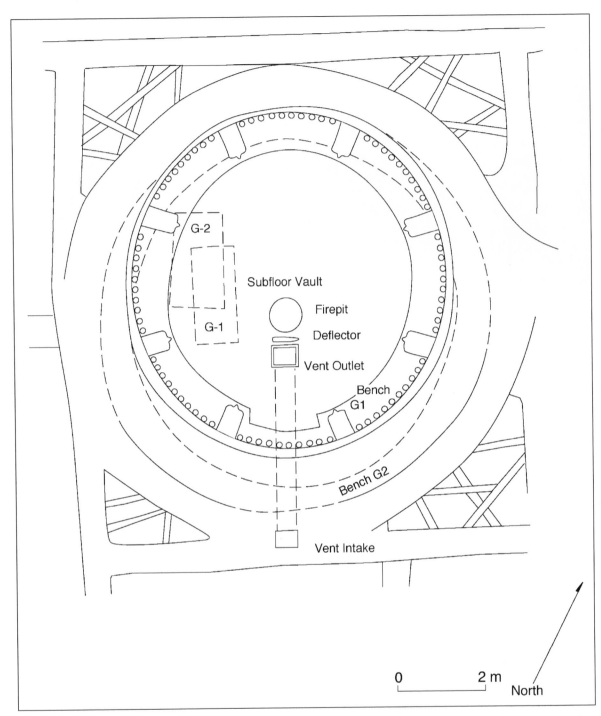

FIGURE 2.8. Kiva G, Chetro Ketl, showing typical Chacoan kiva features. (After Miller 1937; redrafted by David Underwood)

"type" is entirely appropriate. As a type, however, they are not limited to Chaco. They form one of the few definable groups in Pueblo II and Pueblo III round rooms at Mesa Verde (McClellan 1969:131), they are documented as far south as Zuni (Hodge 1923), and various elements, such as the subfloor vault, range farther still. Rightly or wrongly, this type of round room is referred to Chaco wherever it or elements of it are found. Perhaps this is justified, since the Chacoan circular

FIGURE 2.9. Wainscoting in Kiva G-1, Chetro Ketl. (Courtesy of Palace of the Governors [MNM/DCA], neg. 67049; from Lekson 1984a:58, Figure 3.7B)

room is definitely associated with large-scale construction in the canyon. Small round rooms of various other forms (discussed below) are also found in the large buildings, but most and probably all of them are later additions to existing structures.

The later Chacoan round room was an above-ground structure, built in a square enclosure on the first or (occasionally) second story of the building. The interior diameters of excavated examples appear trimodal at 6.0–6.5 m, 7.5–8.0 m, and 8.5–9.0 m (Figure 2.10). The inclusion of unexcavated, elevated (almost certainly Chacoan) round rooms suggests trimodality is the product of sampling error. For combined excavated and unexcavated round rooms, the mean (7.08 m, s.d. = 1.37, $N = 65$) diameter is nearly coincident with the mode (about 7.25 m).

The insertion of a circle into a square created four empty corners which were often crossed by masonry or beam buttresses supporting the rear of the exposed arc of the circular room. These corners were sometimes filled with trash, rubble, shale, or soil. Occasionally, they were left unobstructed and were used as incidental rooms (see below).

A consistent set of features, aligned north-south, occupied the southern half of the floor (Figure 2.7). Offset slightly to the south in the Chacoan round room was a deep, circular or square firepit. This pit was usually masonry lined. In front of the firepit was the opening of a subfloor ventilator shaft. In a few rooms, between the ventilator opening and the firepit stood an upright slab or a short, low, and thin wall called a deflector. It deflected the flow of air from the ventilator and reflected the heat and light of the firepit.

About three-quarters of Chacoan round rooms had floor vaults, or subfloor rectangular boxes west of the firepit. Because these vaults were frequently filled and plastered (occasionally over board covers), it is likely that the real proportion of round rooms with this feature is considerably

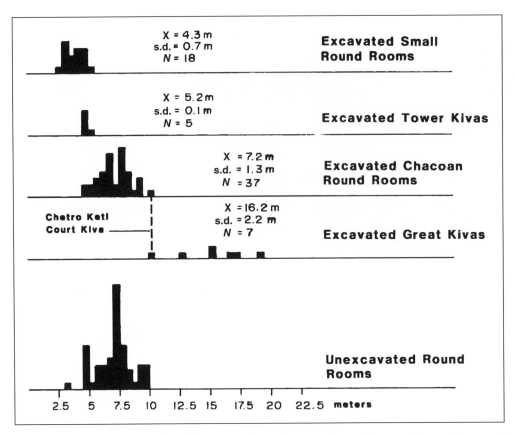

FIGURE 2.10. Interior, above-bench diameters of round rooms. (From Lekson 1984a:55, Figure 3.5)

higher than the three-quarters reported in the literature and notes. The function of these features is obscure. The board-covered cavity has suggested to some researchers that the vaults were "foot drums" or resonators for dancing, but since many were filled with sand, this seems unlikely.

Relatively few Chacoan round rooms had niches in the bench or wall, although for some reason Judd (1964) considered a large niche at the northern point of the bench standard. No elevated Chacoan round room had a "sipapu," the symbolic hole in the floor seen in many prehistoric pit-structures and historical kivas.

A low masonry bench ran around the entire circumference of the room, with a short recess (Figures 2.7 and 2.8) usually to the south. There is some evidence (at Pueblo Bonito) of a shelf over the recess, continuing the level of the bench and creating a very large niche. The width of the bench (mean = 0.62 m, s.d. = 21, $N = 37$) varied with the diameter of the room; the larger the room diameter, the wider the bench ($r = 0.7451$, $N = 37$), whereas

the height, about 0.66 m (s.d. = 0.18 m, $N = 37$), did not vary with room size.

Built on the bench were six or eight evenly spaced pilasters (Figures 2.7 and 2.8). In Chacoan round rooms, they usually consisted of a short section of beam seated in the wall and laid horizontally on the bench, extending to the center-point of the room. The beam segment was often encased in a masonry box; less frequently, a round cavity was carved out of the top of the beam to hold small caches of beads, etc. Three variations on this basic pattern are notable: in four rooms, the beams were of squared wood of about the same size as the beam-and-box unit; in two other rooms, pilasters consisted of three or four smaller beams placed side by side, again with a masonry box built around them; and in one other room (which Judd considered "foreign"), two beam and box units were built one upon the other to form a double-height pilaster.

Rising from the back of the bench (particularly in rooms exceeding 6.75 m in diameter, as discussed

24

below) was "wainscoting" (also called "bench backing" or "bench padding"). This is one of the most peculiar features of Chacoan round room. Wainscoting consisted of wooden boards or (more often) thin, upright poles supporting wattlework or jacal, rising from the back of the bench between pilasters. The poles lean outward from the wall toward the center of ceiling, perhaps 10° to 15° from vertical (Figures 2.9 and 2.11). The space behind the boards or wattlework was packed with vegetal material, possibly with trash, and the front was plastered with mud. Although Reiter (1946:85) states that no backing taller than about 0.70 m was preserved, Judd (1964:181, Plate 56 lower) shows a post-and-wattle backing that was more than 2 m tall. Reiter also states that the top of the backing was finished, with the mud plaster continuing across the vegetal packing and onto the vertical masonry wall behind it (Miller 1937; Reiter 1946).

It appears likely that wainscoting represents the surviving lower portions of a dome-shaped false ceiling. Imagine a large, hemispherical basket, the diameter of a round room, inverted and set on the bench: that was the "wainscoting." The wattle-work was plastered to create a smooth dome ceiling under a flat, load-bearing roof supported by beams (much like that of a square room). The space between the load-bearing flat roof and the "false ceiling" wicker dome was probably left unfilled. It appears that many (most?) Chacoan round rooms had this type of ceiling (it also appears at a number of "outliers," such as Chimney Rock and Aztec Ruins). The inverted basket recalls the symbolism of Rio Grande kivas (Swentzell 1989). But Chacoan round rooms were still houses!

The development of the type. The best evidence of the development of the Chacoan round room of the 1075–1130 period is found in the northern plaza of Pueblo Bonito. The Pueblo Bonito series will be supplemented by examples from Chetro Ketl.

Early 900s round rooms are known only from early Pueblo Bonito. The earliest round rooms at Pueblo Bonito (the unnumbered structures below Rooms 83 and 324) were fully subterranean and slightly less than 5 m in interior diameter. No details of floor features, roofing, etc., are known.

The next step in the development is not much better documented than the first. It is represented by the round pitstructures fronting Pueblo Bonito

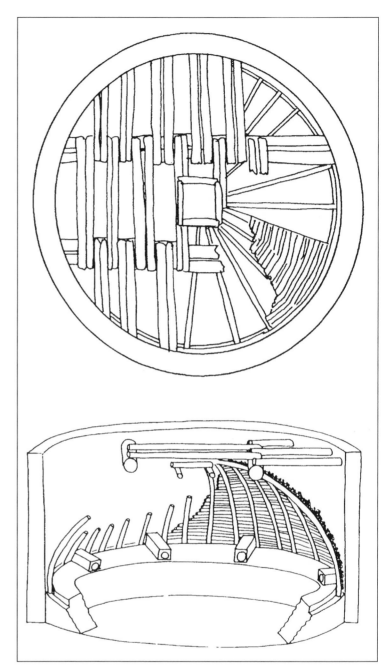

FIGURE 2.11. Chaco kiva roofing: an inverted "basket" of jacal, plastered on the interior face, is inferred from "wainscoting" reported in most Chacoan kivas. (Reconstruction by the author)

(900–915): round rooms that were, again, subterranean, but considerably larger (7.0 to 7.3 m in diameter) than their predecessors. Few construction details are known from these rooms, but Judd notes that they were "bowl-shaped"; that is, the walls sloped outward above the bench, which was between 0.6 and 1.0 m high and close to 1.0 m wide. A larger pitstructure, in the middle of the Pueblo Bonito 900–1060 plaza, was about 9.75 m in diameter at the top of its walls, and about 3.7 m deep. This may have been a great kiva. Only the north half of this unit was exposed, but Judd noted:

> An encircling bench, 25 inches high and averaging 34 inches wide was surfaced with sandstone slabs and plastered. In it, in the portion we exposed, were the remains of two pilasters, each consisting of small sandstone chips set in adobe mud and enclosing a 6-inch log that lay flat upon the slab surface, its butt end inserted into the masonry and packed about with shale. . . . Here again, as with that under room 83, a 4-pilaster kiva is indicated (1964:67).

There are no tree-ring dates from this room, but it certainly dates to the early 900s. In this second group of round rooms, we see two details foreshadowing later developments: first, the use of radial beam pilasters, and second, a diameter of slightly over 7 m.

Several of the 7-m-diameter pitstructures fronting Pueblo Bonito (900–915) were later modified or rebuilt. Modifications of these earlier rooms may represent the next step in the development of the Chacoan round room, intermediate between the pitstructure and elevated round room. Only nine subterranean Chaco-type round rooms have been excavated (Pueblo Bonito Kivas L, M, N, R, and probably Kivas S and 67; Kivas F and G-5 at Chetro Ketl; and Kiva 10 at Pueblo Alto). They were built sometime between the early 900s and the late 1080s or 1090s; I suspect they date to between 1030 and 1070. Of all nine, only Kiva G-5 at Chetro Ketl remains exposed.

Kiva G-5 dates to about 1035–1040. Because it largely escaped later rebuilding, it will be considered at some length. Kiva G-5's interior diameter of 7.9 m is only slightly larger than the Pueblo Bonito (900–915) pitstructures; its depth of 3.7 m is close to that of the possible great kiva at Pueblo Bonito (900–915). "The main wall was constructed with the inner face sloping slightly outward" (Miller 1937:82), like the "bowl-shaped" pitstructures of the early 900s at Pueblo Bonito.

The bench of Kiva G-5 had been razed; originally it measured about 0.8 m wide and 0.6 m in height. No pilasters survived intact on the bench, but a series of "three complete niches and part of a fourth," indicating six evenly spaced niches around the back of the bench (Miller 1937:83), undoubtedly represents mortises left for the insertion of the butt ends of the radial pilaster beams. An offset at the top of the wall indicated the beam seating of a flat roof. A deep, circular, masonry-lined firepit was the only floor feature found.

One of the features of subterranean Kiva G-5 may have presaged later elevated forms. This was a straight wall tangent to the exterior wall of the round room, exposed only for a short length. This wall appears to have been built into the Kiva G-5 excavation (Miller 1937:99). Does this represent an early subterranean form of the later elevated Chacoan round room enclosure? The depth of the wall was not determined, and it may not have continued to the floor level of Kiva G-5. (Similar walls were noted for subterranean Kivas L and 2-C at Pueblo Bonito.)

Kiva G-5 and the eight other subterranean round rooms form a group that appears to be transitional between earlier (900s) and later (post-1070) round rooms. All of these units were subterranean. Eight of them had six pilasters (the number of pilasters at Kiva 10, Pueblo Alto, is unknown), a transition between the rooms of the early 900s with four pilasters each and those postdating 1075 with eight or ten. The walls of at least three (Kiva G-5 at Chetro Ketl, Kiva R at Pueblo Bonito, and Kiva 10 at Pueblo Alto) and probably all of these transitional units slope outwards, like earlier pitstructure walls.

Interior diameters ranged from 6.7 to 8.0 m (except Kiva R at Pueblo Bonito, which was 9.3 m in diameter). Wainscoting would be expected in almost all later (post-1075) round rooms of this diameter, but it was present in only half of this group. Only one floor vault was present, whereas at least three-quarters of all later round rooms had floor vaults. All rooms (where data were available) had subfloor ventilators except Kiva G-5 at Chetro Ketl. In Kiva G-5, the lack of evidence of an above-floor ventilator suggests that a subfloor unit was present, although it was not found.

The elevation of these rooms into rectangular enclosures and the more standardized use of floor vaults and wainscoting produced the "classic" archetypical Chacoan round rooms.

Large round rooms, and the Court Kiva at Chetro Ketl. The very largest Chacoan round rooms (9.0 to 10.5 m diameter) represent an important subset of the group. The 9–10.5 m group (the secondary mode in Figure 2.10) includes both elevated and subterranean rooms. The two excavated examples (Kiva C at Pueblo del Arroyo and Kiva D at Pueblo Bonito) are identical to smaller Chacoan units in floor features, bench characteristics, and so on. The other round rooms of this size are all subterranean, and—with three exceptions—unexcavated (five, all in the plaza of Pueblo Bonito: Kivas 67, P, O, an unnumbered earlier version of Kiva O, and the large unnumbered unit in the southeast plaza). The three excavated examples include Kiva R (Pueblo Bonito) and the Court Kiva (Chetro Ketl); a third, Kiva J at Talus Unit, was only partially excavated. Little is known about the interior features of Kiva J; Kiva R appears to have been a fairly typical Chaco-type structure, lacking the usual floor vault.

The Court Kiva at Chetro Ketl was originally built as a typically equipped Chacoan unit (Vivian and Reiter 1960; Woods 1934). At 10.25 m in diameter, it was the largest of all Chacoan round rooms. It was subsequently converted to a great kiva by the addition of the characteristic great kiva features: masonry piers, fire box, raised vaults, etc. The largest Chaco-type round room thus became the smallest great kiva. Chacoan round rooms and great kivas are fairly distinct, but in the Court Kiva (and perhaps other very large Chacoan units) there is a suggestion of a continuum of size.

NON-CHACOAN ROUND ROOMS

About 22 round rooms excavated at Pueblo Bonito, Pueblo del Arroyo, Chetro Ketl, Kin Kletso, and Pueblo Alto are neither great kivas nor tower kivas nor "Chaco-type." As shown in Figure 2.10, the average interior diameter of small round rooms (mean = 4.3, s.d. = 0.7, N = 20) is considerably smaller than that of the Chacoan round rooms. There is little overlap between the two: hence the term "small round rooms." This category was defined originally by the absence of architectural details characteristic of great kivas, tower kivas, and Chaco-type rooms, and the presence of some features not found in the previously defined three types. The "keyhole" plan of many of these smaller

rooms has been singled out as particularly suspicious. Judd (and many others) has interpreted these differences as indicating that many of the smaller units are "foreign" architectural intrusions into Chacoan buildings. While this interpretation may be correct, many of the small kivas have subfloor ventilators, bench recesses, and even floor vaults, features associated with Chacoan round rooms, although none of the smaller units has the full complement of features and details. It is also worthwhile to consider the wide variability in round rooms at smaller sites at Chaco Canyon (Truell 1986) when pronouncing on "foreign" intrusions.

More than half of the small round rooms are in fact round, and not "keyhole." Most are still rather different from Chacoan round rooms; only three have a bench recess, and only two of those three have subfloor ventilators. Neither of these two most-nearly-"Chaco-type" (Kiva J at Pueblo del Arroyo, Kiva U at Pueblo Bonito) has radial beam pilasters or floor vaults (but then no Chacoan round room of less than about 5.5 m in diameter has a floor vault). Both of these rooms are elevated in square enclosures that appear to have been built specifically for the purpose. They may actually represent the smallest Chacoan round rooms. (Because the analysis centers on the interpretation of unexcavated sites, diameter rather than architectural detail is the criterion for inclusion in the Chaco-type or small round room groups.)

Other small round rooms show a variety of forms, including "keyhole" shapes with no pilasters (4) or with tall pier pilasters (2). All but two very late units (at Pueblo Alto) have subfloor ventilators: one has a south bench recess, and one has a floor vault.

All the excavated, elevated, small round rooms are later additions or modifications of existing buildings. There are no tree-ring dates from any of these small round rooms; however, all probably date to the early to mid-1100s.

Unexcavated round rooms of 5.0 m diameter or less are probably similar "small" rooms. Most of these unexcavated rooms also appear to be later additions to or modifications of existing buildings.

At least two, and probably more, of the few subterranean small round rooms are equally late. Units 2-E and sub-286 at Pueblo Bonito, despite tree-ring dates of 1058 and 1088, are probably

27

quite late. The subterranean rooms at Chetro Ketl (Kivas A, B, D, and E) are associated with a very late plaza surface.

These subterranean rooms are less elaborate than their elevated counterparts, with the exception of Kiva 2-D and sub-162 at Pueblo Bonito. Kiva 2-D is an odd oval room with a subfloor vent, located next to two equally odd subterranean rectangular rooms with corner vent-fireplaces (Rooms 350, 351). Sub-162, an unnumbered round room beneath the later Chacoan round room (Kiva 162), is "keyhole" in shape, with a bench recess and four pier pilasters.

Some of these small round rooms may, in fact, be "foreign" architectural intrusions into Chacoan buildings, but the continued use of earlier Chacoan details, such as bench recesses and subfloor ventilators, suggests that many, perhaps most, of the smaller round rooms represent a late expression of the Chacoan buildings tradition.

Incidental Rooms

Rooms created more-or-less incidentally to more formal construction projects are often oddly shaped rooms at the conjunction of building programs built on different axes. Or (more frequently) they represent the subrectangular voids between round rooms and their square enclosures. These corners, often crossed by masonry or timber buttresses or packed with fill, occasionally accommodated oddly shaped rooms and passages (e.g., stairways from surrounding rectangular rooms to the terrace level atop the circular room), or even fully rectangular rooms. Several of these rooms at Pueblo Bonito (especially those around Kiva B) contained firepits, heating pits, bins, and—perhaps—mealing bins. Domestic features in incidental rooms may have been late introductions; Kiva B is a late addition to a roomblock, which probably postdates 1105.

Holsinger (1901) had great fun with incidental rooms; he described shapes ranging from diamonds to crescents to bizarre compound forms with partial incurving arcs, multiple corners, and reentrants. These incidental rooms were located around much-remodeled round rooms. As a product of formal design, this range of room shapes is misleading, as well as incidental to the basic formal vocabulary of round and rectangular rooms.

Balconies

Evidence from the exterior walls of several great houses (Pueblo Bonito, Chetro Ketl, Pueblo del Arroyo, possibly Hungo Pavi) indicates the presence of balconies on the second- and third-story levels (Figure 2.2). Early photos show cantilever beams supporting these features on the north-facing wall of Pueblo del Arroyo, but those beams were gone by the time the site was excavated. Indeed, it is likely that balcony beams were frequently "harvested" for firewood by early explorers and ranchers—the probable fate of surviving wooden ramps and stairways (if any) as well.

Balconies, as they are known from Pueblo del Arroyo and from sheltered sites such as Balcony House at Mesa Verde, were narrow (probably about 1 m wide), continuous ledges running the full length of a building, on the exterior wall. They were apparently constructed much like a roof/ceiling: cantilever primary beams supported secondary beams/closing materials, and the surface was formed by clay and sand. Presumably, the wood elements were lashed together. The exterior edge of clay and sand is a bit of a mystery: what prevented the earth component from simply falling off the edge?

Balconies offered access to rear row rooms through the nearly ubiquitous "storage doors" visible in rear walls, now filled in with masonry. Presumably, these doors were open or temporarily sealed with slabs, and access was possible along the balcony ledge.

Terraces

Terraces were the roofs of lower story rooms located in front of upper story rooms. Although terraced construction is considered typical of Chacoan (and all Puebloan) buildings, very few were consistently stepped up a story at each row's remove from the plaza. More frequently, the plaza-facing row of rooms was one story, and the rooms behind it were two stories from front to rear. Only the rear row of rooms along the back walls of buildings like Peñasco Blanco, Pueblo Bonito, Chetro Ketl, Hungo Pavi, and Wijiji stood one story higher than the intermediate two-story rooms; wings were not generally terraced beyond the first row of rooms. Large sections of Chetro Ketl, Pueblo del Arroyo, and the later (1110–1140)

28

buildings were not terraced at all, in this sense. Although ramada or portal structures are likely on first-story terraces, there is not much evidence beyond a hint of a line of ramadas on the first-story terrace of the east wing of Pueblo Bonito.

ROOM SUITES

By tracing doorway connections, archaeologists can delimit sets of rooms that have been called "suites" (Figure 2.12). Suites are often assumed to reflect the social units that occupied them: families, households, etc. For recent analyses of Chaco great house connections, see Bernardini 1999 and especially Bustard 2003.

The extant walls of Chacoan ruins are an apparent advantage for the archaeologist; many walls stand high enough to show doors. Most Southwestern sites are not so well preserved. Unfortunately, two problems more than offset the advantage of studying the standing walls.

First, in spite of all the standing walls, the record is actually rather fragmentary. Chacoan building

was multistoried. The reason that many first stories are standing is that the first-story walls were unusually wide, being designed to support second stories. We can see the first-story doorway connections, but the upper story connections and the very important hatchways through floors into those stories are usually absent. Therefore, the following discussion will be limited to ground floor plans.

Second, Chacoan buildings were not simply residences. Consider two early construction programs at Pueblo Bonito and Chetro Ketl. Both were additions to existing buildings, which had long rear walls unbroken by doors. At both buildings, a row of rooms was added to the blank rear wall. The new rooms were connected by doorways up and down the row; however, no doors were cut through the older rear wall into the original building. Both early Pueblo Bonito and Chetro Ketl had 20 to 30 rooms that were connected in a line only to each other. Were these residential suites? Probably not.

At Pueblo Bonito and Chetro Ketl, the older buildings comprised a series of gratifyingly well defined suites, each of about four or five rooms.

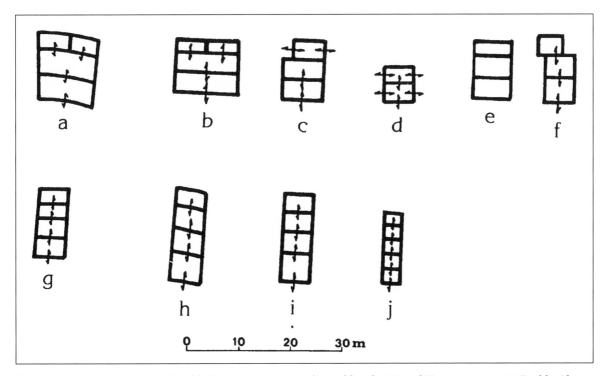

FIGURE 2.12. Room suites: (a) Pueblo Bonito I, 920–935; (b) Pueblo Alto IA and IB, 1020–1040; (c) Pueblo Alto, 1050–1060; (d) Pueblo Bonito, 1050–1060; (e) Chetro Ketl, 1050–1055; (f) Pueblo del Arroyo, 1065–1075; (g) Pueblo Bonito, 1060–1075; (h) Pueblo Bonito, 1075–1085; (i) Pueblo del Arroyo, 1095–1105; (j) Wijiji, 1105+. (From Lekson 1984a:63, Figure 3.8)

The additions along the rear of these buildings crosscut the older suites but at the same time continued, almost exactly, the cross-wall spacing of the older building; the additions repeated exactly the size and arrangement of the older rear row of rooms. Surely, this alignment has implications for functions and use. The additions were community-wide construction projects, but the rooms themselves may have been allotted to the particular suites they backed.

These two construction programs, and others like them, discourage the simple equation of room suites with social units, such as households. The problem is one of detecting the less-than-obvious non-suites, or conversely, discovering the interconnected rooms that might mean something in terms of the social units occupying them.

Several construction programs of the early 900s were designed as series of suites, each consisting of two large rooms backed by a pair of smaller rooms (Figure 2.12). This pattern is identical to the suites at contemporaneous small sites (Truell 1983); formal similarity suggests a functional parallel.

At small sites, the units composed of one large room and two small rooms are almost certainly suites and probably represent some form of household (Truell 1983). If these units were significant at small sites, then we can assume that the large-room-with-paired-small-rooms units were in fact units of some meaning in Chacoan building. This gives us a referent for the development of Chacoan room suites.

The paired-room unit remained in Chacoan building from the early 900s until the early 1000s (Figure 2.12). This is not to say that it was the exclusive arrangement of interconnected rooms, simply that among the possibilities, the paired-room unit remained patterned and definable. After about 1030 (certainly by 1050), paired-room suites were no longer built.

During the middle 1000s, paired rear rooms were deleted from suite arrangements and were replaced by a single room. This marks an important point of transition from the paired room unit to the final Chacoan suite arrangement—the linear suite (Figure 2.12). From about 1060 on, all patterned suites are linear, with the cross-walls aligned from the front to the rear. In linear suites, rooms decrease in size from front to back. Since the rooms are all of equal length, changes in size obviously are the result of variation in width. In most cases, the front room was square, and rooms to the rear, rectangular.

The importance and clarity of suites in Chacoan building design seem to decrease through time. Pueblo Bonito in the 900s consisted almost entirely of a row of identical paired-room suites; later building might include only one or two linear suites in a building program of 35 ground floor rooms (e.g., Pueblo del Arroyo). Either the formal concept of suites was changing and becoming less patterned, or many of the later structures were not designed for the same activities that were housed in the paired-room suites and probably continued in the linear suites. For a number of reasons, discussed more fully below, I favor the latter interpretation.

UNITS OF DESIGN/UNITS OF CONSTRUCTION

Rooms may have been the smallest formal unit of archaeological analysis at Chaco, but the suite was almost certainly the basic unit of design in earlier building programs (900–1050). Early Chacoan design was thus the product of, first, determining the number of suites required and then—using the suite width as a module—designing a building containing the appropriate number of modules. Construction programs ordinarily consisted of four or more suites. The unit of design (the suite) did not equal the unit of construction (the roomblock). The process of design, based on suites but producing roomblocks, could not correspond to the individual domestic groups occupying the finished structure.

This situation is more confusing in later Chacoan building, where suite patterns are poorly defined or even absent. In the latest Chacoan structures, such as Kin Kletso, there are no evident suite patterns, yet the entire building of interconnected rooms was clearly planned as a unit. What then was the unit of design? Presumably, the building itself had replaced the suite as the unit of design.

PLAZAS

Archaeologists speak of "plazas" or "plaza areas" at Anasazi sites of the 700s and 800s. Like the term "kiva," this is a projection from later pueblo

30

architecture that may be unwarranted. The earliest formal enclosed plazas in pueblo buildings appear at Chaco appear in the early 1000s (contra Adams 1991).

Chaco great house plazas were bounded by roomblocks and were leveled and sometimes (perhaps usually) surfaced. More important, whereas earlier plazas were simply the heavily used areas between roomblock and pitstructure, the Chacoan plaza is essentially a bounded area beyond the pitstructure or round room. At some Chacoan buildings, the area between the roomblock and pitstructure shows many of the same kinds of use as the analogous space in smaller, earlier sites. At Pueblo Bonito, for example, there are large firepits and other features along the front of earlier roomblocks, between the rooms and the subterranean round rooms that continue in a line along its front. The formal plaza, a Chacoan development that may survive into the modern pueblos, is the bounded area beyond this zone of domestic use. This kind of architectural space may have been present at a few earlier sites, particularly the large pithouse aggregations of southeastern Utah and southwestern Colorado of the 800s. In many ways, the formal plaza is a correlate of large-scale masonry architecture and the massing of roomblocks. Not all Chacoan buildings had plazas, of course, but it is difficult to conceive of a formal plaza without something very like Chacoan building.

The uses of these plazas are unknown. Although excavations have revealed zones of use along the edges of these spaces, presumably continuing the earlier function of use areas between rooms and pitstructures, the area beyond these zones is a closed book. The very few test excavations conducted in formal plazas have produced few clues to their use.

BUILDINGS

By the early 1100s a bewildering variety of building types was in use at Chaco. The many buildings were the product of more than two and a half centuries of formal change and innovation. In this section, formal change is described in four temporal segments: tenth-century building, a "hiatus" from 960 to 1020, eleventh-century building, and early twelfth-century forms.

Tenth-Century Building (850–960)

Early tenth-century construction was first noted at Pueblo Bonito: "the crescentic house cluster that identifies the original settlement stands out conspicuously" (Judd 1964:57). Building in the first half of the tenth-century was not confined to Pueblo Bonito. Peñasco Blanco and Una Vida also have initial sections that date to this period (Figure 2.13). Three aspects of tenth-century building at these sites stand out in contrast to earlier and contemporary smaller sites: the presence of multiple stories, the very large size of rooms and pitstructures, and the scale of design and construction units.

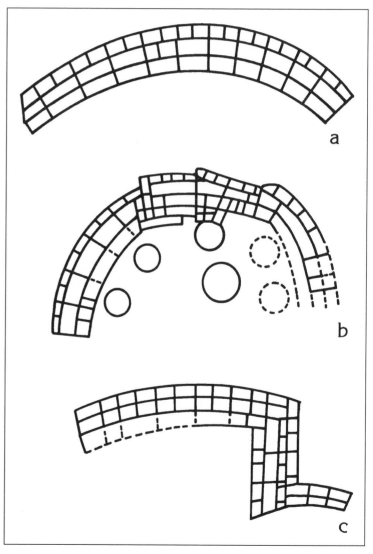

FIGURE 2.13. Early 900s building: (a) Peñasco Blanco, (b) Pueblo Bonito, (c) Una Vida. (From Lekson 1984a:65, Figure 3.9)

Windes and Ford (1992, 1996) document initial construction at Pueblo Bonito by the mid to late ninth century. However, the earliest definable construction events now apparently date to the early tenth century. Early 900s building at all these sites appears to have included sections of multiple stories. As described above, Type I masonry may have been unstable under loads developed in multistoried building. At the large sites, the tenth-century sections were later surrounded by more massively built eleventh-century additions, and this buttressing and enclosure preserved Type I multiple stories that may not otherwise have survived. Any other Type I building that was not incorporated into later structures, and instead fell into inconspicuous ruin, might not be recognized today as anything unusual.

The arrangement of rooms in suites parallels that seen at many earlier and contemporaneous small sites (Truell 1983). As noted above, suites consist of large rooms backed by paired smaller rooms. As in small sites, subterranean round rooms were located in front of the rows of rooms. Floor areas in plaza-facing rooms are generally about 40 m^2, about four times the size of their counterparts in small sites. Similarly, rear row rooms and subterranean round rooms are two or three times the size of their small-site counterparts.

The number of suites in a single construction program varies from building to building, and between programs at each building. The eastern and central parts of early Pueblo Bonito (Figure 2.13) consist of small segments of one or two suites with a notable irregularity in the size of front rooms and the number of rear rooms associated with each front room (see also Bernadini 1999; Windes and Ford 1992). The west arc, however, consists of five very regular suites and clearly represents a single construction program. The situation at Una Vida is more obscure, but early Una Vida (Figure 2.13) consisted of no more than three suites. Unexcavated Peñasco Blanco is even more difficult to interpret, but the initial building at that site may have included up to 11 units.

With the possible exception of Una Vida (which may have consisted of an 11-room-wide, two-room-deep, curved, multistoried block), tenth-century building at these sites was remarkably uniform. At Pueblo Bonito, Peñasco Blanco, and Una Vida, initial building was an arc of multiple suites comprising a large room paired with two small rooms. Along the front of the arc of rooms was a line of subterranean round rooms, one for every two or three suites.

The "Hiatus" (960–1020)

For sixty years, from about 960 to 1020, there seems to have been a hiatus in building. Two construction stages probably date to this period. Both are very incompletely known and not very well dated: initial construction at Hungo Pavi, dating to somewhere between 945 and 1010, and Chetro Ketl, beginning about 1010.

The actual scale of building at Hungo Pavi is unknown; the length of the projected rear wall suggests that it approached the size of the three earlier buildings. However, there is a significant difference in form. The rear wall of Hungo Pavi was straight, whereas the three early 900s buildings were arcs with markedly curved rear walls. The earliest building at Chetro Ketl was also rectangular rather than curved. These two sites may represent a transition between the early tenth-century plans and the earliest well-documented eleventh-century plans (Figures 2.13 and 2.14).

Was there a major reduction in building during this period? The early tenth-century buildings continued to be occupied; there is a clear continuity in form, as we shall see, between them and the first well-documented eleventh-century building. Considered with the limited but suggestive evidence of formal transition at Hungo Pavi and Chetro Ketl, this suggests that building continued at a more extensive level than is evident from tree-rings or exposed buildings.

Earlier, large-scale construction seems to have progressed in a series: Peñasco Blanco (900–915), Pueblo Bonito (920–935), Una Vida (930–950). Perhaps this series continued, first at Hungo Pavi (954–1010) and then Chetro Ketl (1010+). I suspect the apparent "hiatus" is a true reduction in building, perhaps exaggerated by vagaries of preservation and the history of archaeology in the canyon. In addition to Hungo Pavi and Chetro Ketl, it is likely that sections of Pueblo Bonito, Una Vida, and Peñasco Blanco (dated to either side of the hiatus) were actually constructed during this span.

Eleventh-Century Building (1020–1115)

Eleventh-century Chacoan architecture has long been considered a radical departure from earlier Chacoan building. Judd (1964:24) thought that the occupants of the early 900s arcs were ethnically distinct from the eleventh-century builders at Pueblo Bonito. However, as we shall see, this is probably not the case; early eleventh-century building clearly continues the 900s forms. Through a series of stages, the tenth-century plan was gradually transformed during the eleventh century into compact, rectangular units of the twelfth century.

1020–1050. The first eleventh-century construction (Figure 2.14) includes the creation of two new buildings (Pueblo Alto and the currently visible version of Chetro Ketl) in the central canyon area. Early eleventh-century construction at Pueblo Alto and Chetro Ketl show an unmistakable continuity with tenth-century building. This is most obvious at Pueblo Alto.

Pueblo Alto consisted of two rows of large rectangular rooms, each about 40 m², backed by a row of paired smaller rooms, each about 8–10 m². Along the front of the rectangular rooms are two or three large, subterranean round rooms (8–9 m in diameter). The arrangement and sizes of rooms are identical to parts of early tenth-century Pueblo Bonito, with "Old Bonito's" curved plan straightened out into a long rectangle.

Early construction at Chetro Ketl (Figure 2.14) was greatly obscured by later building, but again, continuity with tenth-century building is evident. A row of subterranean round rooms runs along the front of two rows of rectangular rooms. Although the front row rooms are larger than the rear row rooms, there is no clear association of paired rear row and large front row rooms. Subsequent (almost immediate?) additions of a row of rooms to the front and rear of the initial roomblock created a plan with a large front room, a slightly smaller room behind it, and two smaller rooms behind that. Although the arrangement of rectangular and round rooms recalls the tenth century, the connections and layout of individual suites perhaps anticipate the later eleventh-century linear suite.

The third notable instance of early eleventh-century construction was at Pueblo Bonito. It too demonstrates continuity with tenth-century building, but in an entirely different way. New construction

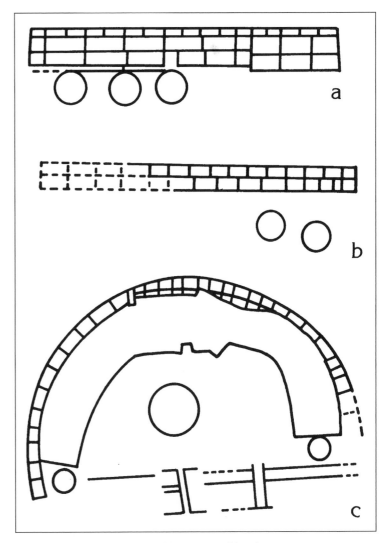

FIGURE 2.14. 1020–1050 building: (a) Pueblo Alto, (b) Chetro Ketl, (c) Pueblo Bonito. (From Lekson 1984a:67, Figure 3.10)

at Pueblo Bonito (Figure 2.14) consisted of a row of small, multistoried rectangular rooms added to the rear wall of the existing early 900s structure. Pueblo Bonito (1050–1060) preserved the earlier building by enclosing it in a shell of more massive construction.

In addition to the rear row of rooms, walls (perhaps representing rows of rooms) were built across the open plaza of Pueblo Bonito (1050–1060). This is the earliest direct evidence for enclosed plazas at Chaco. (See Windes and Ford 1992 for an argument for an earlier enclosed plaza at Peñasco Blanco.)

Even with the addition of rear row rooms, the enclosed plaza, and a few minor alterations of

33

plaza-facing rooms and walls, the earlier (tenth-century) Pueblo Bonito remained essentially unchanged. The tenth-century structures of "Old Bonito" remained useful throughout the eleventh century (and even into the twelfth). The form of "Old Bonito" remained an acceptable solution to Chacoan design problems in the early 1000s.

1050–1060. During the next decade, wings of one or two stories were added to the existing structures at Pueblo Alto, Chetro Ketl, Pueblo Bonito, and perhaps Hungo Pavi (Figure 2.15). There is little direct tree-ring dating of this construction;

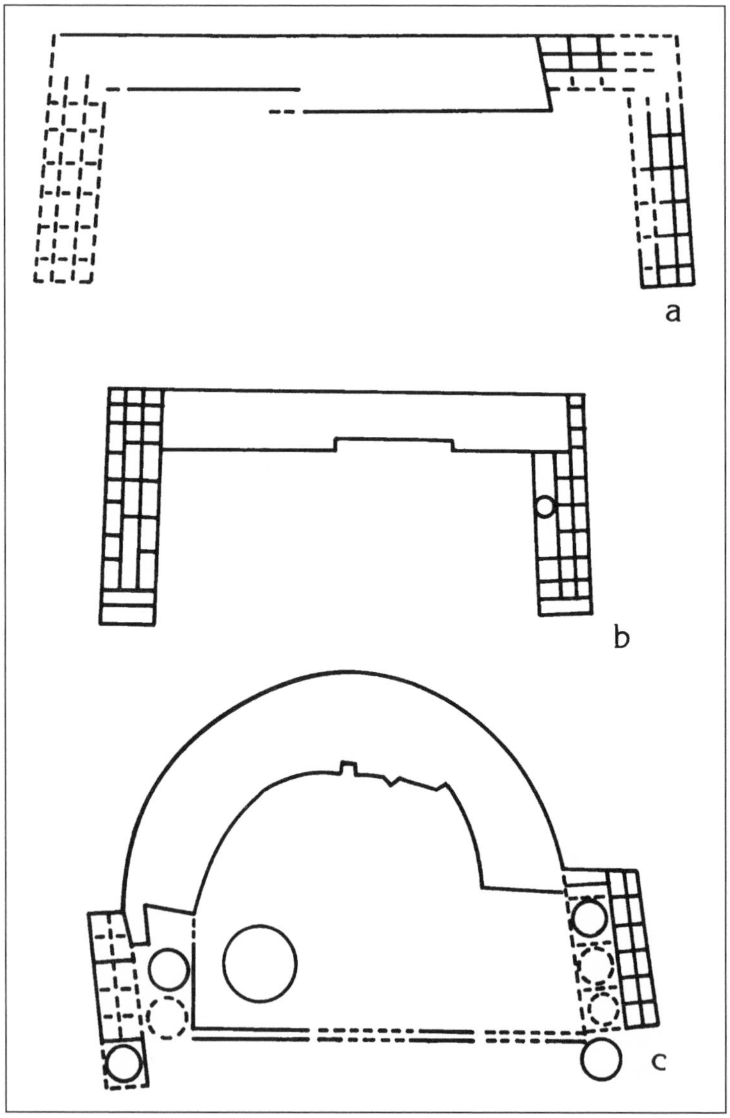

FIGURE 2.15. 1050–1075 building: (a) Chetro Ketl, (b) Pueblo Alto, (c) Pueblo Bonito. (From Lekson 1984a:69, Figure 3.11)

34

Stephen H. Lekson

bracketed by earlier and later building, it postdates 1040 and antedates 1075. The decade from 1050 to 1060 seems most likely. Wings created the three-sided plan so characteristic of Chacoan building, and so vexingly difficult to name: "C", "E", "[", "O", etc.

Wings are not added at right angles to the older buildings, but are generally about 5° off. Oddly enough, the wings added to Pueblo Bonito and Hungo Pavi are almost parallel (that is, they are off 5° in the same direction), whereas those added to Pueblo Alto and Chetro Ketl diverge (at a combined angle of about 10°). In the latter cases, the angle of the wings may simply continue the slightly diverging end walls of the older structures that they abut.

Each wing is about half the size of the building to which it was added; thus the addition of two wings doubled the size of the building. At Chetro Ketl, Pueblo Bonito, and perhaps Pueblo Alto, there is evidence of long parallel walls (or perhaps a row of very narrow rooms) connecting the two wings and enclosing the plaza. Enclosed plazas are certainly possible at the other two buildings, but direct evidence is lacking.

The tenth-century suite lost definition in the construction events of 1050–1060. The association of subterranean round rooms with any of the wings added during this period is also doubtful. The only exceptions are the round room perhaps associated with the west wing of Pueblo Alto and another round room, which may have been added to the east wing at Chetro Ketl. At both sites, however, extensive trenching indicates that these pitstructures are the only ones that possibly date to this period. A few elevated round rooms may have been present, as at Pueblo Bonito, although these are very problematic assignments. They were inferred from fragmentary remains of an early version of Kiva G at Pueblo Bonito. (The currently visible round rooms fronting Pueblo Bonito construction of this period almost certainly postdate 1075.)

Whatever the status of round rooms, rectangular rooms certainly do not continue the tenth-century pattern. The last vestige of the large-room-and-two-small-rooms suite may be the east wing of Pueblo Alto; however, even here the pattern is confused by an odd, very small round room that divides the two large rooms. In almost all building programs, paired rear row rooms are absent.

With the possible exception of construction at Pueblo Alto, the size differences between most front and rear row rooms are minor or nonexistent; that is, rear row rooms are about the same size as front row rooms. The decreasing sizes evident in the later, linear suite pattern are not evident in the wings built during 1050–1060.

1060–1075. Major construction during this period consisted of additions to and asymmetric extension of existing buildings. A single new building, Pueblo del Arroyo, was begun.

New stories were added at Chetro Ketl, and at Pueblo Bonito. Rooms were built over existing rear and middle rows. As noted above, the interpretation of upper story additions is fraught with difficulties and ambiguities. The newer rooms naturally repeat the size and shape of the older rooms below them. Did the additions also repeat the functions of the older rooms? Since the upper story additions deprived the lower story rooms of exterior access, the function of those lower story rooms apparently did not require it. The older rooms apparently continued to be serviceable since they were not filled with trash, sealed off, or otherwise abandoned. The duplication of the lower story forms on the new upper story may represent an increase in the area devoted to the same function(s). Rear-row rooms were probably designed for storage; thus the upper stories added to Chetro Ketl and Pueblo Bonito during the 1060–1075 period may represent significant additions of storage space, without proportionate additions of habitation space.

Upper story additions are only one part of 1060–1075 construction, which also included asymmetric extensions of existing buildings (such as Peñasco Blanco, Pueblo Bonito, and Una Vida). These extensions were two stories tall, at least in their rear rows, and were about the same size as the wings added in the previous period (1050–1060).

The single new building, Pueblo del Arroyo, is similar in scale to the other 1060–1075 construction programs. For example, the asymmetric extension of Peñasco Blanco and initial building at Pueblo del Arroyo both have two rows of generally larger rooms backed by a row of much smaller rooms—the smaller size being in part determined by closer spacing of cross-walls. In number of rows and relative room sizes, these units recall the building characteristic of 1020–1050.

On the other hand, the 1060–1075 additions to Pueblo Bonito and Una Vida consisted of up to four rows of rooms. Room size decreased from front to rear solely as a function of decreasing room depth, not cross-wall spacing, creating the linear suites described above. Pueblo Bonito contains the earliest clear example of a linear suite; this pattern of rooms may also be present at Una Vida.

The earliest of these four programs, Peñasco Blanco (1050–1065), shows formal continuities with earlier building forms, whereas the latest program, Una Vida (1070–1075), anticipates the massed rooms and the linear suites of 1075–1115.

1075–1115. The most massive Chacoan construction went up between 1075 and 1115 (Figure 2.16). Six programs were exceptionally large: the east and west wings of Pueblo Bonito, the rear row of rooms (along with two end roomblocks) at Peñasco Blanco, the north and south wings of Pueblo del Arroyo, and Wijiji, a large great house built in a single program. These six units were much larger than any preceding construction stage: four or five rooms deep (the rear row of rooms at Peñasco Blanco, although only one room wide, made that unit five rooms deep) and—where evidence exists—a minimum of three stories tall.

The earliest of these programs at Pueblo Bonito and Peñasco Blanco added rooms to the rear of existing buildings. These rooms were probably road-related (Windes 1987:362ff). At Peñasco Blanco, the work was very similar to the first eleventh-century addition to Old Bonito; new construction at Peñasco Blanco enclosed the exposed rear wall of an early tenth-century arc. Rear rooms added to existing buildings recall the rows of upper story rooms added to Pueblo Bonito and Chetro Ketl during the preceding period, but on a much more massive scale. Building at Pueblo del Arroyo created two wings that were almost independent of the older, central roomblock. The last major building of this period was Wijiji, an entirely new building. Between 1075 and 1115 there is a progression from the addition of rows of (functionally specific?) rooms to existing buildings to the construction of largely independent wings and roomblocks to the creation of massive new buildings like Wijiji, presaging twelfth-century construction of structures like Kin Kletso and New Alto.

35

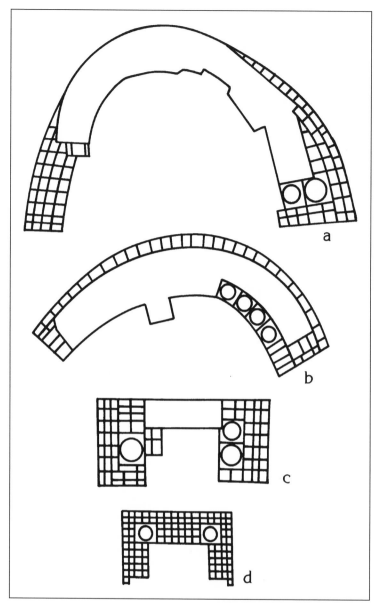

FIGURE 2.16. 1075–1115 building: (a) Pueblo Bonito,
(b) Peñasco Blanco, (c) Pueblo del Arroyo, (d) Wijiji.
(From Lekson 1984a:71, Figure 3.12)

The great majority of elevated round rooms have been assigned to this period; however, although many of the round rooms assigned to this period probably date no earlier than 1075, many may be later, perhaps much later. The uncertainty of dating precludes any extensive discussion of round rooms here.

Twelfth-Century Building (1115–1140?)
Buildings of the twelfth century generally correspond to the so-called McElmo phase (Vivian and Mathews 1965; Vivian 1990). The reality of this phase is a matter of some moment. The McElmo phase was first defined by Vivian and Mathews (1965) as an intrusion of northern San Juan groups into Chaco Canyon. Their argument was criticized and rejected by Lekson (1984:267–269), and later revived and championed by Vivian (1990:372–376). Some find Vivian's (1990) arguments persuasive (e.g., Van Dyke 2004); I do not, and I do not see McElmo as a cultural intrusion, but instead as a culmination of Bonito phase architectural traditions, which corresponded (perhaps coincidentally) to a broad, region-wide ceramic shift to carbon paints (often associated with the Northern San Juan area, but also implicated in northeastern Arizona traditions). "McElmo" sites are characterized by a particular ground plan (Figure 2.17), the use of McElmo-style masonry (with massive, tan sandstone rather than the tabular, darker brown stone previously preferred), and a well-dated assemblage of carbon-painted ceramics. "McElmo" sites include Kin Kletso, New Alto, Casa Chaquita, and Tsin Kletzin. To this conventional list, I add Pueblo del Arroyo, or at least its north and south wings (built in the preceding period), and Wijiji; Vivian's McElmo phase does not include these two sites.

Pueblo del Arroyo (discussed above) is one of Vivian and Mathews's Bonito phase towns; however, its north and south wings (Figure 2.17) mark a clear transition into the later Chacoan building forms of the "McElmo" phase. Pueblo del Arroyo's north and south wings each consist of large Chacoan round rooms surrounded on three sides by two or three rows of rooms. The rooms are remarkably uniform in size. Judd (1959:6) noted that much of this building, and particularly these wings, made use of recycled stone. Some construction is of the

Linear suites are evident at Pueblo Bonito, at both ends of the Peñasco Blanco addition, and in the south wing of Pueblo del Arroyo; however, most of the building during the 1075–1115 span consists of a tremendous number of interconnected interior rooms, or—in the case of Peñasco Blanco—rear rooms. In the east wing at Pueblo Bonito (added to the rear of an existing structure), in both wings at Pueblo del Arroyo, and at Wijiji, rooms are remarkably uniform in size.

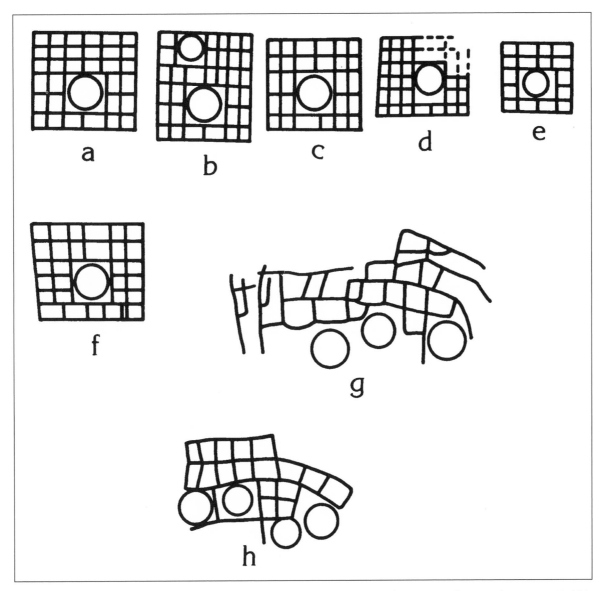

FIGURE 2.17. 1115+ building: (a) New Alto; (b) Kin Kletso, west; (c) Kin Kletso, east; (d) Casa Chiquita; (e) Rabbit Ruin, west; (f) Escalante Ruin; (g) Big Juniper House; (h) Bc 50. (From Lekson 1984a:73, Figure 3.13)

massive sandstone employed in the later, McElmo-style masonry. Reuse suggests a decreasing availability of tabular sandstone in the central canyon area; thus the wings of Pueblo del Arroyo may show the beginnings of both the ground plan and the stone selection that characterize subsequent twelfth-century "McElmo" construction. Wijiji, which shares "McElmo" room sizes and very low numbers of kivas, was built entirely of tabular sandstone, which would have been available in a part of the canyon that had previously seen no great house construction.

McElmo-style masonry appears at other, existing great houses. The first major twelfth-century construction in the central canyon was the Kiva G complex at Chetro Ketl (1110–1115). This unit is constructed almost entirely of pecked massive sandstone, in a style that would easily be lost at Kin Kletso, the "McElmo" phase type site. Much of the latest, plaza-facing construction at Pueblo Bonito was undertaken with masonry of McElmo style.

Tsin Kletzin is built of massive sandstone in the McElmo style, but this is an asymmetric building with an enclosed plaza, resembling earlier ground

37

plans more than it does Kin Kletso. Tsin Kletzin is located on the crest of South Mesa, well away from the most accessible sources of tabular sandstone.

Small-scale repairs and additions undoubtedly continued throughout the twelfth century at the existing buildings. Two of the largest "outliers," Kin Bineola and Aztec Ruin, were largely or entirely built in the early 1100s.

OTHER CONSTRUCTION

Mounds or Platforms

Several extraordinary features at Chaco have been called "trash mounds": one at Peñasco Blanco, one at Pueblo Alto, two at Pueblo Bonito, and one at Chetro Ketl (Figure 2.18). These mounds stood up to 6 m above the surrounding ground surface and were typically about 60 m by 40 m in plan.

Archaeologists, familiar with the comparatively small middens typical of "unit pueblos," were impressed by the size of the Chacoan mounds but saw them only as expanded versions of the unit pueblo middens.

If the mounds were simply middens, they should be present at other Chacoan sites occupied at the same time as Pueblo Bonito, Pueblo Alto, Chetro Ketl, and Peñasco Blanco. The absence of trash mounds at several structures (e.g., Una Vida and Hungo Pavi) with construction histories paralleling those of the structures with mounds strongly suggests that the mounds are, in fact, architectural.

Most Chacoan mounds were composed mainly of trash. Large proportions of this trash were clearly redeposited (Judd 1964). And, in addition to trash, the mounds typically include a great deal of sterile sand and construction debris (Judd 1964;

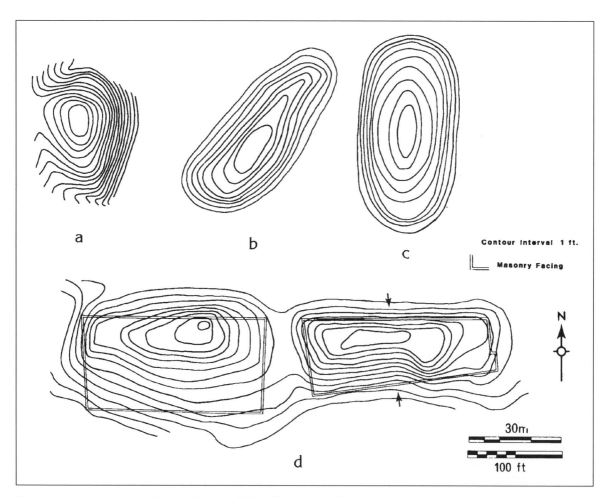

FIGURE 2.18. Mounds: (a) Peñasco Blanco; (b) Pueblo Alto; (c) Chetro Ketl, reconstructed; (d) Pueblo Bonito. (From Lekson 1984a:75, Figure 3.14)

Stephen H. Lekson

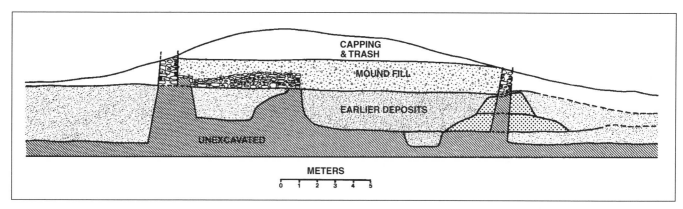

FIGURE 2.19. Stratigraphy of the East Mound, Pueblo Bonito. (Simplified; after Judd 1964: Figure 24; from Lekson 1984a:76, Figure 3.15)

Roberts 1927; Windes 1987). Many archaeologists argue that Chaco mounds are more than simple middens; these features are probably earthen architecture (Stein and Lekson 1992; Stein et al., Chapter 8, this volume; but see Wills 2001 for strong arguments against an architectural origin of these mounds).

Our knowledge of mound structure comes from trenches and small pits designed to test midden stratigraphy. We know less about their construction than we might wish, but differences in construction (stratigraphy) from mound to mound are suggestive (Hawley 1934; Judd 1964; Roberts 1927; Windes 1980, 1987). Some mounds were constructed initially of masonry debris overlain by layers of trash and sand (Pueblo Alto, Peñasco Blanco). Others were largely constructed of razed building debris (Pueblo Bonito, Chetro Ketl). Mounds with nearly identical final forms were made up of very different strata, and similar strata were deposited in very different sequences. Form seems to have been more important, or at least more consistent, than content.

The most spectacular and convincing examples of mound architecture at Chaco are the paired earthen structures in front of Pueblo Bonito. These two rectangular, masonry-faced features had flat surfaces 3–4 m above the surrounding ground level (clearly evident in period photographs, reproduced in Windes 1987: Figure 8.10). These surfaces were later buried under other deposits. When they were excavated, no one recognized the possibility of architectural mounds in the Anasazi area. As a result, the Pueblo Bonito mounds were repeatedly trenched by archaeologists who studied their

stratigraphy but failed to see their architecture (Figure 2.19). Even though Judd realized that the mounds were "not a normal trash pile" (Judd 1964:212), he continued to trench them as if they were. He did not excavate horizontally. Thus, we have no idea what sort of structures, if any, occupied the tops of the mounds.

On the basis of ceramics and the few available tree-ring dates, Windes (1980) concluded that the mounds at Pueblo Bonito, Pueblo Alto, and Chetro Ketl were constructed in the late eleventh or early twelfth century. The Peñasco Blanco mound contains earlier, tenth-century ceramics. Either the Peñasco Blanco mound is the earliest Chacoan mound, or the mound was constructed with redeposited earlier trash. The position of the mound outside a late (post-1090), plaza-enclosing arc of rooms supports this interpretation.

Tri-Walled Structures

Tri- and bi-walled structures are circular rooms surrounded by one or two concentric rows of rooms (see Figure 2.20, the Hubbard Triwall at Aztec Ruins, the best preserved of the excavated examples). They are an unusual form, and since most of the known examples are located north of the San Juan River, archaeologists were excited when one was uncovered behind Pueblo del Arroyo. Most tri- and biwalls were found at sites with Mesa Verde components, so it had been assumed that they were a thirteenth-century Mesa Verde form.

The Pueblo del Arroyo Triwall was excavated in two separate projects, first by Karl Ruppert (Judd 1959) and later by Gordon Vivian (Vivian 1959).

39

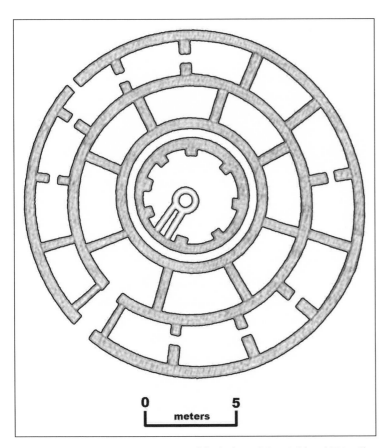

FIGURE 2.20. Simplified plan of the Hubbard Triwall, Aztec Ruins. (After Vivian 1959)

Ruppert cleared most of the triwall structure. The recovered ceramics, according to Judd, included "a preponderance of Chaco-San Juan [Chaco McElmo Black-on-white] sherds . . . and a high proportion of Mesa Verde Black-on-white" (1959:118). The latter statement is contradicted by Roberts's (1927) analysis of the Pueblo del Arroyo ceramics. He recorded fewer than 60 sherds of Mesa Verde black-on-white from all the excavations at Pueblo del Arroyo, and more than 40 of those were in the fill of Kiva G, part of the main building to which the triwall was appended. Roberts summarized the triwall sherds as follows: "The potsherds from the [triwall] were practically all of the Chaco-San Juan Group. The few exceptions were typical proto-Mesa Verde [McElmo] pieces" (1927:240).

The decorated ceramics recovered by Vivian (1959:68) included only about 1% Mesa Verde Black-on-white. Vivian interpreted the presence of this small amount of Mesa Verde as coming "from a time of reoccupation of the canyon when the tri-wall was being razed for building stone" (1959:68). The northern distribution of triwalls influenced Vivian's assignment of the Pueblo del Arroyo example to his McElmo phase, which he thought was intrusive from the San Juan area; however, he noted that the Pueblo del Arroyo Triwall was the earliest of that building type.

The major pottery types in the Pueblo del Arroyo assemblage were McElmo, Chaco/Gallup, and Escavada Black-on-whites (probably including Red Mesa and Mancos; Vivian 1959: Figures 18 and 19). The decorated redwares were limited to Wingate and Puerco Black-on-red. This assemblage agrees with the early 1100s ceramics found at almost every major Chacoan building. A single tree-ring date of 1109 from the Pueblo del Arroyo Triwall confirms early 1100s construction.

Triwalls are a late architectural type in the Chacoan regional system, coincident with the shift of the regional focus from Chaco to the San Juan River and the north (Lekson 1984b). As a class of building, they are of only limited interest in the great pueblo architecture of Chaco Canyon. The single example, at Pueblo del Arroyo, had been prehistorically razed; little is known of the internal features of the central circular room and the concentric rows of rooms.

Roads

Prehistoric roads appear to radiate from Chaco to the edges of the San Juan Basin and beyond (Kincaid 1983; Nials, Stein and Roney 1987; Roney 1992, among others). The extent and meaning of the extra-canyon roads are currently issues of intense research (e.g., Kantner and Mahoney 2000). This discussion is limited to better-documented roads within Chaco Canyon (see Stein et al., Chapter 8, this volume). Roads within the canyon were often very well constructed, and they often included formal, even monumental, ramps, stairs, curb walls, and berms.

Holsinger (1901) was the first to report roads within the canyon. Many subsequent workers have investigated these roads, particularly in the Pueblo Bonito–Chetro Ketl–Pueblo Alto area (Kievit 1998; Vivian 1997a, 1997b; Windes 1987). Unfortunately, historical ranching, commercial activities, a century of archaeology, and National Park Service improvements have made the canyon floor a maze

40

of linear features; definitive mapping of the prehistoric road network within the canyon is difficult.

Notwithstanding the difficulties in producing an "accurate" map, roads were obviously an important part of Chacoan building. The evidence of stairs cut into the sandstone cliffs, massive masonry ramps, and several sections of prehistoric cut-and-fill attest to the labor investment in the roads, and their importance in the overall community plan. Numerous roads crisscrossed the canyon, running from building to building and sometimes to natural features. Their impact on the landscape should not be underestimated. The roads were undoubtedly one of the major land modifications in the Chacoan architectural repertoire.

Long, Low Walls

Long, low masonry walls are visible in several areas of Chaco Canyon; most were less than 1 m in height but 1 m or more in width. Some of these walls run along the edges of roads and are probably road-related features, whereas several others seem to delineate large enclosed areas around major buildings. In particular, there are several long, low walls around Pueblo Alto, and another extends from Pueblo Bonito toward Chetro Ketl.

The lack of rubble at the base of these walls suggests that they were never very tall. Physically, they would not have prevented access to the areas they define; however, even their low height may have been an architectural convention sufficient to channel or exclude traffic. The low walls formalize areas and areal relationships.

The extent and arrangement of these walls is no better known than the intra-canyon road system. The walls around Pueblo Alto have not been buried or otherwise obscured, unlike the walls on the canyon floor. The low walls at Pueblo Bonito were discovered only by excavation, and further excavation would doubtlessly disclose many more walls in the central canyon area.

CHACO ARCHITECTURE

Chacoan architectural traditions are defined by great houses, but they were not limited to those structures. Roads, mounds, and other landscape monuments extended the field of design to much larger areas; Chaco Canyon itself was probably a designed settlement, which some call a city (Lekson, Windes, and McKenna 2006). Design extended to the larger Chacoan region, with roads and "outlier" great houses transposing Canyon elements to distant settings. It is even possible that regional-scale design principles structured Chaco architecture and the Chaco settlement plan (Doxtater 2002; Lekson 1999).

Great houses, however, were the central objects, the defining structures of Chacoan architecture as we perceive it today. What were these buildings?

After more than a century of study, Pueblo Bonito, Chetro Ketl, and the other great houses have been interpreted in many different ways. Early speculation made them the abandoned palaces of ancient Aztecs (Simpson 1850). Throughout much of the twentieth century, great houses were seen as pueblos; that is, as independent agricultural villages comparable to Hopi, Zuni, Acoma, and the Rio Grande pueblos (Hewett 1936; Judd 1954, 1964; Vivian 1990). Mesoamerican themes reappeared mid-century, but with a reversed flow: several archaeologists argued that great house architecture was unprecedented in the Anasazi or ancestral Pueblo area and must have been inspired or directed by an incursion of Mexican colonists (anticipating by half a millennium similar actions of Spanish conquistadors) (Ferdon 1955). Appeals to Mexico reached a crescendo in the mid-1970s (Di Peso 1974; Hayes 1981; Kelley and Kelley 1975) but were thereafter eclipsed by understandings of Chaco as a locally developed, complex society (e.g., Schelberg 1984; see also discussion in Judge 1989). In both Mexican and local-complexity scenarios, great houses were not equated with modern pueblos: they were elite residences for foreign or domestic leaders. More recently, great houses have become ritual or ceremonial centers (e.g., Judge 1989; Renfrew 2001; Wills 2000). The possibility of elite residence has not vanished (Lekson 1999; Lekson, Windes, and McKenna 2006; Neitzel 2003), nor has the notion of Mesoamerican intrusion (Turner and Turner 1999). And throughout these academic debates, the pueblo model of great houses remains the most widely accepted popular perception, and it still finds favor with many important archaeologists (Vivian 1990).

It might be possible to find some common ground among these competing arguments, but I can't see it. I see compelling evidence for elite residence, even palatial functions for great houses; others consider the same evidence and see ritual centers or pueblos. You will find elements of all these interpretations, and more, in the following chapters.

Adler, Michael
1993 Why Is a Kiva? New Interpretations of Prehistoric Social Integrative Architecture in the Northern Rio Grande Region of New Mexico. *Journal of Anthropological Research* 49:319–346.

Adler, Michael, and Richard H. Wilshusen
1990 Large-Scale Integrative Facilities in Tribal Societies. *World Archaeology* 22(2):133–146.

Adams, E. Charles
1991 *The Origin and Development of the Pueblo Katsina Cult.* University of Arizona Press, Tucson.

Bernardini, Wesley
1999 Reassessing the Scale of Social Action at Pueblo Bonito, Chaco Canyon, New Mexico. *Kiva* 64: 447–470.

Bustard, Wendy
2003 Pueblo Bonito: When a House Is Not a Home. In *Pueblo Bonito*, edited by Jill E. Neitzell, pp. 80–93. Smithsonian Books, Washington, DC.

Cater, John, and Mark Chenault
1988 Kiva Use Reinterpreted. *Southwestern Lore* 54(3):19–32.

Crown, Patricia, and W. H. Wills
2003 Modifying Pottery and Kivas at Chaco: Pentimento, Restoration, or Renewal? *American Antiquity* 68:511–532.

Di Peso, Charles C.
1974 *Casas Grandes: A Fallen Trading Center of the Gran Chichimeca.* Amerind Foundation, Dragoon, AZ.

Doxtater, Dennis
2002 A Hypothetical Layout of Chaco Canyon Structures via Large-Scale Alignments between Significant Natural Features. *Kiva* 68:23–47.

Ferdon, Edwin N.
1955 *A Trial Survey of Mexican-Southwestern Architectural Parallels.* School of American Research Monograph 21. Santa Fe.

Gillespie, William B.
1974 *Culture Change at the Ute Canyon Site.* M.A. thesis, Department of Anthropology, University of Colorado, Boulder.

Hawley, Florence
1934 *The Significance of the Dated Prehistory of Chetro Ketl.* University of New Mexico Bulletin 246, Monograph Series 1(1). University of New Mexico Press, Albuquerque.

Hayes, Alden C.
1981 A Survey of Chaco Canyon Archeology. In *Archeological Surveys of Chaco Canyon*, by Alden C. Hayes, David M. Brugge, and W. James Judge, pp. 1–68. Publications in Archeology 18A, Chaco Canyon Studies. National Park Service, Santa Fe.

Hewett, Edgar L.
1936 *The Chaco Canyon and Its Monuments.* University of New Mexico, Albuquerque, and School of American Research, Santa Fe.

Hodge, Frederick Webb
1923 *Circular Kivas near Hawikuh, New Mexico.* Contributions from the Museum of the American Indian 7(1).

Holsinger, S. J.
1901 Report on Prehistoric Ruins of Chaco Canyon, New Mexico. Ordered by General Land Office Letter "P," December 18, 1900. General Land Office. Ms. on file, National Anthropological Archive, Smithsonian Institution, Washington, DC.

Judd, Neil M.
1954 *The Material Culture of Pueblo Bonito.* Smithsonian Miscellaneous Collections 124. Smithsonian Institution, Washington, DC.

1959 *Pueblo del Arroyo, Chaco Canyon, New Mexico.* Smithsonian Miscellaneous Collections 138(1). Smithsonian Institution, Washington, DC.

1964 *The Architecture of Pueblo Bonito.* Smithsonian Miscellaneous Collections 147(1). Smithsonian Institution, Washington, DC.

1967 The Passing of a Small PIII Ruin. *Plateau* 39(3): 131–133.

Judge, W. James
1989 Chaco Canyon/San Juan Basin. In *Dynamics of Southwest Prehistory*, edited by Linda S. Cordell and George J. Gumerman, pp. 209–261. Smithsonian Institution Press, Washington, DC.

1991 Chaco: Current Views of Prehistory and the Regional System. In *Chaco and Hohokam: Prehistoric Regional Systems in the American Southwest*, edited by Patricia L. Crown and W. James Judge, pp. 11–30. School of American Research Press, Santa Fe.

Kantner, John, and Nancy Mahoney, eds.
2000 *Great House Communities across the Chacoan Landscape.* Anthropological Papers 64. University of Arizona Press, Tucson.

Kelley, J. Charles, and Ellen Abbott Kelley
1975 An Alternative Hypothesis for the Explanation of Anasazi Culture History. In *Collected Papers in Honor of Florence Hawley Ellis*, edited by Theodore R. Frisbie, pp. 178–223. Papers of the Archaeological Society of New Mexico 2. Hooper Publishing, Norman, OK.

Stephen H. Lekson

Kievit, Karen A.

1998 Seeing and Reading Chaco Architecture at AD 1100. Unpublished Ph.D. dissertation, Department of Anthropology, University of Colorado, Boulder.

Kincaid, Chris, ed.

1983 *Chaco Roads Project Phase I: A Reappraisal of Prehistoric Roads in the San Juan Basin.* Bureau of Land Management, New Mexico State Office, Santa Fe, and Albuquerque District Office.

Kuckelman, Kristin A., ed.

2003 *The Archaeology of Yellow Jacket Pueblo (Site 5MT5): Excavations at a Large Community Center in Southwestern Colorado* [HTML Title]. Available online at <http://www.crowcanyon. org/yellowjacket>.

Lekson, Stephen H.

1981 Cognitive Frameworks and Chacoan Architecture. *New Mexico Journal of Science* 21(1):27–36.

1984a *Great Pueblo Architecture of Chaco Canyon.* Publications in Archeology 18B, Chaco Canyon Studies. National Park Service, Santa Fe.

1984b Dating the Hubbard Tri-wall and Other Tri-wall Structures. *Southwestern Lore* 49(4):15–23.

1999 *Chaco Meridian: Centers of Political Power in the Ancient Southwest.* Altamira, Walnut Creek, CA.

Lekson, Stephen H., Thomas C. Windes, and Peter J. McKenna

2006 Architecture. In *The Archaeology of Chaco Canyon, An Eleventh-Century Pueblo Regional Center,* edited by Stephen H. Lekson, pp. 67–116. School of American Research Press, Santa Fe.

Lipe, William D.

1989 Social Scale of Mesa Verde Anasazi Kivas. In *The Architecture of Social Integration in Prehistoric Pueblos,* edited by William D. Lipe and Michelle Hegmon, pp. 53–71. Occasional Papers 1. Crow Canyon Archaeological Center, Cortez, CO.

Marshall, Michael P., John R. Stein, Richard W. Loose, and Judith E. Novotny

1979 *Anasazi Communities of the San Juan Basin.* Public Service Company, Albuquerque, and New Mexico State Historic Preservation Bureau, Santa Fe.

Mathien, Frances Joan

2005 *Culture and Ecology of Chaco Canyon and the San Juan Basin.* Publications in Archeology 18H. National Park Service, Santa Fe.

McClellan, George E.

1969 *The Origin, Development, and Typology of Anasazi Kivas and Great Kivas.* Ph.D. dissertation, University of Colorado, Boulder.

McKenna, Peter J., and Marcia L. Truell

1986 *Small Site Architecture of Chaco Canyon, New Mexico.* Publications in Archeology 18D, Chaco Canyon Studies. National Park Service, Santa Fe.

Miller, James Marshall

1937 The G Kivas of Chetro Ketl. Unpublished M.A. thesis, University of Southern California, Los Angeles.

Morris, Earl H.

1921 *The House of the Great Kiva at Aztec Ruin.* American Museum of Natural History Anthropological Papers 26(2). New York.

1928 *The Aztec Ruin.* American Museum of Natural History Anthropological Papers 26. New York.

Neitzel, Jill E., ed.

2003 *Pueblo Bonito: Center of the Chacoan World.* Smithsonian Books, Washington, DC.

Nials, Fred, John Stein, and John Roney

1987 *Chacoan Roads in the Southern Periphery: Results of Phase II of the BLM Chaco Roads Project.* Cultural Resources Series 1. Bureau of Land Management, New Mexico State Office, Santa Fe.

Pepper, George H.

1920 *Pueblo Bonito.* American Museum of Natural History Anthropological Papers 27. New York.

Powers, Robert P., William B. Gillespie, and Stephen H. Lekson

1983 *The Outlier Survey: A Regional View of Settlement in the San Juan Basin.* Reports of the Chaco Center 3. Division of Cultural Research, National Park Service, Albuquerque.

Reiter, Paul D.

1933 The Ancient Pueblo of Chetro Ketl. Unpublished M.A. thesis, Department of Anthropology, University of New Mexico, Albuquerque.

1946 Form and Function in Some Prehistoric Ceremonial Structures in the Southwest. Unpublished Ph.D. dissertation, Department of Anthropology, Harvard University, Cambridge, MA.

Renfrew, Colin

2001 Production and Consumption in a Sacred Economy: The Material Correlates of High Devotional Expression at Chaco Canyon. *American Antiquity* 66:14–25.

Roberts, Frank H. H., Jr.

1927 The Ceramic Sequence in the Chaco Canyon, New Mexico, and Its Relation to the Cultures of the San Juan Basin. Unpublished Ph.D. dissertation, Harvard University, Cambridge, MA.

Rohn, Arthur H.

1983 Budding Urban Settlements in the Northern San Juan. In *Proceedings of the Anasazi Symposium 1981,* edited by Jack E. Smith, pp. 175–180. Mesa Verde Museum Association, Mesa Verde.

Roney, John R.

1992 Prehistoric Roads and Regional Interaction in the Chacoan System. In *Anasazi Regional Organization and the Chaco System,* edited by David E. Doyel, pp. 123–131. Anthropological Papers 5. Maxwell Museum of Anthropology, University of New Mexico, Albuquerque.

Schelberg, John D.

1984   Analogy, Complexity, and Regionally Based Perspectives. In *Recent Research on Chaco Prehistory*, edited by W. James Judge and John D. Schelberg, pp. 5–21. Reports of the Chaco Center 8. Division of Cultural Research, National Park Service, Albuquerque.

Simpson, James Hervey

1850   Journal of a Military Reconnaissance from Santa Fe, New Mexico, to the Navajo Country. *Report of the Secretary of War to the 31st Congress, 1st Session, Senate Executive Document* 65:55–168. Washington, DC.

Smith, Watson

1952   When Is a Kiva? In *Excavations in the Big Hawk Valley, Wupatki National Monument, Arizona*, by Watson Smith, pp. 154–162. Museum of Northern Arizona Bulletin 24. Flagstaff.

Stein, John R., and Stephen H. Lekson

1992   Anasazi Ritual Landscapes. In *Anasazi Regional Organization and the Chaco System*, edited by David E. Doyel, pp. 87–100. Anthropological Papers 5. Maxwell Museum of Anthropology, University of New Mexico, Albuquerque.

Steward, Julian

1937   Ecological Aspects of Southwestern Society. *Anthropos* 32:87–104.

Swentzell, Rina

1989   Pueblo Space, Form and Mythology. In *Pueblo Style and Regional Architecture*, edited by Nicholas C. Markovich, Wolfgang F. E. Preiser, and Fred G. Sturm, pp. 23–30. Van Nostrand Reinhold, New York.

Truell, Marcia L.

1986   A Summary of Small Site Architecture in Chaco Canyon, New Mexico. Part II in *Small Site Architecture of Chaco Canyon, New Mexico*, by Peter J. McKenna and Marcia L. Truell, pp. 115–502. Publications in Archeology 18D, Chaco Canyon Studies. National Park Service, Santa Fe.

Turner, Christy G. II, and Jacqueline A. Turner

1999   *Man Corn.* University of Utah Press, Salt Lake City.

Van Dyke, Ruth M.

2004   Memory, Meaning, and Masonry: The Late Bonito Chacoan Landscape. *American Antiquity* 69:413–431.

Vivian, R. Gordon

1936   Restoring Rinconada. *El Palacio* 41:89–97.

1959   *The Hubbard Site and Other Tri-wall Structures in New Mexico and Colorado.* Archaeological Research Series No. 5. National Park Service, Washington, DC.

Vivian, R. Gordon, and Tom W. Mathews

1965   Kin Kletso: A Pueblo III Community in Chaco Canyon, New Mexico. *Technical Series* 6(1):1–115. Southwest Parks and Monuments Association, Globe, AZ.

Vivian, R. Gordon, and Paul Reiter

1960   *The Great Kivas of Chaco Canyon and Their Relationships.* School of American Research and Museum of New Mexico Monograph 22. Santa Fe.

Vivian, R. Gwinn

1990   *The Chacoan Prehistory of the San Juan Basin.* Academic Press, San Diego.

1997a   Chacoan Roads: Morphology. *Kiva* 63:7–34.

1997b   Chacoan Roads: Function. *Kiva* 63:35–67.

Wills, W. H.

2000   Political Leadership in Chaco Canyon, New Mexico, AD 1020–1140. In *Alternative Leadership Strategies in the Prehispanic Southwest*, edited by Barbara J. Mills, pp. 19–44. University of Arizona Press, Tucson.

2001   Ritual and Mound Formation during the Bonito Phase in Chaco Canyon. *American Antiquity* 66:433–451.

Windes, Thomas C.

1984   A New Look at Population in Chaco Canyon. In *Recent Research on Chaco Prehistory*, edited by W. James Judge and John D. Schelberg, pp. 75–87. Reports of the Chaco Center 8. Division of Cultural Research, National Park Service, Albuquerque.

1987   *Investigations at the Pueblo Alto Complex, Chaco Canyon, New Mexico, 1975–1979.* Publications in Archeology 18F, Chaco Canyon Studies. National Park Service, Santa Fe.

1993   *The Spadefoot Toad Site: Investigations at 29SJ629, Chaco Canyon, New Mexico,* 2 vols. Reports of the Chaco Center 12. Branch of Cultural Research, National Park Service, Santa Fe.

Windes, Thomas C., and Dabney Ford

1992   The Nature of the Early Bonito Phase. In *Anasazi Regional Organization and the Chaco System*, edited by David E. Doyel, pp. 75–85. Anthropological Papers 5. Maxwell Museum of Anthropology, University of New Mexico, Albuquerque.

1996   The Chaco Wood Project: The Chronometric Reappraisal of Pueblo Bonito. *American Antiquity* 61:295–310.

Woods, Janet Mc.

1934   Excavation of the Court Kiva, Chetro Ketl. Archive 1919, 1941, 2125, National Park Service Chaco Archives, University of New Mexico, Albuquerque.

Stephen H. Lekson

3

Gearing Up and Piling On

Early Great Houses in the Interior San Juan Basin

Thomas C. Windes

THE NORTHERN, WESTERN, AND SOUTHWESTERN peripheries of the geological San Juan Basin enjoyed extensive, persistent Puebloan occupation from Basketmaker II through Pueblo III times. Conversely, the interior of the basin (Figure 3.1), which is drained by the Chaco River, had its population peaks but generally was sparsely inhabited for much of the Puebloan era. Given the differential natural resources, soils, and climate of the two areas, it is not surprising that societies based on agricultural economies found the interior basin a harsh and difficult place to establish long-term occupation and subsistence. But for a relatively short period of time, the use of the land and resources in these two adjoining regions flip-flopped dramatically. Key early great houses from Chaco Canyon and to the west illuminate the rise of the Chacoan system and great house architecture and emphasize the importance of the Pueblo I era.[1]

The 800s in the greater San Juan Basin reflect tumultuous times (all dates in this chapter are AD). Extensive studies in the northern San Juan region show that for a short period of time huge communities formed and then disbanded, depopulating entire river valleys in the highlands (e.g., Varien et al. 1996; Varien and Wilshusen 2002; Wilshusen 1999; Wilshusen and Ortman 1999). Simultaneously, within the lower San Juan Basin (south of the San Juan River), new communities, often with a large building in association, formed after minimal

and widely dispersed prior occupation. Clearly, large numbers of people were on the move, particularly by the late 800s.

Based on ceramic time (Table 3.1), the interior basin filled with new inhabitants between about 875 and 1050, culminating in the centralization of great houses in the lower Chaco Canyon between 1050 and 1100. Just prior to the first influx of migrants in the late 800s and early 900s, sites were dominated by Lino Gray and White Mound Black-on-white (775–850), and today they rarely exhibit much surface archaeological material. The few surface remains have minimal relief, and the refuse is sparse. Houses are small, rarely exceeding room space for two to four families. The sense is that they are very short-lived habitations, even in communities such as those along the Fajada South Fork.

At about 875, something dramatic happened throughout the San Juan Basin. New communities and isolated great houses were founded, and the amount of refuse skyrockets at most small houses and at many of the new great houses. Both site longevity and activity intensity/diversity produced unprecedented amounts of refuse. In the northern San Juan, poor building materials and harsh environments are believed to have restricted use of structures to a mere 10–15 years (Ahlstrom 1985; Cameron 1990; Schlanger 1985, 1987) or, at best, 40–50 years (Wilshusen 1991) except at the large villages. Yet, these same materials of adobe, some

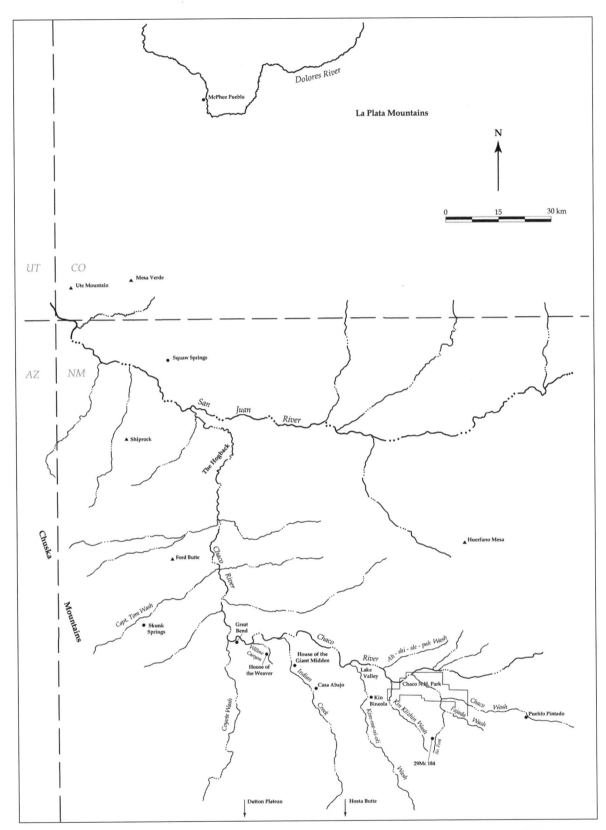

FIGURE 3.1. The Chaco River and its tributaries in the interior San Juan Basin. Many proto- and early great houses were built along its course in the 800s. (From Windes 2006)

46

Thomas C. Windes

TABLE 3.1. Ceramic Assemblage Time in the San Juan Basin Interior: Cibola Tradition

TIME (AD)	PROMINENT WHITEWARES	LESSER WHITEWARES	PROMINENT GRAYWARES	LESSER GRAYWARES
600–750	La Plata B/w	Lino B/g	Obelisk Gray, Lino Gray Plain gray	
750–850	White Mound B/w	La Plata B/w	Lino Gray Plain gray	
850–875	White Mound B/w	La Plata B/w Kiatuthlanna B/w	Lino Gray Plain gray	Wide neckbanded
875–900	Kiatuthlanna B/w	White Mound B/w Red Mesa B/w	Plain gray Wide neckbanded[a]	Lino Gray
900–925	Red Mesa B/w	Kiatuthlanna B/w	Plain gray Wide neckbanded[b]	Narrow neckbanded
925–1000	Red Mesa B/w	—	Plain gray Narrow neckbanded[b]	Neck indented corrugated
1000–1050	Red Mesa B/w	Gallup B/w Puerco B/w	Plain gray Narrow neckbanded[b] Neck indented corrugated	Indented corrugated
1050–1100	Gallup B/w	Puerco B/w	Indented corrugated	

Note: Rare numbers (absent to >1%) of San Juan and Chuskan redwares present in all periods. Depending on site location, equivalent types of Chuskan and rarely Kayentan and Mesa Verdean types are present.

Indented corrugated = overall indented corrugated vessels.

[a] Much is clapboard variety.

[b] Majority is clapboard variety.

stone, and wood were the construction mainstays for small houses in the interior basin that now often spanned more than a century of use (e.g., Marshall and Bradley 1994; McKenna 1984; Truell 1992; Windes 1993), though not necessarily continuous (e.g., Windes 1993:401–402, 404). Some communities lasted into the 900s but were then abandoned, while others continued in use into the 1000s. By the early 1000s, at least in the Chaco Canyon region, there is a decline in small houses (Windes 1987[I]:393–402, 1993:404). Small-house inhabitants dispersed from the basin interior back into the peripheral regions. Never again were there such alluring attractions that brought a flood of people into the interior San Juan Basin.

The appearance within the San Juan Basin of a limited number of houses built with stone stands in sharp contrast to the normal regional construction techniques and represents a type of architecture that was not common previously. From a practical point of view, this technique produced structures that were built to last, employing stone that was highly resistant to deterioration and fire. The visual aspects of masonry architecture would

also have signaled cultural values of prestige and power (Hegmon 1989; Nielsen 1995). Initially, these houses tended to be small and of one or two stories, but some of them grew as additions were made later on.

In the interior basin, three highly noticeable aspects of the new sites contrast sharply with previous occupations: the use of substantial stone architecture in a few scattered structures, the creation of massive refuse mounds that are not only dense with artifacts but piled vertically, and the placement of great houses in settings with a commanding view of the region. A refocus on the architectural and cultural landscape modifications that relate to our understanding of these early great houses leads to new conclusions about the rise of Chacoan culture.

In the 1970s, two pioneering studies (Marshall et al. 1979; Powers et al. 1983) alerted Southwestern archaeologists to the extent of and wide variation in the new-style structures and site clustering; however, systematic regional survey and extensive documentation of the majority of these important sites are still mostly lacking. Even existing reports

47

of great houses, great kivas, and large middens, as well as their temporal contexts, cannot be taken at face value given the wide range of reporting biases from differing institutional agendas and personal field experience, education, and backgrounds. These handicaps distort our understanding of the Puebloan use of the San Juan Basin because they have been assembled from a mishmash of contract investigations focused on linear rights-of-way, well pads, and other piecemeal work. Large-scale, systematic surveys are still needed for the interior drainages, which were conduits for movement during the ebb and flow of San Juan Basin use.

Although widespread recognition of the big "bumps" (Figure 3.2) on the landscape (Lekson 1991, 1999) drew initial archaeological attention to the identification of great houses in the greater San Juan Basin, little effort has been expended on explaining the initial rise of these structures. Much work has been conducted in the San Juan Basin, but a systematic reexamination of sites defined as potential early great houses has been lacking. The complex nature of these structures, often overlying earlier constructions, and the distribution of cultural materials at the sites do not lend themselves to cursory inspections, mapping, and ceramic tallies. These early great houses comprised the initial "footprint" of a new social dynamic that has been

variously described as "Chacoan." Whether it was a system, a phenomenon, an emerging hierarchial society, a relocation of prior communities, or whatever, is still hotly debated (Mills 2002), but the lack of focus on origins ill serves our understanding and interpretations of the later Classic and post-classic Bonito phases.

THE LANDSCAPE AND ENVIRONMENTAL SETTING

Buildings and refuse symbolize larger relationships with physical landscapes that few investigators have fully appreciated. The interior San Juan Basin provides a diversity of landscape features: badlands, stark plains, mesas, buttes, volcanic cones, mountain peaks, hidden valleys, and other viewsheds that connect to physical and spiritual worlds that were highly important to the inhabitants (e.g., Doxtater 2002; Kievit 1998; Ortiz 1969; Swentzell 1997; Van Dyke 2003). Occasionally, physical links between the inhabitants and their landscape can be discerned from the networks of prehistoric roads and shrines. These links may extend back in time to the beginnings of the new settlements, helping to connect them with the earlier homesteads, past histories, and past settlement memories, and enabling the inhabitants to forge new ritual landscapes (e.g., Fowler and Stein 1992; Van Dyke 2003). The economic landscape brings an additional dimension to the communities that utilize it. Some of these important connections are discussed here as part of ongoing research that reemphasizes their importance within great house settings.

It is hard to imagine that the dry interior San Juan Basin was ever as attractive as the wetter but cooler drainages north of the San Juan River. But the interior basin lies between alternating summer-dominant and bimodal summer-and-winter precipitation regimes (Dean 1996). This may have influenced farming and settlement strategies over time and in turn helped to spur the shifting mobility patterns common to the region.

Dean's (1996) modeling of the environment indicates that an expansion into the San Juan Basin from the surrounding regions occurred during an episode of high variability in precipitation between 750 and 1000. But the model is too broad to pinpoint specific environmental episodes, if any, that might have sparked such widespread mobility in

FIGURE 3.2. The "big bump" profile of the Chaco East Community great house (29MC560). (Photograph by Richard Moeller, January 2003; from Windes 2006)

Thomas C. Windes

the late 800s. Burns (1983) proposes food short-falls in the northern San Juan in the late 800s correlating with the northern settlement dislocations, and Wiseman (1982) shows a concordant dispersal of inhabitants along the Chuksan slope into more marginal environments during wetter times. Still, at this point we do not understand enough about paleoenvironmental conditions in and around the San Juan Basin peripheries to know what thresholds were exceeded to cause migrations and the significant social adjustments that resulted in the influx of peoples into the basin interior.

Although our knowledge of early great houses south of the San Juan River is limited, those examined here suggest that in general many of the inhabitants of the northern settlements and those along the Chuskan slope may have moved into the interior San Juan Basin when the northern region was abandoned. The readaptation may have not been as dramatic as the stark differences between the northern highland and southern basin landscapes suggest. Although upland, dryland farming dominated the economy of the northern settlements in the central Mesa Verde–Dove Creek–Dolores area, the location of many of the largest settlements in river and drainage valleys suggests that runoff/floodwater farming could have been practiced. Oddly, little or no credence is given to the possibility of floodwater farming as an alternative or supplemental means for crop production in the north (e.g., Peterson 1987), which would have hastened crop growth and shortened the required growing season in areas at risk for early or late frosts. Still, most if not all early great houses and their communities in the southern San Juan Basin are found in association with drainages, as are many of their large counterparts to the north, with a particularly heavy clustering along tributaries to the Chaco Wash and Chaco River. In the south, the opportunities for dryland farming are limited given the lower precipitation rates (6–8 inches), so farming practices are expected to have been more diverse and spread out. The various farming strategies available to pueblo inhabitants are typically given little more than lip service, however, and are seldom systematically explored to provide viable estimates of the subsistence economy.

In a real sense, the interior San Juan Basin is harsh and unpredictable (Lekson 1984; Powers et al. 1983; Schelberg 1992), but some areas are clearly more favorable than others. These areas, attractive in the late 800s, were all associated with drainages. Given our knowledge of farming technologies of the time, we might expect that much of the attraction was a result of environmental factors that had become more favorable in the basin interior (Sebastian 1992), while deteriorating in peripheral areas (Wilshusen and Wilson 1995). On the other hand, some areas along the basin periphery, such as the Chuskas, may have experienced more favorable conditions that allowed or forced competing populations to push into more marginal areas (e.g., Wiseman 1982). But the environment cannot be downplayed (Varien 2002) as a critical causal factor for expansion into the basin because the climate of the interior prohibits sustained farming except for periods of extended rainfall or high water tables.

Three prominent tributaries of the Chaco River between Chaco Canyon and the Chuska Mountains (Coyote Wash, Indian Creek, and Kim-me-ni-oli/Lake Valley) may have provided pathways for the spread of people from the south (Figure 3.1). But vast areas of the San Juan Basin remain archaeologically unknown, and if there was a conduit for movement into the interior basin, the Chaco River could have been the primary access, particularly for those coming from the west and north. With the knowledge gained from research in the past few decades, we need to reevaluate great house sites, especially with regard to their complex temporal and architectural histories and their potential origins.

MOUNDS AS FEATURES ON THE CULTURAL LANDSCAPE

Many of the Chacoan great houses have an attendant mound(s) of cultural material, often exceeding 1,000 m³, which also sets them apart from normal house sites. Not only do these mounds greatly exceed normal accumulations found at small-house sites, they also are prominent markers on the landscape (Cameron 2002; Stein and Lekson 1992; Windes 1987[I]). To provide scale, compare them with examples of discarded refuse from excavated small-house sites. External middens at three contemporary small houses in Chaco Canyon with

49

between two and five households that were occupied for more than a century have volumes of approximately 41 m³ (McKenna 1984:92–93), 65 m³ (Windes 1993:245), and 570 m³ (Truell 1992: 193–202), several orders of magnitude smaller than many of the great house middens. The largest volume of 570 m³ was calculated for a small house of five households occupied for more than 400 years (Truell 1992:193), a time span greatly exceeding the length of occupation/use of many great houses. Keep in mind, however, that neither for Chacoan small houses nor for great houses can we be sure of continuous occupation during the span of use (e.g., Windes et al. 2000). In the north, the late 800s Pueblo I Duckfoot site yielded 67,000 sherds from the extramural midden of 108 m³ (Lightfoot 1994; Lightfoot et al. 1993:124) that was generated over 20 years by three households totaling between 14 and 25 people. The numbers and types of artifacts discarded are even more telling of the vast discrepancy between small-house and great house middens and deserve detailed study.

A recent focus on mounds and earthen architecture at great houses in central Chaco Canyon and other large sites in the region (Cameron 2002; Marshall 1997; Toll 2001; Van Dyke 2000; Wills 2001; Windes 1987[II]) builds on earlier work by John Stein and his colleagues (Fowler and Stein 1992; Fowler et al. 1987; Stein and Lekson 1992; Stein and McKenna 1988; Stein et al., Chapter 8, this volume) that examines these features within the overall cultural landscape of Chacoan sites. Fowler and Stein (1992) argue, for example, that these mounds are sacred in character and are encoded to reflect deep ties to and continuity with the past (see also Van Dyke 2003). They also appear placed as part of a larger scheme of landscaping around the great houses, serving as markers, boundaries, and points of entry for prehistoric roads. The prominence of many of these late mounds suggests to Schlanger (personal communication 2005) that they may have intentionally been made voluminous to create the impression of occupational longevity and ties to the land to achieve greater status for the inhabitants.

Mounds in front of great houses in downtown Chaco achieved their greatest volumes during the 1050–1100 period, but the deposits did not conform to materials discarded by small-house inhabitants.

Instead, only low quantities of the usual ash, charcoal, and vegetal material have been found in mounds, and almost no burials. In addition, their great size, internal layering (Toll 1985; Windes 1987[II]), and the presence of construction debris makes these features extraordinary, particularly in light of their relatively rapid accumulation over 50 years or less (Toll 1985; Windes 1987). The formal nature of these mounds *and* the projected low numbers of associated residents suggest both ritual and intermittent activities at the sites (e.g., Lekson 1991; Stein and Lekson 1992; Toll 1985, 2001). Wills (2001:434, 446–447), however, has argued that the mounds were not intentionally placed and built as part of ritual activity but instead represent debris from construction activities correlated with the number of rooms at the sites, site location, and occupation duration.

In previous works (Windes 1987[II]:561–667), I have argued for the special character of the great house mounds deposited between 1050 and 1100. These deposits were coeval with a proliferation of activities involving architecture and material goods that have been used to define the classic period of Chacoan culture. Aside from the unusual size and contents of the mounds, it is the discrepancy between the large amount of materials and the estimated low numbers of residents that is noteworthy. Large mounds might be considered normal if the huge number of residents originally postulated for the large great houses (e.g., Drager 1976; Hayes 1981; Judd 1959, 1964; Pierson 1949; Vivian 1990) were accurate. But any correlation between house size and mound volume (Wills 2001) is tenuous at best and based on far too small a sample. There are many striking examples of relatively small great houses with substantial mounds, including those described here at Casa del Rio, Great Bend, Willow Canyon, and Lake Valley (Table 3.2), as well as some large great houses (e.g., Una Vida and Wijiji) without mounds. This variability defies explanations that link refuse accumulation to domestic activities.

Large mounds are not unique to the 1000s; they also occur at some early great houses. These early mounds provide new evidence that can be used to examine the relationship, if any, between mound size and the number of residents. At least five early great houses (Peñasco Blanco, Casa del Rio, Lake

TABLE 3.2. Middens from Selected Early and Proto–Great Houses

SITE	MAXIMUM DEPTH (cm)	VOLUME (m³)	CERAMIC SURFACE DENSITY (per m²)	ESTIMATED NUMBER OF MIDDEN SHERDS[†] (1000s)	GROUNDSTONE SURFACE DENSITY (per m²)
Peñasco Blanco East Midden	366	1430–1840[a]	17.8[b]	585–1460	unknown
Casa del Rio Midden 1	165–505	1702	22.5	609–1520	.08
Lake Valley Midden 2	150+	2475	39.8	886–2210	.02
Kin Bineola					
Midden 2	75	113	15.2	45–100	.01
Midden 5	30	106	10.0	42–95	.00
House of the Giant Midden	75	350	25.0	125–313	.04
Great Bend East Midden	70	330	40.3	118–295	.07
29MC184 Houses A-B Middens	10–20	50–60	03.8	14–17	.00

[†] Windes (1987[II]: Table 8.14). Range computed from high and low densities recorded in all great house middens after the highest and lowest densities were eliminated. Thus, high = 893 and low = 396 sherds/m³. Surface densities not computed into this result.

[a] Windes (1987[II]: Table 8.14).

[b] Density probably reduced by tourist theft.

Valley, Willow Canyon, and Great Bend) have mounds that contrast with the better-known, later mounds in the Chaco Canyon core and at some of the outlying great houses. These early mounds all have ash, charcoal, and bits of burned stone that indicate discard of household and firepit refuse; at least two have evidence of burials. Domestic refuse and burials are largely absent by the mid-1000s, however, when huge new deposits accumulated in front of many new or remodeled great houses (Toll 1985; Windes 1987[II]). The change in mound contents before and after about 1000 or 1050 indicates a dramatic change in great house activities and the intensity of occupation within these structures.

GREAT HOUSES: THE PERCEIVED BEGINNINGS

Most Southwestern archaeologists are acutely aware of evidence for underlying progenitors of what later expanded into the huge, multistoried buildings known as Peñasco Blanco, Pueblo Bonito, and Una Vida. It is here, some say (e.g., Cordell 1994; Judge et al. 1981:81; Lekson 1999:51; Plog 1997:111; Sebastian 1990, 1992; Stuart 2000:107; Vivian 1990:194), that it all began. The proximity of these three early structures, their preservation, the extent of excavation, and the ease of visitation has resulted in an overemphasis on these three at the expense of other, likely contemporaneous, if not earlier, "big bumps" that remain relatively out of reach, out of sight, and out of mind for most Chacoan investigators.

Indeed, the common definition of a Chacoan great house relies on attributes widely recognized nearly a quarter of a century ago (e.g., Hayes 1981; Judge et al. 1981; Marshall et al. 1979; Powers et al. 1983) during the initial focus on San Juan Basin great houses. The highly visible and appealing construction styles in vogue during the mid-to-late 1000s became (and remain) the hallmark of great house recognition: core-and-veneer masonry, multistory construction, oversized kivas, kivas built within the house architecture, a great kiva in the plaza or nearby, and a large midden. These highly visible attributes, touted in brochures and texts and on tours, have been noted by generations of field-school students who passed through the park during the requisite summer field trip. Thus, these sites provided the lasting, albeit distorted, image of a typical Chacoan great house.

Just two centuries before the appearance of these finely finished edifices, the stacking of stone to form crude massive walls was a new and rare style within the San Juan Basin (Table 3.3). Some walls were built with local, hard, dark-brown quartzitic sandstone from deposits of the Menefee Formation, which outcrops everywhere in the basin. The naturally occurring large, flat slabs

51

TABLE 3.3. Ceramic Assemblage Time in the San Juan Basin Interior: Architectural Trends

APPROX. TIME (AD)	TYPICAL HOUSE MASONRY	PROTO-GREAT HOUSE MASONRY	GREAT HOUSE MASONRY[†]
750–850	Slab foundations Mud walls with some spalls	Slab and block foundations Partial stone masonry	?
850–875	Slab foundations Mud walls with some spalls	Slab and block foundations Partial stone masonry	Type I masonry
875–900	Slab foundations Mud walls with some spalls/stones	Slab and block foundations Partial stone masonry	Type I masonry
900–925	Slab or block foundations Mud walls with some spalls/stones	Slab and block foundations Partial stone masonry	Type I masonry
925–1000	Block foundations Mud walls with some stone	?	Type I masonry

[†] Type I masonry of large, tabular slabs set horizontally in single or double-width courses, often two-story.

were shaped around the edges by hand and set in horizontal stacks. House mounds covered with these slabs, generally about 30–60 cm in the widest dimension, indicate the type of construction first described by Jackson (1878) and then formalized by Judd (1964:Plate 10), Hawley (1934:13), and Lekson (1984:17) as Type I masonry. Although the stone is tough and highly resistant to weathering (unlike that used later in much core-and-veneer masonry), it generally limits buildings to two stories when used in single-width construction. This stone slab material, set in abundant mortar and often faced with stone spalls, is indicative of Type I masonry in the 800s and 900s and a hallmark of early great house construction (also see Neitzel, Chapter 5, this volume). Type I masonry alone does not equate with great house architecture, but it does signify a shift in construction philosophy that merits more investigation as it relates to political and social differentiation.

At Pueblo Bonito and Una Vida, at least, the earliest structures were small masonry buildings (Windes and Ford 1992) with layouts that resemble the classic Pueblo I house form (Figure 3.3). An initial core unit at Peñasco Blanco, if any, has not been identified. Unfortunately, what little excavation was done in these early great houses failed to adequately record features that could reflect habitation or other uses in the core units.

Otherwise, the earliest architecture at the best-known trio of great houses in Chaco Canyon was different from the norm, although once dismissed as not "incompatible with the early Pueblo II San

Juan pattern" (Hayes 1981:55). Early Peñasco Blanco, Pueblo Bonito, and Una Vida stand out from the vast majority of contemporary structures of the 800s on the basis of vertical size and mass, created by the extensive use of stone masonry as a construction medium, and multistory construction. Contemporary structures in the region generally favored the use of upright sandstone slabs for the basal wall supports, capped by adobe turtlebacks or puddled adobe to form walls. Sometimes, spalls and larger stones were incorporated within the adobe walls, but the primary wall material remained adobe. Adobe walls demand extensive upkeep, but they eventually weather to grade. Although plentiful stone was readily available, it was generally not used for primary wall construction in small houses in the basin until well into the 1000s.

Not surprisingly, many unimpressive bumps have escaped recognition as unusual buildings potentially akin to the big three in Chaco Canyon, at least in architectural style. In fact, within Chaco Canyon and its environs, other large, early buildings have generally failed to be included within the group of important Chacoan great house sites. On the other hand, others have been classified as Chacoan great houses when there is minimal wall debris and mounding; two of these are discussed below as proto–great houses. Clearly, standards for and experience in recognizing early great houses, as well as a lexicon of terms, need to be developed. Context, however, more than any other standard, sets great houses apart from other

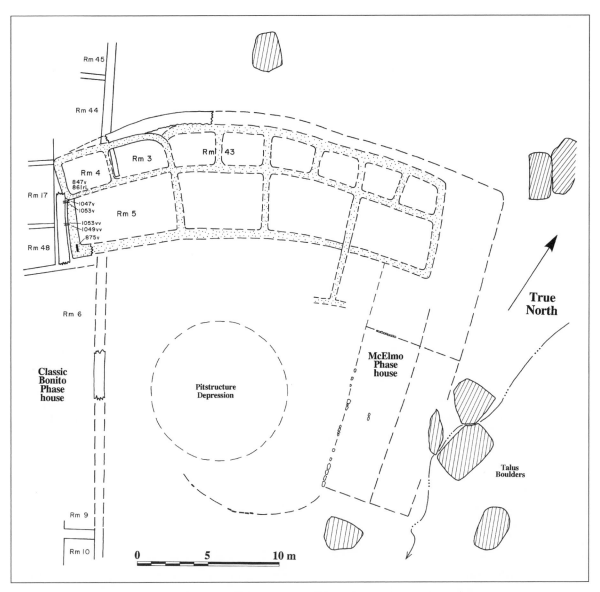

FIGURE 3.3. The initial building plan (dot pattern) at Una Vida with an early 1100s house attached to the top and right. The main great house is to the left (back wall). (Original by the author, 2002; from Windes 2006)

house structures (e.g., Lekson 1991; Powers et al. 1983:308).

The Earliest Chaco Canyon Area Great Houses?

29MC184 IN THE FAJADA WASH, SOUTH FORK COMMUNITY (LA 40081)

Before the construction of stacked stone masonry structures, habitation within the Chaco areas was generally limited to scattered small houses without community structures (Windes 2006). The total population was low, and there was little suggestion

by the early 800s of the events to follow. The lone exception is a Pueblo I community of small houses and a community structure located about 10 km south of Fajada Butte and Chaco Canyon along the South Fork tributary of Fajada Wash. The specific houses of interest here occupy a low ridge; their middens were tested in 1975. The surrounding valley was inventoried in the 1990s (Windes 2006). Despite their decidedly unmonumental architecture, the houses illustrate the shift in the 800s in the San Juan Basin that gave rise to the early great houses. A number of aspects of two of the little

53

house bumps among the four Pueblo I houses at the site qualify them as early or proto–great houses despite their diminutive size.

Site 29MC184 comprises four house mounds arranged linearly. Two resemble other houses in the community with basal wall slabs and adobe wall construction (Figure 3.4). Mound height for these ruins seldom exceeds 10 cm and is mostly level with the surrounding terrain. The two other houses in the 29MC184 community are aberrant in that they exhibit partial use of Type I stone masonry; in a ruined state, the house mounds measure a meter high. Although these monuments are not impressive compared with the later, massive, multistory great house constructions, they are sharply distinguished from their nearby neighbors. To those living in the outlying adobe houses, these stone houses would have been examples of display and power: they

were larger than most houses in the community (encompassing about eight households in total), and every other Pueblo I site within the community was visible from them. In addition, a probable community structure (i.e., a great kiva—29MC620) was located nearby, below the mesa to the north, a mere 230 m away. This community structure, however, is not observable from any Pueblo I house. A short prehistoric road connects the community structure and the two small masonry houses, confirming temporal and social linkage. Other roads appear to run through the community (Richard Friedman, personal communication 2004).

The 29MC184 community of Pueblo I sites in the South Fork of Fajada Wash (occupied mostly at about 800 and dominated by White Mound Black-on-white and Lino Gray ceramics) is the largest of its kind known thus far in or around Chaco Canyon,

FIGURE 3.4. The upright slab wall foundation stones for a small, adobe, 800s house in the Chaco area. House C in 29MC184; looking east toward Chacra Mesa. (Photograph by John M. Campbell, © 2003; from Windes 2006)

Thomas C. Windes

with a second smaller cluster of eight houses (in an area of 0.8 km²) located at the head of Kin Klizhin Wash immediately to the west. Although the South Fork Valley runs for 15 km north-south, almost all of its Pueblo I houses are clustered within a 3.4-km² area around 29MC184. Using criteria proposed by Wilshusen and Blinman (1992),[2] and subsequently modified by the author, the momentary population could have been about 230 people within 43 households, which easily fits within the proposed size range for Pueblo I villages in the northern San Juan (but see Lightfoot 1994:148–149). Whereas northern villages were formed of numerous, contiguous house blocks, like those at McPhee Village (and Casa del Rio; see below), the 29MC184 community houses were dispersed and seldom exceeded 2–4 households per house. The local pattern mirrors the late Pueblo I settlements found at Cedar Hill (Wilshusen and Wilson 1995) near Aztec, New Mexico, and may reflect the transition in community organization from the long, contiguous house units of the northern regions.

The presence of much nonlocal chipped stone and ceramics suggests that the inhabitants of this short-lived 29MC184 settlement migrated to the area from the south, but nothing in the material culture of the two houses indicates differential access to material goods or special craft activities relative to other sites within the community. Consistent finds of expedient micro-drills and worked red dog shale indicate a budding ornament industry that by 875 exploded in the greater San Juan Basin and Chaco Canyon. Finally, the setting of the communities in both the South Fork and upper Kin Klizhin Wash allowed direct observation of prominent peaks (Fajada and Huerfano buttes) not visible from many locations within the two areas, and a deliberate community effort to maintain visual contact. These connections were not systematically maintained during the subsequent Pueblo II house occupation of the area, however, suggesting that the importance of these northern landmarks had declined or that there was a break in cultural continuity.

Peñasco Blanco, Pueblo Bonito, Kin Nahasbas, Una Vida, and the East Canyon

Because of a few tree-ring dates, partial excavation, and exposed early architecture, Pueblo Bonito,

Peñasco Blanco, and Una Vida have become the focus for understanding the rise of great houses in the basin. But several other sites within Chaco Canyon (Figure 3.5) and the basin provide a fuller picture of these early structures (Table 3.4), and there are even more potential examples. Much of the region to the west, southwest, and south of Chaco is relatively unexplored or poorly recorded, but minimally an east-west strip of early great houses started at the east end of Chaco Canyon and terminated in the west along the eastern Chuska slope. In addition, great houses and attendant communities of small houses may be scattered along every major tributary flowing into Chaco Wash and the Chaco River.

The earliest constructions at Pueblo Bonito (Figure 3.6) and Una Vida (Figure 3.7) employed stone masonry and two-story construction, neither of which are found in contemporary, small-house occupations in the vicinity. Both were also built on the north side of the canyon, not generally favored for occupation until later times. These initial great houses were *not* substantially larger than contemporary nearby houses in terms of room area or numbers of rooms. Their core units survived centuries of remodeling and renovation and clearly were viewed as important links to the past and places of ritual importance (see Ashmore, Chapter 7, this volume; Neitzel 2003, and Chapter 4, this volume), judging from the wealth of ritual materials found in the earliest rooms at Pueblo Bonito.

When the next phase of construction occurred (in the 860s at Pueblo Bonito, the 920–950s at Una Vida, and perhaps the early 900s at Peñasco Blanco), huge new rooms were arranged in three-room suites (Windes 1987[I]:356–362; Windes and Ford 1992:79), but not for habitation. For the first time, three-story construction (Figure 3.8) is a certainty (at Una Vida) despite the continued use of Type I masonry, which might seem inadequate to support such massive structural loads. In addition, at Una Vida, the original orientation (facing east) was abandoned when new rooms were built. The shift in layout to the south suggests that long-term architectural planning had begun and, unlike at Pueblo Bonito, that expansion did not conform to the original building plans. In addition, the viewscape (Kievit 1998) had shifted from the relatively restricted eastern canyon to the more open

55

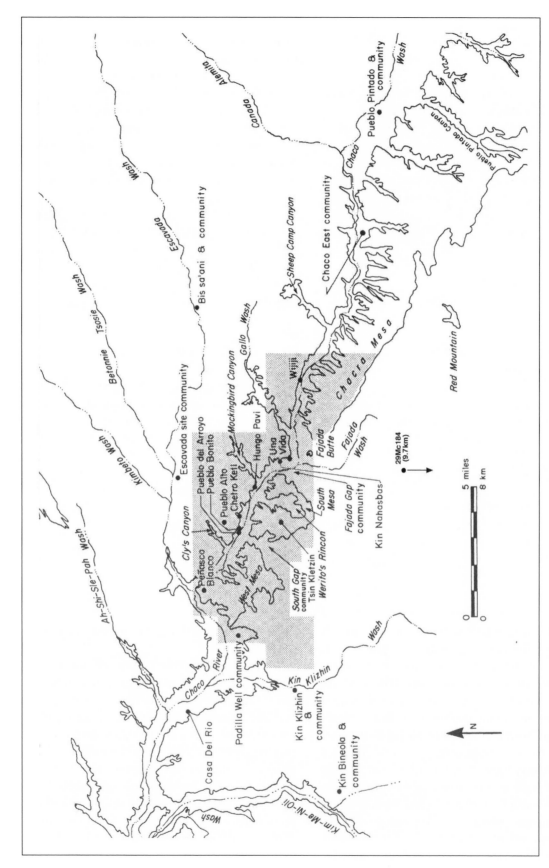

FIGURE 3.5. Great houses and communities in the Chaco Canyon area. (From Windes 2006)

Thomas C. Windes

TABLE 3.4. Households and Other Data from Early Great Houses and Proto–Great Houses (East to West)

| GREAT HOUSE | INITIAL NUMBER OF HOUSEHOLDS | INITIAL NUMBER OF STORIES | MOUNDED EARLY MIDDEN PRESENT | CHUSKA CERAMICS[†] | | |
				CHUSKAN %	OVERALL SAMPLE	ASSEMBLAGE TYPE
East Community	0–7?	1	no	6	189	mixed[a]
29MC184	8	1	no	1	2,859[b]	
Una Vida	4; 10[c]	2; 3[c]	no	14	269[d]	mixed
Kin Nahasbas	0–5?	1	no	10	1,435[e]	
Pueblo Bonito	3–4; 6[e]	2	unknown	20	1,645[f]	
Peñasco Blanco	unknown	2	yes	12	3,063[f]	mixed
Casa del Rio	4–6	1	yes	33	1,411[g]	mixed
Lake Valley	2–3?	1	yes	59	478	
Kin Bineola	0–12?	2	indeterminate	14	1,176[h]	
Casa Abajo	1–2?	1	no	9	300	mixed
House of the Giant Midden	2	1	no	46	339	
Willow Canyon[i]	1–2	1	yes	66	1,222	
Great Bend	2–3?	1–2	indeterminate	76	353	mixed
Hogback (Component A at LA 11594)	2–3	1–2	no	65	513	mixed

Note: Chuskan ceramics from associated Pueblo I house middens adjacent to or underneath early/proto–great houses at Casa del Rio, House of the Giant Midden, and Great Bend are 26%, 55%, and 65%, respectively.

[†] Overall total refers to the earliest assemblages; mixed assemblages contain both early and late Pueblo II pottery. Obvious, late Pueblo II pottery (e.g., indented corrugated, Gallup B/w) has been eliminated from these calculations.

[a] From the great house berm.
[b] The majority of Chuskan sherds (18 of 28) are probably from a single culinary jar.
[c] Second calculation for households and stories derived from secondary, 900s building constructions.
[d] From the floor fill over Floor 2 in Room 23.
[e] From Test Trench 3 under the great kiva walls and surface transects T4, T5, and T8.
[f] Pueblo Bonito sample from West Plaza, Trench 2, Levels D–K (Windes 1987 [II]: Table 8.22); Peñasco Blanco sample from midden Sections 1 and 2 (Windes 1987[II]: Tables 8.35 and 8.36).
[g] Casa del Rio, Mound 1.
[h] Kin Bineola, Middens 2–5.
[i] Early Type I masonry structures present but no sizable early great house. Data for the House of the Weaver.

southern basin, past Fajada Butte. An easterly house direction suggests summer occupation (e.g., Windes et al. 2000), but it is to the south that the landscape offers dramatic connections to the Chacoan world in terms of important peaks and mountains (including nearby Fajada Butte and the prominent horizon marker of Hosta Butte, with its many shrines), prehistoric roads, and occupied areas that may have served as additional farming locations, such as the large Pueblo I community along the South Fork of the Fajada Wash drainage discussed above. South is also the best direction to take advantage of winter passive solar heating. This shift in architecture emphasizes the growing

premium on addressing the world beyond the canyon.

Una Vida and Pueblo Bonito are not the only early great houses within the canyon. Kin Nahasbas (Mathien and Windes 1988, 1989) dates to perhaps as early as the late 800s, according to ceramics and radiocarbon dates, and contains two possible circular towers, which would be unique for the period. Although Kin Nahasbas seldom receives recognition as an early great house, its position provides a critical visual link to all other early great houses within the canyon core. It contains the earliest great kiva known within a great house, if we rely on its Type I

FIGURE 3.6. Pueblo Bonito, looking north through the center core of the original roomblock of Type I masonry. Lower set of latilla holes and latillas in center of photograph are from rooms that were built ca. 891. Third- and fourth-story walls in the background and low wall in center foreground were added in the 1040s. (Photograph by John M. Campbell, © 2003; from Windes 2006)

masonry construction, as well as an oversized pit-house that resembles the community structures in the large Pueblo I houses north of the San Juan, such as McPhee Pueblo. The abundant refuse around the site is not mounded or concentrated in a single large pile.

Another Type I masonry great house, 29MC560 (Figure 3.2; LA 100,060) lies in the Chaco East Community (Windes et al. 2000). Although single story, the rooms are of formidable height, resulting in a mound almost 4 m high (Figure 3.9). The earliest visible ceramics are associated with construction debris and date to the mid-to-late 900s. Refuse mounding began by the mid-1000s but without a coeval building expansion such as those in the downtown Chaco great houses.

A Northern Perspective

Work in the Dolores River valley of southwestern Colorado between 1978 and 1985 resulted in the first in-depth study of the Pueblo I (700–900) occupation in the region. Studies south of the San Juan River have focused primarily on the following Pueblo II (900–1100) period and on Chacoan culture, expansion, and dominance. Oddly, despite knowledge of the widespread abandonment of the northern San Juan villages at about 900 and the subsequent rise of Pueblo II villages in the southern San Juan, only recently has there been any in-depth examination (cf. Wilshusen and Ortman 1999; Wilshusen and Van Dyke 2006; Windes 2006; Windes and Ford 1992) linking these potentially overlapping cultural events.

58

FIGURE 3.7. The earliest house units at Una Vida, ca. 847–875, employing Type I masonry. Room 5 in foreground and Room 3 in background. Beam hole at base of wall contained an intramural pine log that was cut in 875. Wall to left is Type III-style masonry added in the mid 1000s above Rooms 17 and 48. Looking north. (Photograph by the author, 2002; from Windes 2006)

FIGURE 3.8. The third-story section of Type I masonry at Una Vida, built ca. 920s–950s. Looking west-northwest at the outside walls of Rooms 28 and 77. (Photograph by John M. Campbell, © 2003; from Windes 2006)

59

FIGURE 3.9. Bulldozed room on the west side of the East Community great house (LA 100,060). Note the Type I masonry and the wall cross-sections, and the scatter of large slabs from collapsed walls. Left-to-right: Eileen Bacha, Peg Kaiser, and Ursula Moeller. (Photograph by Richard Moeller, January 2003; from Windes 2006)

An absence of masonry construction was the 800s norm in the San Juan Basin, but inhabitants in some areas began to experiment with its use. Our knowledge of this technique is poor, but the Dolores Project provides examples that tie to later events in the southern San Juan Basin. Large Pueblo I villages outside of Dolores and north of the San Juan River, however, were not unlike their contemporary cousins to the south and west, which employed mud as the primary construction material (e.g., Brew 1946; Morris 1939; Windes 2006), although the occasional use of stone is documented (e.g., Martin 1939; Roberts 1939:147). Some Pueblo I houses excavated during the Dolores Project were built with a mixture of sandstone, river cobbles, jacal, and adobe (e.g., Kane 1986; Kane and Robinson 1988; Wilshusen 1988), but others (e.g., Grass Mesa; Lipe et al. 1988) continued to favor adobe and jacal construction.

Adobe-and-jacal (post-and-adobe; see Varien 1999) construction was common in the wooded regions but was rare within the interior San Juan Basin, probably because of limited wood resources. Adobe-and-jacal structures required

high maintenance and were short-lived (Ahlstrom 1985; Cameron 1990; Schlanger 1985, 1987; Schlanger and Wilshusen 1993; Wilshusen, ed. 1995; Wilshusen 2002). More important from an archaeological point of view, once abandoned, these structures left little mound relief and essentially melted back to ground level, rarely leaving even the tips of a few upright slabs or cobbles to mark the former wall locations. In the Dolores region by the 760–850 period, when true masonry makes its first appearance (Wilshusen 1988:621, 627), at least the lower courses of the walls of surface rooms were built of stone. By the next phase (850–900), surface structures were built with half- or full-height masonry walls (Wilshusen 1988:623); finally, between 900 and 975, masonry became the dominant form of construction. This sequence may duplicate the use of Type I stone masonry in Pueblo I houses in the Ackmen-Lowry area (Martin 1939).

Stone was not favored as the primary material for house construction in the interior San Juan Basin, however, until the mid-eleventh century. It may have been more common a century earlier in

60

the north (Wilshusen 1988:627), although Varien (1999) maintains that full-height, load-bearing masonry does not appear in the north until very late in the 1000s. Digging earth for adobe and having abundant water supplies does not seem to provide an advantage in terms of time or effort over quarrying and setting stone, even if the pit-structure excavations naturally provided material for the surface-room constructions (Wilshusen 1988, 1989a). According to Varien (1984:4), replication experiments with construction of Pueblo I–style surface structures built with jacal rather than stone were 1.5 times more labor intensive. This difference would be alleviated in the San Juan Basin, however, because a lack of wood for jacal construction would eliminate the need to invest labor in harvesting and preparing any wood wall elements.

Arguably, the use of stone in Pueblo I houses at Dolores could have been partially environmentally determined. Because of wide fluctuations in temperatures and moist conditions, particularly compared with the southern San Juan Basin, stone masonry would have required far less maintenance (Wilshusen 1988:627; 2002), but it was not universally employed in Dolores houses. The southern San Juan Basin can get just as cold, with recorded temperatures reaching −37 and −38F° three times in the Chaco area between 1960 and 1992 and the average coldest day of the year being −14F° (Windes 1993: Table 3.2), but cold spells may not last as long as in the higher elevations, where it is also far more moist. Since freeze-and-thaw cycles can have a profound effect on earthen architecture, the use of stone masonry would extend structure life (Varien 1984; Wilshusen 1988, 1989a, 2002).

A DOLORES EXAMPLE: MCPHEE PUEBLO

Although seldom acknowledged, recognition of the links between the north and south San Juan Basin has been hampered by institutional, cultural, and political realities such as the difficulties of working across state lines, and complex permitting procedures. The New Mexico boundaries with Arizona and Colorado (partitioning the San Juan Basin) have been derisively called by some the "Adobe Curtain," an obvious analogy to the barriers posed by the Iron Curtain during the Cold War. This barrier continues to impede shared archaeological understanding for those who work in the Four Corners region, except for some contract archaeologists who operate along and across the borders.

Given this myopia, it is understandable that, among others, McPhee Pueblo, a massive stone masonry Pueblo I structure in the Dolores River Basin, has seldom been linked to the Chacoan World (but see Wilshusen and Ortman 1999; Windes 2006; Windes and Ford 1992). Mark Varien (personal communication 2004) relates that McPhee's similarity to Pueblo Bonito was much discussed, especially by Neal Morris of the Dolores Archaeological Project, but that this similarity failed to make it into print. McPhee Pueblo had an estimated mound height of about two meters (Joel Brisbin, personal communication 2002) before impact of the spade, but researchers in both the northern and southern San Juan Basin fail to appreciate its architectural status in comparison with the beloved behemoths of the south.

Some of McPhee's most substantial construction, consisting of single- and double-width horizontal slab masonry (Figures 3.10 and 3.11), is identical to the Type I masonry employed in early Peñasco Blanco, Pueblo Bonito (Figure 3.6), and Una Vida (Figure 3.7). Stone masonry construction is found as early as the 860s and 870s at McPhee Pueblo (Brisbin et al. 1988), overlying the initial residences of jacal and upright slab footings dated to between 780 and 860. This sequence of architectural superimposition is also found at some great house sites in the southern San Juan Basin (e.g., Casa del Rio and Skunk Springs). Although the information is sketchy, there is evidence at McPhee of wall foundations (Brisbin et al. 1988:93), a trait common to Chacoan great house construction (Lekson 1984:15). By the 920s to 940s at McPhee Pueblo, extensive remodeling widely employed substantial, double-coursed stone masonry that duplicated masonry construction employed in Chaco Canyon and the San Juan Basin. Since publication, a reevaluation of the corrugated ceramics associated with the 920–940 period at McPhee suggests that the remodeling events took place at about 1000 (Mark Varien, personal communication 2004).

Given the type of construction, crescentic layout, and the large rooms, and given the abundant feature

61

FIGURE 3.10. McPhee Pueblo, Room 1, Surface 2, third building period (860–910), Unit 1. Note the Type I masonry and the storage bin in the floor. (Courtesy of Anasazi Heritage Center, DAP 002120)

and material evidence for ritual and political authority at McPhee, it is difficult not to see this pueblo as similar to the early great houses in Chaco Canyon. If McPhee Pueblo had been discovered within the San Juan Basin, its big-bump-on-the-landscape profile would have characterized it easily as an early Chacoan great house.

Much of McPhee Pueblo and several adjacent pueblos comprising McPhee Village employed stone masonry to some degree (Kane 1986; Kane and Robinson 1988; Wilshusen 1988:623). Other villages, such as House Creek, Rio Vista, and Grass Mesa (Lipe et al. 1988), contained surface room-blocks built of adobe and jacal. The two different construction technologies, village layouts, and community pitstructures suggested to Wilshusen and Ortman (1999:391) that two different social groups lived together in the Dolores Valley. Although

some stone (but mostly adobe) is used in Pueblo I houses elsewhere in the region (e.g., those found in the bean fields around Dove Creek, Colorado; David Breternitz, personal communication 2002; Lightfoot 1994:18–19), McPhee Pueblo construction is notable in this regard. For this reason, McPhee Pueblo is a logical starting point to examine early "great house" architecture. McPhee Pueblo provides a reasonable facsimile of an early Bonito-style building in a context other than the southern San Juan Basin. The estimated population in the eight large villages of the Dolores Valley at its peak, between 865 and 875 (2,860; Wilshusen 1991:211), is on par with some estimates for Chaco during its heyday (2,500–5,800; e.g., Drager 1976:168; Hayes 1981:50–51; Lekson 1999:63, 78; Loose and Lyons 1976:150; Pierson 1949:58)—numbers that provoke discussions about chiefdoms and

Thomas C. Windes

FIGURE 3.11. McPhee Pueblo, Non-Structural Unit 1, Surface 2, third building period (920–940), Unit 1, a plaza-facing outdoor work area/living room backed by storage rooms. Note the Type I masonry and the masonry storage cist in the corner. (Courtesy of Anasazi Heritage Center, DAP 002201)

complexity (e.g., Kosse 1996; Lekson 1999:164, 2002; Vivian 1990; Wilcox 1993).

The initial layout of McPhee Pueblo, consisting of 20–25 rooms set in a crescentic shape common to sites of the era, including those in the southern San Juan Basin, dates to between 780 and 860 (Brisbin et al. 1988:72–74). This early residence was built with jacal walls footed with sandstone slabs. Presumably, the typical roof of wooden beams covered with brush and mud completed the structure. This construction style is widespread on the Colorado Plateau and, with the exception of wooden elements placed horizontally in the walls of some Chaco great houses, commonplace within the San Juan Basin.

McPhee Pueblo was rebuilt in the 850s or 860s, with the final form represented by two horseshoe-shaped houses (Figure 3.12) of 50 rooms each (Brisbin et al. 1988:76–77) and, more importantly, by the extensive use of stacked stone, Type I masonry, for the small (5.0–7.7 m²), rear storage rooms (Brisbin et al. 1988: Figures 2.20–2.26). The large (12.8–21.2 m²), front living rooms, however, were primarily of adobe and basal-slab construction, unlike their big-room counterparts in Chaco. Approximately 18–20 habitation suites were represented, yielding an estimated 105 residents. By 874 or 875, a large (67 m²), squarish masonry pitstructure (#3) built in the plaza provided integrative facilities for the residents (Brisbin et al. 1988:229–230).

The vast majority of the refuse from McPhee Pueblo was deposited between 860 and 910, although the mound it created served during the

63

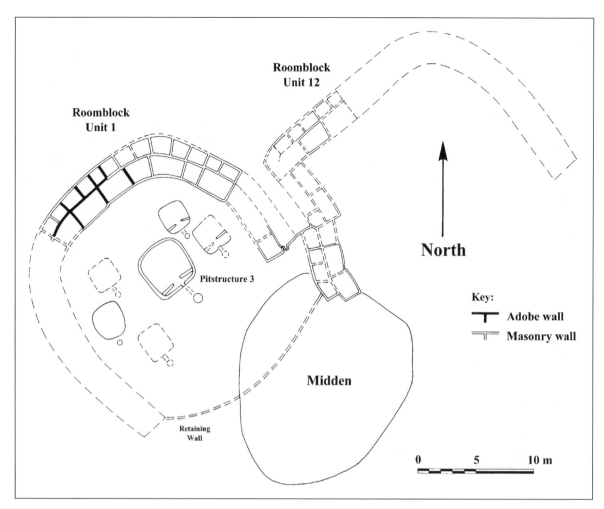

FIGURE 3.12. Plan of McPhee Pueblo, second building period (860–890). (Redrafted from Brisbin et al. 1988: Figure 2.92; from Windes 2006)

entire site occupation (Brisbin et al. 1988:243–247). This mound contained abundant cultural material, including ash, charcoal, building stone, and burials, typical of domestic refuse. The overall deposit was a maximum of 1.2 m deep and was estimated by the author to have been about 630 m^3 in volume.

By the 890s the pueblo was abandoned, and then a final reoccupation after 950 (Richard Wilshusen, personal communication 2003) or in the 1000s (Mark Varien, personal communication 2004) lasted for about 10 to 20 years. More rooms, built over the earlier ones, employed massive, double-coursed masonry. Although no multistory construction was noted for any phase of construction, the massive style, like that in Chaco Canyon, suggests that loads of more than a single story might have been planned. Final construction

and remodeling occurred about 980, with new partition walls and a suite of rooms added over the rubble from the second construction phase (Brisbin et al. 1988:317–318). Final abandonment occurred soon afterward.

The architectural history of McPhee Pueblo reveals remarkable similarities to early great houses in Chaco Canyon and the San Juan Basin in terms of construction materials, construction techniques, the large rooms, site layout, refuse deposition, and dates. Some of the roofing elements at McPhee Pueblo, Pueblo Bonito, and Una Vida were even cut in the same year (861), a striking coincidence given the paltry numbers of early dated specimens recovered from the three excavations. Only in projected household numbers are there major differences—McPhee being much larger.

64

Early Great Houses Outside the Chaco Core

Outside of Chaco Canyon, several examples of early great houses provide a fuller picture of events that draw the focus away from the downtown core. Although the canyon certainly emerged as a central place in the middle 1000s, the construction of early great houses in the late 800s and 900s is demonstrably a basin-wide event and concentrated along the vast drainage encompassing the Chaco Wash and River, and their adjacent tributaries, reaching from the Hogback near Shiprock, New Mexico, to the east end of Chaco Canyon, a distance of about 105 km.

Proto–Great Houses on the Chacoan Landscape

Several sites illustrate the very early shift to stone masonry architecture and discard behavior that characterizes the change in occupation and construction within the San Juan Basin in the late 800s. The use of stone masonry in some structures suggests a certain "gearing up" of social distinction, setting such sites apart from the vast majority, but many of them still cannot be considered great houses. All fit Wilshusen's (1988:621–623) observation for the Dolores Region between 760 and 900, where stone masonry was first used sparingly but then more abundantly through time and more often in the back rooms, where the protection of perishable storage goods would be paramount. But many lack the mass and scale relative to other contemporary sites in the area. The partial stone architecture and prominent settings were aberrant characteristics that served to warrant status as great houses in some published accounts. But the change is relatively minor, and the label "great house" is overemphasizing the architectural distinction within the interior basin community sites. The change in architectural technology is important to note for sites in transition from the common adobe-and-spall construction to partial use of Type I masonry, and thus, these sites are labeled proto–great houses. Wilshusen and Van Dyke (2006) classify these basin structures as incipient or candidate great houses. Two of them provide examples of the problems faced by archaeologists in identifying and classifying these early sites.

Work by Michael Marshall and John Stein provides some of the first documentation of early great houses. Some of the settlements reported by Marshall et al. (1979) and Marshall and Bradley (1994) are worthy of reexamination in light of knowledge of Chaco gained over the past two decades. The identification of a corridor to the west of Chaco along the Chaco River and to the south that is spotted with great houses served to refocus the author's investigation on their beginnings. The sites are all located along the major tributaries within 30 km south of the Chaco River or within the river's environs. Despite the small sample, some trends were noted that were not evident before the in-field reexamination. All appear to have been first constructed in the late 800s. Each was found within a scatter of small-house sites, but each lacked the dense site clustering evident in communities by the 900s. Although the areas around the sites have not been fully surveyed, no great kivas were evident. Overall, a lack of community cohesion among the small populations of these sites suggests a lack of empowerment for potential leaders (i.e., Sebastian 1992), but all had a visual command of landscape around the basin and the nearby drainage. Finally, most had a view of Hosta Butte above the Dutton Plateau far to the south near Crownpoint, New Mexico, a sight common to many later great houses but often not visible within the many valleys and other low areas in the basin interior.

House of the Giant Midden

Several potential great houses (Marshall and Bradley 1994; Marshall et al. 1979) have been identified along Indian Creek just west of Lake Valley, New Mexico. One such site, 10.2 km south of the Chaco River, has been named the House of the Giant Midden (LA 89433), with estimated midden deposits of 1,200 m³ and a Late Basketmaker III/early Pueblo I great house. This enticing description seems to mark a great house of very early vintage, but recent reexamination of the site suggests that it could be best designated a proto–great house, if one at all.

The site consists of a 50-m-long, crescent-shaped house marked by very slight mounding, a light scatter of spalls, and a few upright slabs indicative of adobe wall construction typical of the Pueblo I

65

period in the basin. A sample of ceramics from the midden in front of the eastern end of the house yielded only plain gray and wide neckbanded culinary ware and predominantly Kiatuthlanna Black-on-white service ware, marking the earliest occupation at about 875. A smaller structure of 8–12 rooms was either built over or appended to the western end of the Pueblo I house. This 13-m-long section was originally designated the "great house" because of the concentration of large slabs along the back wall. But the Type I, stacked-slab stone masonry was used sparingly—only for the lower back walls of a few rooms. Little mound relief was created by the collapsed walls. A sample of ceramics from the midden in front of this part of the house revealed only slightly later deposition (900–925). The single midden was dense with cultural material and stained dark with ash and charcoal. It created little relief (less than 75 cm), although it covered a considerable area (17.5 by 50 m; 985 m^2) and was reestimated at about 350 m^3 in volume.[3]

Despite the impressive refuse at the site, neither the midden size nor the masonry fits the great house standard. Nevertheless, the site is indicative of the increased use of stone masonry and the prolific discard of cultural material, marking a new era in the San Juan Basin. Starting in the late 800s, a cluster of contemporary houses was built near the House of the Giant Midden with similar but smaller middens, dense with cultural material. Marshall and Bradley (1994) indicate a nearby great kiva, which upon reinspection proved to be several ephemeral, small-house remains. No obvious evidence of a great kiva was seen in the community.

CASA ABAJO
South of the House of the Giant Midden, 18 km up Indian Creek, is another "great house" first documented by Marshall et al. (1979:45–49). The use of Type I masonry in single- and double-width walls is evident in this single-story, nine-room house. But the house lacks rubble from the upper walls, suggesting that they were constructed of adobe, leaving the stone masonry walls a mere 50 cm in maximum height (Figure 3.13). The room outlines are clearly defined by standing walls, but the house lacks mounding because there is little stone rubble within the rooms. The earliest ceramics from the slope refuse indicate deposition that started by 875 and continued into the early 1100s with some use in the 1200s. Despite the extensive temporal range of ceramics in the refuse, there is little overall volume (estimated at 128 m^3). This structure is similar to the House of the Giant Midden in that it stands out from contemporary structures in the valley, but its partial use of Type I masonry relegates it to proto–great house status, at best.

Within 100 m of Casa Abajo is a classic slab-foundation Pueblo I house, built originally with adobe and exhibiting ceramics of a slightly earlier age (850–875) than found at Casa Abajo. This building is a dramatic example of the shift in architectural construction style from that evident at Casa Abajo. Other sites in the vicinity were not examined. Casa Abajo was built on an elevated, south-facing slope, which provided extensive visibility of the valley and the horizon, particularly to Hosta Butte and to the south along the Dutton Plateau.

FIGURE 3.13. Looking across the pile of wall masonry of Casa Abajo and south down Indian Creek. (Photograph by Richard Moeller, January 2003; from Windes 2006)

Great Houses on the Chacoan Landscape

True early great houses are distinguished from their contemporary neighbors by their relative size (a large house mound), the use of stacked stone masonry, and monumental refuse piles that are piled up rather than broadcast over a large area. In addition, the surrounding landscape was often modified to enhance and delineate the great house. The trend was for the early great houses to be located along or adjacent to the Chaco River, while the proto–great houses were located to the south along its dry tributaries. In all cases, Type I masonry was present in varying amounts, but the monumental character of the associated midden deposits suggests much of the deposition represents nonresidential activities. In each case, the masonry structure was too small by several degrees of magnitude to have housed enough residents to have created so much refuse, assuming that it was generated by normal, day-to-day activities within the projected occupation span.

The great house locations appear far more suitable for agricultural production than those of the proto–great houses along the southern tributaries (except at Kin Bineola). The Chaco River, a broad, braided wash with a shallow (<60 cm) water table and bordered in places with sand dunes and high cliffs, presents a relatively ideal location for farming, even during dry times, in contrast to the very arid adjacent landscapes. The amount of groundstone present on these great house sites, in the form of manos, metates, and lapidary abraders, is far above normal and suggests that food processing and ornament production were primary activities. The large and small sites in the greater Chaco area observed by the author over the decades seldom have much groundstone on them, particularly those along the tributaries of the Chaco River.

The band of early great houses with large midden deposits starts with Peñasco Blanco, sitting at the point where Chaco Canyon debouches into the Chaco River, and extends downstream along the south side of the Chaco River to the Hogback community near Shiprock, a distance of about 105 km. Sites discussed here are Casa del Rio, Lake Valley, Great Bend, and the Hogback (8.4 km, 19.7 km, 50 km, and 105 km, respectively, downstream of Peñasco Blanco). Willow Canyon, located 44 km downstream from Peñasco Blanco and about 5 km south of the Chaco River, was also examined.

Significantly, the strip of the Chaco River running roughly east-west from Peñasco Blanco to the Great Bend is paralleled along the south by an east-west prehistoric road, the Great West Road, that is only partly documented (e.g., Marshall and Bradley 1994: Figure 62d). Parts of it are visible in the Indian Creek and Willow Canyon areas. Additional unpublished work has been conducted along the road between Indian Creek and Willow Canyon by archaeologist Tim Kearns. I suspect that this road connects Peñasco Blanco to Skunk Springs (on the Chuskan Slope) and all the great houses along the Chaco River strip. If true, then the corridor across the basin connecting Chaco Canyon with the Chuskan world may have been used for the distribution of food and material goods. Certainly the high densities of Chuskan materials (ceramics and chipped stone) found in great- and small-house sites along the route attest to the importance of travel between the Chuskas and Chaco Canyon.

Two other great houses (29MC184, discussed above, and Kin Bineola), lacking significant refuse deposits, are found along southern tributaries to the Chaco River. Other early great houses of unknown size and midden extent have been noted elsewhere (e.g., Peach Springs and Standing Rock along the Dutton Plateau slope; see Gilpin and Purcell 2000; Marshall et al. 1979; Powers et al. 1983), many of them along the same southern tributaries, but they were not investigated for this study (see Kantner 1996:Table 2).

CASA DEL RIO
One of the most striking examples of an early great house uncomplicated by extensive remodeling and deposition is located just 8.4 km west of Chaco Canyon along the Chaco River. This site, Casa del Rio (Figure 3.14; LA 17221), was initially reported as a multistory great house from the 1000s containing about 125 rooms (Marshall et al. 1979:31–32), but recent work has reexamined its setting and early occupation. Its most startling feature, a huge refuse mound (Midden 1), towers above the collapsed Type I masonry architecture of the single-story great house. The great house, in turn, overlies an adobe and slab Pueblo I house mound whose size (112 m in length) rivals those of the large villages along the northern tributaries of the San Juan River and in the Dolores Valley. No attendant small-house community is evident in the immediate area (just two small houses), although the locality has not been thoroughly surveyed.

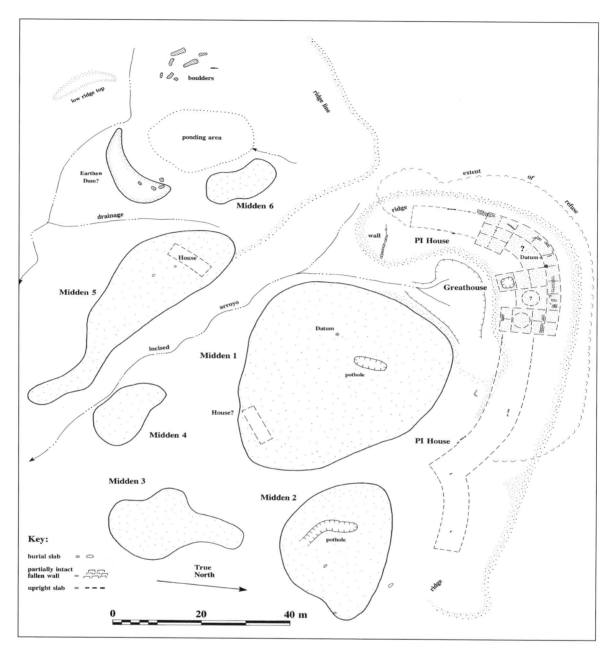

FIGURE 3.14. Plans of the Pueblo I and later great house at Casa del Rio. (Original by Jamie Schubert, Eileen Bacha, Peg Kaiser, Valerie Barnes, Cheryl Synka, and Holly Flynn, 2002; from Windes 2006)

An estimated 16 households (about 88 residents, as per Wilshusen and Blinman 1992:257–258, but see Lightfoot 1994:148–149) occupied the adobe Pueblo I house. This house size is within the range for the northern villages (Wilshusen 1999; Wilshusen and Blinman 1992; Wilshusen and Ortman 1999) but greatly exceeds any known contemporary house within the Chaco Canyon area. By any standard, it was a very large house, fronted by massive amounts of refuse that probably do not exceed a meter in depth. At least 1,150 m² of refuse is exposed on the surface of the three earliest mounds (Middens 2–4), although more extends under the 1,776 m² covered by the later great house mound (Midden 1). Taking these as the total extent of the early refuse, and assuming an average depth of 50 cm, the total volume might be estimated at about 1,463 m³ for an occupation of about 50 years or

Thomas C. Windes

less (at around 800, based on ceramic dates), conforming to those of the northern villages (Wilshusen and Blinman 1992).

In contrast to the large Pueblo I house, the late Pueblo I/early Pueblo II house is a smaller, compact masonry structure built over the adobe Pueblo I house. This architectural sequence duplicates the construction history observed at McPhee Pueblo (Brisbin et al. 1988), House of the Giant Midden, and Skunk Springs (Marshall et al. 1979; Windes and Ford 1992). The earlier house must have been abandoned before construction started on the great house, although the interval between occupations may have been quite short. Construction of the early great house appears to have started by the late 800s (based on ceramic time). The new building employed large stone slabs set horizontally in the wall (i.e., Type I masonry), similar to the earliest constructions within great houses in the Chaco core. Some front rooms may have been very large (e.g., 18 m²), although not all cross-walls are visible. Many sections of wall fell intact, particularly along the back, which preserved the original crescentic house layout. The collapsed house rubble created a mound 1 to 2 m high—a big bump—that sharply contrasts with the house underneath it. This early great house could not have exceeded 21–27 rooms and could not have housed the large number of residents that lived in the preceding Pueblo I roomblock. In fact, the size of the early great house (with a maximum 4 or 5 households) is similar to that of a small house excavated in Chaco Canyon (29SJ627; Truell 1992) that was occupied twice as long as the Casa del Rio great house and yielded, at best, 570 m³ of midden refuse with far less dense cultural material (e.g., an estimated 17,356 sherds).

Midden 1 at Casa del Rio compares favorably in size with the great house mounds in downtown Chaco and is estimated to be approximately the same volume as that at Peñasco Blanco (see Windes 1987[II]: Table 8.14): 1,702 m³. The density of surface ceramics (22.5 sherds/m² based on a 3.5% surface sample yielding 1,411 sherds) is similar to other great house deposits. Thus, based on excavated mound deposits elsewhere (Windes 1987[II]: Table 8.14), Midden 1 at Casa del Rio could contain between 0.6 and 2.3 million sherds. There is no appreciable difference in volume and artifact density between the great house midden and the adjacent Pueblo I mounds, but the refuse is deposited differently—one concentrated and piled vertically, the other broadcast laterally into multiple piles with little mound relief. The Pueblo I deposits do little to alter the landscape, but in the spring when it is covered with lush vegetation Midden 1 can be seen from as far as 5 km away. On the downslope side, Midden 1 reaches nearly 5 m in elevation and may have once equaled the rooftop elevation of the great house on the ridge behind it.

The mound's size is extraordinary, but was it created in an act of ritual behavior (e.g., Fowler and Stein 1992; Lekson et al. 1988; Stein and Lekson 1992; Toll 1985, 2001; Wills 2001)? It is difficult to believe that the few inhabitants of the great house could have been responsible for the quantity of cultural materials contained in the mound. Aside from some minor renovations to the house, little construction debris would have been generated to create the bulk of the mound, as argued by Wills (2001) for other great houses. The ceramic evidence indicates a lengthy occupation covering the tenth, eleventh, and early twelfth centuries, but there is little evidence of construction in the 1000s and 1100s, which contrasts with the flurry of construction in nearby Chaco Canyon. The vast bulk of the mound appears to be from 900s household deposition. The deposits are dark from carbonized firepit remains, and the mound contains evidence for at least one burial. Deposits from the Pueblo I house and the great house look remarkably similar; however, during the wet summer of 2000, despite their spatial overlap, the mounds had markedly different plant cover. The great house mound was densely covered in Russian thistle (*Salsola kali*), which failed to grow on the wolfberry (*Lycium pallidum*)–covered earlier deposits. This difference was replicated in the same month at house deposits in the early Pueblo Pintado community at the eastern end of Chaco Canyon and can likely be attributed to dissimilar composition of deposits from the different periods. These mounds would be a fruitful location for a study of differences in food and other organic materials between the two occupations.

In other ways, Casa del Rio stands out from every other site in the area. Numerous ground-stone artifacts (more than 500 were mapped) litter all houses and middens, particularly on Midden 1. If there was ever a site that screamed "surplus" from extensive food processing, this is it. The arid desolation of the Casa del Rio location makes surplus food production seem counterintuitive. However, an unusual combination of topographic and geomorphological features near Casa del Rio may have led to abnormally high crop yields that resulted in surpluses even during droughts (Windes 2006). The broad expanse of the braided streambed of the nearby Chaco River, with its shallow water table of 58 cm (measured in dry June 2003), would have provided an ideal area safe from floods (Figure 3.15). Such a location would have been rare, if not unique, in the Chaco Canyon area in terms of potential food production; this provides a promising venue for future research in an area that is otherwise decidedly marginal.

Besides manos and metates (tools related to food processing), most of the remaining groundstone was for lapidary work, evidenced by the turquoise and red dog shale debris littering the site. Some very fine, delicate abraders were found that were similar to those recovered in association with jewelry production at a small site in Chaco Canyon (Fretwell 2006; Mathien 1993; Windes 1993). Clearly, another major activity at the site was craft production. The presence of ornaments and exotic materials has been suggested as evidence of social power (e.g., Lipe 2002:229), but such items are common to many big and small Chacoan sites which became widespread by the late 800s.

In summary, the Casa del Rio great house mound greatly exceeds the expected volume of materials generated by a few households (4 or fewer) for a similar duration seen in contemporary small houses

FIGURE 3.15. Overview of the broad, braided, sandy wash of the Chaco River near Lake Valley, New Mexico. (Photograph by John M. Campbell, © 2004; from Windes 2006)

Thomas C. Windes

(e.g., McKenna 1984; Truell 1992; Windes 1993), especially if Kohler and Blinman's (1987) estimate of 600 sherds per household per year is realistic. In addition, the deposits suggest domestic household refuse and an emphasis on activities associated with ornament and food production. The height of the mound also deviates from that of earlier deposits, enabling it to be seen from some distance.

Casa del Rio was not isolated from the canyon communities. The troughlike depression partly encircling Midden 1 on its upslope side between it and the great house suggests a formalized traffic or road area. Several prehistoric roads that align directly with the great house are nearby (Ireland 2001; Marshall et al. 1979:32) and must be part of the Great West Road, which runs south of the Chaco River after leaving Peñasco Blanco for the Chuska Valley.

In addition to the network of roads that suggest direct, on-the-ground ties to the region, Casa del Rio is clearly visible from the western communications shrine (Hayes and Windes 1975; McKenna and Windes 1975; Windes 2006) that overlooks the entire region from West Mesa to as far west as the Chuska Mountains. Although most of the shrines have been argued to date to the late 1000s, datable material culture on them is sparse. The shrine overlooking Casa del Rio is built with Type I, compound stone masonry and is associated with a number of round, solid stone columns or cairns, some exceeding 2 m in height. Like the roads, the communication system may have been in place far earlier than is generally assumed, linking great houses across the basin in the late 800s or early 900s.

Whatever was going on, the site generated enormous amounts of household materials that were deposited in an unusual manner compared with the depositional patterns of the preceding occupation. It would be difficult to attribute the primary deposition of this refuse to a ritual status, although clearly it contributes to the overall cultural landscape of the great house and its prominent setting above the Chaco River. Still, either the small number of inhabitants produced a prodigious amount of refuse or they had outside help to create such a volume. The Chuskan material (Table 3.4) reveals strong interaction with the west and may have been brought to the site during specific gatherings.

LAKE VALLEY

The Lake Valley site is 11.3 km downstream from Casa del Rio along the Chaco River at the mouth of Lake Valley and the Yellow Point–Kim-me-ni-oli Wash, which has its headwaters far south in the Dutton Plateau. About 1.6 km south of the confluence with the Chaco River is an impressive settlement of three houses with immense deposits of refuse (Marshall et al. 1979:73–75). This site is like other early great house settlements in terms of its association with a nearby cluster of small, adobe, Pueblo I houses on a bluff overlooking the Chaco River that ceramically just antedate the beginnings of the Lake Valley site.

The site location appears favorable in several ways: the proximity of the Chaco River, with its shallow water table (measured at 70 cm depth in July 2003); the adjacent Kim-me-ni-oli Wash with headwaters in the southern high plateau, which has seen much historic use from damming, ditching, and farming; the widespread sand dunes; and the potential for creating large, shallow, lakes. In about 1935, nearby Juan's Lake was formed by flood runoff from Kim-me-ni-oli Wash. It contained water for a number of years (including the entire span of 1979–1982), although in 2003 it was dry. Peach trees, watermelon, corn, and alfalfa were grown in the area into the 1970s, although little farming takes place today (see Miller et al. 1991:6–7 for an overview).

An awe-inspiring midden (Midden 2), encompassing 110 by 30 m with a maximum depth of about 1.5 m visible in a road cut (mean depth about 75 cm) and a volume of about 2,475 m^3, fronts House 2, a small bump of a house mound. This house contains some Type I masonry built over by later block masonry. Little of the original house can be seen, but ceramics from the midden verify its early beginnings at about 875. The other houses are late. None of the houses is very large, and the earliest one must have been quite small and unimposing, which makes the volume of refuse astounding. Marshall et al. (1979:75) estimate an overall volume for the eight middens at 9,041 m^3, but even half that, which is more reasonable, is an extraordinary amount of refuse for a settlement with only a few residential structures. Midden 2, dark from ash and charcoal, is littered with small stones. Given the small amount of architecture represented in the three houses, it can scarcely be imagined that construction debris (i.e., Wills 2001) is responsible for much of the midden's volume.

A common constituent of the midden is red dog shale, a burned lignite coal that occurs in numerous hills, some nearby. Although most of the red dog shale is unworked, some was ground and shaped. Turquoise and other stones are also represented in the ornaments found on the midden. Groundstone (59 manos and fragments, 11 metate fragments, and uncounted lapidary abraders) was particularly common on the midden surface. The ceramic sample (n = 478) along the road cut yielded 40 sherds/m². If the mound is as dense as that of Peñasco Blanco's earliest deposits (Sections 1 and 2; Windes 1987[II]: Table 8.14), then it could contain between 2.1 and 3.4 million sherds.

Although the ceramic sample is a tiny one (12 m²) relative to the midden's surface area, surface inspection suggests that much of its volume was generated between 875 and 1000. The only surface ceramic sample from Peñasco Blanco's midden yielded less than half of the surface density noted here, indicating that the number of sherds estimated for Midden 2 is reasonable.

KIN BINEOLA
About 12 km south of the Chaco River and further upstream along Kim-me-ni-oli Wash is another prominent great house (Figure 3.16) of considerable size (Kin Bineola, LA 18705). Most of the early, Type I, two-story architecture is incorporated as the base for later, third-story construction (Figures 3.17 and 3.18). This initial building was T-shaped (although additional wings may be buried)

FIGURE 3.16. Overview of Kin Bineola in 1899. Frederic W. Putnam (on horseback) and assistant. Looking west across the Kim-me-ni-oli Wash. (Photograph by Richard Wetherill, courtesy of American Museum of Natural History, AMNH 147)

Thomas C. Windes

FIGURE 3.17. Looking northwest into the second tier of rooms in the West Roomblock at Kin Bineola around the Room 28 area. Note the irregular remodeling of later masonry atop the Type I masonry in the lower stories. (Photograph by Richard Moeller, January 2003; from Windes 2006)

and had at least 64 rooms (Figure 3.19). The long axis is about 83 m. Tree-ring dates from two rooms (50 and 51) place initial construction in the 940s, although a single cutting date of 923 from the central roomblock suggests some earlier construction.[4] The only extramural deposits that can be linked temporally with this construction and possible occupation are masonry debris piles of little volume or relief along with some refuse piles from the 900s (Windes 1982). Unlike at Casa del Rio, this great house was expanded in the early 1100s, and an elevated mound of refuse, similar to those of the late 1000s in Chaco Canyon, was formed. Whatever activities took place at Kin Bineola, they did not generate much cultural material until a brief flurry of deposition during the last building expansion. Ditch systems are well-known around the site (e.g., Vivian 1990), but surface evidence

for intensive food production in terms of manos and metates is rare. Without a consistent, shallow water table or extensive, favorable wet periods, it is difficult to see this as a reliable horticultural area. The site sits in a cove below the surrounding terrain that blocks off much of the surrounding region, but it provides a commanding view of the southern horizon, including the Dutton Plateau and prominent Hosta Butte. This siting maintains the preference for a southern orientation exhibited by many great houses in the Chaco area.

WILLOW CANYON

During the early hunt for great houses, Marshall et al. (1979:91–93) noted a number of unusual structures on the mesa tops overlooking Willow Canyon, a locality first recorded by Stewart Peckham in 1962. Within Willow Canyon, a southern

FIGURE 3.18. Close-up of Type I masonry in Room 36 at Kin Bineola. Note face of chinking embedded in thick adobe scratch coat. (Photograph by Richard Moeller, January 2003; from Windes 2006)

tributary of the Chaco River near the Great Bend, a dense settlement was found at the confluence of the main canyon and a large eastern tributary. In May 2003, well into a second year or more of drought, the broad, flat bottomlands of both drainages were covered in high grasses, suggesting good agricultural potential and a primary reason for the community placement. Many typical 800s houses with upright slab foundations and little mound relief were scattered about the area, particularly on the ridges and higher elevations to the south and west. Most were short-lived occupations, but the residences were only modest in numbers and might not have housed enough people to account for the sudden concentration of houses in the main community. Although it has been noted previously (Marshall et al. 1979:91–93; Marshall and Bradley 1994:347–348), the Willow Canyon community has never been formally documented. Marshall and

Bradley's cursory inspection indicated an early Pueblo II occupation, one that contained high house mounds of "phenomenal concentration," and large midden deposits of "extraordinary dimension." In the 1960s a small cluster of four houses with a possible great kiva was noted about 1 km northwest of the main community, but this cluster could not be relocated. To the west, 700 m from the Willow Community on the opposite side of the canyon bottom and about 400 m north of the cluster, was a single-story house of 12–15 rooms (LA 139391) built partly of Type I masonry.

The community contains an unusually large number of structures built partly with Type I masonry, giving it more examples of Type I masonry construction than any other in the revisited sites discussed here. This contrasts with the usual finding of a single masonry structure per community during this time period.

74

Thomas C. Windes

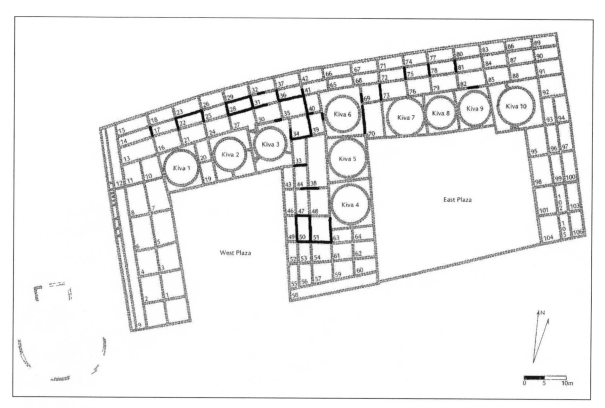

FIGURE 3.19. Plan of Kin Bineola showing the earliest constructions (walls in black). (Revised by author and Beth Bagwell from Marshall et al. 1979:60; from Windes 2006)

The main community of about 12–15 houses (Figure 3.20) is tightly packed into a small, 200 by 200 m area with a dense collection of cultural material. Ceramics are primarily Chuskan-made. The concentration of trash and houses is similar to that of the Standing Rock Community (Marshall et al. 1979:231–233). Mapping of the Willow Canyon community with a GPS unit in July 2003 revealed that surface refuse covers 7,700 m², or roughly 19% of the total community area. The largest midden is 82 m long, and a second of equal length parallels it a few meters away. Together, these two middens, covering 3,006 m² and reaching maximum depths of about one meter, contain approximately 1,277 m³ of refuse. The remaining 10–13 middens are shallow, but their 25–50 cm average depth might yield as much as 1,900 to 3,800 m³ of refuse. This is a lot of refuse, and the bulk of it appears to have been deposited in the late 800s and 900s, although 1000s material is also common. The feature density is such that houses and middens blend into each another. Some earlier houses may be buried within later middens.

The community houses are all of masonry except for a single, large, slab-foundation and adobe house, measuring 21 m long and dating to about 800, positioned in the center of the cluster. This slab-and-adobe house may be the earliest in the community. Three or four houses on the surrounding mesa tops were built partly of Type I masonry. The community layout appears to be of two semiconcentric rings of houses focused on a single house (LA 139390) in the center along the south edge, with a second house (LA 139389) situated on the highest ridge and dominating the community landscape. These two houses had identical room layouts of the same size, were built of Type I masonry, and were founded at about 875. Surface inspection suggests many of the other houses were also started early, with use continuing into the 1000s. Only the two houses mentioned above were mapped (with an alidade) and the earliest areas of their middens were sampled. The interesting, compact layout of this community of houses is similar to the initial community at Pueblo Pintado but contrasts with the spread of the houses at the South Fork and

75

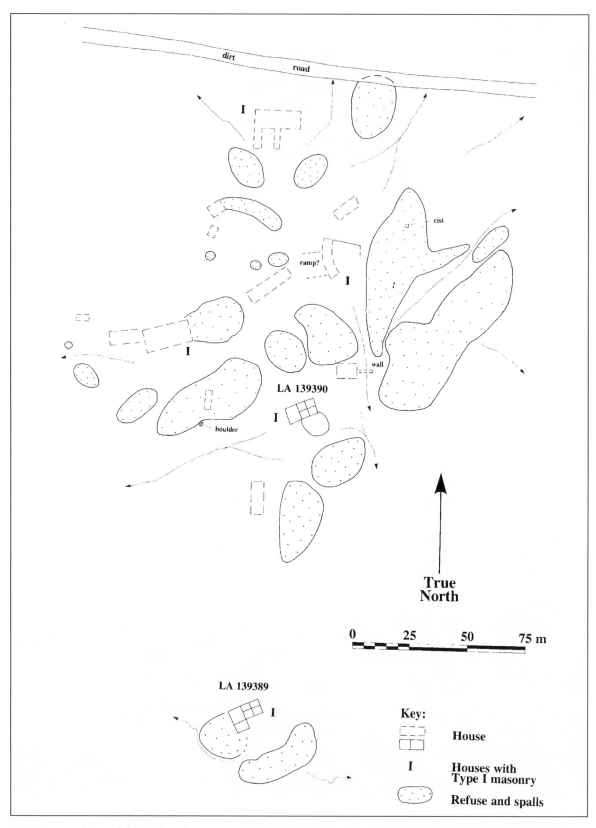

In the figure: labels visible — dirt road, I, cist, ramp?, wall, LA 139390, boulder, I, I, I, LA 139389, I

True North

0   25   50   75 m

Key:

House

I   Houses with
     Type I masonry

Refuse and spalls

FIGURE 3.20. Map of the Willow Canyon community. (Original by the author, Eileen Bacha, and Peg Kaiser, January 2003; from Windes 2006)

Thomas C. Windes

Cedar Hill Pueblo I communities (Wilshusen, ed. 1995). Although none of the houses appears to have been multistory, three or four of them were built of Type I masonry.

On top of the mesa south of the community, two structures documented by Marshall et al. (1979:91–93) are worthy of note. One (LA 18236) is a late 800s structure that employed Type I and block masonry. The building is a single room, 8 by 4 m, perched high above the valley with an incredible spectrum of prominent features on the horizon: the Chuska, Lukachukai, Ute, La Plata, and San Juan mountains; Ford Butte, Shiprock Peak, and the Hogback to the north; Huerfano Mesa to the northeast; and the Dutton Plateau to the south. Interestingly, Hosta Butte is not visible, although it is commonly visible at many great houses and proto–great houses to the east and southeast of

Willow Canyon. A fallen wall of Type I masonry, a single course wide, indicates that wall height was minimally 1.5 m (Figure 3.21). A probable pit-structure is located just to the south, and a few upright slabs indicate other associated features. The quantity of refuse is limited. Just downslope on the next bench to the east is a large, upright-slab-enclosed area (LA 18234), measuring 16 by 18 m. Marshall et al. (1979:93) suggest a house is associated with this enclosure, but this supposition is tenuous. Its size suggests some type of specialized, community use area. Overall, the architecture, associated walled plaza, and view indicate the special function of these features. Despite their diminutive size, these features stand architecturally apart from a nearby slab-and-adobe Pueblo I house located about 200 m to the west that is typical of most of the valley's many Pueblo I houses.

FIGURE 3.21. Intact, fallen Type I masonry wall in the large room at LA 18236 at Willow Canyon. Looking west toward the Chuska Mountains. Eileen Bacha and Tom Windes. (Photograph by Richard Moeller, January 2003; from Windes 2006)

On top of the west mesa is an unusual Pueblo I house built with upright slabs and stacked Type I masonry (Figure 3.22) that is similar to construction at McPhee Pueblo and to the use of masonry in early Chaco Canyon great houses. A proto–great house designation might be apt for this building. The collapsed house masonry forms a mound 84 to 120 cm high, but an intact section of wall fall indicates that the original building height was between 2 and 2.5 m. This building, the House of the Weaver (LA 18235; Figure 3.23), contained several cists and four large rooms that range between 21 and 35 m². The house has a slab- and masonry-enclosed plaza (14 by 28 m), and widespread refuse that covers 26 by 60 m but, because it is quite shallow, would yield little in the way of volume. Nevertheless, the density of cultural material is high, with an estimated 5,000 sherds in the refuse. The site has no pitstructure depressions;

perhaps none are present given the shallow deposits and the exposed bedrock. The house's location, high atop the mesa overlooking Willow Canyon, affords a spectacular view of much of the greater San Juan Basin, including all the mountains and volcanic peaks to the west and north just beyond the Arizona and Colorado borders. Nearby and to the east, below the mesa top, are several more small Pueblo I houses built primarily of adobe and spalls, the norm for the region.

This community provides an excellent example of the early influx of agriculturalists into the basin interior. The community is situated along the prehistoric Great West Road (Windes 2006). The Willow Canyon community also provides a good example of architectural and community continuity from mid Pueblo I times through late Pueblo II or early Pueblo III that could link settlements like McPhee Village with the later examples of great

FIGURE 3.22. The House of the Weaver (LA 18235) showing the wall construction of upright slabs and stacked Type I masonry. (Photograph by the author, 2004; from Windes 2006)

Thomas C. Windes

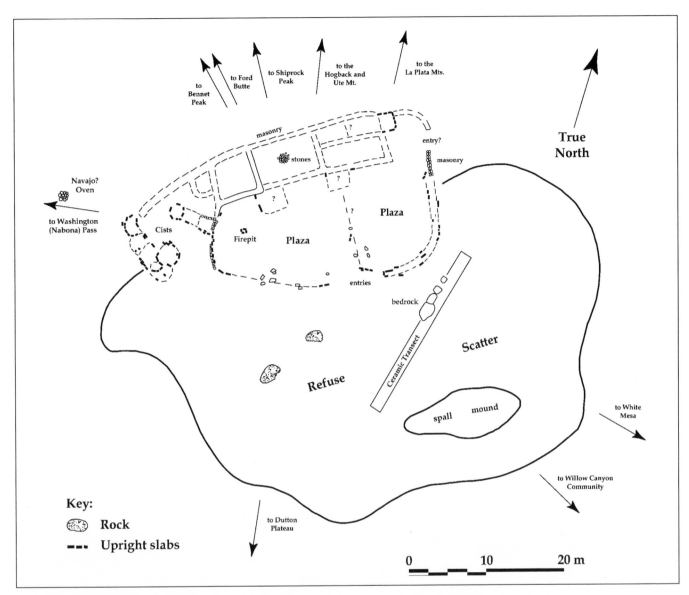

FIGURE 3.23. Map of the House of the Weaver (LA 18235). (Original by the author, Randi Gladwell, Teri Orr, and Steve Emmons, 2003; from Windes 2006)

house communities in and around Chaco Canyon. Finally, the Willow Canyon settlement provides a prime study area for examining the transition from scattered hamlets into a clustered house community, as well as the shift from simple earthen architecture to stone construction.

GREAT BEND

Great Bend, an isolated great house (LA 6419) first recorded by Stewart Peckham in 1962, is located where the Chaco River turns north toward the San Juan River. It is about 5 km west of Willow

Canyon. The site sits atop a sharp ridge that overlooks the canyon (Marshall et al. 1979:33–36, 262a). The walls of the canyon tower over the great house remains in a setting similar to Chaco Canyon. Several slab-and-adobe Pueblo I houses sit on the adjacent ridges; other sites may be present, but the area has not been systematically surveyed.

The Great Bend site duplicates others along the Chaco River in terms of the temporal sequence of house forms. Thirty meters directly behind the great house is a classic slab-foundation and adobe-and-spall-walled Pueblo I house (LA 6418), 22–30 m

79

long, with a small midden that yielded ceramics from the 850–880 period. In contrast, the great house reveals both Type I and block core-and-veneer masonry marking its long construction history (Figure 3.24). Another small, late, block-masonry house is located on a ridge 50 m away. Little of the original great house form is visible on the surface, but it could not have been very large, perhaps less than eight rooms. Ceramics in the midden reveal deposition between 875 and the 1200s, but the bulk of the limited sample (10 m²) in the midden center is primarily from the late 800s and 900s. The midden is 12 by 50 m and less than a meter deep, although it spills down a steep slope an additional 18 m. The contents are dark with ash, and the numerous large, thin slabs scattered on its surface attest to looted burials. Sherd density is 40/m², and the estimated volume of this primary midden is 330 m³, although some has

been lost through erosion and channeling. Numerous groundstones, as well as spalls, red dog shale, and ornaments, are present on the surface.

Great Bend lies adjacent to a massive dune field that borders the Chaco River to the north and beyond (Schultz 1983). Immediately across from the site to the north, the river is broad and flanked along one side by a pair of parallel sand-dune ridges that capture overflow floods between them. During the drought (in June 2003), the water table was reached at a depth of 70 cm, although no pooling occurred. The lush vegetation suggests that this area was advantageous for farming. A deep side drainage just east of the site also provides good potential for runoff farming. The deep, main canyon location prevents extensive visibility except for a view to the northwest of the north end of the Chuskas and the south end of the Lukachukai Mountains. If the site is tied to others by a visual

FIGURE 3.24. Room rubble from collapsed Type I masonry walls at the Great Bend great house. (Photograph by Richard Moeller, January 2003; from Windes 2006)

80

Thomas C. Windes

communications network, the necessary shrines must be located on the surrounding, unsurveyed heights. The prehistoric road observed heading west from Willow Canyon probably intercepts the Great Bend site and continues to the Chuskan slope.

THE HOGBACK

This community (see Marshall et al. 1979) lies along the Chaco River a mere 11 km south of the San Juan River between Fruitland and Shiprock, New Mexico, and close to the Four Corners Power Plant, silhouetted along the skyline. The location is a typical one, affording the resources of the high water table of the Chaco River just below (standing water was encountered at 50 cm when measured in May 2003, a drought year); the lush river oxbows with thick, knee-high grasses; and a major topographic barrier (the 200-m-high Hogback) that would impede storms and create heavy downpours. A major side drainage (Chinde Wash) enters the Chaco River directly east of and across from the settlement. There is an extensive view reaching to the Chuska and La Plata mountains (still snow-capped in May), important topographic landmarks.

It is not known if the 30–35 houses in the community are coeval, although the abundance of 900s surface ceramics suggests a sizeable early settlement. Two great kivas on the south terrace appear to date to the 1000s, but more substantial sampling is warranted to describe the settlement history adequately. A single structure dwarfs all others and provides a significant community landmark. This great house (Component A of LA 11594), measured with a surveying compass, is 2 m in relief and forms a roomblock 26 m long. The remains of Type I masonry are evident among later-style masonry, but this early masonry is still between 174 and 187 cm high, suggesting a very tall single story or an early two-story structure. Ceramics ($n = 655$) indicate occupation of the house beginning by the early 900s; many of the ceramics were Chuskan made, revealing strong ties to the nearby Chuskan-slope communities.

The Hogback Community appears to be the latest great house occupation in the sample. It has substantial numbers of houses built and occupied in the 900s and 1000s, but it was not part of the initial thrust along the Chaco River. Further to the north across the San Juan River, at Squaw Springs,

another huge community has been noted (Marshall and Stein 1978), but only a small part is documented. McKenna (personal communication 2004) believes that a substantial part of the undocumented community may be Pueblo I. If so, this community may provide an important link in our understanding of the breakup of the large Pueblo I communities to the north and the subsequent movement of people to the south along the Chaco River and into the interior San Juan Basin.

CHACOAN READAPTATION OF
A NORTHERN THEME?

The appearance of stone masonry houses and heaped-up middens in the late 800s was a new phenomenon to southerners accustomed to small, mundane hamlets. The inspiration for monumental architectural and landscape modification may have been rooted in the northern San Juan rather than in Chaco Canyon. Our understanding of Pueblo I social and political complexity in the interior San Juan Basin improves when we consider it along with the breakup of the late Pueblo I villages north of the San Juan River. Wilshusen and Wilson (1995) and Wilshusen and Van Dyke (2006) link the dissolution of settlements in the San Juan to the beginnings of the Bonito phase in an important examination of this social continuum. We can expect that the breakup of large villages to the north would have had social consequences reflected in the readaptation to the landscape and settlement in the drier, treeless south.

Some evidence of northern groups is evident in the cultural material in the Chaco area. The initial inhabitants of the Pueblo Pintado community used enough pottery manufactured north of the San Juan River to suggest migration, although additional study is warranted (Windes 2006; Windes et al. 2000). Eric Blinman (personal communication, 2005) reports much of the pottery recovered from nearby Raton Springs also has northern origins. A second early house cluster at Pueblo Pintado has very different pottery that suggests southern origins. The Fajada South Fork community also reveals strong material ties to the south. Immediately west of Chaco Canyon, however, material culture reveals strong ties all the way to the Chuska Valley, which suggests expansion of populations from the eastern

Chuskan slope. The San Juan Basin was occupied during Pueblo I times, but in the late 800s the population swelled dramatically, beyond normal growth expectations. The migrations into the interior San Juan Basin came from all directions except the east; this movement is particularly evident along the primary drainage of the interior San Juan Basin, the Chaco River and its tributaries, yet there appears to be relatively little occupation in the highlands between the drainages. The migration likely spread along drainages, and new settlements typically formed where multiple drainages come together (e.g., Judge et al. 1981). This choice reveals a striking reliance on a combination of floodwater and ground-water farming, the most viable horticultural strategy in the dry, interior basin. Concentrations of early great houses and small-house clusters are also particularly evident in areas where the sharp topography of cliffs, mesas, and hills affected storms sweeping across the San Juan Basin, causing localized rainfall and increased local runoff (see Windes 2006). This phenomenon is documented by Vivian (1990) along the lower Chaco Canyon.

SUMMARY AND CONCLUSIONS

The piling up of stone masonry and refuse in the 800s is visible evidence of a "reformatted" use of the landscape (Wilshusen and Wilson 1995). The rare use of stone masonry in construction sets off a few sites from the general population in the San Juan Basin interior and marks them as different. Practicality could provide a driving force behind the shift in construction technology, but it was too rarely used in the tenth century to provide a simple functional explanation for the change. Instead, these stone masonry structures tend to be located on topography that dominates the landscape and provides commanding views of nearby river valleys, drainages, and small houses. The mounded refuse and masonry construction brings the visual aspects of dominance into play—a visual display of hierarchy (Nielsen 1995; Sebastian 1990, 1992).

Despite the strong links between the northern and southern San Juan Basin occupations, there is little doubt that the Chuskan region was a major contributor to the influx of immigrants into the interior basin; witness the massive flow of ceramics

(Table 3.4) and lithics into the interior great houses and associated communities and the classic fall-off distribution of the artifacts. Unfortunately, our understanding of the Chuskan settlements lacks the strength and cohesion provided by studies of the northern Pueblo I and Pueblo II periods generated by the Dolores Archaeological Project and subsequent projects.

Although problems outside the San Juan Basin must have contributed to this population movement (e.g., Wilshusen and Ortman 1999), some attraction drew people into the interior basin. Given the relatively low population of the Chacoan region in the 700s and 800s, the possibility of escaping strife caused by deteriorating conditions and the pressures of increasing populations outside the interior San Juan Basin must have been enticing. In addition, the high incidence of burned dwellings as a possible indication of warfare or witchcraft (e.g., LeBlanc 1999; Turner and Turner 1999; Walker 1998), common outside the basin in the Pueblo I period (except in the north before 900: Kuckelman et al. 2000:152), is practically nonexistent for surface remains and excavated Pueblo I sites within the interior in the 800s and 900s, particularly in the Chaco Canyon region. Lekson (2002) views this period in the 900s (and later) as one of limited strife—"Pax Chaco"—and this may have been true of the basin interior, at least.

When the push-and-pull of events began to stir these communities in the 800s (e.g., Cameron 1995; Wilshusen and Van Dyke 2004), those along the peripheries might have sent small groups to scout new territories for possible migration. For farmers, these routes of exploration would have been by necessity along the many drainages within the interior San Juan Basin. Favored areas, particularly along the Chaco River, would have been settled, and corporate structures would have served as a focus for community inhabitants and as a base for control of the local areas and for further expansion. The new, strongly built structures could serve as visible symbols of power and safety during stressful times. Strong ties with former homelands would be logical extensions for cultural continuity, resulting in artifactual, topographic, and architectural connections between the areas. The association of communities along the productive Chaco River and the Great West Road suggests that the

Thomas C. Windes

major conduit of movement across the interior basin was funneled along the corridor provided by the Chaco River. If food surplus was a major factor in the establishment of the river communities, groups could exercise considerable control over movement within the interior basin and the transport of goods along the tributaries throughout the region. Only by the 1000s does the influence along the river wane and power become centralized in lower Chaco Canyon.

If there is continuity with the past, as many have argued (e.g., Lekson 1999; Fowler and Stein 1992; Van Dyke 2003; Vivian 1990), then there can be little doubt that memory of past glories and prime settlements linked the initial Chaco core great house settlement with previous times. Given the importance of North in Chacoan cosmology (Ashmore, Chapter 7, this volume; Lekson 1999:130), it may be that Lekson's argument can be extended back from Chaco as a prime center to north of the San Juan River, and to areas such as the Dolores Valley. The alignment is not on the prime meridian, but north nevertheless. To take it further, the twin giant Basketmaker III villages centered at Shabik'eshchee and 29SJ423 (Wills and Windes 1989; Windes 2006) must also be considered prime pathways for later developments in Chaco. Couldn't there have been multiple movements south-to-north and back again in the greater San Juan Basin during the course of Puebloan prehistory?

Use of the basin interior as a refuge would not have lasted long given the swelling population unless a new social order developed that allowed resolution of disputes over limited economic resources. Our knowledge of settlement density in the interior basin is incomplete, but it appears that clustered settlements were widely dispersed at first so that conflict over scarce resources may not have been intense. Settlement dispersal is also evident in Chaco Canyon when great houses first appeared, but by the early 900s, crowding would have necessitated some institutionalized dispute resolution.

The numbers of households that make up northern villages (e.g., Wilshusen 1999; Wilshusen and Blinman 1992; Wilshusen and Ortman 1999; Wilshusen and Wilson 1995) are far greater than the numbers in or near the earliest great houses (Casa del Rio, Great Bend, Lake Valley, Peñasco Blanco, Pueblo Bonito, Una Vida, and Willow Canyon) in the Chaco area. Numbers of households in early great houses appear to have been small (2–6 households; Table 3.4) with concomitantly few inhabitants. This is similar to what is found in other new communities in Chaco (e.g., the Pueblo Pintado community) and far to the south (Van Dyke 1999: Table 3) in the same period (875–925), but here the community great houses were built much later.

As these initial settlements grew, community-level decision-making and dispute resolution would be needed, which is assumed to be manifested architecturally in the presence of a great kiva. None of the late 800s/900s great house settlements along the Chaco River has an identifiable, contemporary great kiva in association. Only the Hogback community exhibits great kivas, and these structures appear to date to the 1000s. We might expect that the regional abandonment of the northern San Juan in the late 800s would transfer social values and organizations along with populations to new areas of settlement. The lack of great kivas in association with early great houses supports Wilshusen and Wilson's (1995) model in which the political economy is reinvested in scattered settlements lacking strong communal control. The largest late 800s great houses in our sample also seem to lack localized community control for the simple reason that clustered settlement appears absent.

Thus, the social integration of these settlements and centers appears to follow a McPhee Village pattern with communal structures in the form of oversized pitstructures rather than the Grass Mesa (Dolores) area pattern where a great kiva served as the community structure. It is possible, of course, that two community integration models based on different organizing principles (e.g., Wilshusen and Wilson 1995) existed, one with large, squarish pithouses and one with circular great kivas.

Judd's (1964) work at Pueblo Bonito suggests that unusually large, circular pitstructures were associated with the early occupation, but little is known about them. More striking is the huge circular pithouse (ca. 44 m² of floor area) found under the great kiva at Kin Nahasbas (Mathien and Windes 1989), with floor features and contents that are similar to those of the oversized community pitstructures at Dolores. The recovery of ritually placed selenite wands, Washington (Narbona)

Pass chert, and iron concretion nodules in two large pits north of the firepit suggests parallels with Wilshusen's roofed sipapus in the north (Wilshusen 1989b). To the south, early great kivas seem common (e.g., Kantner 1996; Van Dyke 2002 and Chapter 4, this volume), which is not generally the case with the early communities in the interior basin.

At this point, the evidence indicates that great kivas, present in the two large Basketmaker villages in Chaco, reoccur as a phenomenon of social integration in the interior basin at about 1050, clearly marking a major shift in social organization (see Van Dyke, Chapter 4). In addition, Wilshusen and Ortman's (1999) argument that the spatial arrangement of the post-Dolores communities reflects different social integrative mechanisms may be applicable to the Chaco settlements.

Basically, compact communities have oversized pitstructures, and dispersed ones, a great kiva. Early and late Chacoan settlements are marked by several different settlement patterns (see Orcutt 1987:617): a dispersed one covering several square kilometers, a highly compact one with adjacent houses within throwing distance of one another, and one with a great house but little supporting or adjacent community. There are also settlements without a great house. Each of these settlement types requires more research to understand their sociopolitical organization and the movement of diverse cultural groups into the interior San Juan Basin.

The clustered settlement is often seen with houses aligned as if facing avenues or streets (e.g., the Hogback, Navajo Springs, Pueblo Pintado, Skunk Springs, and Willow Canyon). The close proximity of the houses indicates social cohesion and group participation within the same social unit (Fretwell 2006). The widely dispersed settlements suggest less strong ties and perhaps immigrants arriving from divergent localities and different kin groups. All these early settlement types are present in the San Juan Basin, but the only one with a probable great kiva is the dispersed community at 29MC184 along the South Fork Valley.

We do not yet know when the expansion occurred at the few great houses that later blossomed into gigantic structures because very few of them have been excavated. Pueblo Bonito grew large with the western (and eastern?) additions in the 860s, and Una Vida expanded in the 940s. But many early great houses do not exhibit the massive additions seen at great houses in the Chaco Core in the 1000s. In at least some cases, however, these early buildings are buried under the later 1000s construction (e.g., Great Bend, Lake Valley, Morris 41, Padilla Well, Peach Springs).

The site histories in the present sample are widely divergent. The 29MC184 houses were occupied only briefly before abandonment; then there was a temporal break before early Pueblo II houses were built in the area. The East Community great house exhibits little subsequent construction after its initial construction except to enclose the plaza area with a block masonry wall. However, the large midden deposit mirrors those of the other, later 1000s mounds in the canyon in terms of its large size, temporal span, and cultural material. That is, the large volume of cultural material that was deposited is not temporally linked with the early surface architecture. Thus, activities at the site took a dramatic shift from when the house was first constructed, and little cultural material was deposited, to events in the late 1000s. This behavior mirrors that manifested at Kin Bineola, where there is little evidence for major extramural deposition at the site for 150 years until the late 1000s/early 1100s, when the great house was enlarged and a large midden began.

Casa del Rio and Peñasco Blanco, and other great houses along the Chaco River, present different scenarios. At these houses, massive external deposition seems to have immediately followed great house construction; it then diminished or ceased in the 1000s, at the time when the building boom was taking place in downtown Chaco. Clearly, the variety of activities that were being practiced at the various early great houses abruptly shifted in the 1000s.

Some of the earliest great houses are concentrated along the Chaco Wash and Chaco River and their southern tributaries. The shallow water table along the Chaco River and the broad expanse of the riverbed may have provided the best opportunity for producing surplus food of any area within the interior San Juan Basin. Perhaps it is not surprising that so many early great houses are found along the Chaco River (e.g., the Hogback, Great Bend, Willow Springs, Lake Valley, Casa del Rio, and Peñasco Blanco; Marshall et al. 1979), with perhaps more as yet undiscovered. The largest known examples of massively piled-up refuse occur along the Chaco River, where the most reliable farming in the interior basin may have been possible. In addition, at Peñasco Blanco, a large sand dune and masonry dam may have blocked the Chaco Wash, creating a shallow lake (Force et al. 2002; Force 2004) that would have enhanced farming. Few sites can match the huge quantities of refuse generated at Peñasco Blanco, Casa del Rio, and Lake Valley, yet these sites lack an immediate community of contemporary small houses that could have contributed greatly to the profusion of discarded material. Other nearby early great houses of striking size, Kin Bineola, Pueblo Bonito, Una Vida, and the East Community great house, which were along tributaries of the Chaco River, do not have quantities of refuse that suggest similar discard behavior in the late 800s and 900s. Unlike the great mounds of the mid and late 1000s, the early mounds reflect primarily domestic trash. The great house inhabitants at Peñasco Blanco and Casa del Rio may have generated the majority of the refuse, but it is hard to reconcile this behavior with contemporary occupations of equal duration and household size that discarded far less.

Dense communities of small houses adjacent to great houses appear by the very late 800s or by the early 900s, when such communities proliferate. Thus, we must ask, what was the early role of great houses? The known examples of discard at the early great houses (Table 3.2) suggest domestic refuse and the likelihood that they were domestic structures, unlike the primary role for these structures in the 1000s (cf. Vivian 1990; Wills 2001). Despite the domestic appearance of the refuse, the massive quantities indicate an intensity and duration of discard that was seldom apparent in earlier periods except at the two huge Basketmaker III settlements in Chaco Canyon (Roberts 1929; Wills and Windes 1989; Windes 2006). On the other hand, the amount of turquoise and the evidence of craft activities suggest that these early structures may have served partly as ritual centers, like their 1000s counterparts (see Durand 2003; Neitzel 2003 and Chapter 5, this volume).

Although downtown Chaco has been characterized in the past as a center of Chaco power and ritual activities, there is little to suggest that this core was dominant before about 1050 or somewhat later. Yes, the downtown great houses were large and prominent early architectural constructions, but they were not several degrees of magnitude larger than the other contemporary great houses. What is unique is that Peñasco Blanco, Pueblo Bonito, Kin Nahasbas, and Una Vida were built close together, unlike any other early great house locations, and exhibited multistory construction. But could the clustering be accounted for in large part by the unusual canyon topographical setting that offered multiple locales advantageous for farming? The density of great houses and associated small houses in downtown Chaco can be challenged by that around McPhee Pueblo in the Dolores Valley and by the Newcomb–Skunk Springs communities on the Chuskan slope. Even the series of great houses that includes Peñasco Blanco, Padilla Well (probably underlain by an early great house that is not described here), Casa del Rio, Lake Valley, and Kin Bineola rivals the downtown Chaco sites in the late 800s and 900s. Any uniqueness assigned to the early core sites must withstand testing against a much larger sample of great houses within the San Juan Basin that await reinvestigation or discovery. For instance, the perceived regional planning assigned to the downtown core sites (e.g., Doxtater 2002; Lekson 1999; Stein et al., Chapter 8, this volume; Sofaer 1997, and Chapter 9, this volume) must take into account placement of the many other early great houses. It is difficult to defend the uniqueness of the early core great houses and their deliberate placement when there are so many others that remain undocumented or poorly documented.

When the architectural boom first began in the 1000s, it was not at any of the early Chaco core great houses. The earliest example of tree-ring-dated core-and-veneer masonry was at a new great house, Hungo Pavi, between about 1004 and 1010,[4] coeval with or somewhat prior to the core-and-veneer building at Chetro Ketl (Lekson et al., Chapter 6)—both within the core area. This is followed by a staggered series of constructions within and beyond the canyon. This does not support the model of initial concentration of political power (i.e., Sebastian 1992) at the earliest great houses in the core area to the detriment of nearby community

Gearing Up and Piling On

loci, particularly if the general area was beginning to experience small-house abandonment (e.g., Windes 1987, 1993). Yet, considerable social energy was invested in downtown Chaco after 1040 or 1050, perhaps to the detriment of many other great houses in the area. When Pueblo Alto was built in the 1040s, if not earlier,[5] it provided the key site that integrated the canyon with the entire San Juan Basin and beyond in terms of visual connections, roads, and prominent landscapes. At this point, Chaco may have become the Center Place and assumed greater political network leadership (Blanton et al. 1996; Earle 2001) or centralized ritual (Renfrew 2001) that reached well beyond the core area.

But the key to these later events may reside in the small communities along the Chaco River in the late 800s and 900s with possible economic control over food surpluses that may have been carried east to Chaco Canyon, west to the Chuska Mountains, and south along the major southern tributaries. Recent efforts to determine the origins of corn consumed in the area indicate that at least some of it was nonlocal (Benson et al. 2003, 2006). Perhaps there is a positive correlation between the solidly built early great houses and food production, but the presently inadequate sample will not resolve these issues. As Wilshusen and Blinman (1992) cautioned long ago, much greater emphasis must be paid to the Pueblo I era, for therein lie the seeds of the rise and spread of Chacoan culture. Without substantial research into the late 800s and 900s occupations within the San Juan Basin, we can do little to adjust and refine the myriad models purporting to explain the Chaco system. Continued emphasis on the events in downtown Chaco Canyon during the 1000s is inadequate for this task.

ACKNOWLEDGMENTS

A vast pool of volunteers helped over the decades of fieldwork in and around Chaco, which could not have been done without their skills, energy, and time. My special thanks to the many Sierra Club service trips into the Fajada South Fork ably led by Bonnie Sharpe and her assistants, Tom Meehan and Cheryl Srnka. A number of others have also helped over the years, including Rachel Anderson, Valerie Banks, GB Cornucopia, Steve Cowan, Diane and Holly Flynn, Richard Friedman, Paul LaQuatra, Tom Meehan, Richard and Ursula Moeller, Jeremy Moss, Colby Phillips, Courtney Porreca, Jamie Schubert, Cheryl Srnka, John Stein, Jim Trimball, Ruth Van Dyke, and Al Webster. Late-hour help in the reinvestigations of the early great houses, for which I am most grateful, was given by Eileen Bacha, Stephanie Ford, Richard Friedman, Randi Gladwell, Peg Kaiser, Richard and Ursula Moeller, and Colby Phillips. My special thanks to Clay Mathers, of Statistical Research, Inc., who provided digital graphics assistance. I am particularly appreciative of Eileen Bacha, Peter McKenna, Mark Varien, and Gwinn Vivian, who took the time to read, edit, and comment on a draft of this chapter.

NOTES

1. All interior basin sites discussed here were revisited by the author in December 2002 and January 2003. Data may differ from Marshall et al. (1979) and Marshall and Bradley (1994), particularly in estimated midden volumes and recognition of the earliest deposits. In no case are ceramic samples adequate to represent the entire site occupation or its intensity by period. The focus here is on recognition of the initial great house constructions, whereas Marshall and colleagues focused on the final site use.

2. Wilshusen and Blinman (1992:257–258) propose a correlate between house length and number of households, but the sample is biased by the inclusion of mostly large houses, which are common to the northern San Juan. Employing the formula to the small sample of excavated or surface-delineated Pueblo I roomblocks in Chaco produces household numbers inflated by approximately one-third. To adjust for the very small house sizes common to the 29MC184 community, the combined wall lengths in the community were used instead of individual house lengths. This adjustment produced an estimated 43 households, whereas the northern San Juan method yielded 79 households.

3. Generally, the Marshall et al. (1979) and Marshall and Bradley (1994) midden volumes were calculated as if the feature were a cube (length by width by depth), but most middens are rounded and contain approximately half the volume calculated for a cube. Estimates here are made as if the mean midden depth is approximately half of the estimated maximum depth. The Midden 1 volume for Casa del Rio, however, was made by an engineering firm based on a 50-cm contour map.

Thomas C. Windes

Despite such rough estimates, the magnitude of the volumes is evident.

4. Tree-ring dates from great houses listed here are from the Chaco Wood Project.

5. This connection with the outside may have been earlier, depending on the nature of the earlier structure under Pueblo Alto, which suggests an early small (great?) house in the late 900s (Windes 1987[I]).

REFERENCES

Ahlstrom, Richard V. N.
1985   *The Interpretation of Archaeological Tree-Ring Dates*. Ph.D. dissertation, Department of Anthropology, University of Arizona, Tucson. University Microfilms, Ann Arbor.

Benson, Larry, Linda Cordell, Kirk Vincent, Howard Taylor, John Stein, G. Lang Farmer, and Kiyoto Futa
2003   Ancient Maize from Chacoan Great House: Where Was It Grown? *Proceedings of the National Academy of Science* 100:13111–13115.

Benson, L., J. Stein, H. Taylor, R. Freidman, and T. C. Windes
2006   The Agricultural Productivity of Chaco Canyon and the Source(s) of Pre-Hispanic Maize Found in Pueblo Bonito. In *Histories of Maize: Multidisciplinary Approaches to the Prehistory, Linguistics, Biogeography, Domestication, and Evolution of Maize*, edited by J. E. Staller, R. H. Tykot, and B. F. Benz, pp. 289–314. Elsevier/Academic Press, Burlington, MA.

Blanton, R. E, G. M. Feinman, S. A. Kowalewski, and P. N. Peregrine
1996   A Dual Processual Theory for the Evolution of Mesoamerican Civilization. *Current Anthropology* 37:1–14.

Brew, John Otis
1946   *Archaeology of Alkali Ridge, Southeastern Utah*. Papers of the Peabody Museum of American Archaeology and Ethnology XXI. Harvard University, Cambridge, MA.

Brisbin, Joel M., Allen E. Kane, and James N. Morris
1988   Excavations at McPhee Pueblo (Site 5MT4475), A Pueblo I and Early Pueblo II Multicomponent Village. In *Dolores Archaeological Program: Anasazi Communities at Dolores: McPhee Vilage*, compiled by A. E. Kane and C. K. Robinson, pp. 63–401. Engineering and Research Center, U.S. Bureau of Reclamation, Denver.

Burns, Barney Tillman
1983   Simulated Anasazi-Storage Behavior Using Crop Yields Reconstructed from Tree Rings: A.D. 652–1968. Unpublished Ph.D. dissertation, Department of Anthropology, University of Arizona, Tucson.

Cameron, Catherine M.
1990   The Effect of Varying Estimates of Pit Structure Use-Life on Prehistoric Population Estimates in the American Southwest. *Kiva* 55:155–166.
1995   Migration and the Movement of Southwestern Peoples. *Journal of Anthropological Archaeology* 14:104–124.
2002   Sacred Earthen Architecture in the Northern Southwest: The Bluff Great House Berm. *American Antiquity* 67:677–695.

Cordell, Linda
1994   *Ancient Pueblo Peoples*. Smithsonian Books, Washington, DC.

Dean, Jeffrey S.
1996   Demography, Environment, and Subsistence Stress. In *Evolving Complexity and Environmental Risk in the Prehistoric Southwest*, edited by Joseph A. Tainter and B. Bagley Tainter, pp. 25–56. Addison-Wesley, Reading, MA.

Doxtater, Dennis
2002   A Hypothetical Layout of Chaco Canyon Structures via Large-Scale Alignments Between Significant Natural Features. *Kiva* 68(1): 23–47.

Drager, Dwight L.
1976   Anasazi Population Estimates with the Aid of Data Derived from Photogrammetric Maps. In *Remote Sensing Experiments in Cultural Resource Studies*, assembled by Thomas R. Lyons, pp. 157–171. Reports of the Chaco Center 1. National Park Service, Albuquerque.

Durand, Kathy Roler
2003   Function of Chaco-Era Great Houses. *Kiva* 69(2):141–169.

Earle, Timothy
2001   Economic Support of Chaco Canyon Society. *American Antiquity* 66:26–35.

Force, Eric R.
2004   Late Holocene Behavior of Chaco and McElmo Canyon Drainages (Southwest U.S.): A Comparison Based on Archaeologic Age Controls. *Geoarchaeology: An International Journal* 19(6):583–609.

Force, Eric R., R. Gwinn Vivian, Thomas C. Windes, and Jeffrey S. Dean
2002   *The Relation of "Bonito" Paleo-channels and Base-level Variations to Anasazi Occupation, Chaco Canyon, New Mexico*. Archaeological Series 194. Arizona State Museum, University of Arizona, Tucson.

Fowler, Andrew, and John R. Stein
1992   The Anasazi Great House in Space, Time, and Paradigm. In *Anasazi Regional Organization and the Chaco System*, edited by David E. Doyel, pp. 101–122. Maxwell Museum of Anthropology, Anthropological Papers 5. University of New Mexico, Albuquerque.

Fowler, Andrew, John A. Stein, and Roger Anyon
1987   An Archaeological Reconnaissance of West-Central New Mexico: The Anasazi Monuments Project. Ms. on file, New Mexico Office of Cultural Affairs, Historic Preservation Division, Santa Fe.

Fretwell, Hannah
2006   Social Information in Early Chacoan Ornaments: A Study of Basketmaker III and Pueblo I Assemblages. In *Early Puebloan Occupations in the Chaco Region: Excavations and Survey of Basketmaker III and Pueblo I Sites, Chaco Canyon, New Mexico*, Vol. II, edited by T. C. Windes and June-el Piper. Reports of the Chaco Center 13. Branch of Cultural Research, National Park Service, Santa Fe. (in press)

Gilpin, Dennis, and David E. Purcell
2000   Peach Springs Revisited: Surface Recording and Excavation on the South Chaco Slope, New Mexico. In *Great House Communities across the Chacoan Landscape*, edited by J. Kantner and N. M. Mahoney, pp. 28–38. Anthropological Papers 64. University of Arizona Press, Tucson.

Hawley, Florence
1934   *The Significance of the Dated Prehistory of Chetro Ketl, Chaco Canyon, New Mexico*. University of New Mexico Bulletin, Monograph Series 1(1). Albuquerque.

Hayes, Alden C.
1981   A Survey of Chaco Canyon Archeology. In *Archeological Surveys of Chaco Canyon, New Mexico*, by Alden C. Hayes, David M. Brugge, and W. James Judge, pp. 1–68. Publications in Archeology 18A, Chaco Canyon Studies. National Park Service, Washington, DC.

Hayes, Alden C., and Thomas C. Windes
1975   An Anasazi Shrine in Chaco Canyon. In *Collected Papers in Honor of Florence Hawley Ellis*, edited by Theodore R. Frisbie, pp. 143–156. Papers of the Archaeological Society of New Mexico 2. Santa Fe.

Hegmon, Michelle
1989   Social Integration and Architecture. In *The Architecture of Social Integration in Prehistoric Pueblos*, edited by W. D. Lipe and Michelle Hegmon, pp. 5–14. Occasional Papers of the Crow Canyon Archaeological Center 1. Cortez, CO.

Ireland, Arthur K.
2001   Analysis of Aerial Photography of the Area of Chaco and Kin Klizhin Washes between the Western Boundary of Chaco Culture National Historical Park and the Community of La Vida Mission, New Mexico. Ms. on file, Anthropology Projects, National Park Service, Santa Fe.

Jackson, William H.
1878   Report on the Ancient Ruins Examined in 1875 and 1877. In *Tenth Annual Report of the United States Geological and Geographical Survey of the Territories Embracing Colorado and Parts of Adjacent Territories*, by F. V. Hayden, pp. 411–450. U.S. Government Printing Press, Washington, DC.

Judd, Neil M.
1959   *Pueblo del Arroyo, Chaco Canyon*. Smithsonian Miscellaneous Collections 138(1). Washington, DC.

1964   *The Architecture of Pueblo Bonito*. Smithsonian Miscellaneous Collections 147(1). Washington, DC.

Judge, W. James, H. Wolcott Toll, William B. Gillespie, and Stephen H. Lekson
1981   Tenth Century Developments in Chaco Canyon. In *Collected Papers in Honor of Erik Kellerman Reed*, edited by Albert H. Schroeder, pp. 65–98. Papers of the Archaeological Society of New Mexico 6. Albuquerque.

Kane, Allen E.
1986   Prehistory of the Dolores River Valley. In *Dolores Archaeological Program: Final Synthetic Report*, compiled by D.A. Breternitz, C. K. Robinson, and G. T. Gross, pp. 353–435. Engineering and Research Center, U.S. Bureau of Reclamation, Denver.

Kane, A. K., and C. K. Robinson
1988   *Dolores Archaeological Program: Anasazi Communities at Dolores: McPhee Village*, 2 vols. Engineering and Research Center, U.S. Bureau of Reclamation, Denver.

Kantner, John
1996   Political Competition Among the Chaco Anasazi of the American Southwest. *Journal of Anthropological Archaeology* 15:41–105.

Kievit, Karen A.
1998   Seeing and Reading Chaco Architecture at AD 1100. Unpublished Ph.D. dissertation, Department of Anthropology, University of Colorado, Boulder.

Kuckelman, Kristin A., Ricky R. Lightfoot, and Debra L. Martin
2000   Changing Patterns of Violence in the Northern San Juan Region. *Kiva* 66:147–165.

Kohler, Timothy A., and Eric Blinman
1987   Solving Mixture Problems in Archaeology: Analysis of Ceramic Material for Dating and Demographic Reconstruction. *Journal of Anthropological Archaeology* 6:1–28.

Kosse, Krisztina
1996   Middle Range Societies from a Scalar Perspective. In *Interpreting Southwestern Diversity: Underlying Principles and Overarching Patterns*, edited by Paul R. Fish and J. Jefferson Reid, pp. 87–96. Anthropological Research Papers 48. Arizona State University, Tempe.

88

LeBlanc, Steven A.

1999   *Prehistoric Warfare in the American Southwest.* University of Utah Press, Salt Lake City.

Lekson, Stephen L.

1984   *Great Pueblo Architecture of Chaco Canyon, New Mexico.* Publications in Archeology 18B, Chaco Canyon Studies. National Park Service, Albuquerque.

1991   Settlement Pattern and the Chaco Region. In *Chaco and Hohokam: Prehistoric Regional Systems in the American Southwest,* edited by Patricia L. Crown and W. James Judge, pp. 31–55. School of American Research Press, Santa Fe.

1999   *The Chaco Meridian.* Altamira Press, Walnut Creek, CA.

2002   War in the Southwest, War in the World. *American Antiquity* 67:607–624.

Lekson, Stephen L., Thomas C. Windes, John R. Stein, and W. James Judge

1988   The Chaco Canyon Community. *Scientific American* 259:100–109.

Lightfoot, Ricky R.

1994   *The Duckfoot Site, Vol. 2: Archaeology of the House and Household.* Occasional Papers of the Crow Canyon Archaeological Center 4. Cortez, CO.

Lightfoot, Ricky R., Mary C. Etzkorn, and Mark D. Varien

1993   Excavations. In *The Duckfoot Site, Vol. 1: Descriptive Archaeology,* edited by R. R. Lightfoot and M. C. Etzkorn, pp. 15–129. Occasional Papers of the Crow Canyon Archaeological Center 3. Cortez, CO.

Lipe, William

2002   Social Power in the Central Mesa Verde Region, AD 1150–1290. In *Seeking the Center Place: Archaeology and Ancient Communities in the Mesa Verde Region,* edited by M. D. Varien and R. H. Wilshusen, pp.203–232. University of Utah Press, Salt Lake City.

Lipe, William, James N. Morris, and Timothy A. Kohler

1988   *Dolores Archaeological Program: Anasazi Communities at Dolores: Grass Mesa Village.* Engineering and Research Center, U.S. Bureau of Reclamation, Denver.

Loose, Richard W., and Thomas R. Lyons

1976   The Chetro Ketl Field: A Planned Water Control System in Chaco Canyon. In *Remote Sensing in Cultural Resource Studies: Non-destructive Methods of Archeological Exploration, Survey, and Analysis,* assembled by Thomas R. Lyons, pp. 133–156. Reports of the Chaco Center 1. National Park Service, Albuquerque.

Marshall, Michael P.

1997   The Chacoan Roads: A Cosmological Interpretation. In *Anasazi Architecture and American Design,* edited by Baker H. Morrow and V. B. Price, pp. 62–74. University of New Mexico Press, Albuquerque.

Marshall, Michael P., and Ronna J. Bradley

1994   El Llano-Escalon and Standing Rock Communities. In *Across the Colorado Plateau: Anthropological Studies for the Transwestern Pipeline Expansion Project, Vol. IX: A Study of Two Anasazi Communities in the San Juan Basin,* by Ronna J. Bradley and Richard B. Sullivan, pp. 313–381. UNM Project 185-461B. Office of Contract Archeology and Maxwell Museum of Anthropology, University of New Mexico, Albuquerque.

Marshall, Michael P., and John R. Stein

1978   *Archeological Investigations in the Squaw Springs District of the Ute Mountain Indian Reservation, Northwestern New Mexico.* Environmental Quality Services, Albuquerque Area Office, Bureau of Indian Affairs.

Marshall, Michael P., John R. Stein, Richard W. Loose, and Judith E. Novotny

1979   *Anasazi Communities of the San Juan Basin.* Public Service Company of New Mexico and New Mexico Historic Preservation Bureau, Albuquerque and Santa Fe.

Martin, Paul S.

1939   *Modified Basket Maker Sites, Ackmen-Lowry Area, Southwestern Colorado.* Anthropological Series XXIII(3). Field Museum of Natural History, Chicago.

Mathien, Frances Joan

1993   Ornaments and Minerals from 29SJ 629. In *The Spadefoot Toad Site: Investigations at 29SJ 629, Chaco Canyon, New Mexico,* edited by Thomas C. Windes, pp. 269–316. Reports of the Chaco Center 12. Branch of Cultural Research, National Park Service, Santa Fe.

Mathien, Frances Joan, and Thomas C. Windes

1988   Kin Nahasbas Ruin, Chaco Culture National Historical Park, New Mexico. Historic Structure Report. Ms. on file, Chaco Archives (CHCU 51432), University of New Mexico, Albuquerque.

1989   Great House Revisited: Kin Nahasbas, Chaco Culture National Historical Park. In *From Chaco to Chaco: Papers in Honor of Robert H. Lister and Florence C. Lister,* edited by Meliha S. Duran and David T. Kirkpatrick, pp. 11–34. Papers of the Archaeological Society of New Mexico 15. Albuquerque.

McKenna, Peter J.

1984   *The Architecture and Material Culture of 29SJ1360, Chaco Canyon, New Mexico.* Reports of the Chaco Center 7. Division of Cultural Research, National Park Service, Albuquerque.

McKenna, Peter J., and Thomas C. Windes
1975   29SJ1088, Abstract of Site Notes. Chaco Archives (CHCU 51405), University of New Mexico, Albuquerque.

Miller, Ralph L., Mary Alice Carey, and Carolyn L. Thompson-Rizer
1991   *Geology of the La Vida Mission Quadrangle, San Juan and McKinley Counties, New Mexico.* U.S. Geological Survey Bulletin 1940. U.S. Government Printing Office, Denver.

Mills, Barbara J.
2002   Recent Research on Chaco: Changing Views on Economy, Ritual, and Power. *Journal of Archaeological Research* 10:65–117.

Morris, Earl H.
1939   *Archaeological Studies in the La Plata District, Southwestern Colorado and Northwestern New Mexico.* Carnegie Institution of Washington, Publication 519. Washington, DC.

Nielsen, Axel E.
1995   Architectural Performance and the Reproduction of Social Power. In *Expanding Archaeology*, edited by J. M. Skibo, W. H. Walker, and A. E. Nielsen, pp. 47–66. University of Utah Press, Salt Lake City.

Neitzel, Jill E.
2003   Artifact Distributions at Pueblo Bonito. In *Pueblo Bonito: Center of the Chacoan World*, edited by Jill E. Neitzel, pp. 107–126. Smithsonian Books, Washington, DC.

Orcutt, Janet D.
1987   Changes in Aggregation and Spacing, A.D. 600–1175. In *Dolores Archaeological Program: Supporting Studies: Settlement and Environment*, compiled by K. L. Peterson and J. D. Orcutt, pp. 617–648. Engineering and Research Center, U.S. Bureau of Reclamation, Denver.

Ortiz, Alfronso
1969   *The Tewa World: Space, Time, Being and Becoming in a Pueblo Society.* University of Chicago Press, Chicago.

Peterson, Kenneth Lee
1987   Concluding Remarks on Prehistoric Agricultural Potential in the Dolores Project Area. In *Dolores Archaeological Program: Supporting Studies: Settlement and Environment*, compiled by K. L. Peterson and J. D. Orcutt, pp. 235–246. Engineering and Research Center, U.S. Bureau of Reclamation, Denver.

Pierson, Lloyd M.
1949   The Prehistoric Population of Chaco Canyon, New Mexico: A Study in Methods and Techniques of Prehistoric Population Estimation. Unpublished M.A. thesis, Department of Anthropology, University of New Mexico, Albuquerque.

Plog, Stephen
1997   *Ancient Peoples of the American Southwest.* Thames and Hudson, London.

Powers, Robert P., William B. Gillespie, and Stephen H. Lekson
1983   *The Outlier Survey: A Regional View of Settlement in the San Juan Basin.* Reports of the Chaco Center 3. Division of Cultural Research, National Park Service, Albuquerque.

Renfrew, Colin
2001   Production and Consumption in a Sacred Economy: The Material Correlates of High Devotional Expression at Chaco Canyon. *American Antiquity* 66:14–25.

Roberts, Frank H. H., Jr.
1929   *Shabik'eshchee Village: A Late Basketmaker III Site in the Chaco Canyon, New Mexico.* Bureau of American Ethnology, Bulletin 92. Smithsonian Institution, Washington, DC.
1939   *Archeological Remains in the Whitewater District, Eastern Arizona*, Part I. Bureau of American Ethnology, Bulletin 121. Smithsonian Institution, Washington, DC.

Schelberg, John S.
1992   Hierarchical Organization as a Short-term Buffering Strategy in Chaco Canyon. In *Anasazi Regional Organization and the Chaco System*, edited by David E. Doyel, pp. 59–71. Maxwell Museum of Anthropology, Anthropological Papers 5. University of New Mexico, Albuquerque.

Schlanger, Sarah H.
1985   *Prehistoric Population Dynamics in the Dolores Area, Southwestern Colorado.* Ph.D. dissertation, Washington State University, Pullman. University Microfilms, Ann Arbor.
1987   Population Measurement, Size, and Change: A.D. 600–1175. In *Dolores Archaeological Program: Supporting Studies: Settlement and Environment*, compiled by K. L. Peterson and J. D. Orcutt, pp. 569–616. Engineering and Research Center, U.S. Bureau of Reclamation, Denver.

Schlanger, Sarah H., and Richard H. Wilshusen
1993   Local Abandonments and Regional Conditions in the North American Southwest. In *Abandonments of Settlements and Regions*, edited by C. M. Cameron and S. A. Tomka, pp. 85–98. Cambridge University Press, Cambridge.

Schultz, J. D.
1983   Geomorphology and Quaternary History of the Southeastern [*sic:* Southwestern] Chaco Dune Field, Northwestern New Mexico. In *Chaco Country: A Field Guide to the Geomorphology, Quaternary Geology, Paleoecology, and Environmental Geology of Northwestern New Mexico*, edited by Stephen G. Wells, David W. Love, and Thomas W. Gardner, pp. 159–166. American

90

Geomorphological Field Group, 1983 Field Trip
Guidebook. Adobe Press, Albuquerque.

Sebastian, Lynn
1990   Sociopolitical Complexity and the Chaco
System. In *Chaco and Hohokam: Prehistoric
Regional Systems in the American Southwest*,
edited by Patricia L. Crown and W. James
Judge, pp. 109–134. School of American
Research Press, Santa Fe.
1992   *The Chaco Anasazi: Sociopolitical Evolution in
the Prehistoric Southwest*. Cambridge University Press, Cambridge.

Sofaer, Anna
1997   The Primary Architecture of the Chacoan Culture: A Cosomological Expression. In *Anasazi
Architecture and American Design*, edited by
Baker H. Morrow and V. B. Price, pp. 88–132.
University of New Mexico Press, Albuquerque.

Stein, John R., and Stephen H. Lekson
1992   Anasazi Ritual Landscapes. In *Anasazi Regional
Organization and the Chaco System*, edited by
David E. Doyel, pp. 87–100. Maxwell Museum
of Anthropology, Anthropological Papers 5.
University of New Mexico, Albuquerque.

Stein, John R., and Peter J. McKenna
1988   *An Archaeological Reconnaissance of a Late
Bonito Phase Occupation near Aztec Ruins
National Monument, New Mexico*. Division of
Anthropology, National Park Service, Santa Fe.

Stuart, David E.
2000   *Anasazi America and American Design*. University of New Mexico Press, Albuquerque.

Swentzell, Rina
1997   A Puebloan Perspective. In *Anasazi Architecture*, edited by Baker H. Morrow and V. B.
Price, pp. 149–158. University of New Mexico
Press, Albuquerque.

Toll, H. Wolcott
1985   Pottery, Production, Public Architecture, and
the Chaco Anasazi System. Unpublished Ph.D.
dissertation, Department of Anthropology, University of Colorado, Boulder.
2001   Making and Breaking Pots in the Chaco World.
American Antiquity 66:56–78.

Truell, Marcia L.
1992   *Excavations at 29SJ627, Chaco Canyon, New
Mexico*, Vol. I. Reports of the Chaco Center 11.
Branch of Cultural Research, National Park
Service, Santa Fe.

Turner, Christy G., II, and Jacqueline A. Turner
1999   *Man Corn: Cannibalism and Violence in the
Prehistoric American Southwest*. University of
Utah Press, Salt Lake City.

Van Dyke, Ruth M.
1999   The Andrews Community: A Chacoan Outlier
in the Red Mesa Valley, New Mexico. *Journal
of Field Archaeology* 26:55–67.

2000   Chacoan Ritual Landscapes: The View from the
Red Mesa Valley. In *Great House Communities
across the Chacoan Landscape*, edited by John
Kantner and Nancy Mahoney, pp. 91–100.
Anthropological Papers of the University of Arizona 64. University of Arizona Press, Tucson.
2002   The Chacoan Great Kiva in Outlier Communities: Investigating Integrative Spaces across the
San Juan Basin. *Kiva* 67:231–247.
2003   Memory and the Construction of Chacoan Society. In *Archaeologies of Memory*, edited by R. M.
Van Dyke and S. E. Alcock, pp. 180–200. Blackwell Publishers, Oxford, UK, and Malden, MA.

Varien, Mark D.
1984   Honky House: The Replication of Three
Anasazi Surface Structures. Unpublished M.A.
thesis, Anthropology Department, University of
Texas, Austin.
1999   Regional Context: Architecture, Settlement Patterns, and Abandonment. In *Sand Canyon
Archaeological Project: Site Testing Report*,
Version 1.0, edited by Mark D. Varien.
<http://www.crowcanyon.org/ResearchReports/SiteTesting/start.html> (Archaeological
Research; Publications). Last accessed: 1-20-05.
2002   Persistent Communities and Mobile Households: Population Movement in the Central
Mesa Verde Region, AD 950 to 1290. In *Seeking
the Center Place: Archaeology and Ancient
Communities in the Mesa Verde Region*, edited
by M. D. Varien and R. H. Wilshusen, pp.
163–184. University of Utah Press, Salt Lake
City.

Varien, Mark D., and Richard H. Wilshusen, eds.
2002   *Seeking the Center Place: Archaeology and
Ancient Communities in the Mesa Verde
Region*. University of Utah Press, Salt Lake City.

Varien, Mark D., William D. Lipe, Michael A. Adler, Ian
M. Thompson, and Bruce A. Bradley
1996   Southwestern Colorado and Southwestern Utah
Settlement Patterns: A.D. 1100 to 1300. In *The
Prehistoric Pueblo World, A.D. 1150–1350*,
edited by Michael A. Adler, pp. 86–113. University of Arizona Press, Tucson.

Vivian, R. Gwinn
1990   *The Chacoan Prehistory of the San Juan Basin*.
Academic Press, New York.

Walker, William H.
1998   Where Are All the Witches of Prehistory? *Journal
of Archaeological Method and Theory* 5:245–308.

Wilcox, David R.
1993   The Evolution of the Chacoan Polity. In *The
Chimney Rock Archaeological Symposium*,
edited by J. M. Malville and G. Matlock, pp.
76–90. Rocky Mountain Forest and Range
Experiment Station, General Technical Report
RM-227. Fort Collins, CO.

Wills, W. H.

2001   Ritual and Mound Formation during the Bonito Phase in Chaco Canyon. *American Antiquity* 66:433–451.

Wills, W. H., and Thomas C. Windes

1989   Evidence for Population Aggregation and Dispersal during the Basketmaker III Period in Chaco Canyon, New Mexico. *American Antiquity* 54:347–369.

Wilshusen, Richard H.

1988   Architectural Trends in Prehistoric Anasazi Sites during A.D. 600 to 1200. In *Dolores Archaeological Program: Supporting Studies: Additive and Reductive Strategies*, compiled by E. Blinman, C. J. Phagan, and R. H. Wilshusen, pp. 599–633. Engineering and Research Center, U.S. Bureau of Reclamation, Denver.

1989a   Architecture as Artifact—Part II: A Comment on Gilman. *American Antiquity* 54:826–833.

1989b   Unstuffing the Estufa: Ritual Floor Features in Anasazi Pit Structures and Pueblo Kivas. In *The Architecture of Social Integration in Prehistoric Pueblos*, edited by W. D. Lipe and Michelle Hegmon, pp. 89–111. Occasional Papers of the Crow Canyon Archaeological Center 1. Cortez.

1991   *Early Villages in the American Southwest: Cross-Cultural and Archaeological Perspectives*. Ph.D. dissertation, University of Colorado, Boulder. University Microfilms, Ann Arbor.

1999   Pueblo I (A.D. 750–900). In *Colorado Prehistory: A Context for the Southern Colorado River Basin*, edited by W. D. Lipe, M. D. Varien, and R. H. Wilshusen, pp. 196–241. Colorado Council of Professional Archaeologists, Denver.

2002   Estimating Population in the Central Mesa Verde Region. In *Seeking the Center Place: Archaeology and Ancient Communities in the Mesa Verde Region*, edited by Mark D. Varien and Richard H. Wilshusen, pp. 101–120. University of Utah Press, Salt Lake City.

Wilshusen, Richard H., comp.

1995   *The Cedar Hill Special Treatment Project: Late Pueblo I, Early Navajo, and Historic Occupations in Northwestern New Mexico*. La Plata Archaeological Consultants Research Papers 1. Dolores, CO.

Wilshusen, Richard H., and Eric Blinman

1992   Pueblo I Village Formation: A Reevaluation of Sites Recorded by Earl Morris on Ute Mountain Ute Tribal Lands. *Kiva* 57:251–269.

Wilshusen, Richard H., and Scott G. Ortman

1999   Rethinking the Pueblo I Period in the San Juan Drainage: Aggregation, Migration, and Cultural Diversity. *Kiva* 66:369–399.

Wilshusen, Richard H., and Ruth M. Van Dyke

2006   Chaco's Beginnings: The Collapse of Pueblo I Villages and the Origins of the Chaco System. In *The Archaeology of Chaco Canyon: An Eleventh-Century Pueblo Regional Center*, edited by Stephen H. Lekson, pp. 211–259. School of American Research Press, Santa Fe.

Wilshusen, Richard H., and C. Dean Wilson

1995   Reformatting the Social Landscape in the Late Pueblo I–Early Pueblo II Period: The Cedar Hill Data in Regional Context. In *The Cedar Hill Special Treatment Project: Late Pueblo I, Early Navajo, and Historic Occupations in Northwestern New Mexico*, compiled by R. H. Wilshusen, pp. 43–80. La Plata Archaeological Consultants Research Papers 1. Dolores, CO.

Windes, Thomas C.

1982   Lessons from the Chacoan Survey: The Pattern of Chacoan Trash Disposal. *New Mexico Archeological Council Newsletter* 4(5–6):5–14.

1987   *Investigations at the Pueblo Alto Complex*, 2 vols. Publications in Archeology 18F, Chaco Canyon Studies. National Park Service, Santa Fe.

1993   *The Spadefoot Toad Site: Investigations at 29SJ629, Chaco Canyon, New Mexico*. Reports of the Chaco Center 12. Branch of Cultural Research, National Park Service, Santa Fe.

2006   *Early Puebloan Occupations in the Chaco Region: Excavations and Survey of Basketmaker III and Pueblo I Sites, Chaco Canyon, New Mexico*. Reports of the Chaco Center 13. Branch of Cultural Research, National Park Service, Santa Fe. (in press)

Windes, Thomas C., Rachel M. Anderson, Brian K. Johnson, and Cheryl A. Ford

2000   Sunrise, Sunset: Sedentism and Mobility in the Chaco East Community. In *Great House Communities across the Chacoan Landscape*, edited by John Kantner and Nancy Mahoney, pp. 39–60. Anthropological Papers of the University of Arizona 64. University of Arizona Press, Tucson.

Windes, Thomas C., and Dabney Ford

1992   The Nature of the Early Bonito Phase. In *Anasazi Regional Organization and the Chaco System*, edited by David E. Doyel, pp. 75–85. Maxwell Museum of Anthropology, Anthropological Papers 5. University of New Mexico, Albuquerque.

Wiseman, Regge N.

1982   Climatic Changes and Population Shifts in the Chuska Valley: Shifts in the Chuska Valley: A Trail Correlation. In *Collected Papers in Honor of John W. Runyan*, edited by G. X. Fitzgerald, pp. 111–125. Papers of the Archaeological Society of New Mexico 7. Albuquerque.

4

Great Kivas in Time, Space, and Society

Ruth M. Van Dyke

Few architectural forms have so captivated the public imagination as the great kiva. The circular masonry "great bowls" in front of Pueblo Bonito and Chetro Ketl attracted the attention of early canyon excavators, such as Judd and Hewett. The reconstructed and stabilized Casa Rinconada has become a modern-day pilgrimage site for people of a variety of faiths and religious proclivities (Finn 1997). Great kivas are part of the suite of architectural characteristics—including great houses, road segments, and earthworks—that characterize Classic Bonito phase Chacoan architecture (1040–1100; all dates are AD). The structures are usually considered to have functioned as public, integrative spaces where groups of people came together to perform ceremonies, discuss matters of concern, and conduct other social, ritual, or economic transactions (Adler 1989; Adler and Wilshusen 1990:138–143; Hegmon 1989). But Chacoan great kivas also embody symbolic meanings specific to canyon society in the eleventh century. The structures are part of the architectural representation of ideas that helped legitimate Chacoan social and political authority. These ideas include balanced dualism, center place, directionality, social memory, and cyclical time (Van Dyke 2007).

My goals in this chapter are both descriptive and interpretive. In the pages that follow, I have assembled a summary description of the great kivas of Chaco Canyon. Although canyon great kivas have been the focal points of a great deal of investigation over the past century, sources of information about them are usually partial, occasionally

conflicting, and often confusing. Some early investigations are only sketchily reported or remain entirely unpublished. Authors called kivas by various names and organized them in different ways—some (e.g., Hewett 1936) chose to number multiple construction episodes in the order encountered (latest to earliest), whereas others (e.g., Mathien and Windes 1988) chose to number them in the order constructed. In 1960, Vivian and Reiter produced a descriptive summary of excavated great kivas from Pueblo Bonito, Chetro Ketl, and Kin Nahasbas, as well as the "isolated" great kiva known as Casa Rinconada. Vivian and Reiter attempted to sort out contradictions among photographs and notes from the Judd, Hewett, and Hyde expeditions, while adding their own stratigraphic layer of notes and interpretations to the mix. This chapter represents, in part, an updated supplement to Vivian and Reiter's synthesis, expanded to include unexcavated and isolated great kivas in Chaco Canyon. In the pages that follow, I provide a description of every great kiva in the canyon, synthesizing information gleaned not only from published sources but also from site forms and field records housed in the Chaco Archives.

I also explore the functions and meanings represented by great kivas in Chaco Canyon. The great kiva is not a purely Chacoan phenomenon—great kivas in a variety of shapes and sizes are widely distributed in space and time across the ancient puebloan Southwest (e.g., Anyon 1984; Herr 1994, 2001; Lipe et al. 1988; Riggs 2001:201).

93

The Chacoan great kiva emerged from antecedent Basketmaker III and Pueblo I forms. Great kivas were largely absent from Chaco Canyon during the early Pueblo II period. During the Classic Bonito phase, however, Chacoan architects appropriated and transformed the great kiva into a formalized, iconic symbol.

The incorporation of great kivas into the Chacoan architectural repertoire during Chaco's "Golden Century" is associated with concomitant changes taking place in Chacoan society. The great kiva likely functioned as a space for special meetings and rituals, but the structure also became part of a suite of architectural elements representing components of the Chacoan worldview. The development of the formal great kiva in Chaco Canyon is linked to ideas about cyclical time, social memory, directionality, and balanced dualism that were integral to an ideology legitimating Chaco as a center place.

GREAT KIVA ANTECEDENTS

Oversized, circular pitstructures are found in Basketmaker III communities in Chaco Canyon, throughout the San Juan Basin, and in adjacent areas (e.g., Eddy 1966, 1972; Kearns et al. 2000; Marshall et al. 1979:285–286; Morris 1980; Reed and Wilcox 2000:86–88; Roberts 1929; Wills and Windes 1989; Windes 1975, 2006). They are also well-known from Pueblo I contexts north of the San Juan River (e.g., Lightfoot et al. 1988:584–618; Martin and Rinaldo 1939; Morris 1939), and from late Pueblo I/early Pueblo II sites across the central San Juan Basin (e.g., Marshall et al. 1979; Van Dyke 1999; Van Dyke and Powers 2002; Windes 2006).

There is quite a bit of variability among these early, large, circular pitstructures, and between these early pitstructures and Classic Bonito phase Chacoan great kivas (Lightfoot et al. 1988:617–618; McLellan 1969:178). The terms *communal pitstructure*, *oversized pitstructure*, *great pitstructure*, and *great kiva* have been used in different ways by different authors in reference to Basketmaker III features.

Chaco Canyon is home to two large Basketmaker III villages, both of which contain very large pitstructures. At Shabik'eshchee Village on Chacra Mesa at the east end of Chaco Canyon, a 12-m-diameter, slab-lined pitstructure is situated in the midst of a community of smaller pitstructures (Roberts 1929:73–81; Wills and Windes 1989). The interior of this "great kiva," as Roberts called it, is encircled by a slab-faced bench topped with plaster. The roof was supported by four posts braced with sandstone slabs. Additional features included a slab-lined, rectangular hearth; a deflector slab; and a ventilator. A similar, 10-m-diameter structure was excavated by Windes (1975, 2006) at 29SJ423, an early Basketmaker III village on a promontory 500 m south of Peñasco Blanco at the west end of Chaco Canyon. This structure contained a bench, a rectangular firepit, four to six roof support posts, and a number of sealed floor pits. Turquoise chips and a bead were found under some of the roof supports. These Basketmaker III structures undoubtedly are related to the great kivas built in Chaco Canyon some three centuries later, if not through direct cultural continuity, then as inspiration.

The great kiva form continued to develop during the Pueblo I period. Between 750 and 850, much of the population of the central San Juan Basin moved to the Four Corners area, north of the San Juan River. Here, an intense period of aggregation led to the formation of communities such as McPhee and Grass Mesa villages. Archaeologists working at Pueblo I sites north of the San Juan use the terms *great pitstructure* and *great kiva* to distinguish between two discrete forms that may represent two ways of organizing ritual, or perhaps even two ethnicities (Schachner 2001; Wilshusen and Ortman 1999). *Great pitstructures* contain few or no floor features and are spatially situated away from domestic sites; *great kivas* contain special floor features such as roofed sipapus and are spatially incorporated into the plazas of domestic sites (Adler and Wilshusen 1990:139; Lightfoot 1988; Orcutt et al. 1990:200; Wilshusen 1989; Wilshusen and Wilson 1995:52). By around 880, however, the ritual system that helped to hold these villages together appears to have failed or broken down (Schachner 2001), and the population again shifted south into the San Juan Basin (Wilshusen and Ortman 1999; Wilshusen and Van Dyke 2006; Wilshusen and Wilson 1995; Windes 2006 and Chapter 3, this volume).

Many areas of the San Juan Basin, including Chaco Canyon, show evidence of a dramatic increase in settlement in the late Pueblo I/early

Pueblo II period, between 875 and 950. At least 30 late Pueblo I/early Pueblo II communities are found across the San Juan Basin, ranging from the La Plata Valley in northwest New Mexico to the area along the Chuskan slopes to the west, across the western San Juan Basin along Indian Creek and the Chaco Wash corridor, through Chaco Canyon, on the South Chaco slopes, in the Red Mesa Valley, and along the Rio Puerco of the West (Van Dyke 2008: Chapter 4; Wilshusen and Van Dyke 2006; Windes 2006 and Chapter 3, this volume). In addition to slab-footed domestic architecture, at least 20 of these communities contain proto–great houses built of Type I masonry (Windes, Chapter 3, this volume). At least 13 contain large, circular depressions, sometimes lined with upright slabs, which may represent late Pueblo I/early Pueblo II great kivas. Three contain large surface enclosures defined by single or double rows of upright slabs that represent nonsubterranean, great kiva–like communal spaces. At some of these communities, occupation ended at around 950. At many others, occupation continued through the Classic Bonito phase and even into the 1200s.

Some scholars have described late Pueblo I/early Pueblo II San Juan Basin communities as centered around great kivas (e.g., Eddy 1977; Martin and Rinaldo 1939; Powers et al. 1983:26; Van Dyke 1999; Van Dyke and Powers 2002; Vivian 1990: 174), yet Windes and colleagues (2000:39) point out a remarkable deficit of great kivas in Chaco Canyon during the same period. Great kivas are conspicuously absent from Padilla Well, South Gap, Fajada Gap, Chaco East, and Pueblo Pintado—five communities settled along Chaco Wash in the late 800s or early 900s. However, oversized pitstructures dating to the early 900s are present at Kin Nahasbas and Pueblo Bonito, a possible 900s great kiva is located at Una Vida, and one isolated 900s great kiva (29SJ1253) is situated in Fajada Gap, across from Kin Nahasbas (see below).

In an attempt to resolve this apparent contradiction—were there many 900s great kivas, or weren't there?—I recently conducted a systematic examination of the 35 late Pueblo I/early Pueblo II communities in the San Juan Basin (Van Dyke 2008: Chapter 4). The investigation revealed some interesting patterns. Although at least 24 communities contain proto–great houses, and at least 19 contain

some type of circular, great kiva–like structure, there is little overlap between the two types of architecture. Only nine communities contain both proto–great houses *and* great kivas (or some other type of circular communal structure). And, the 15 communities that contain proto–great houses but lack great kivas or similar enclosures are located mostly in the core area of Chaco Canyon, west of the canyon, or on the south Chaco slope.

Two kinds of community and ritual organization—represented by horseshoe-shaped roomblocks and great kivas—were present in aggregated Pueblo I communities north of the San Juan (Schachner 2001; Wilshusen and Ortman 1999). As Puebloan peoples moved back into the San Juan Basin during the late Pueblo I/early Pueblo II period, these two groups may have maintained their distinctiveness and, with a few exceptions, may have founded separate communities centered around either proto–great houses or great kivas (Van Dyke 2008: Chapter 4). Great kiva–centered communities developed in the La Plata Valley, the Red Mesa Valley, and other southwest basin locations. Late Pueblo I/early Pueblo II Chaco Canyon, by contrast, was a major locus of settlement for proto-great-house-centered communities. These early distinctions may have contributed to the concept of balanced dualism that pervades subsequent Chacoan, and Puebloan, worldviews.

CANYON GREAT KIVAS

Because Chaco Canyon was heavily settled by proto–great house people, few tenth-century great kivas are present. However, a burst of formal great kiva construction took place in Chaco Canyon during the Classic Bonito phase (1040–1100). During the eleventh century, great kivas were built in Chaco both in association with great houses and in "isolated" contexts more than 100 m from a great house. Great houses in Chaco Canyon with associated great kivas include Pueblo Bonito, Chetro Ketl, Kin Nahasbas, Una Vida, Hungo Pavi, and Peñasco Blanco (Figure 4.1). In addition, four "isolated" great kivas are found on the south side of Chaco Canyon.

Most canyon great kivas are unexcavated depressions, so information concerning them is limited. Like great houses, great kivas were repeatedly

95

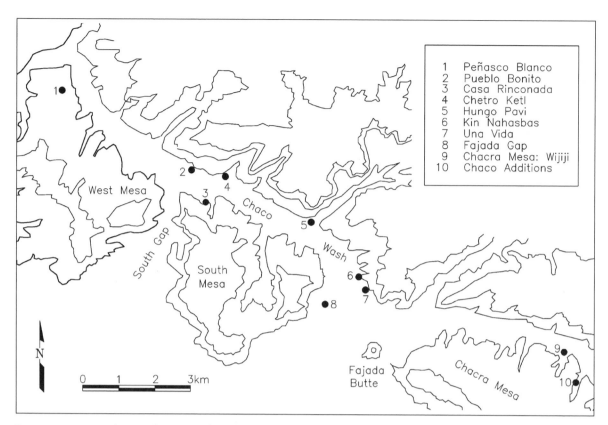

FIGURE 4.1. Map showing locations of great kivas in Chaco Canyon.

remodeled in the course of a succession of construction episodes. Dating often rests on stratigraphic relationships; absolute dates are largely obtained through dendrochronology. If sequential construction events at the same spot are counted separately, a total of 21 great kivas were built in Chaco Canyon between 900 and 1120 (Table 4.1). If sequential events are lumped together and only discrete great kiva locations are counted, there are eighteen great kivas in Chaco Canyon—fourteen associated with six great houses, and four "isolated" great kivas.

Below, I describe the ten excavated great kivas built in seven locations at Pueblo Bonito, Chetro Ketl, and Kin Nahasbas. I then present information from the seven unexcavated great kivas at Una Vida, Hungo Pavi, and Peñasco Blanco, and I review the four "isolated" great kivas—one excavated, and three unexcavated.

Pueblo Bonito

At least four great kivas were built over the course of about 200 years at Pueblo Bonito (Figure 4.2).

The primary information for these structures has been gleaned from Judd (1964), Vivian and Reiter (1960:63–71), and Lekson (1984:142–143) (Figure 4.3). Construction of Pueblo Bonito began in the mid-800s and continued through the early 1100s (Windes and Ford 1992). Dating of the great kivas is based on masonry styles and stratigraphic relationships. The great kivas are discussed below in chronological order. Two and possibly as many as three great kivas may have been open and in use at the same time, but this cannot be definitely ascertained given the available data.

Possible Great Kiva under Kiva 2C

The earliest great kiva at Pueblo Bonito is an unnumbered pitstructure beneath Kiva 2C, in the central plaza area directly north of Kiva A. Here, Judd (1964:179, Plate 23) partially excavated a 10-m-diameter pitstructure dated on the basis of stratigraphy and Type I masonry to 900–950. Lekson (1984:143) proposes this structure may be a great kiva based on its size, but with a floor area of 38 m², the structure is within the range known

96

TABLE 4.1. Great Kivas in Chaco Canyon

LOCATION	IDENTIFICATION	DATE (AD)	ABOVE-BENCH DIAMETER (m)	EXCAVATED?	SOURCES
Pueblo Bonito	Great Kiva under Kiva 2C	900–950	10	Judd 1921–1923	Judd 1964; Lekson 1984
	Kiva Q	1040–1050	14.6	Judd 1924	Judd 1925a, 1925b, 1964; Lekson 1984; Vivian 1940; Vivian and Reiter 1960
	SW Plaza Great Kiva	1050–1060	19.4	Judd 1924	Judd 1964; Lekson 1984; Roberts 1927; Vivian and Reiter 1960
	Kiva A	1100+	17	Judd 1921	Hewett 1936; Judd 1922, 1964; Lekson 1984; Martin 1936; Vivian and Reiter 1960
Chetro Ketl	CKII	1060–1090?	16.5	SAR 1921, 1929–1933	Bradfield 1921; Chapman 1922; Hawley 1934; Hewett 1921, 1922, 1936; Leinau 1934; Lekson 1983, 1984; Miller 1937; Reiter 1933; Vivian and Reiter 1960
	CKI	1090?–1120	18.4	SAR 1929–1933	Hawley 1934; Hewett 1936; Leinau 1934; Lekson 1983, 1984; Miller 1937; Reiter 1933; Vivian and Reiter 1960
	Court Kiva	1060–1120	10	SAR 1934	Hawley 1934; Lekson 1983, 1984; Vivian and Reiter 1960; Woods 1934
Kin Nahasbas	Pitstructure 1	900–950	7	NPS 1983	Mathien and Windes 1988
	Great Kiva 1	1030–1070	15.5	SAR 1935	Luhrs 1935; Mathien and Windes 1988; Vivian and Reiter 1960
	Great Kiva 2	1060–1100+	15.5	SAR 1935	Luhrs 1935; Mathien and Windes 1988; Vivian and Reiter 1960
Una Vida	Great Kiva 1	930–950	17	No	Gillespie 1984
	Great Kiva 2	1000s	18	No	Gillespie 1984
Hungo Pavi	Plaza Great Kiva	1060–1080	15	No	Lekson 1984
Peñasco Blanco	Plaza Great Kiva 1	1000–1100?	13	No	Lekson 1984
	Plaza Great Kiva 2	1000–1100?	15	No	Lekson 1984
	South Great Kiva	1000–1100?	17	No	Lekson 1984
	Northwest Great Kiva	1000–1100?	23	No	Lekson 1984, personal observation
Casa Rinconada	29SJ386	1060–1109	19.5	SAR 1930–1931	Vivian and Reiter 1960
Fajada Gap	29SJ1253	900–1050	20	no	Marshall et al. 1979
Chacra Mesa: Wijiji	29SJ1642	900–1100	17	no	Marshall et al. 1979
Chacra Mesa: Chaco Additions	29SJ2557	1000–1225	13	no	Van Dyke and Powers 2002

for domestic pitstructures. Other evidence that does not corroborate interpretation of this structure as a great kiva includes the fact that no roof support posts were present in the partially preserved north section of the floor. Furthermore, Judd (1964: Plate 23) depicts a radial beam pilaster on a bench, which is not a great kiva feature.

KIVA Q

Kiva Q, located immediately west of Kiva 2C in the northwest part of the plaza, was excavated by Judd (1925a) and subsequently backfilled. It was cleared of backfill in January 1940 in connection with stabilization (Vivian 1940:127–130) and is open and visible today. Kiva Q is described by Judd

97

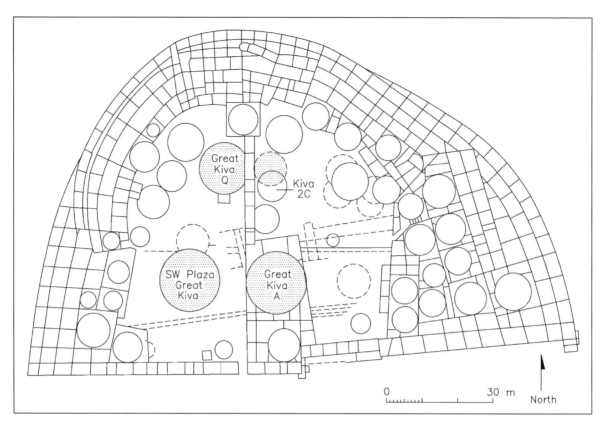

FIGURE 4.2. Plan of Pueblo Bonito, showing locations of great kivas. (After Lekson 1984:111, Figure 4.17)

(1964:207–211), Vivian and Reiter (1960:62–66), and Lekson (1984:142–143). It is dated by means of masonry and stratigraphy to the mid-eleventh century. The extensive reconstruction and stabilization of the walls (Judd 1964:209–210; Vivian and Reiter 1960:65) may explain inconsistencies between Judd's discussion of the masonry and the accompanying photographs (Judd 1925a:228). Where the masonry is best preserved, Vivian and Reiter consider it to appear most like Hawley's Type II, which is tree-ring dated to 1030–1070. Lekson considers Kiva Q to most likely belong to his Stage II building episode, which places construction between 1040 and 1050. Kiva Q is beneath Stage VIIE construction, which postdates 1085.

Kiva Q has a diameter of 12.1 m at the floor and an exterior diameter of 14.6 m. A masonry bench circles the entire structure. The roof was supported by wooden posts rather than masonry pillars. Each of the four roof support sockets contains a thick, irregularly shaped sandstone slab at its base. Each socket was lined with masonry, packed with shale, and covered with a tabular stone apron. A roof support fragment reputedly was recovered by Judd from one of the sockets. Two masonry floor vaults are attached to the roof support sockets. In contrast to floor vaults of later construction, these are not completely subterranean but extend approximately 30 cm above and 15 cm below the floor. Another unusual feature is the presence of a sipapu—a 35-cm-diameter, circular, masonry-walled opening midway between the two northern roof support sockets. The sipapu is 23 cm deep; at its base, it contains a thin stone slab with a circular hole in it. Kiva Q also contains a raised, rectangular, masonry firebox with a circular interior firepit, and a thin, shale-lined trench that probably served as the base for a moveable fire screen. Vivian and Reiter (1960:63) speculate that four pole sockets above the bench on the north side of the kiva may have supported a balcony. Kiva Q is purportedly associated with an unusual, south-facing antechamber. Vivian and Reiter (1960:65) question whether interpretation of this room as an antechamber to the great kiva might not be an error of reconstruction.

98

FIGURE 4.3. Judd's Pueblo Bonito great kiva excavation. (Photograph by O. C. Havens, 1924, courtesy of Smithsonian Institution, NAA neg. 28444A)

Judd (1964:211) mentions a predecessor to Kiva Q, a razed structure discovered in 1924 during trenching. Only remnants of benches, pillars, vaults, and the floor were present, and the floor diameter is estimated at 16 m. Judd mentions that it is near Roberts's (1927) trash excavations, which suggests there may be some confusion with the Southwest Plaza Great Kiva, discussed below.

SOUTHWEST PLAZA GREAT KIVA
A third great kiva is located in the southwest plaza at Pueblo Bonito. Written sources contain considerable confusion about this partially razed structure. Roberts (1927:40–41) mentions a 15-m-diameter kiva in the west plaza of Pueblo Bonito that does not appear on any plans. This structure was supposedly built relatively late in the life of the pueblo in an area that had previously been used as a midden. It was eventually backfilled, the stone robbed, and the area reused for trash disposal.

Given the vague general location and the lack of any known similar structures in the west plaza, it appears likely that this structure is the Southwest Plaza Great Kiva. Lekson (1984:142) contends the Southwest Plaza Great Kiva likely was intermediate between Great Kivas Q and A. He places the structure within his Stage III construction phase (1050–1060). The Southwest Plaza Great Kiva is estimated to have had a diameter of 16.3 m at floor level and 19.4 m at the top of the walls.

KIVA A
Kiva A (Figure 4.4) is part of a group of rooms that divides the east and west plazas. It is enclosed in a rectangular area with a three-room antechamber complex situated to the north and six possibly unassociated rooms located to the south. It is open and visible today. Kiva A was excavated by Judd in 1921 (Judd 1922:115, 1964:198–207). Despite Hewett's (1936:78) assertion that Kiva A was

99

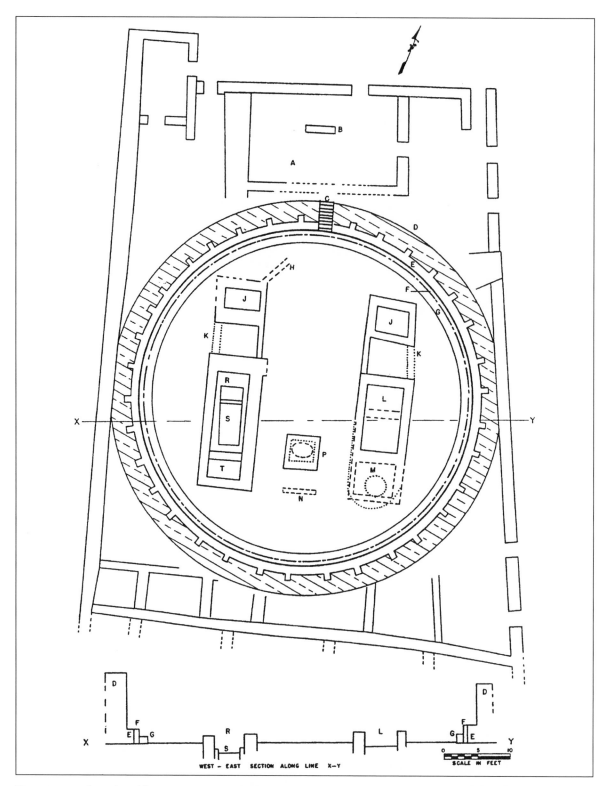

FIGURE 4.4. Plan of Pueblo Bonito, Great Kiva A. A, central room, north antechamber group; B, masonry block "altar"; C, recessed stairway; D, outer wall; E, primary bench; F, bench veneer; G, secondary bench; H, wall extension from support column; J, north roof support columns; K, walls of modern appearance joining columns and vaults; L, east vault; M, southeast support column; N, fire screen; P, firebox; R, west vault; S, subfloor enclosure in west vault; T, southwest roof column. (Vivian and Reiter 1960:66, Figure 31, courtesy of SAR Press)

Ruth M. Van Dyke

excavated by the Hyde Expedition between 1896 and 1899, Vivian and Reiter (1960:67) clarify that only surrounding areas and the antechamber were cleared at that time. Kiva A is described by Judd (1922:115, 1964:198–207), Vivian and Reiter (1960:66–70), and Lekson (1984:142). Kiva A is the largest and the latest great kiva at Pueblo Bonito. Its floor dates from the 1100s or later (Lekson 1984:142).

Kiva A is partially elevated within the surrounding block of rooms. It has a diameter of 13.7 m at floor level and an exterior diameter of 17 m. Judd (1922:115–116) estimated an original ceiling height of about 3.5 m. Inside, the great kiva is encircled by a twice-remodeled masonry bench. Thirty-four 25 by 23 cm wall niches are evenly spaced around the circumference of the great kiva, approximately 1 m above the bench. Two additional, smaller (15 by 15 cm) niches are found on the north side. A series of small, horizontal pole sockets is also found in the kiva wall on the north side. Masonry floor vaults and roof supports take up much of the floor space. Judd contends (1922:16, 1964:201–202) the roof supports were seated in low-grade coal, but Vivian and Reiter (1960:70) noted no trace of it. The roof support columns appear to be hollow. They may have constituted supports for higher, wooden posts (Martin 1936:47), or the masonry may have encircled timbers (Vivian and Reiter 1960:70). Additional floor features include a masonry firebox and an adobe-and-pole fire screen. The north antechamber was excavated but insufficiently described by the Hyde Expedition. Twenty years later, Morris observed that the "altar" was still standing (Vivian and Reiter 1960:70). Each room in the three-room antechamber complex has a door to the exterior.

ADDITIONAL POSSIBILITIES

Lekson (1984:143) notes that other unusually large, unexcavated, circular subterranean structures at Pueblo Bonito may represent great kivas. Possibilities include Kiva O in the southeast plaza and an unnumbered structure northwest of Kiva O, both about 11.3 m in diameter.

Chetro Ketl

Great kivas were built in two locations at Chetro Ketl during the late eleventh and early twelfth centuries (Figure 4.5). The Great Kiva exhibits two construction episodes (CKII and CKI). It is located in the southeast corner of the plaza. The Court Kiva is a regular kiva that was converted into a great kiva. It is located in the central plaza approximately 30 m west of the Great Kiva. Both structures were excavated by the School of American Research and the Museum of New Mexico under Hewett's direction in the 1920s and 1930s. Although a complete excavation report for Chetro Ketl was never produced (but see Lekson 1983 and Vivian et al. 1978), a great deal of information on the Great Kiva was published in various forms by Hewett and his students. The primary information for Chetro Ketl great kivas is derived from Reiter (1933), Hawley (1934), Leinau (1934:33–38), Hewett (1936:68–100), Miller (1937), and Vivian and Reiter (1960:27–50). Vivian and Reiter worked on the excavation of Chetro Ketl and incorporate a number of personal observations and communications from other excavators into their summary. Some summary information also appears in Lekson (1983, 1984:152–192).

Hewett and his students first undertook excavation of "the great bowl" in 1921, with Wesley Bradfield as field director and Sam Hudelson as a field supervisor (Bradfield 1921; Chapman 1921; Hewett 1921, 1922). During this phase of the excavation, the uppermost, later great kiva was cleared. Vivian and Reiter term this structure "CKI," and despite the numeric and chronological reversal, this designation is retained in the ensuing discussion. After the 1921 season, Hewett's work in Chaco Canyon was discontinued to make way for Judd's National Geographic expedition. Hewett resumed work in Chaco in 1929. In that year, tests confirmed that earlier floors lay beneath CKI. Subfloor excavations began in 1930 and continued for three seasons under the direction of W. W. Postlethwaite and Janet Woods. During these years, the earlier great kiva, or CKII, was cleared (Figure 4.6). CKII and CKI are discussed below in order of construction. The Court Kiva was tested by Hewett in 1931 and was excavated under the direction of Postlethwaite and Woods in 1934 (Vivian and Reiter 1960:43–50; Woods 1934). Dating of all the Chetro Ketl great kivas is based on stratigraphy and masonry styles. All three generally date to the latter half of the eleventh century, and the Court

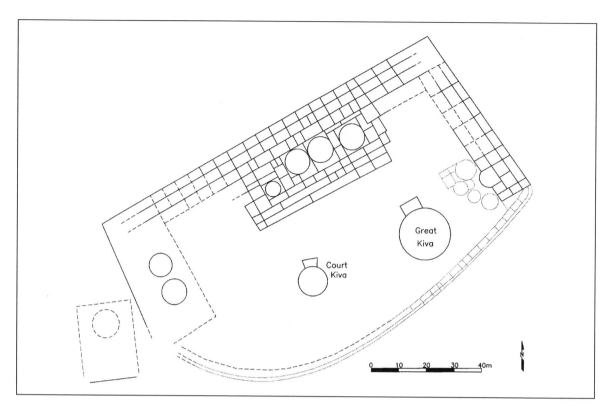

FIGURE 4.5. Plan of Chetro Ketl, showing locations of great kivas. (After Lekson 1984:153, Figure 4.39)

Kiva and CKI appear to have been remodeled and used into the twelfth century.

CKII

The earliest version of the Chetro Ketl Great Kiva was dubbed CKII by the excavators, since it was the lower, second version excavated. The great kiva was built on the site of unrelated, earlier foundation walls (Vivian and Reiter 1960:36). Lekson associates these walls with his Stage VB, which would place initial construction of the great kiva after 1050 and perhaps as late as 1075 (Lekson 1984:187). Hawley (1934:25–26) considered the CKII masonry to date to between 1062 and 1090. CKII has an average diameter of 16.5 m above the bench, wall remnants approximately 0.85 m high, and a maximum depth of 4.25 m below CKI plaza level. An 80-cm-high, 60-cm-wide bench encircles the interior and was constructed as a single unit with the walls. Wall features include 10 masonry-sealed niches measuring 15 by 25 cm and 45 cm deep. When opened in 1932, each was found to contain a string of beads and turquoise pendants (Hewett 1936:87–93) (Figure 4.7). An antechamber

on the north side opened to the great kiva and to the plaza to the north.

Three floor levels are associated with CKII. The lowest and earliest was found about 10 cm above the base of the bench. Features include floor vaults, roof support pits, and a probable firebox (Figure 4.8). A second floor was found 30 cm higher, atop an intentional layer of sand and adobe fill. The second floor used the same floor vaults and roof support pits as the first, but it contained a new or remodeled firebox. A third floor was identified flush with the bench atop another layer of intentional sand and adobe fill. This surface is associated with a firebox, a deflector, and higher extensions of the roof support pits and floor vaults. No bench is identified at this level, although one may have been removed during construction of CKI.

The masonry floor vaults average 120 by 230 cm and are 75–120 cm deep. The partly subterranean vaults have flagstone floors, small square openings in the side and end walls, and steps along one side. In the west vault, a layer of juniper bark and lignite lay under the flagstone. The vaults were raised and remodeled to meet each new floor level.

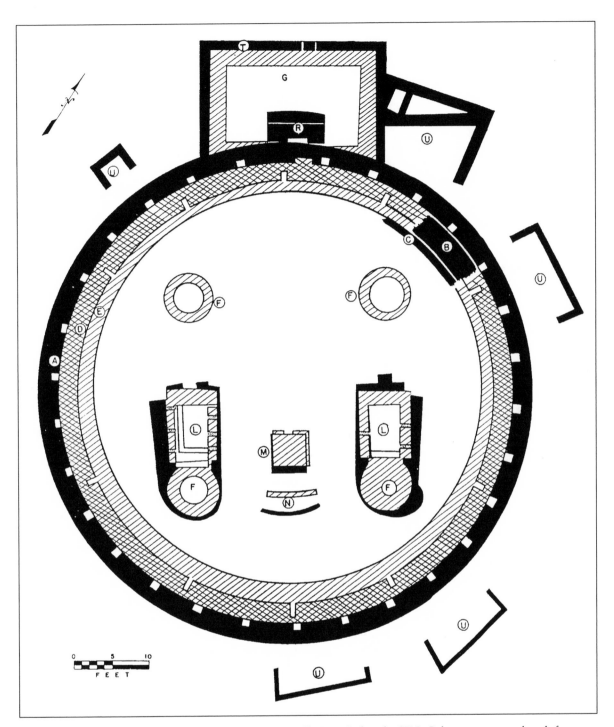

FIGURE 4.6. Plan of Chetro Ketl, CK I & II. A, outer wall, CK I; B, bench, CK I; C, late veneer over bench face; D, fill over wall, Chetro Ketl II; E, bench, CK II; F, seating pits; G, antechamber area, CK II; L, vaults: dotted areas show vents of lower structure; M, firebox; N, fire screens; R, masonry "altar"; T, antechamber wall, CK I; U, peripheral rooms. (Vivian and Reiter 1960:28, Figure 12, courtesy of SAR Press)

Fill intentionally deposited under the third floor contained beads, sherds, wood fragments, turquoise fragments, and pendants.

The roof support pits were used throughout the life of the great kiva and show evidence of at least three episodes of remodeling. However, it is difficult

Great Kivas in Time, Space, and Society

FIGURE 4.7. Opening wall niches at Chetro Ketl. (Photograph by Paul Reiter, courtesy of Chaco Culture National Historical Park, Chaco Archives, CHCU 101494)

to associate particular remodeling events with particular floors. The pits are lined with masonry and contain a vertically stacked series of stone disks approximately 1 m in diameter. The disks are separated by layers of adobe. Some upper surfaces show marks of the timbers they supported. Higher disks were added as remodeling events raised the overall level of the great kiva. The masonry linings were also raised to extend the pits to new floor levels. The northeast roof support pit contained four disks, the northwest pit contained three, and the southern pits contained at least one apiece. Beneath the lowest disk in the northern pits, a leather bag containing pulverized turquoise was covered with alternating layers of lignite and adobe. The roof support pits contained massive uprights packed with shale that supported a four-square timber framework for the roof. A 65-cm-diameter spruce log was found in the southeast pit. The CKII roof appears to have been completely

removed and replaced during construction of the slightly larger CKI.

CKI

At some point in the late 1000s, the Chetro Ketl great kiva underwent very extensive remodeling—the kiva chamber and its antechamber were enlarged. The result was the version of the great kiva originally excavated by Hewett and his students in 1921, dubbed CKI. As with CKII, Hawley (1934:25–26) considered most of the CKI masonry to date to between 1062 and 1090, with some late veneers dating to between 1100 and 1116. CKI averages 18.4 m in diameter above the bench. The same roof support pits were employed for this version, however, so CKI must have required a new roof, with longer radial logs extending around the circumference of the four-square framework. Remains of radial pine vigas, juniper splints, and juniper bark were found in the northwest quadrant of CKI.

A meter of fill was placed atop the old floor. The fill layer contained concentrations of shale and lignite, a small hearth in its midst, and four strings of beads and ornaments (Vivian and Reiter 1960:37). An enigmatic, thin layer of sand at the bottom of the intentional fill may represent ritual closure of the earlier structure. The new great kiva wall was built as a single unit. It is 4.25 m high and 75–90 cm wide. A 1.5-m-deep foundation becomes gradually wider and is packed with shale. A set of 29 evenly spaced wall niches average 30 by 33 cm and 38 cm deep. Two additional, smaller niches do not conform to the spacing and may represent pole sockets. A 1-m-wide, 85-cm-high bench encircles CKI. A "secondary bench," part of the earliest CKI floor foundation, protrudes for about 15 cm. On the south side of the great kiva, a 90-cm gap in the main bench exposes a section of the outer wall of CKII. The original antechamber was partly filled and the walls reduced to form benches for a new, larger antechamber. This antechamber retains openings to the north and into the great kiva. Nine steps lead down into the great kiva; the third and fourth were of hewn planks still in place at the time of the 1921 excavation. Several other, later peripheral rooms do not open into the antechamber or the great kiva. Two floors, separated by 15 cm of sandy fill, were identified in CKI. Floor features

FIGURE 4.8. Chetro Ketl, CKI excavation. (Photograph by Paul Reiter, courtesy of Chaco Culture National Historical Park, Chaco Archives, CHCU C100363)

are common to both levels. A faced masonry rectangular firebox contains a circular, fire-reddened hearth. A small ash pit is located between the firebox and a curved masonry deflector. Roof support pits from CKII were remodeled as discussed above and continued in use during CKI. Well-faced masonry floor vaults were built directly over the CKII vaults below.

Fire-reddening on the outer bench veneer and wall, and a compact layer of ash found in the west floor vault, led Vivian and Reiter (1960:42) to speculate that the roof of CKI may have burned. However, no mention is made by the excavators of charred roofing remains or charcoal and ash in the postabandonment fill.

COURT KIVA
Vivian and Reiter (1960:50) comment that, while CKII and CK I are examples of Chacoan great kiva construction at its finest, construction of the

contemporaneous Court Kiva seems a bit sloppy and crude by comparison. The Court Kiva was originally a small or regular kiva that was remodeled to exhibit great kiva features. The original kiva was a little more than 10 m in diameter. Its features included a low, encircling bench; eight radial, horizontal wooden pilasters; a ventilator; a masonry-lined firepit; and a rectangular masonry box. There may have been a deflector as well. The wall behind the benches was padded with juniper bark, and the well-packed adobe floor was 5–8 cm thick. Entry was through the roof. Hawley (1934) dated the blocky sandstone masonry to 1100–1116.

The original Court Kiva appears to have been abandoned for some period of time—this area of the site is subject to flooding, and there were about 30 cm of waterlain sands, gravels, and adobe lenses atop the original kiva floor. These deposits left about 30 cm of the bench exposed. At this point, the structure was remodeled and converted

105

into a great kiva (Figure 4.9). The bench is covered by a veneer and built up an additional 30 cm, although the addition did not extend for its full width, producing a slightly stepped bench. A recess appears in the bench on the south side near the original location of the ventilator. A rectangular masonry firebox with a round firepit was constructed over the earlier firepit. No deflector is present. Two rather crooked floor vaults were built. Four masonry columns about 60 cm square were

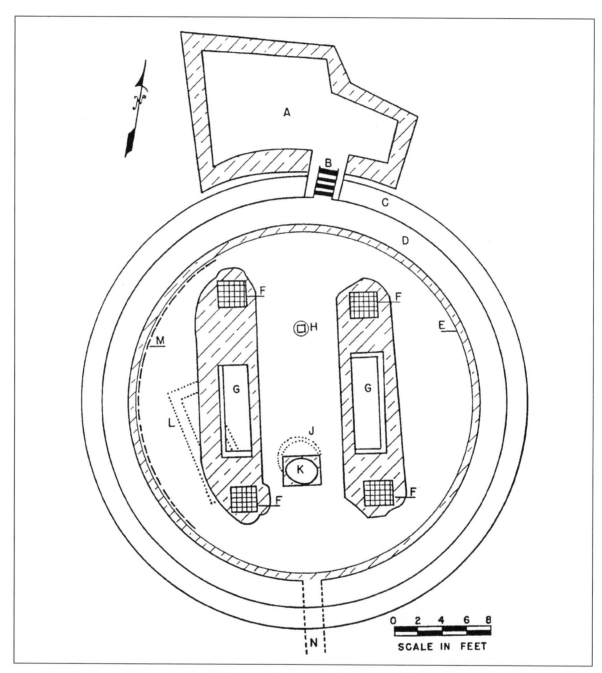

FIGURE 4.9. Plan of Chetro Ketl Court Kiva. A, north antechamber (great kiva); B, stairway (great kiva and small kiva); C, outer wall (great kiva and small kiva); D, bench (great kiva and small kiva); E, bench veneer (great kiva); F, roof supports (great kiva); G, vaults (great kiva); H, sipapu; J, firepit (small kiva); K, firebox (great kiva); L, probable floor resonator (small kiva); M, vertical slab veneer; N, ventilator shaft (small kiva). Based on a plan by J. Woods. (Vivian and Reiter 1960:43, Figure 20, courtesy of SAR Press)

constructed to serve as roof supports, but no evidence of roofing materials was recovered. An antechamber was added to the north; it is not regularly shaped, nor is it oriented precisely with respect to the kiva. A new kiva entrance was cut through the wall to the antechamber. Two steps led down to the kiva bench. No excavation was undertaken in the surrounding plaza, so it is not known whether there are any peripheral rooms.

Four floors are apparent. The lowest and earliest (Floor 1) contains a sealed sipapu, which may, in fact, have been constructed as part of the earlier kiva. Sipapus are often found in small kivas but are not known from any other Chacoan great kiva. The masonry-lined, square sipapu in the Court Kiva was packed with adobe and had a piece of flat sandstone at its base and another as its cover. Inside, turquoise fragments, two white quartz pebbles, two brachiopods, and a few bird bones were covered with a limestone polishing stone. A 10-cm-thick layer of adobe and waterlain silt and sand lay between Floor 1 and the subsequent adobe surface of Floor 2. Another 10-cm layer of silt and sand lay between Floor 2 and Floor 3. The vaults, firebox, and bench were heightened in association with Floor 3 to accommodate the rise in the floor surface. A further 10- to 15-cm-thick layer of waterlain sands and adobe lenses separated Floor 3 from Floor 4, the latest and final floor. Final repairs to the bench, vaults, and firebox are associated with Floor 4.

Kin Nahasbas

Kin Nahasbas is located northwest of Una Vida atop a sandstone hill connected to the north wall of Chaco Canyon by a narrow ridge. It consists of a small, 15- to 20-room great house, an associated great kiva, and an extensive trash midden (Figure 4.10). The great kiva, its antechamber, and one nearby room were excavated by the School of American Research in 1935 under the direction of Dorothy Luhrs. In 1983, the great kiva was reinvestigated and additional excavation was undertaken by the Chaco Project as part of stabilization assessment. Kin Nahasbas is described by Luhrs (1935), Vivian and Reiter (1960:53–61), and Mathien and Windes (1988). Luhrs's original investigation paid little attention to the associated roomblock, and over the years, the myth grew that Kin

Nahasbas is an isolated great kiva. Mathien and Windes's (1988) report puts that myth to rest and includes a thorough description of the associated pueblo. There are no tree-ring dates from the site. Dating is based on ceramics, masonry styles, stratigraphy, and radiocarbon samples collected by Mathien and Windes from the trash midden. Ceramics from the trash midden indicate a lengthy occupation at Kin Nahasbas stretching from the early 900s through the early 1100s (Mathien and Windes 1988:79–93). Mathien and Windes identify two construction phases at the pueblo. A block of rooms termed the Old House exhibits Type I masonry similar to that dating to the early to mid 900s at nearby Una Vida and elsewhere. Immediately to the east, the New House is a symmetrical addition containing 13 rooms and exhibiting masonry dating from the late 1000s to the early 1100s.

The great kiva is directly south of the Old House, but it is not attached, nor is the great kiva enclosed in a plaza. There is evidence for multiple reconstructions or remodeling episodes over the life of the great kiva. Luhrs recognized early and late masonry in the structure. Mathien and Windes documented these as two superimposed great kivas (Great Kiva 1 and Great Kiva 2), and they discovered an earlier, antecedent pitstructure (Pitstructure 1) beneath the great kiva. These structures are described in chronological order below.

Pitstructure 1

Under the two superimposed great kivas at Kin Nahasbas, Mathien and Windes (1988:22) found "the earliest and the only tenth-century great house pitstructure for which a floor has been cleared." This pitstructure had an estimated diameter of only about 7 m, which is "several standard deviations above the mean floor areas for pitstructures of the period" (Mathien and Windes 1988:30), suggesting that it may have functioned as a great kiva. Most of floor was destroyed by subsequent construction, but features excavated into the floor remain. These include a firepit, a heating pit, three postholes, and a number of small, amorphous, subfloor pits that Mathien and Windes interpret as ladder rests associated with a roof entry. Pitstructure 1 cannot be dated, but Mathien and Windes reason that it is most likely associated with the early 900s construction of the Old House on the hill above.

FIGURE 4.10. Plan of Kin Nahasbas. (Mathien and Windes 1988:20, Figure 4)

GREAT KIVA 1

The great kiva at Kin Nahasbas was extensively remodeled or reconstructed. Both Mathien and Windes (1988:30–40) and Lurhs (1935) recognized multiple floor vaults and overlapping walls of differing masonry styles as evidence for an early version of the great kiva. Mathien and Windes (1988:31) contend that Great Kiva 1 contained a bench, a firebox, a deflector, four seats for wooden roof supports, and two floor vaults. Remodeling makes it difficult to separate features used during this period from those used later on. The deflector is the only feature that positively belongs solely to Great Kiva 1, as the deflector groove was com-

pletely plastered over in the course of remodeling. Luhrs (1935:27, 30) considered Great Kiva 1 masonry to resemble a style dating to between 1030 and 1070 (Hawley 1934:21–25), and Vivian and Reiter (1960) agree with that designation.

GREAT KIVA 2

Great Kiva 2 is the structure that drew the School of American Research to excavate the site in 1935 (Luhrs 1935; Vivian and Reiter 1960:53–61; Mathien and Windes 1988:32, 40–69). Masonry styles place construction between 1062 and 1090, and ceramics support use of the structure into the early 1100s. The great kiva has a diameter of 14.5 m at the floor and 15.5 m at the top of the walls (Figure 4.11). The great kiva was excavated into the talus slope, so the north side was subterranean but the south side was only partially so. On the south side, the great kiva is buttressed by an immense double wall, 1.5 m wide. The floor was formed by sandstone bedrock leveled with fill and covered with plaster. Features are the same as those assigned above to Great Kiva 1: a bench, a firebox, a deflector, four seats for wooden roof supports, and two floor vaults. The plastered bench encircled the interior. The rectangular firebox stands 75 cm high. Roof support pits were cut into bedrock, but despite this were treated like roof support pits at contemporaneous great kivas at Pueblo Bonito and Chetro Ketl. The pits were lined with masonry, a large stone disk was placed at the bottom, and wooden posts were packed in with gray shale. A stone apron covered each pit. Wood remains were found in the pits and in various other contexts during excavation. The great kiva appears to have been roofed atop a central square of logs that rested on the four support columns. No wall niches were observed, but wall remnants were only 3 m high at the time of Luhrs's excavation. The floor vaults were excavated into sandstone but lined with masonry, except for their outward-facing walls. Each was rather crudely remodeled to be smaller, and a stone disk like those at the base of the roof support pits was found at the bottom of each. A small (3 by 5 m) antechamber is attached to the north side of the structure. A three-step masonry stairway leads through the north wall of the antechamber into the Old House.

Una Vida

At least one and possibly two great kivas were built over the course of perhaps two centuries in the plaza at Una Vida (Figure 4.12). Neither structure has been excavated. Construction at Una Vida began in the 860s and continued to the end of the 1000s. Una Vida was minimally probed and sketchily reported by Hewett in the 1930s and by Gordon Vivian in the 1950s (Gillespie 1984:87–88). The Chaco Center collected some additional data prior to backfilling in 1979 (Akins and Gillespie 1979), but none of these activities involved the great kivas. Available information for these structures is summarized by Gillespie (1984:79–94).

Dates are suggested by Gillespie based on spatial relationships.

Great Kiva 1 is in the plaza, northwest of a later, conspicuous depression (Great Kiva 2, described below). Gillespie (1984:90) associates this great kiva with his Stage II construction, dated to between 930 and 950. He estimates a diameter of approximately 17 m. Great Kiva 2 is prominently placed in Una Vida's plaza approximately 15 m southwest of the northeast wing and 35 m southeast of the northwest wing of the great house, within the plaza's enclosing wall. Gillespie does not describe the structure, but the accompanying map (Gillespie 1984:80) shows Great Kiva 2 to have a diameter of approximately 18 m. Great Kiva 2 cannot be associated with a specific construction episode but surely predates the construction of the arc of rooms that encloses Una Vida's plaza. The arc was added after 1095 (Gillespie 1984:94), so Great Kiva 2 was likely constructed sometime in the 1000s.

Hungo Pavi

Hungo Pavi has not been excavated. Tree-ring dates suggest the great house was built in two stages—the first in the early 1000s, and the second between 1060 and 1080 (Lekson 1984:152; Windes, personal communication 2001). A great kiva depression located in the plaza is depicted by Lekson (1984:147) as being associated with the second construction stage. This unexcavated great kiva has a diameter of approximately 15 m (Figure 4.13).

Peñasco Blanco

The Peñasco Blanco great house has not been formally excavated, although some 12 rooms were probed by Navajo workmen during the Wetherill/Pepper era, and several rooms were cleared by a National Park Service Ruins Stabilization crew in the early 1970s. Four great kiva depressions are associated with the great house (Figure 4.14)—none has been excavated. Two great kivas are located in the plaza, one is located south of the great house, and one is northwest of the great house (Lekson 1984:109). Tree-ring data gathered by the Chaco Center indicate construction at Peñasco Blanco was initiated between 900 and 915 and continued into the 1120s (Lekson 1984:104–109). However, there are no dates for the unexcavated

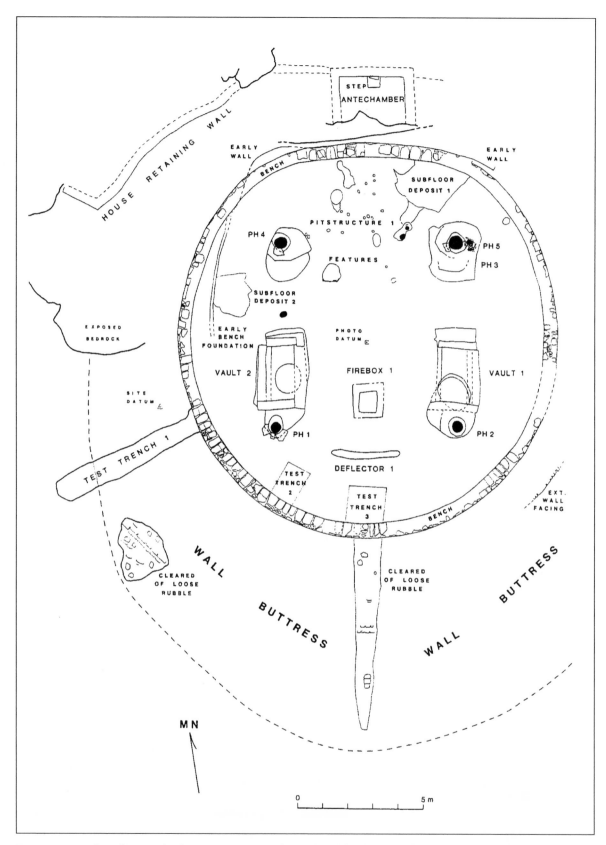

Labels within the figure:

STEP
ANTECHAMBER

HOUSE RETAINING WALL

EARLY WALL   EARLY WALL

BENCH

SUBFLOOR DEPOSIT 1

PITSTRUCTURE 1

PH 4   PH 5
                                        PH 3

FEATURES

SUBFLOOR DEPOSIT 2

EARLY BENCH FOUNDATION

EXPOSED BEDROCK

PHOTO DATUM

VAULT 2   FIREBOX 1   VAULT 1

SITE DATUM

PH 1   PH 2

TEST TRENCH 1

DEFLECTOR 1

EXT. WALL FACING

TEST TRENCH 2

TEST TRENCH 3   BENCH

CLEARED OF LOOSE RUBBLE   CLEARED OF LOOSE RUBBLE

WALL   BUTTRESS

BUTTRESS   WALL

MN

0   5 m

110   FIGURE 4.11. Plan of Kin Nahasbas Great Kiva 2 and associated features. (Mathien and Windes 1988:32, Figure 9)

Ruth M. Van Dyke

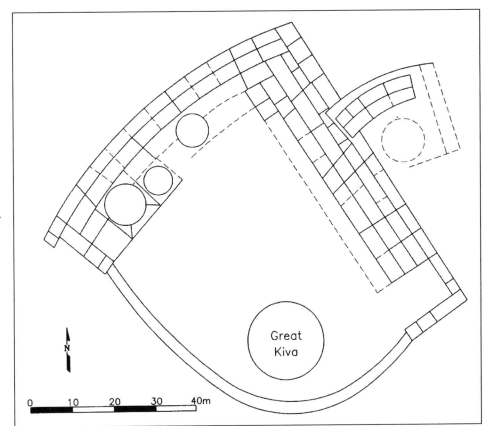

FIGURE 4.12. Plan of Una Vida, showing location of great kiva. (After Lekson 1984:80, Figure 4.1)

Great Kiva

0   10   20   30   40m

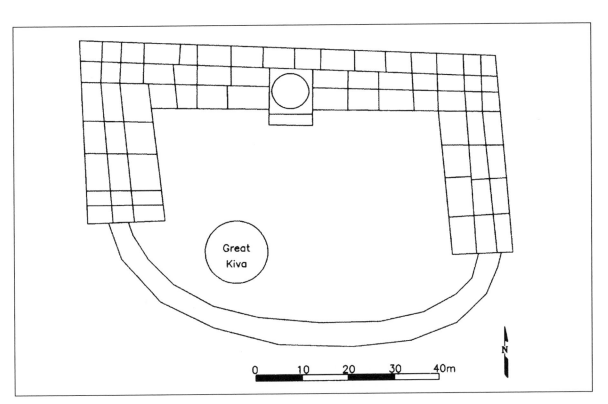

Great Kiva

0   10   20   30   40m

FIGURE 4.13. Plan of Hungo Pavi, showing location of great kiva. (After Lekson 1984:145, Figure 4.31)

Great Kivas in Time, Space, and Society

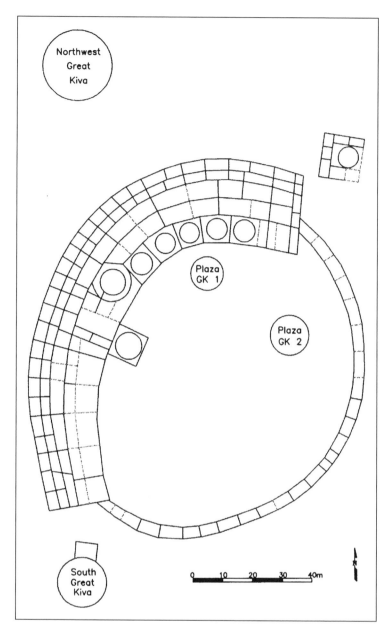

FIGURE 4.14. Plan of Peñasco Blanco, showing locations of four great kivas. (After Lekson 1984:95, Figure 4.8)

great kivas, and Lekson makes no attempt to assign them to construction sequences.

The south great kiva is a dramatic depression with approximately 2 m of relief at its center. Sandstone rubble up to 2 m wide is in evidence, particularly on the west side of the structure, suggesting the presence of massive core-and-veneer masonry walls. The interior diameter of this great kiva is estimated at 17 m; its exterior diameter is approximately 25 m. The structure is oriented due

north-south and contains an antechamber on the north side.

Plaza Great Kiva 1 is located in the northwest portion of the Peñasco Blanco plaza. This rather shallow depression has a relief of approximately 50 cm and an estimated interior diameter of 13 m. The north side of the structure abuts the exterior wall of the Peñasco Blanco roomblock. Plaza Great Kiva 2 is an obvious circular depression located in the northeast area of the plaza. There is little masonry in evidence except for scattered spalls around the edges, particularly on the north side. The structure has a relief of approximately 75 cm, an interior diameter estimated at 15 m, and an exterior diameter of approximately 20 m.

The northwest great kiva is congruent with 29SJ415, recorded in 1972 by Beardsley (as documented in the NPS Chaco Archives, Albuquerque). This great kiva is located 30 m northwest of Peñasco Blanco. It has a diameter of approximately 23 m and is 1.5 m deep. Although Beardsley reports exposed masonry and apparent partial excavation of this structure, these attributes were not apparent upon a visit to the site by the author in 2001. A light scatter of sandstone rubble with occasional cobbles appears around the edges of the structure, and a possible antechamber is present on the north side. Based on Hayes's interpretation of surface ceramics, Beardsley considered the structure to date to the Pueblo I period. Windes (personal communication, 2001), however, contends that the structure and associated ceramics date to the Pueblo II–III periods.

Isolated Great Kivas

Four great kivas are located on the south side of Chaco Canyon. Although they are often termed "isolated" great kivas because they are not directly associated with great houses, small sites are in their vicinity. Of the four, only Casa Rinconada has been excavated and is well-known. The isolated great kivas are discussed below in order from west (Casa Rinconada) to east.

Casa Rinconada (29SJ386)

Perhaps the best known of Chaco Canyon great kivas, Casa Rinconada is located on the south side of the canyon atop a small ridge adjacent to a 300-m-wide rincon. The structure was excavated into the sandstone and shale that comprise the ridge. Ten small sites are located in the immediate vicinity. Casa Rinconada was excavated by the School of American Research under Hewett's direction in 1930 and 1931. Vivian and Reiter were involved in the excavation, and their report on great kivas (Vivian and Reiter 1960:8–26) constitutes the primary reference for the structure. Partial reconstruction was undertaken by Gordon Vivian in 1933. Roland Richert of the National Park Service stabilized the floor features and capped the outer wall in 1955. In the wake of intensive "alternative" religious activities in Casa Rinconada in the late 1980s (Finn 1997), the National Park Service officially closed the structure to visitors in 1996 by adding masonry to block entrance to the kiva interior.

Unlike the great kivas at Chetro Ketl and Kin Nahasbas, Casa Rinconada was not the subject of extensive remodeling—only one version of the structure is present, with minor alterations (Figure 4.15). Initial construction took place in the latter half of the 1000s, and a McElmo-style veneer was added in the early 1100s. The main chamber has a diameter of 19.5 m. It is encircled by a continuous bench 84 cm high and 79 cm wide. The slightly banded, core-and-veneer wall is nearly 1 m wide and, at the time of excavation, extended for 2.9 m above the bench. The 34 wall niches are divisible into two sets based on size and position. Twenty-eight are of uniform size (30 by 38 cm by 30 cm deep), evenly spaced around the circumference approximately 85 cm above the bench. Six additional, irregular niches are lower in the wall. Groups of three small, 8-cm-diameter poles were set in sockets in the wall spaced at 70 cm intervals. Eighteen sockets were still present in the walls at excavation, and another 30–32 sets can be extrapolated to have originally existed. The purpose of the poles is not known, but they are considered to have extended into the main chamber for at least 15 cm.

Antechambers reached by stone steps from the bench are located to the south and north of the main chamber. The southern antechamber consists of one room with openings into the great kiva and to the exterior. The northern antechamber consists of a group of four or five rooms. With the exception of a passageway and a low bench in two of the northern rooms, they do not contain any features.

Peripheral rooms to the east and west of the main chamber are represented by fragmentary walls. One of these, to the northeast, opens into the main chamber of the great kiva by means of a door or window. The others cannot be definitely connected with the great kiva's interior. Across from this northeast opening, in the southwest wall, is a partially preserved, irregular wall niche.

Floor features include a masonry firebox, a deflector built of masonry with abundant mortar and upright poles, two masonry floor vaults, an incomplete or partially razed subfloor vault, four roof support pits, a stone-lined circular trench, and a subterranean passageway. Each of the masonry-lined roof support pits was built over a large, circular stone slab 120 cm in diameter set 70 cm below floor level. Vivian and Reiter (1960:15) state it was not feasible to remove the disks to see if additional ones were stacked underneath, as at Chetro Ketl. The pits were packed with rubble on the inside, and one contained a log 60 cm in diameter. The two southern roof support pits are connected with floor vaults. The northeast pit is isolated and contains space for a second, smaller timber beside the major roof support post. The northwest pit is in the middle of a stone-lined circular trench nearly 5 m in diameter. The subterranean passageway emerges within its circumference. Vivian and Reiter (1960:20) speculate that the pit may have housed a shelter that enabled religious practitioners to make surprise appearances from the subterranean passageway. The passageway is unique among excavated great kivas. It originates within the northwest pit and extends beneath the bench and main chamber wall and the primary antechamber room to emerge in the northernmost antechamber room. The passageway is approximately 85 cm wide, 90 cm deep, and 12 m long. Stone steps are found at each entrance. There is no evidence of passageway roofing, but Vivian and Reiter (1960:17) consider it likely that the passage was roofed.

Casa Rinconada contains two floors separated by approximately 10 cm of fill. Remodeling was minimal. The subterranean passageway and northwest pit were filled prior to construction of the second, higher floor. The bench was extended in height and width. Minor additions to floor vaults and roof support pits raised these features slightly.

113

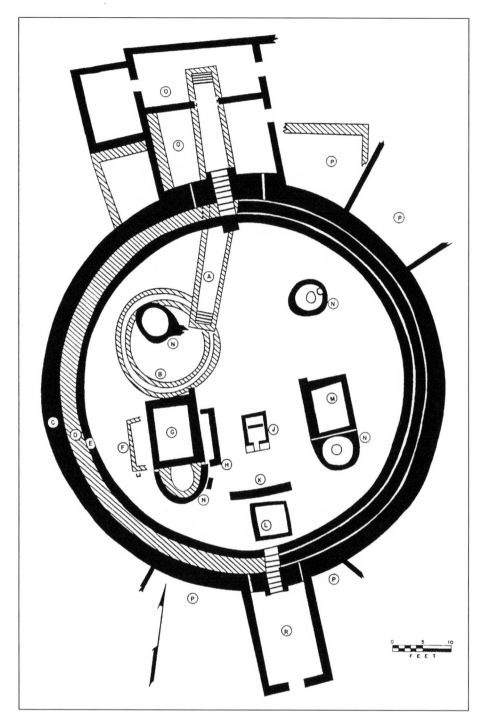

FIGURE 4.15. Plan of Casa Rinconada. A, subfloor passage, lower floor level; B, circular trench, lower floor level; C, outer wall; D, original bench, later covered with veneers; E, later bench veneer; F, earlier partial vault; G, west vault; H, vault extension; J, firebox; K, fire screen; L, subfloor enclosure; M, east vault; N, the seating pits; O, north antechamber; P, partial peripheral rooms. (Vivian and Reiter 1960:10, Figure 4, courtesy of SAR Press)

The interior of the firebox was reduced by the addition of a cross-wall and fill.

FAJADA GAP (29SJ1253)
Isolated great kiva 29SJ 1253 is located just below a ridge west of the confluence of Chaco Wash and Fajada Wash. A Basketmaker III site (29SJ1252) is located on the ridge to the east. The great kiva was recorded by Windes in 1972 and 1988. A brief description appears in Marshall et al. (1979:273), but the following information was obtained from the site form on file at the Chaco Archives. The kiva depression is 20 m in diameter and 3 m deep. Several concentrations of spalls and sandstone

Ruth M. Van Dyke

masonry are scattered just outside the great kiva's circumference. An antechamber measuring approximately 7 m north-south by 6 m east-west is attached to the north side of the structure. Surface ceramics from the great kiva berm date primarily to the 900s and early 1000s, with some intrusives from the late 1000s and early 1100s. The decorated assemblage is dominated by Red Mesa Black-on-white. About 8% of the ceramic assemblage consists of Chuskan wares.

CHACRA MESA NEAR WIJIJI (29SJ1642)

Isolated great kiva 29SJ1642 is found atop a prominent natural ridge projecting from the south side of Chacra Mesa just below and northwest of Shabik'eshchee Village (Figure 4.16). Wijiji is located 1,500 m to the northwest on the north side of the canyon, so the great kiva is colloquially known as "the one across from Wijiji," although the two structures are not in direct association or proximity. Test excavations were conducted at this great kiva by Gwinn Vivian in 1970, and site forms were complete by Tom Windes in 1972 and 1999. A brief description of the structure also appears in Marshall et al. (1979:273–274), but the following information was obtained from Vivian's field notes and Windes's site forms. Vivian excavated four shallow test pits, one at each cardinal direction along the edges of the depression, in order to locate the great kiva walls. A section of small, thin, tabular Chacoan masonry was exposed. The kiva is 17 m in diameter and is estimated to be approximately 2 m deep. A 14 by 12 m concentration of masonry rubble on the north side of the structure may represent an antechamber. Vivian's test pit on the north side located the entryway in this area. Windes also noted several spall and masonry concentrations downslope to the northeast or northwest that may represent a small, 2- to 4-room pueblo. A moderate to dense scatter of trash is found below the great kiva along its eastern flanks. The dense trash suggests the spot may have been the site of a domestic structure before the great kiva was constructed. Surface ceramics from the

FIGURE 4.16. 29SJ1642, the great kiva across from Wijiji. (Photograph by Gwinn Vivian)

great kiva berm date to the 900s and 1000s. The ceramic assemblage contains a great deal of Red Mesa Black-on-white with some Gallup Black-on-white and lots of indented corrugated grayware.

Chaco Additions Survey (29SJ2557)

Isolated great kiva 29SJ2557 is located in a side canyon of Chacra Mesa immediately southeast of Shabik'eshchee Village and east of 29SJ1642. The foundations of a small great house (29SJ2384) are at the mouth of the side canyon, approximately 400 m to the north. 29SJ2557 was recorded by the Chaco Additions survey in 1983 (Van Dyke and Powers 2002). The kiva depression is 13 m in diameter. Three rooms and a trash mound are associated (Figure 4.17). There are no contemporary sites nearby. Surface ceramics from the trash mound are securely dated to between 1000 and 1225. About 13% of the ceramic assemblage consists of Chuskan wares.

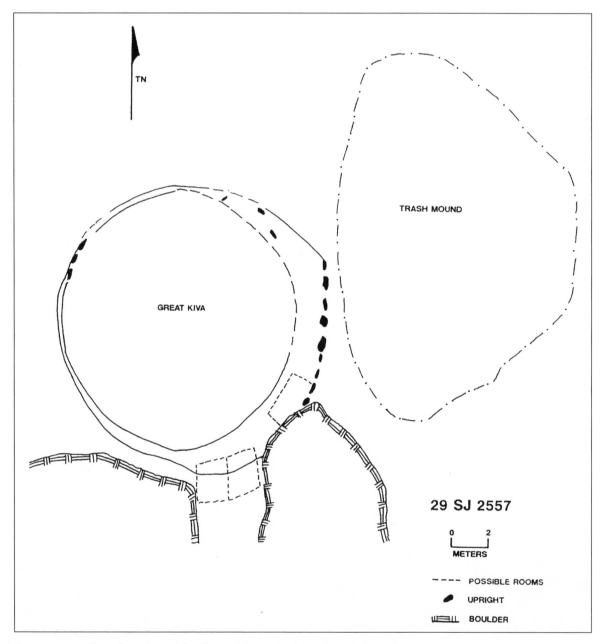

FIGURE 4.17. Plan of 29SJ2557, the Chacra Mesa great kiva. (Van Dyke and Powers 2002)

Ruth M. Van Dyke

Synthesis

Although a few great kivas were present in the canyon during the 900s, the Classic Bonito phase is characterized by a dramatic boom in formal great kiva construction. These new structures, whether associated with great houses or placed among small sites on the south side of Chaco Canyon, are characterized by uniformity in size, orientation, and appearance. Great kiva diameters exceed 9–10 m and more typically approach 15–20 m. When associated with a great house, they are located in an open space or plaza, often in front and to the south or southeast. Great kivas are subterranean, or semisubterranean. Entry is generally through an antechamber on the north side; a southern entry is sometimes present as well. Subterranean walls are lined with banded masonry, and above-ground walls are of core-and-veneer construction. Formalized interior features include an encircling bench; wall niches; paired masonry floor vaults; a central, elevated masonry firebox; and four masonry-lined pits for wooden roof supports or masonry pillars. Niches may be set in the wall, and a deflector is sometimes found in front of the firebox. Great kivas were roofed by means of four pillars that supported a four-log framework surrounded by radial beams; the roof framework was overlain with layers of smaller posts, bark, and earth.

Cardinal directions were important in many aspects of Classic Bonito architecture, and great kivas are no exception (Lekson 1999; Marshall 1997; Sofaer et al. 1989; Stein et al. 1997; Van Dyke 2007). Chacoan great kivas are usually oriented on a north-south axis. When great kivas are associated with great houses, antechambers and interior features are aligned with the perpendicular axis of the great house. Floor vaults, roof support pillars, and niches generally express bilateral symmetry along the north-south kiva axis.

Great kivas were also constructed during the Classic Bonito phase in outlier communities throughout the San Juan Basin and adjacent areas (Fowler et al. 1987; Herr 2001; Marshall et al. 1979:263–328; Powers et al. 1983; Van Dyke 2002). As in the canyon, Classic Bonito outlier great kivas are part of a larger architectural package that includes great houses, earthworks, and road segments. Most outlier great kivas are located close to great houses, either in front or to the side

of the great house to the southeast, sometimes enclosed within a plaza retaining wall. Isolated great kivas at outliers tend to date to the 900s. Recently (Van Dyke 2002) I investigated great kiva presence/absence for a sample of 56 outliers. Twenty-nine of these communities contain one great kiva, 11 contain multiple (2 or 3) great kivas, and 16 lack great kivas altogether. The study shows that the presence/absence of great kivas is inversely related to distance from Chaco Canyon, generally supporting Doyel et al.'s (1984) notion of a Chaco Halo, or reflecting the heritage of the canyon as a locus of proto–great house rather than great kiva–centered settlement.

As in the canyon, outlier great kiva size is fairly uniform—it is not related to great house size, nor is it related to estimated community population (Van Dyke 2002). Although great kiva diameter ranges between 10 and 23 m, the coefficient of variation for a sample of 44 Classic Bonito phase outlier great kivas is 0.20, reflecting the fact that most great kiva diameters fall within 15 to 17 m (see also Herr 1994:57, 59). The uniformity in orientation, symmetry, and interior features seen in canyon great kivas is also present in five excavated outlier great kivas (Table 4.2) in the communities of Village of the Great Kivas (Roberts 1932), Fort Wingate (Peckham 1958), Aztec (Morris 1921), Salmon (Marshall et al. 1979:304), and Lowry (Martin 1936).

Although great kivas continued to be built at outliers into the 1100s, the structures are conspicuously absent from Late Bonito great houses in Chaco Canyon, such as Pueblo del Arroyo, Wijiji, Tsin Kletsin, New Alto, Kin Kletso, and Casa Chiquita. Although no new great kivas were built in Chaco Canyon during the early twelfth century, Kiva A at Pueblo Bonito and CKI at Chetro Ketl were remodeled and remained in use during this period. Possible interpretations for these spatial and temporal patterns are discussed below.

GREAT KIVAS AND CHACOAN SOCIETY

The spatial and temporal patterns discussed above hold a great deal of information about Classic Bonito Chacoan society. During the eleventh century, Chaco became a center for ritual gatherings attended by people who lived in outlying communities across

TABLE 4.2. Excavated Classic Bonito Phase Great Kivas outside Chaco Canyon

LOCATION	DATE (AD)	ABOVE-BENCH DIAMETER (m)	FEATURES	SOURCES
Village of the Great Kivas	Pueblo II–III	23.7	north antechamber, bench, firebox, floor vaults, masonry roof support pillars	Roberts 1932
Fort Wingate	Pueblo II–III	12.3	bench, firebox, floor vaults (west only, but east may have been dismantled prehistorically), masonry roof support pillars	Peckham 1958
Aztec West	1110–1120	14.7	northwest antechamber with stairs, peripheral rooms, bench, wall niches, firebox, floor vaults, masonry and horizontal wood roof support pillars with four stone disks at base of pits	Morris 1921
Salmon	1088–1107	14.0	northwest antechamber with stairs, bench, firebox, floor vaults, masonry roof support pillars	Marshall et al. 1979
Lowry	1086–1120	14.3	northeast stairs, peripheral rooms, bench, wall niches, beam sockets on walls, floor vaults, plastered hearth, masonry and horizontal wood roof support pillars, on site of earlier great kiva	Martin 1936

the San Juan Basin. The incorporation of formal great kivas into the Classic Bonito architectural repertoire represents the integration of peoples from great kiva–centered communities into a ritual order centered in Chaco Canyon. The legitimation and support of this ritual order was deeply intertwined with aspects of a Puebloan worldview that had been developing across the preceding centuries. Great kivas likely served as spaces for special ritual events and meetings. Like all Classic Bonito Chacoan architecture, great kivas were not only functional spaces. They were also symbolically charged buildings that represented ideas such as center place, directionality, balanced dualism, and cyclical renewal. In this final section of this chapter, I explore possible functions and meanings of the great kivas of Chaco Canyon.

Great Kivas as Ritual Venues
We have surprisingly little hard evidence to tell us what transpired in Chacoan great kivas. These structures were likely group meeting places or arenas for ritual performances. Great kivas are circular and therefore would be good spaces for face-to-face interactions, heightening their socially integrative potential. The structures possess acoustic properties that would have lent themselves well to ceremonial activities. Floor vaults may have been used as foot drums, overlain with wooden planks that would make a booming noise when people jumped or danced on them. A subterranean passageway leading into a screened area in the great kiva at Casa Rinconada would have facilitated entrances at dramatic moments. Caches of turquoise, beads, and other items found in sealed wall niches and at the base of seating pits in some great kivas have been interpreted as votive deposits.

The best evidence for great kivas as ritual spaces is presented by the structures' highly standardized sizes, layouts, features, and orientations. In a cross-cultural study of integrative spaces, Adler and Wilshusen (1990) found that high-level integrative facilities—structures used for specialized, ritual activities by an entire community or communities—tend to have a standardized size. By contrast, low-level integrative facilities—structures used for a variety of activities by subsets of the community—tend to vary in size with respect to population. As described in the preceding pages, standardization in size is one of the characteristics of the Classic Bonito phase great kiva (Herr 1994; Van Dyke 2002). To some extent, uniformity in great kiva diameter may reflect limitations in roofing technology, which would have presented difficulties for constructing a roofed kiva with a diameter much in excess of 20 m (Haury 1985:420). However, technical limitations cannot explain uniformities in orientation and in floor and wall features.

Ruth M. Van Dyke

The standardization of orientation, layout, and interior features may be construed as strong evidence for the use of great kivas as stages for ritual events. Religious architecture tends to be conservative, incorporating iconographic material symbols easily recognized by ceremonial participants and observers (Adler and Wilshusen 1990). Abstract, religious ideas are often communicated through repetition (Rowlands 1993). Thus it is likely that the repetitive, conservative, increasingly formalized iconographic form of the great kiva was more important to the builders than the mere need to establish a meeting space. Great kivas represented a shared idea and provided a locus for a suite of religious activities that crosscut other differences within the canyon as well as among the outliers.

Ceremonies or other activities in the great kivas are unlikely to have been staged for the general public. Some degree of exclusive access is likely, based on space limitations. It is unlikely that any Chacoan great kiva could have contained more than a small fraction of the resident or visiting population. Using an estimate of one square meter of floor space per person, approximately 250 people could fit in a great kiva with an 18-m-diameter floor, such as Casa Rinconada, but this discounts the area taken up by the floor features and leaves no room for activities inside the structure. A more realistic estimate is derived by imagining a row of spectators shoulder to shoulder every 75 cm around the circumference. In this scenario, approximately 75 people could stand around the 56 m circumference of an 18 m great kiva, leaving room for activity in the central area.

Great Kivas and Chacoan Ideology
Great kivas were formalized during the Classic Bonito phase at a time when construction in Chaco proceeded on a more intense scale than anything in the preceding century (Lekson 1984:66–72, 261). As many as eleven great kivas may have been in simultaneous use in the canyon during this period. Why the boom in great kiva construction, and why the push toward heightened formalization?

These were times of agricultural plenty. Sebastian (1991:120–132) argues that power during initial construction at Chaco in the preceding century was based on generosity leading to prestige, but this strategy would no longer suffice when those

with less did not have to depend on the munificence of those with more. She contends Chacoan leading families made a shift during the eleventh century to ranked inequality grounded in religious monopolies. Whichever variety of Chacoan explanation one chooses, it is undeniable that whatever was happening in Chaco peaked during the latter half of the eleventh century. It is during this period that Chaco's two would-be "big men" were buried with pomp and circumstance beneath Room 33 in the oldest section of Pueblo Bonito (Pepper 1909, 1920; Judd 1954:338–339). The times were characterized by massive construction and conspicuous consumption. The canyon became a locus for periodic gatherings of basin residents who likely visited Chaco to witness or participate in rituals linked to solstices, equinoxes, or lunar events (Sofaer 1997; Stein et al. 1997). Increasing formalization and repetitive iconography inside great kivas communicated symbolic messages. Access to ceremonies in great kivas probably was not universal. Special ritual information would not have been available to all. This scenario fits well with the notion of canyon groups seeking to legitimate power through control of ritual.

The built environment of Classic Bonito Chaco Canyon enhanced visitors' aesthetic experiences of place. Great kivas, great houses, earthworks, and roads created spatial perceptions and relationships that resonated with important elements of the visitors' worldview. Like contemporary Puebloans, Chacoans likely held a cosmographic vision of their world (Marshall 1997). Chaco Canyon was a center place, and ceremonies there helped to keep the world in balance. The construction of great kivas in Chaco Canyon integrated peoples from outlying great-house- and great-kiva-centered communities. The repetitive iconography conveyed by great kivas (and great houses) emphasized the importance of social memory, cyclical renewal, balanced dualism, and directionality. As visitors to Chaco resonated aesthetically with the ideas expressed in the architecture, they bought into a Classic Bonito Chacoan ideology that legitimated the ritual order and the authority of those who held ritual knowledge.

Establishing continuity with a real or imagined past—the construction of social memory—is a common way to consolidate social identities and legitimate authority (Eagleton 1991; Van Dyke and Alcock 2003). Chacoan architecture often contains references and linkages to the past (Ashmore, Chapter 7, this volume; Van Dyke 2003, 2004b). The Chacoan great kiva creates an architectural continuum with the communal pitstructures of the Basketmaker III/Pueblo I periods, evoking the communal ideologies of an imagined past. This helped to naturalize new and unequal distributions of labor and prestige. Great kivas represent an idealized Basketmaker III and Pueblo I past woven into the fabric of the Classic Bonito landscape.

Crown and Wills (2003) argue that remodeled small kivas, and repainted and refired cylinder jars, represent a kind of cyclical "ritual renewal" at Chaco. Cyclical renewal is part of the construction of social memory (Van Dyke 2008). Like great houses, Chacoan great kivas were repeatedly remodeled over the course of three centuries of building in the canyon. Stein et al. (1997) argue that a new great kiva was built at Pueblo Bonito near the start of every major construction phase. Traces of partially obliterated older forms were present beneath new forms, just as traces of earlier designs are found under repainted cylinder jars, and just as knowledge gleaned from past experience informs present social decisions and interpretations. A repetitive cycle of transformation, built on the past-yet-not-the-past, naturalizes the present social order and keeps the world in balance. Balance relies upon opposing dualisms, which come together at a center place.

The incorporation of great kivas into Chacoan architecture was important to the development of Chaco Canyon as a Puebloan center place. Placement of great kivas next to great houses symbolized (as well as practically facilitated) the integration of great-kiva-centered and great-house-centered peoples and rituals. Balance at Chaco not only involved the integration of different ethnic groups, it also was grounded in beliefs that were cosmographically expressed on the landscape (Marshall 1997; Sofaer 1997; Stein and Lekson 1992; Van Dyke 2004a, 2008).

A concern with directionality is clearly expressed through Chacoan architecture and road alignments (Lekson 1999; Marshall 1997). Directions—particularly cardinal directions, with oppositions between north and south, east and west, and vertical and subterranean—were important. Opposing directions converged and were balanced against one another at Chaco Canyon—the center place. Ideas about directionality and balanced dualisms are reflected in the orientation and floor features of great kivas. Paired roof supports and floor vaults oppose each other across the meridian axis that often divides the structures into symmetrical halves.

The pairing of great kivas with great houses also represents a number of opposing dualisms, including subterranean and vertical, visible and hidden, accessible and restricted, and possibly even female and male. Canyon great houses are remarkably visible and vertical edifices, extending up to 10 m or four stories in height. By the mid-1000s, these structures were juxtaposed with great kivas, which were constructed in the plazas of all great houses except Pueblo Alto and Pueblo del Arroyo. These circular spaces represented a subterranean and hidden dimension that balanced the verticality of the great houses—the two intersected in the great house plaza, the center place.

The spatial locations of great kivas also carry meaning. A number of authors have attempted to draw Casa Rinconada into an intricate web of building alignments within Chaco Canyon. Sofaer (1997:125) points out that Casa Rinconada is almost due south of New Alto (1.7 km at 1.3°), and that New Alto is visible from the south Rinconada stairs over the slightly offset north doorway. Some Casa Rinconada features appear to be oriented to solstices (Williamson 1984:132–144; Williamson et al. 1977:207–211), although great kivas in general do not seem to figure into Sofaer's (1997) solar and lunar standstill alignments. Some (Fritz 1978:54; Doxtater 1991) go so far as to postulate Casa Rinconada as a navel of the Chacoan universe. However, it is important not to lose sight of the fact that Casa Rinconada attracts so much attention in part because it has been excavated and reconstructed.

Great kivas on the south side of Chaco Canyon, such as Casa Rinconada, may have been balanced against north-side great houses in a larger landscape sense. Casa Rinconada is located directly across Chaco Wash from Pueblo Bonito, 700 m to the south-southeast. Although downcutting and erosion have long since obliterated any traces, and modern wash entrenchment prevents us from walking this way today, it is likely that a path or perhaps a road segment connected these two eleventh-century structures. The cardinal alignments of both buildings emphasize the meridian that runs through Chaco and keeps the world in balance. The two structures may be meant to represent a paired opposition, with Casa Rinconada as a circular, southern, subterranean place balanced against Pueblo Bonito as a rectangular, northern, vertical place. This pattern reiterates the opposition between north and south, vertical and subterranean, with the central canyon itself as the point of intersection (see also Van Dyke 2008). Pueblo Alto, which sits high on the north side of Chaco Canyon, may not have an associated great kiva because the canyon itself is a subterranean counterbalance.

Accessible/restricted and male/female dualism can be seen, albeit somewhat more tentatively, in the pairing of great houses with great kivas. Elsewhere I have argued that access to great house interiors must have been at least somewhat restricted (Van Dyke 2008). Although everyone may not have had access to great kivas, once inside, the interior space is largely undifferentiated by physical barriers. Great kivas are thus more accessible spaces than great houses. The circular form of the kiva is considered female in some contemporary pueblos. At a Zuni summer rain dance ca. 1969, clowns imitated astronauts landing on the moon by walking on the roof of a kiva. According to the Zuni who related the story, the clowns' purpose was to criticize the astronauts, who showed disrespect for the moon-mother by walking on her and piercing her with probes (Young 1988:114). While great houses are not overtly phallic structures, they may be considered so in contrast to the womblike shapes of great kivas.

Great kivas were part of a powerful set of architectural symbols. When visitors came to Chaco to witness or participate in ritual events, the architecture and landscape of the canyon reiterated the notion that Chaco was the center place, the fulcrum around which balanced opposites revolved, the arena within which the world was repeatedly transformed. Visitors' emotional and aesthetic responses to the architecture encouraged them to lend their physical and spiritual support to Chacoan ceremony. This ideology, of course, also legitimated the power and authority of canyon ritual leaders.

Although great kiva construction in Chaco Canyon fell off after 1100, the structures continued to be an important part of the Chacoan architectural package as transferred and transformed in outlier communities such as Salmon and Aztec. The iconic power of the Chacoan great kiva extended into the post-Chacoan world. For example, Kintigh (1994) contends that the great kiva form was appropriated as a symbolic reference to Chaco during Puebloan aggregation in post-Chacoan times. By the late 1200s, great kivas gave way to plazas on the Colorado Plateau (Adams 1991:153).

Summary

The great kivas of Chaco Canyon are part of a suite of large-scale architectural forms that coalesced during the Classic Bonito phase. The emergence of these formal, masonry-walled, circular, subterranean structures, constructed in front of great houses and among small sites, cannot be understood without reference to developments dating back at least five centuries, from Basketmaker III through Pueblo I times. In this chapter I have attempted a comprehensive look at canyon great kivas, from antecedent origins through probable Classic Bonito functions and meanings. And I have provided a brief, synthetic description of every great kiva currently identified in Chaco Canyon. This picture is still necessarily incomplete, as many canyon great kivas have not been excavated, and outlier great kivas are not addressed except in passing. Some outlier great kivas were the core of late Pueblo I/early Pueblo II communities, while others were introduced along with formal Chacoan great houses during the eleventh century—these patterns deserve further study and discussion, but are beyond the scope of this book.

Like all large-scale Chacoan architecture, great kivas are heavily laden with symbolic and cosmographic meaning. Great kivas were not only locations for ritual, they were also symbolic spaces where worldview intertwined with the social order. By creating continuity with the past, great kivas were part of a naturalizing process legitimating new and less-equal forms of social organization. Repetitive remodeling was part of cyclical renewal. Great kivas symbolically expressed the importance of directionality and balanced dualism in a variety of

121

ways, through their internal features, orientations, and positions on the architectural landscape. Those who participated in or witnessed ritual activities in great kivas would have aesthetically resonated with these symbolic messages. The experiences would have confirmed the validity of a Puebloan worldview that emphasized Chaco Canyon as center place, and ceremony in Chaco as necessary for the balance and continuity of life. Ultimately, this ideology legitimated the authority of Chacoan ritual leaders.

Acknowledgments

I would like to thank Steve Lekson for the invitation to participate in the Chaco Synthesis Architecture Summit in Chaco Canyon during October 2000. Thanks to the conference participants, particularly Wendy Ashmore, Ben Nelson, Anna Sofaer, and Phillip Tuwaletstiwa for thought-provoking discussions during the meeting. Gwinn Vivian, Tom Windes, Barbara Mills, and an anonymous reviewer kindly provided comments on the original draft. I am grateful to Joan Mathien and Joyce Raab, who patiently assisted me in locating and extracting archived materials at the University of New Mexico, and to Randy McGuire, who procured archived materials from the Smithsonian Institution. Photographs in this chapter appear courtesy of the Smithsonian Institution, Gordon Reiter, and Gwinn Vivian. Maps from Vivian and Reiter's (1960) publication appear courtesy of the School of American Research Press, and maps from Mathien and Windes's (1988) report appear courtesy of the National Park Service. Finally, I wish to express my appreciation to the National Endowment for the Humanities, Doug Schwartz, Nancy Owen Lewis, and the staff of the School of American Research in Santa Fe. I completed the original draft of this manuscript while a Resident Scholar at the School of American Research during 2000–2001. Not only did SAR provide me with time and resources to work on this project, but the library there serendipitously provided me with access to many of the early publications of Hewett and his students.

References

Adams, E. Charles
1991   *The Origin and Development of the Pueblo Katsina Cult*. University of Arizona Press, Tucson.

Adler, Michael A.
1989   Ritual Facilities and Social Integration in Non-ranked Societies. In *The Architecture of Social Integration in Prehistoric Pueblos*, edited by William D. Lipe and M. Hegmon, pp. 35–52. Occasional Papers of the Crow Canyon Archaeological Center 1. Cortez.

Adler, Michael A., and Richard H. Wilshusen
1990   Large-scale Integrative Facilities in Tribal Societies: Cross-cultural and Southwestern U.S. Examples. *World Archaeology* 22:133–146.

Akins, Nancy J., and William B. Gillespie
1979   Summary Report of Archaeological Investigations at Una Vida, Chaco Canyon, New Mexico. Ms. on file, NPS Chaco Archives, University of New Mexico, Albuquerque.

Altschul, Jeffrey H., and Edgar K. Huber
2000   Economics, Site Structure, and Social Organization. In *Foundations of Anasazi Culture*, edited by Paul F. Reed, pp. 145–160. University of Utah Press, Salt Lake City.

Anyon, Roger
1984   Mogollon Settlement Pattern and Communal Architecture. Unpublished M.A. thesis, University of New Mexico, Albuquerque.

Bradfield, Wesley
1921   Economic Resources of Chaco Canyon. *Art and Archaeology* 11(1&2):36–38.

Chapman, K. M.
1921   What the Potsherds Tell. *Art and Archaeology* 11(1&2):39–44.

Crown, Patricia, and W. H. Wills
2003   Modifying Pottery and Kivas at Chaco: Pentimento, Restoration, or Renewal? *American Antiquity* 68:511–532.

Doxtater, Dennis
1991   Reflections of the Anasazi Cosmos. In *Social Space: Human Spatial Behaviour in Dwellings and Settlements*, edited by Ole Gron, Ericka Engelstad, and Inge Lindblom, pp. 155–184. Odense University Press, Odense, Denmark.

Doyel, David E., Cory D. Breternitz, and Michael P. Marshall
1984   Chacoan Community Structure: Bis sa'ani and the Chaco Halo. In *Recent Research on Chaco Prehistory*, edited by W. James Judge and John D. Schelberg, pp. 37–54. Reports of the Chaco Center 8. Division of Cultural Research, National Park Service, Albuquerque.

Eagleton, Terry
1991   *Ideology: A Critical Reader*. Verso, London.

Eddy, Frank W.
1966   *Prehistory in the Navajo Reservoir District in Northwestern New Mexico*, Parts I and II. Museum of New Mexico Papers in Anthropology 15. Santa Fe.

Ruth M. Van Dyke

1972 Cultural Ecology and the Prehistory of the Navajo Reservoir District. *Southwestern Lore* 38(1&2):1–75.

1977 *Archaeological Investigations at Chimney Rock Mesa, 1970–1972.* Memoirs of the Colorado Archaeological Society 1.

Finn, Christine
1997 "Leaving More Than Footprints": Modern Votive Offerings at Chaco Canyon Prehistoric Site. *Antiquity* 71:169–178.

Fowler, Andrew, John R. Stein, and Roger Anyon
1987 *An Archaeological Reconnaissance of West-Central New Mexico: The Anasazi Monuments Project.* On file, Office of Cultural Affairs, Historic Preservation Division, Santa Fe.

Fritz, John M.
1978 Paleopsychology Today: Ideational Systems and Human Adaptation in Prehistory. In *Social Archaeology: Beyond Subsistence and Dating*, edited by Charles L. Redman et al., pp. 37–59. Academic Press, New York.

Gillespie, William B.
1984 Una Vida. In *Great Pueblo Architecture of Chaco Canyon, New Mexico*, by Stephen H. Lekson, pp. 79–94. University of New Mexico Press, Albuquerque.

Gilpin, Dennis J., and Larry Benallie
2000 Juniper Cove and Early Anasazi Community Structure West of the Chuska Mountains. In *Foundations of Anasazi Culture*, edited by Paul F. Reed, pp. 161–174. University of Utah Press, Salt Lake City.

Haury, Emil W.
1985 *Mogollon Culture in the Forestdale Valley, East-Central Arizona.* University of Arizona Press, Tucson.

Hawley, Florence M.
1934 *The Significance of the Dated Prehistory of Chetro Ketl, Chaco Canyon, New Mexico.* Monographs of the School of American Research 2. Santa Fe.

Hegmon, Michelle
1989 Social Integration and Architecture. In *The Architecture of Social Integration in Prehistoric Pueblos*, edited by William D. Lipe and Michelle Hegmon, pp. 5–14. Occasional Papers of the Crow Canyon Archaeological Center 1. Cortez.

Herr, Sarah A.
1994 Great Kivas as Integrative Architecture in the Silver Creek Community, Arizona. Unpublished M.A. thesis, Department of Anthropology, University of Arizona, Tucson.

2001 *Beyond Chaco: Great Kiva Communities on the Mogollon Rim Frontier.* Anthropological Papers of the University of Arizona 66. University of Arizona Press, Tucson.

Hewett, Edgar Lee
1921 The Excavation of Chettro Kettle, Chaco Canyon, 1920. *Art and Archaeology* 11:45–58.

1922 The Chaco Canyon in 1921. *Art and Archaeology* 14(3):115–131.

1936 *The Chaco Canyon and Its Monuments.* University of New Mexico and the School of American Research, Albuquerque and Santa Fe.

Judd, Neil M.
1922 Archaeological Investigations at Pueblo Bonito, New Mexico. *Smithsonian Miscellaneous Collections* 72(15):106–117.

1925a Everyday Life in Pueblo Bonito. *National Geographic Magazine* 58:227–262.

1925b Exploration in Pre-historic Pueblo Bonito, Chaco Canyon, New Mexico. *Geographical Society of Philadelphia Bulletin* 23:82.

1954 *The Material Culture of Pueblo Bonito.* Smithsonian Miscellaneous Collections 124. Washington, DC.

1964 *The Architecture of Pueblo Bonito.* Smithsonian Miscellaneous Collections 147(1). Washington, DC.

Kearns, Timothy M., Janet L. McVickar, and Lori Stephens Reed
2000 The Early to Late Basketmaker III Transition in Tohatchi Flats, New Mexico. In *Foundations of Anasazi Culture*, edited by Paul F. Reed, pp. 115–142. University of Utah Press, Salt Lake City.

Kintigh, Keith W.
1994 Chaco, Communal Architecture, and Cibolan Aggregation. In *The Ancient Southwestern Community: Models and Methods for the Study of Prehistoric Social Organization*, edited by W. H. Wills and R. D. Leonard, pp. 131–140. University of New Mexico Press, Albuquerque.

Leinau, Alice
1934 Sanctuaries in the Ancient Pueblo of Chetro Ketl. Unpublished M.A. thesis, University of New Mexico. Ms. on file, NPS Chaco Archives, University of New Mexico, Albuquerque.

Lekson, Stephen H.
1983 *The Architecture and Dendrochronology of Chetro Ketl, Chaco Canyon, New Mexico.* Reports of the Chaco Center 6. Division of Cultural Research, National Park Service, Albuquerque.

1984 *Great Pueblo Architecture of Chaco Canyon, New Mexico.* University of New Mexico Press, Albuquerque.

1999 *The Chaco Meridian: Centers of Political Power in the Ancient Southwest.* Walnut Creek, CA: Altamira Press.

Lightfoot, Ricky R.
1988 Roofing an Early Anasazi Great Kiva. *Kiva* 53:253–272.

123

Lightfoot, Ricky R., Alice M. Emerson, and Eric Blinman

1988   Excavation in Area 5, Grass Mesa Village (Site 5MT23). Chapter 7 in *Dolores Archaeological Program: Anasazi Communities at Dolores: Grass Mesa Village*, edited by William D. Lipe, J. N. Morris, and Timothy A. Kohler, pp. 561–766. USDI Bureau of Reclamation, Denver.

Lipe, William D., Timothy A. Kohler, Mark D. Varien, J. N. Morris, and Ricky Lightfoot

1988   Synthesis. In *Dolores Archaeological Program: Anasazi Communities at Dolores: Grass Mesa Village*, compiled by W. D. Lipe, J. N. Morris, and T. A. Kohler, pp. 1213–1276. Bureau of Reclamation, Engineering and Research Center, Denver.

Luhrs, Dorothy

1935   The Excavation of Kin Nahazbas, Chaco Cañon, New Mexico. Ms. on file, NPS Chaco Archives, University of New Mexico, Albuquerque.

McLellan, George W.

1969   *The Origin, Development, and Typology of Anasazi Kivas and Great Kivas*. Ph.D. dissertation, University of Colorado, Boulder. UMI Publications, Ann Arbor.

Marshall, Michael P.

1997   The Chacoan Roads: A Cosmological Interpretation. In *Anasazi Architecture and American Design*, edited by Baker H. Morrow and V. B. Price, pp. 62–74. University of New Mexico Press, Albuquerque.

Marshall, Michael P., John R. Stein, Richard W. Loose, and Judith E. Novotny

1979   *Anasazi Communities of the San Juan Basin*. Public Service Company of New Mexico, Albuquerque.

Martin, Paul S.

1936   *Lowry Ruin in Southwestern Colorado*. Field Museum of Natural History, Anthropological Series 23(1). Chicago.

Martin, Paul S., and John B. Rinaldo

1939   *Modified Basket Maker Sites, Ackmen–Lowry Area, Southwestern Colorado*. Anthropological Series 23(3). Field Museum of Natural History, Chicago.

Mathien, Frances Joan, and Thomas C. Windes

1988   *Historic Structure Report: Kin Nahasbas Ruin, Chaco Culture National Historical Park, New Mexico*. Branch of Cultural Research, National Park Service, Santa Fe.

Miller, James Marshall

1937   The Great Kivas of Chetro Ketl. Unpublished M.A. thesis, University of Southern California, Los Angeles. Ms. on file, NPS Chaco Archives, University of New Mexico, Albuquerque.

Morris, Earl H.

1921   *The House of the Great Kiva at the Aztec Ruin*. Anthropological Papers of the American Museum of Natural History 26 (Part II). New York.

1939   *Archaeological Studies in the La Plata District: Southwestern Colorado and Northwestern New Mexico*. Carnegie Institution of Washington Publication 519. Washington, DC.

Morris, Elizabeth, ed.

1980   *Basketmaker Caves in the Prayer Rock District, Northeastern Arizona*. Anthropological Papers of the University of Arizona 35. Tucson.

Orcutt, Janet D., Eric Blinman, and Timothy A. Kohler

1990   Explanations of Population Aggregation in the Mesa Verde Region Prior to AD 900. In *Perspectives on Southwestern Prehistory*, edited by Paul E. Minnis and Charles L. Redman, pp. 196–212. Westview Press, Boulder.

Peckham, Stuart L.

1958   Salvage Archaeology in New Mexico 1957–1958: A Partial Report. *El Palacio* 65(5):161–164.

Pepper, George H.

1909   The Exploration of a Burial Room in Pueblo Bonito, New Mexico. In *Anthropological Essays Presented to Frederick Ward Putnam in Honor of His Seventieth Birthday*, pp. 196–252. G. E. Stechert and Company, New York.

1920   *Pueblo Bonito*. Anthropological Papers of the American Museum of Natural History 27. Washington, DC.

Powers, Robert P., William B. Gillespie, and Stephen H. Lekson

1983   *The Outlier Survey: A Regional View of Settlement in the San Juan Basin*. Reports of the Chaco Center 3. National Park Service, Albuquerque.

Reed, Paul F.

2000   Fundamental Issues in Basketmaker Archaeology. In *Foundations of Anasazi Culture*, edited by Paul F. Reed, pp. 3–16. University of Utah Press, Salt Lake City.

Reed, Paul F., and Scott Wilcox

2000   Distinctive and Intensive: The Basketmaker III to Early Pueblo I Occupation of Cove–Redrock Valley, Northeastern Arizona. In *Foundations of Anasazi Culture*, edited by Paul F. Reed, pp. 69–93. University of Utah Press, Salt Lake City.

Reiter, Paul

1933   The Ancient Pueblo of Chetro Ketl. Unpublished M.A. thesis, University of New Mexico. Ms. on file, NPS Chaco Archives, University of New Mexico, Albuquerque.

Riggs, Charles R.

2001   *The Architecture of Grasshopper Pueblo*. University of Utah Press, Salt Lake City.

Roberts, Frank H. H., Jr.

1927   *The Ceramic Sequence in the Chaco Canyon, New Mexico, and Its Relation to the Culture of the San Juan Basin*. Ph.D. dissertation, Harvard University.

1929   *Shabik'eshchee Village: A Late Basket Maker Site in the Chaco Canyon, New Mexico*. Bureau of American Ethnology Bulletin 92. Washington, DC.

1932 *The Village of the Great Kivas on the Zuni Reservation, New Mexico.* Bureau of American Ethnology Bulletin 111. Washington, DC.

Rowlands, Michael
1993 The Role of Memory in the Transmission of Culture. *World Archaeology* 25(2):141–151.

Schachner, Gregson
2001 Ritual Control and Transformation in Middle-Range Societies: An Example from the American Southwest. *Journal of Anthropological Archaeology* 20:168–194.

Sebastian, Lynne
1991 Sociopolitical Complexity and the Chaco System. In *Chaco and Hohokam: Prehistoric Regional Systems in the American Southwest*, edited by Patricia L. Crown and W. James Judge, pp. 109–134. School of American Research, Santa Fe.

Sofaer, Anna
1997 The Primary Architecture of the Chacoan Culture: A Cosmological Expression. In *Anasazi Architecture and American Design*, edited by Baker T. Morrow and V. B. Price, pp. 88–132. University of New Mexico Press, Albuquerque.

Sofaer, Anna, Michael P. Marshall, and Rolf M. Sinclair
1989 The Great North Road: A Cosmographic Expression of the Chaco Culture of New Mexico. In *World Archaeoastronomy*, edited by A. F. Aveni, pp. 365–376. Cambridge University Press, Cambridge.

Stein, John R., and Stephen H. Lekson
1992 Anasazi Ritual Landscapes. In *Anasazi Regional Organization and the Chaco System*, edited by David Doyel, pp. 87–100. Maxwell Museum of Anthropology Anthropological Papers 5. University of New Mexico, Albuquerque.

Stein, John R., Judith E. Suiter, and Dabney Ford
1997 High Noon in Old Bonito: Sun, Shadow, and the Geometry of the Chaco Complex. In *Anasazi Architecture and American Design*, edited by Baker T. Morrow and V. B. Price, pp. 133–148. University of New Mexico Press, Albuquerque

Van Dyke, Ruth M.
1999 The Andrews Community: An Early Bonito Phase Chacoan Outlier in the Red Mesa Valley, New Mexico. *Journal of Field Archaeology* 26(1):55–67.

2002 The Chacoan Great Kiva in Outlier Communities: Investigating Integrative Spaces across the San Juan Basin. *Kiva* 67(3):231–248.

2003 Memory and the Construction of Chacoan Society. In *Archaeologies of Memory*, edited by Ruth M. Van Dyke and Susan E. Alcock, pp. 180–200. Blackwell, Oxford.

2004a Chaco's Sacred Geography. In *In Search of Chaco Canyon*, edited by David Grant Noble, pp. 78–85. School of American Research Press, Santa Fe.

2004b Memory, Meaning, and Masonry: The Late Bonito Chacoan Landscape. *American Antiquity* 69:413–431.

2008 *Experiencing Chaco: Landscape and Ideology at the Center Place.* School of Advanced Research Press, Santa Fe, in press.

Van Dyke, Ruth M., and Susan E. Alcock
2003 Introduction. In *Archaeologies of Memory*, edited by Ruth M. Van Dyke and Susan E. Alcock, pp. 1–30. Blackwell, Oxford.

Van Dyke, Ruth M., and Robert P. Powers
2002 Interpretations and Conclusions. In *An Archaeological Survey of the Additions to Chaco Culture National Historic Park*, edited by Ruth M. Van Dyke. Chaco Center Publications in Archaeology, National Park Service, Santa Fe. Ms. on file, Chaco Culture National Historical Park, New Mexico.

Vivian, Gordon
1940 *Southwestern National Monuments Supplement* (February):127–130.

Vivian, Gordon, and Paul Reiter
1960 *The Great Kivas of Chaco Canyon and Their Relationships.* Monographs of the School of American Research and the Museum of New Mexico 22. Santa Fe.

Vivian, R. Gwinn, Dulce N. Dodgen, and Gayle Harrison Hartmann
1978 *Wooden Ritual Artifacts from Chaco Canyon, New Mexico: The Chetro Ketl Collection.* Anthropological Papers of the University of Arizona 32. University of Arizona Press, Tucson.

Williamson, Ray A.
1984 *Living the Sky.* Houghton Mifflin, Boston.

Williamson, Ray A., Howard J. Fisher, and Donnel O'Flynn
1977 Anasazi Solar Observatories. In *Native American Astronomy*, edited by Anthony F. Aveni, pp. 203–218. University of Texas Press, Austin.

Wills, W. H., and Thomas C. Windes
1989 Evidence for Population Aggregation and Dispersal during the Basketmaker III period in Chaco Canyon, New Mexico. *American Antiquity* 54:347–369.

Wilshusen, Richard H.
1989 Unstuffing the Estufa: Ritual Floor Features in Anasazi Pit Structures and Pueblo Kivas. In *The Architecture of Social Integration in Prehistoric Pueblos*, edited by William D. Lipe and Michelle Hegmon, pp. 89–111. Occasional Papers of the Crow Canyon Archaeological Center 1, Cortez, Colorado.

Wilshusen, Richard H., and Scott G. Ortman
1999 Rethinking the Pueblo I Period in the San Juan Drainage: Aggregation, Migration, and Cultural Diversity. *Kiva* 64:369–399.

125

Wilshusen, Richard H., and Ruth M. Van Dyke
2006   Chaco's Beginnings. In *Archaeology of Chaco Canyon: An Eleventh-Century Pueblo Regional Center*, edited by Stephen H. Lekson, pp. 211–259. School of American Research Press, Santa Fe.

Wilshusen, Richard H., and C. Dean Wilson
1995   Reformatting the Social Landscape in the Late Pueblo I–Early Pueblo II Period: The Cedar Hill Data in Regional Context. In *The Cedar Hill Special Treatment Project: Late Pueblo I, Early Navajo, and Historic Occupations in Northwestern New Mexico*, compiled by Richard H. Wilshusen, pp. 43–80. La Plata Archaeological Consultants, Research Paper 1. Dolores, Colorado.

Windes, Thomas C.
1975   Excavation of 29SJ423, An Early Basketmaker III Site in Chaco Canyon: Preliminary Report of the Architecture and Stratigraphy. Ms. on file, Division of Cultural Research, National Park Service, Albuquerque.

2006   *Early Puebloan Occupations in the Chaco Region: Excavations and Survey of Basketmaker III and Pueblo I Sites, Chaco Canyon, New Mexico.* Reports of the Chaco Center 13.

Branch of Cultural Research, National Park Service, Santa Fe, in press.

Windes, Thomas C., and Dabney Ford
1992   The Nature of the Early Bonito Phase. In *Anasazi Regional Organization and the Chaco System*, pp. 75–86, edited by David E. Doyel. Maxwell Museum of Anthropology Anthropological Papers 5. University of New Mexico, Albuquerque.

Windes, Thomas C., Rachel M. Anderson, Brian K. Johnson, and Cheryl A. Ford
2000   Sunrise, Sunset: Sedentism and Mobility in the Chaco East Community. In *Great House Communities across the Chacoan Landscape*, edited by John Kantner and Nancy Mahoney, pp. 39–59. Anthropological Papers of the University of Arizona 65. University of Arizona Press, Tucson.

Woods, Janet McC.
1934   Excavation of the Court Kiva, Chetro Ketl. Ms. on file, NPS Chaco Archives, University of New Mexico, Albuquerque.

Young, M. Jane
1988   *Signs from the Ancestors: Zuni Cultural Symbolism and Perceptions of Rock Art.* University of New Mexico Press, Albuquerque.

Ruth M. Van Dyke

5

Architectural Studies of Pueblo Bonito

The Past, the Present, and the Future

Jill E. Neitzel

As the largest of the numerous ruins in Chaco Canyon, Pueblo Bonito drew the attention of the first archaeologists who visited the area in the latter part of the nineteenth century. With its multistory walls of fine masonry and its extensive rubble mound, Pueblo Bonito appeared to be a stunning architectural achievement in this remote and desolate canyon (Figure 5.1). Large-scale excavations were initiated by the turn of the century with the purpose of revealing and mapping the building's impressive architecture and, perhaps just as important, recovering the rich artifacts that were assumed to lie buried within its walls. In this paper I focus on Pueblo Bonito's architecture. My goal is to present an overview of what has been learned about the structure after more than a century of study and to identify productive directions for future research.

The history of architectural studies at Pueblo Bonito can be divided into two periods. The first, which began with a brief reconnaissance report in 1850 and culminated with a profusely illustrated, 349-page opus in 1964, was marked by the site's excavation, basic documentation, and dating. The second period began in the final decades of the twentieth century and continues today. Its primary concern has been to use intensive studies of various aspects of both Pueblo Bonito's architecture

and its broader context to learn about the people who built and used the structure. The division between these two periods signifies a shift in priorities, not a complete replacement of interests. The early tasks of mapping and dating, for example, continue to be pursued today, and the more recent preoccupation with using architecture to learn about Chacoan society has roots in earlier efforts. A third period of architectural studies will undoubtedly be defined in the future as researchers continue to address long-standing questions and begin to identify and investigate new ones.

Maps, Reconstructions, and Dates

Basic documentation of Pueblo Bonito has included lengthy descriptions, detailed maps, artists' reconstructions, and fine-grained chronological analyses. This research dominated the first period of architectural studies and has been the subject of ongoing revisions in the second period.

The Early Period

Investigations of Pueblo Bonito began when several exploring expeditions passed through Chaco Canyon during the second half of the nineteenth century. In a report on a military reconnaissance, Lt. James H. Simpson (1850), with the assistance

FIGURE 5.1. Detail of distance view of north wall of unexcavated Pueblo Bonito, 1896. (Courtesy of American Museum of Natural History Library, AMNH 17772, photograph by Granger, Wortman Paleontological Expedition)

of Richard and Edward Kern, published the ruin's first description and a map (see Hine 1962:75–76). Almost three decades later, a report on a geological survey included another description and map along with a reconstruction of what Pueblo Bonito had looked like (Figures 5.2 and 5.3; Jackson 1878). Based on examinations of Pueblo Bonito's surface remains, the two early maps depicted a D-shaped structure comprising rectangular rooms and circular kivas and fronted by two mounds.

Intensive studies of Pueblo Bonito's architecture began in 1896 when the first of two large-scale excavation projects was initiated at the site. The three-year-long Hyde Exploring Expedition, which

FIGURE 5.2. Reconstruction of Pueblo Bonito by William Henry Jackson (1878: Plate LXXII).

Jill E. Neitzel

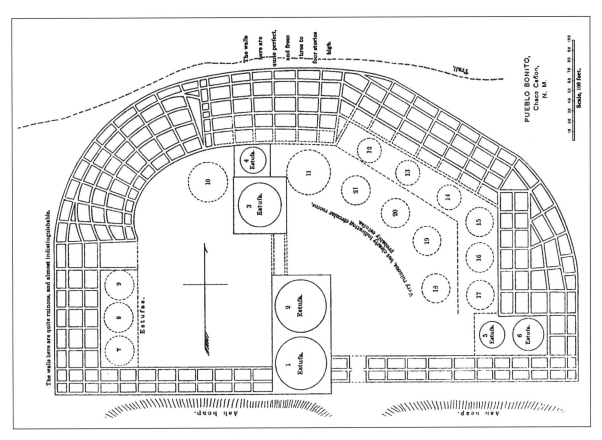

FIGURE 5.3. Plan of Pueblo Bonito by William Henry Jackson (1878).

was sponsored by the American Museum of Natural History, is best known for the bounty of rare and valuable artifacts recovered from a complex of rooms containing burials and ritual caches (Pepper 1905, 1909). In his final report, published 21 years after the project's completion, field director George Pepper (1920) included the first subsurface map of Pueblo Bonito, showing the locations of 198 excavated rooms and kivas as well as other rooms and kivas discerned from surface remains (Figure 5.4). The text consisted of room-by-room descriptions of architectural features and recovered artifacts and a multi-page table listing the dimensions of each excavated room. In his discussion Pepper (1920:375) also noted the presence of two types of masonry—an older one with "undressed stones" forming "purely utilitarian walls" and a later one with "carefully shaped blocks with faced surfaces...laid in varying combination" with the "effect being aesthetic."

Shortly after the publication of Pepper's report, the National Geographic Society in partnership with the Smithsonian Institution undertook a second major excavation project. This endeavor lasted six years (1921–1927) and was followed decades later by a two-volume report by project director Neil Judd. The first volume focused on the site's material culture (Judd 1954) and the second on its architecture (Judd 1964). The time lags in the publication of both Pepper's and Judd's reports are a testament to the overwhelming amount of information recovered during both projects.

Judd's (1964) second volume made seminal contributions to the study of Pueblo Bonito's architecture. In addition to his detailed descriptions of all architectural features, Judd produced a multi-page map of virtually all of the building's rooms and kivas (Figure 5.5), the two mounds outside the front wall, and the extensive foundation complex to the east. Judd also commissioned architect Kenneth Conant to transform the project's architectural data into a series of images of what the building looked like at its peak (see Figure 7.4).

129

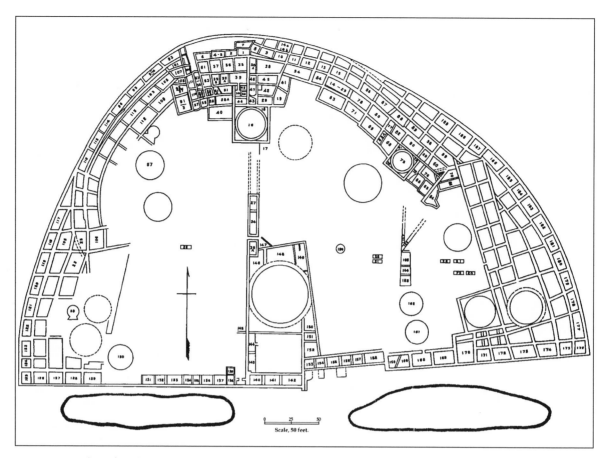

FIGURE 5.4. Plan of Pueblo Bonito by George Pepper (1920).

Judd's most important contribution may have been his delineation of Pueblo Bonito's chronology. Beneath the building's west court, Judd (1954:3, 29, 31, 1964:22, 57, Figure 7) uncovered two pit-structures, which he dated to the Basketmaker III or Pueblo I periods (pre-800), along with a lone ponderosa pine tree, which he did not date. For Pueblo Bonito proper Judd (1964:22) defined two major construction stages. He distinguished these stages, as well as subdivisions within the second, primarily on the basis of distinctive masonry styles (Figure 5.6), whose major types had been noted previously by Pepper (1920:375). Old Bonito, with its relatively crude masonry, was a crescent-shaped cluster of 152 rooms dendrochronologically dated to 828–935 (Judd 1964:51). Constructed with more sophisticated masonry, Late Bonito completed Pueblo Bonito's D-shaped plan. Large roomblocks were added to each end of the original crescent and were then connected by an east-west room wall that enclosed the plaza. Judd (1964:22,

51) estimated that Late Bonito contained 499 rooms, and he used tree-ring dates to place their construction between 1011 and 1126.

Recent Research

The dominant interests of the first period of architectural studies have continued to receive attention as more chronological data have been collected and analyzed. Twenty-two years after Judd published his sequence, Stephen Lekson (1986:109–144) proposed its first significant revisions. Based on his analyses of more than twice as many tree-ring dates as had been reported by Judd (1964:35–38), along with information on masonry styles, stratigraphy, wall abutments, and layout, Lekson identified and mapped seven major construction stages, beginning at 920 and ending after 1085 (Figure 5.7).

Lekson's (1986) sequence was in turn modified by other researchers (e.g., Stein et al. 2003; Windes 2003; Windes and Ford 1996). After analyzing 390 newly collected tree-ring dates Thomas Windes

Jill E. Neitzel

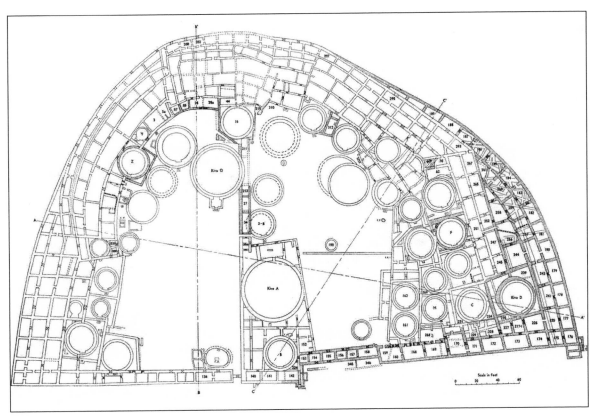

FIGURE 5.5. Plan of Pueblo Bonito by Oscar B. Walsh, 1925. (Adapted by Stein, Ford, and Friedman 2003: Figure 4.6 from Judd 1964: Figures 2–6, courtesy of the authors)

and Dabney Ford (1996) pushed Pueblo Bonito's earliest dated construction event back 60 years to 860.[1] In their opinion the building's initial construction was probably even earlier, given its oldest cutting date of 828, which is the date that Judd (1964) used for the start of his sequence.

In another study, Windes (2003) delineated Pueblo Bonito's extremely complex occupational history, showing how the structure's growth was not the orderly process that might be inferred by looking at the stage-by-stage floor plans. As new construction occurred, portions of previous building were variously repaired, remodeled, abandoned, filled with trash, dismantled, and reused. In the same paper Windes (2003) also extended the dates of Pueblo Bonito's demise. His analyses of tree-ring and archaeomagnetic dates in conjunction with masonry style and ceramic data showed how final construction with tree beams in 1129 was followed by a marked decline in site use through the mid-1100s and into the 1200s. Complete abandonment in the 1300s was marked by a

variety of termination and closure rituals, including widespread burning, the addition of a rubble veneer to Great Kiva A, and the erasure of gylphs on the canyon wall (Stein et al. 2003:56; Windes 2003:30).

These chronological revisions have led to modifications in Pueblo Bonito's stage-by-stage maps (e.g., Stein et al. 2003: Figures 4.13, 4.15, 4.17, 4.19, 4.22; Windes 2003: Figures 3.4–3.7, 3.9–3.11) and to renewed attempts to reconstruct what Pueblo Bonito looked like in three dimensions. The most recent reconstruction by John Stein and his colleagues (2003) depicts the site not just at its peak (Figures 5.8 and 5.9), as in previous efforts, but also at four earlier points in its history.

SOCIAL AND BEHAVIORAL INTERPRETATIONS

The primary concern of the second period of architectural studies has been to learn about the people who built and used Pueblo Bonito. Following on brief comments by Judd (1954, 1964), recent

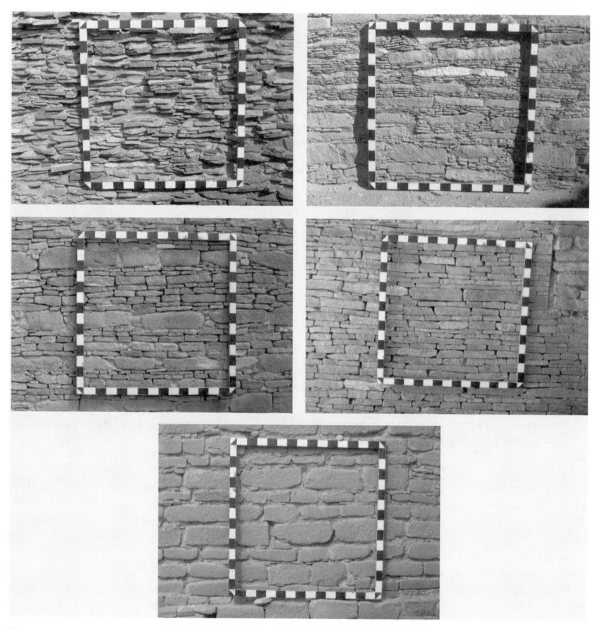

FIGURE 5.6. Five masonry veneer styles used at Pueblo Bonito, from earliest to latest: top left, Type I; top right, Type II; middle left, Type III; middle right, Type IV; bottom, McElmo. 75 cm scale. (Courtesy of Chaco Culture National Historical Park, Chaco Archives, negs. 20009, 19960, 19987, 19994, 19981; photographs by Stephen H. Lekson)

investigations have been numerous and extremely diverse. Most have been directed toward understanding the structure's function, but a few have also produced insights into the organization and size of Pueblo Bonito's resident population.

Judd's Views

In his limited social and behavioral interpretations, Judd (1954:17, 325, 1964:22) called Pueblo Bonito a ruined town that at its peak housed as many as 1,000 people. He emphasized the structure's utilitarian purpose, stating that shelter and subsistence, not building monumental religious structures nor commemorating past leaders, were the primary concerns of its residents (Judd 1964:22). Judd (1954:18–19, 36, 1964:22) saw these residents as consisting of two groups whose presence was signified by the two masonry styles that he associated

Jill E. Neitzel

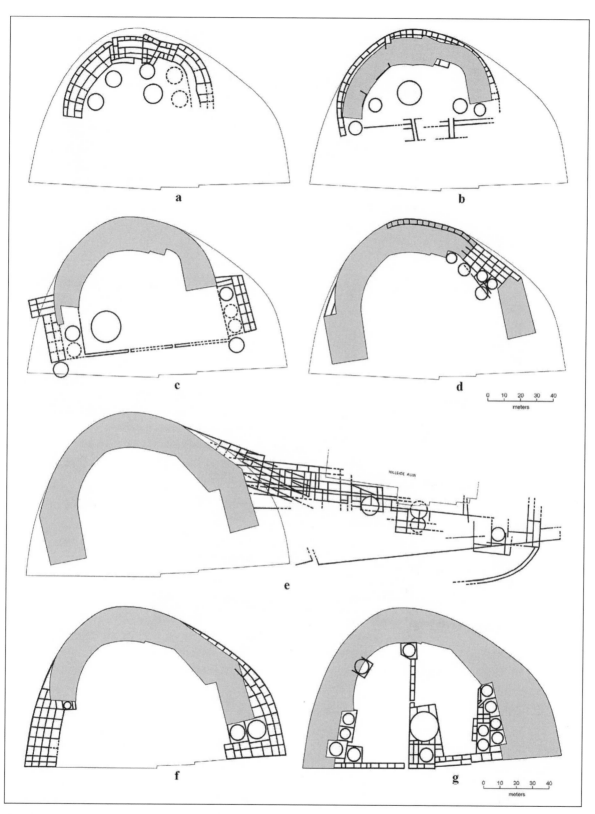

FIGURE 5.7. Floor plans of Pueblo Bonito's major construction stages as defined by Lekson: (a) Stage I, 920–935; (b) Stage II, 1040–1050; (c) Stage III, 1050–1060; (d) Stage IV, 1060–1075; (e) Stage V, 1070–1075; (f) Stage VI, 1075–1085; (g) Stage VII, post-1085. . (Adapted from Lekson 1986: Figure 4.20a–g)

133

CONSTRUCTION STAGE V
A.D. 1115 - 1250

FIGURE 5.8. Reconstruction of Pueblo Bonito proper between 1115 and 1250 (Stein, Ford, and Friedman 2001: Figure 4.23, courtesy of the authors). Note that Stein et al.'s (2003) stage numbers are different from those of Lekson (1986).

PUEBLO BONITO
CONSTRUCTION STAGE V
A.D. 1115 - 1250

FIGURE 5.9. Reconstruction of all of Pueblo Bonito, 1115–1250. (Stein, Ford, and Friedman 2001: Figure 4.24, courtesy of the authors)

with Old and Late Bonito. He described the Old Bonitians as Pueblo Bonito's stubbornly conservative founders and the Late Bonitians as progressive immigrants who lived side-by-side with the Old Bonitians. According to Judd, the Late Bonitians completed Pueblo Bonito's construction and created classic Chaco culture. He also thought that the Late Bonitians were the first to abandon the

Jill E. Neitzel

building, leaving the Old Bonitians as its sole occupants once again.

Function

Most of the numerous social and behavioral interpretations made since Judd's initial comments have been concerned primarily with Pueblo Bonito's role as an elite residence and ceremonial center. Two approaches have been used to assess the residential function. One has involved the identification of habitation rooms based on the presence of hearths and other domestic features; the other has focused on the distribution of habitation suites based on the layout of living and storage rooms (Bernadini 1999; Bustard 2003; Windes 1984). These studies have shown that Pueblo Bonito was a residence throughout its history but that this role was primary only during the structure's initial stage (860–935) (Bustard 2003:91, 92). By 1050, ceremonial functions became paramount and remained so for the rest of the structure's use-life (Bustard 2003; Cooper 1995).

Pueblo Bonito's ceremonial role has been explored through a variety of architectural analyses. The structure evidently had religious significance from the start, as indicated by the relationship between its initial construction and both the lone pine tree and the two pitstructures excavated by Judd (1964). Tom Windes (2003:20) has dated the pine tree to the early part of the 700s and the pitstructures to sometime during that century. How the tree came to grow where it did is unknown, but its presence was so remarkable that it may have been imbued with great symbolic meaning (Windes 2003:20). John Stein and his colleagues (2003:59) believe that the tree was one reason why the builders of both the pitstructures and Pueblo Bonito chose this location. According to Stein et al. (2003:46, 56, Figure 4.13), both the tree and the pitstructures (or their remains) would have been visible to Pueblo Bonito's first builders, whose Stage I construction was done on the eighth-century ground surface. Stein et al. (1997:133–134) also think that the tree was incorporated into Pueblo Bonito's design through successive construction stages.

The most obvious evidence for Pueblo Bonito's ceremonial purpose is its small and great kivas, which were the settings for religious ceremonies (Lekson 1986:142–143; Pepper 1920:375–376; Van Dyke, Chapter 4, this volume; Vivian and Reiter 1960:63–71; see Adler 1989, 1993, and Lekson 1988:128 for alternate interpretations of kiva function). Estimates of the numbers of small kivas range from 33 (Powers 1984:29) to 60 (Windes, personal communication 2005), depending on how kiva reconstructions are counted. Small kivas were present throughout Pueblo Bonito's use-life, although their locations and characteristics changed. Estimates of the numbers of great kivas indicate a minimum of three or four (Van Dyke, Chapter 4, this volume; Powers 1984:29; Windes, personal communication 2005) with the possibility of more. The earliest well-dated great kiva was constructed between 900 and 950, and the latest in the 1100s (Van Dyke, Chapter 4, this volume). John Stein and his colleagues (2003:58) see a pattern in the construction and retirement of great kivas and find that the last use of the latest great kiva, sometime before 1250, was marked by termination and closure rituals.

In her calculations of the amount of labor used in initial kiva construction, Metcalf (2003) found that it was greatest during Stages III (1050–1060) and VII (post-1085). The Stage III peak reinforces the conclusion that the structure's primary function was becoming increasingly ceremonial (e.g., Bustard 2003; Windes 2003). The Stage VII peak evidences another change that has also been suggested by analyses of the structure's astronomical alignments (e.g., Farmer 2003). Recent research by Crown and Wills (2003) has shown that the total effort invested in kiva construction was even greater than Metcalf's calculations indicate. Crown and Wills document that both small and great kivas were systematically dismantled and rebuilt an average of two to four times. This process of ritual renewal undoubtedly reinforced the religious importance of these ceremonial chambers as well as of Pueblo Bonito as a whole.

A series of studies has documented Pueblo Bonito's astronomical alignments, providing further evidence of the site's ceremonial function (see Farmer 2003; Reyman 1976; Sofaer 1997 and Chapter 9, this volume; Williamson 1977, 1978, 1987a, 1987b; Zeilik 1984, 1986, 1987). John Stein and his colleagues (1997) have proposed that a north-south orientation was part of Pueblo

Bonito's earliest design in the 800s (also see Stein et al. 2003:46, 57), and James Farmer (2003: Figure 5.2) has shown that subsequent Stage II construction between 1040 and 1050 was aligned with the summer solstice. Cardinal alignments are most apparent in two additions made during Pueblo Bonito's final construction after 1085 (Stage VII), the time of one of Metcalf's peaks in kiva construction. A new north-south row of rooms bisected the plaza and traced the azimuth of the midday sun, and a new east-west row of rooms enclosed the plaza and could be used to mark the mid-year equinoxes (see Farmer 2003:64–65). By marking the passage of time on a daily and sea-sonal basis, Pueblo Bonito's various astronomical alignments undoubtedly played an important role in the Chacoan ceremonial calender. They proba-bly also encoded deeper meanings about the importance of the sun, the cardinal directions, and the moon in Chacoan religion.

Symmetrical patterns in Pueblo Bonito's archi-tecture provide more evidence of Chacoan reli-gious beliefs (Fritz 1978, 1987; Stein et al. 1997, 2003:46, 58). The most obvious symmetry is the division of the plaza into two halves. Other exam-ples include the stage-by-stage expansion of the building's initial D shape, the juxtaposition of the original north-central section with the platform housing Great Kiva A, the location of two great kivas on either side of the north-south axis, and the successive retirement and replacement of great kivas counterclockwise around a center point. These symmetrical relationships probably encode messages about ritual space and time as well other esoteric knowledge (Stein et al. 1997, 2003).

Recent architectural analyses have suggested that, in addition to being an elite residence and a ceremonial center, Pueblo Bonito was also a stor-age facility. Storage rooms were clearly associated with habitation rooms in the structure's initial stage (Bustard 2003:91). It is plausible that the large suites of featureless, spatially segregated rooms built beginning around 1075 (Stage VI) were also used for storage. An alternate interpre-tation is that these roomblocks were built to give Pueblo Bonito a more dramatic exterior appear-ance (see Stein et al., Chapter 8, this volume). A storage function can be argued more strongly for the built-in platforms found in eight rooms, dating

mostly to Stage III (1050–1060) (see Figure 2.6; Bustard 2003:84).

Organization

Recent architectural analyses have revealed less about the organization of the people who built and used Pueblo Bonito than about the structure's function. One intriguing study by Dee Hudson (1972) showed that different measurement systems were used in the Stage VI (1075–1085) east and west wings, suggesting the presence of two groups in a part of the site that Judd associated with the Late Bonitians.

Another approach to using architecture to look at organization has been to measure Pueblo Bonito's various raw materials and labor require-ments for construction. William Lumpkins (1984:20) estimated that Pueblo Bonito contained 1,000,000 dressed stones obtained from as much as 100,000,000 pounds of rock. Equally impressive are Tom Windes and Dabney Ford's (1996:297) calculations that Pueblo Bonito's construction involved 50,000 tree beams, which in later con-struction stages were transported from distant sources (Betancourt et al. 1986). Based on her efforts to quantify the labor used to construct Pueblo Bonito, Mary Pat Metcalf (2003) con-cluded that the building was a monumental struc-ture that required both substantial labor and a stratified political organization to complete. It is important to note again that Metcalf's calculations were based only on initial construction effort. Had she included data on the frequent dismantling and rebuilding of rooms and kivas (Crown and Wills 2003:527–528; Windes 2003), her conclusions about substantial labor and a stratified political organization could have been stated even more emphatically.

Population

Judd's (1954:325, 1964:22) estimate that Pueblo Bonito housed 1,000 people was lower than the 1,200 figure proposed previously by Pierson (1949),[2] and the numbers generated from subse-quent architectural studies have been even lower. The lowest has been 70 people (Bernardini 1999) with a series of others between the two extremes (Drager 1976; Hayes et al. 1981; Neitzel 2003a:8–9, 2003c:147–148; Windes 1984, 2003:32). Recent analyses of the distributions of domestic features and habitation suites have revealed that Pueblo Bonito contained only a small number of households (Bernardini 1999; Bustard 2003; Windes 1984). Although Reyman (1987, 1989) has claimed that Pueblo Bonito contained more hearths than were recorded during the site's excavations, it is unlikely that these "missing" features would have been sufficiently numerous to undermine the conclusion that not many people ever lived within the building. The current consensus is that the resident population never exceeded more than several hundred people (Neitzel 2003c:147–148; for more specific, lower estimates see Bernardini 1999 and Windes 1984, 2003:32). According to Windes (2003:32), this peak was reached either in the 800s–900s, during the structure's initial occupation, or in the 1100s, after major construction ended.

CONTEXTUAL COMPARISONS

Despite the tremendous insights that architectural studies have revealed about Pueblo Bonito's function and to a lesser extent about its organization and population, a fuller understanding of these issues requires that the structure be considered within its broader context. One productive approach to contextual analysis is to examine Pueblo Bonito's architecture in relation to its location and the architecture of other great houses. Another is to compare the results of Pueblo Bonito's architectural analyses with those of other studies—most notably, recent mortuary and artifact analyses at Pueblo Bonito and other Chacoan sites.

Function

Contextual comparisons can broaden our understanding of Pueblo Bonito's ceremonial role and can suggest additional functions as well. For example, two aspects of Pueblo Bonito's location support the conclusion that the structure had a ceremonial function. First, Pueblo Bonito was built next to Threatening Rock, a 30-m-high, 22,000-metric-ton sandstone monolith, which in 1941, roughly 600 years after the structure was abandoned, fell and crushed the ruin's northeast section (Figure 5.10). Given the reverence contemporary Native Americans give to unique features on the

FIGURE 5.10. Threatening Rock in 1901, four decades before its collapse. (Photograph by Charles Loomis, courtesy of Palace of the Governors [MNM/DCA], neg. 6153)

landscape, Anne Marshall (2003:12) has argued that Pueblo Bonito was deliberately located next to Threatening Rock because of the rock's religious significance, a reasoning that could also be applied to the lone pine tree. In fact, the proximity of both features may have heightened the holiness of this place (Stein et al. 2003:59).

Another possibly religious aspect of Pueblo Bonito's location is its placement roughly in the middle of Chaco Canyon. Anne Marshall (2003:13) has proposed that the canyon's position at the approximate center of the San Juan Basin may make it the symbolic center of the world and perhaps even "the place where Puebloan people emerged from beneath the earth into this world." If true, then Pueblo Bonito's presence at the center of the center must have imbued the structure with sacred meanings.

Pueblo Bonito's location may have also had several practical benefits. For example, both Anne Marshall (2003:12) and Neil Judd (1925:245, 1964:34) have suggested that this place was ideal for defense because it offered a panoramic view in all directions except north, where visibility was blocked by the canyon wall. The siting of Pueblo Alto on the cliff top may have served to protect Pueblo Bonito's blind side. Being situated against the canyon wall did have two advantages—shelter from northerly winds and solar heating during the winter (Lumpkins 1984:20; Marshall 2003:11). In addition to heightened visibility, Pueblo Bonito's position opposite South Gap also offered two other benefits. One was easy access to the south, which could have been important for travel both to and from the structure by traders and religious pilgrims. This location also allowed a framed view of Pueblo Bonito when it was approached from the south (Marshall 2003:12; Stein and Lekson 1992: Figure 8-9).[3] Some researchers would argue that this enhancement to the structure's appearance may have been intended to impress religious pilgrims and thus may have added to Pueblo Bonito's role as a ceremonial center (Jordan 2002; Judge 1989).

Comparisons of Pueblo Bonito's architecture with that of other great houses offer further insights into the building's ceremonial function. Among all great houses, Pueblo Bonito had the greatest combined total of small and great kivas (Powers 1984:29), indicating that it was the preeminent ceremonial center. Furthermore, ceremonies at Pueblo Bonito and other great houses may have been linked. Not only are Pueblo Bonito's astronomical alignments present at other great houses (Sofaer 1997 and Chapter 9, this volume; Williamson 1987b), but James Farmer (2003) has argued that astronomical events at multiple sites structured a coordinated program of rituals. For example, based on the relative timing of solstice events, Farmer has described how a ritual procession could have begun with observances at the isolated great kiva of Casa Rinconada, then traveled two-thirds of a kilometer directly north for further observances at Pueblo Bonito, and then continued more than 6 km up the canyon, perhaps with stops in between, to Fajada Butte and its famous sun dagger. Farmer (2003:62–65, Figure 5.4; reproduced here as Figure 5.11) has also argued that the engraved spiral at Fajada Butte had great symbolic meaning for ancestral Puebloans, and that the spiral and its meaning were embedded in Pueblo Bonito's design.

Another role—as a mausoleum—can be added to the list of Pueblo Bonito's functions when the results of mortuary analyses are used for contextual comparisons. More than 500 burials and perhaps another 100 individuals represented by incomplete remains have been excavated from sites in Chaco Canyon (Akins 1986: Table 2.1, Table B.1; and personal communication, 2003). Of these, at least 131 individuals were recovered from Pueblo Bonito (Akins 2003:94). With the exception of a few isolated infants and miscellaneous bones, virtually all of Pueblo Bonito's burials were recovered from two sets of four rooms each in the northern and western sections of Old Bonito. Presumably, ceremonies were conduced each time a burial or offering was added to one of the room groups, and these rituals undoubtedly reinforced Old Bonito's ceremonial importance as well as that of the entire structure.

One controversial interpretation of these burials may be relevant to investigations of the kinds of ceremonies that were conducted at Pueblo Bonito. Based on their examination of recovered skeletons and the disturbed contexts in which they were found, Christy and Jacqueline Turner (1999:111–131) concluded that human sacrifice and cannibalism were practiced at the site (see

Pepper 1920:378 for an earlier suggestion of cannibalism). This claim has been rejected by others (e.g., Akins 2003:104–105; Martin et al. 2001:21), who argue that the bone damage was postmortem and that looters caused disturbance within burial rooms. While claims about human sacrifice and cannibalism continue to be debated, researchers do agree that one of the site's two most lavishly interred individuals died from wounds to his head and left thigh (Akins 2003:97). The circumstances of this man's death and how they contributed to his elaborate mortuary treatment remain a mystery (Akins 2003:103). However, the injuries do provide clear evidence that violence was a part of Chacoan life even if human sacrifice and ritual cannibalism were not.

Artifacts offer further information on Pueblo Bonito's various functions. For example, studies of decorated ceramics have shown that both burial room groups began to be used as mortuaries around 1020 and that this function continued until at least 1100–1150 (Akins 2003:105). Also, the uneven distributions of various artifact types support the view that Pueblo Bonito was a ceremonial center and that the north-central section of Old Bonito was its sacred precinct (Neitzel 2003b; Pepper 1920). In addition to the numerous artifacts recovered from the northern burial room group, ritual caches were also found in other nearby rooms. The most notable is Room 28, which is adjacent to the northern burial room group and which contained the site's highest quantities of ceramic cylinder vessels, sandstone jar covers, and whole ceramic jars as well as a variety of other artifacts in lesser quantities. Other nearby rooms each contained the site's highest quantities of different artifact types—groundstone (Room 42), projectile points (Room 39), jet (Room 38), pipes (Room 10), and fossil shell (Room 12)—as well as smaller numbers of other kinds of artifacts. Elsewhere I have suggested that the presence of these same artifacts in lesser quantities in other parts of the site may also represent ritual deposits (Neitzel 2003b).

Another function that can be deduced from Pueblo Bonito's artifacts is that the structure was a major destination for a variety of valuable, long-distance trade goods, including macaws and parrots from as far south as lowland Mexico, copper from northern Mexico, shell from the Gulf of

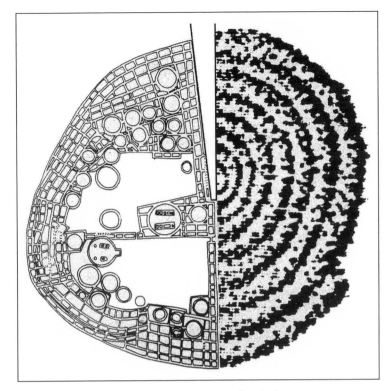

FIGURE 5.11. Pueblo Bonito plan juxtaposed with the Fajada Butte summer solstice sun dagger. (Farmer 2003: Figure 5.4, courtesy of James Farmer, Virginia Commonwealth University)

California and the Pacific Coast, and turquoise from a variety of sources throughout the northern Southwest (Mathien 2003). In comparison with other sites, both Chacoan and non-Chacoan, Pueblo Bonito received significantly greater quantities of these imports (Neitzel 1989b). For example, with its more than 50,000 pieces of turquoise, Pueblo Bonito contained more than four times the amount of turquoise reported for all other Southwestern sites combined (Snow 1973:35). This preeminent position holds to a lesser degree for other imports as well. Within Chaco Canyon, Pueblo Bonito is the site with the most macaws/parrots, copper, and shell (Neitzel 1989b:190–194). Among at least roughly contemporaneous sites outside the canyon, Pueblo Bonito is surpassed only by Wupatki for its quantities of exotic birds, and for all time periods only by the later site of Casas Grandes for its quantities of exotic birds, copper, and shell. Pueblo Bonito also received enormous quantities of more mundane goods such as tree beams (Betancourt, Dean, and Hull 1986; Dean and Warren

139

1983; Windes and Ford 1996; Windes and McKenna 2001), ceramics (Judd 1954:181–184, 234–235; also see Neitzel and Bishop 1990; Toll 1985; Toll and McKenna 1997), and lithics (Cameron 1984, 2001; Lekson 1997). Interestingly, although Pueblo Bonito received large quantities of a diversity of imports, it seems to have exported little. Thus, Pueblo Bonito did not function as a trading center in the usual sense.

Organization

The fairly limited conclusions drawn from architectural analyses about how the people who built and used Pueblo Bonito were organized can be greatly expanded through contextual comparisons. For example, just as Pueblo Bonito's position on the landscape gives the impression that it was at the center of the center, so too does its location relative to other great houses. Spatial comparisons with other great houses can be done at several embedded scales: in relation to its two nearest neighbors, Pueblo del Arroyo and Chetro Ketl (see Stein et al., Chapter 8); to the central canyon great houses (see Figure 9.2; Holley and Lekson 1999: 40; Lekson 1984:70–71, 1999:12; Neitzel 1989a: 512–513); to all canyon great houses; to the structures comprising the so-called Chaco halo (Doyel, Breternitz, and Marshall 1984; Wilcox 1999:130, 132); and finally to all great houses in the San Juan Basin and beyond (Lekson 1991; Marshall et al. 1979; Neitzel 1994; Powers, Gillespie, and Lekson 1983). At each of these levels, Pueblo Bonito is at the approximate geographic center, suggesting that its residents played a key role in the organization of Chacoan society.

This suggestion is confirmed and expanded by two other comparisons between Pueblo Bonito and other great houses. Size comparisons of all recorded great houses reveal a site hierarchy consisting of four tiers with Pueblo Bonito at the apex (Neitzel 1989a; cf. Powers 1984; Schelberg 1984). Labor comparisons of great houses constructed in Chaco Canyon also reveal a hierarchy with Pueblo Bonito at the top (Metcalf 1997, 2003: Table 6.3). These findings indicate that Pueblo Bonito's residents were the most important and powerful people within a stratified society. The four-tier size hierarchy is indicative of a degree of complexity seen cross-culturally in complex chiefdoms, and the fact that many great house construction projects in Chaco Canyon were undertaken simultaneously provides further evidence of the organizational capabilities of the stratified society that was centered on Pueblo Bonito.

Mortuary analyses provide a more detailed picture of this stratified society. The layout of the two burial room groups suggests the presence of two separate populations in the part of the site that Judd (1954:18–19, 36, 1964:22) associated with the Old Bonitians; and biological analyses by Nancy Akins (1986:75, 2003:101, 105) have shown that the two groups represent distinct populations of related individuals, probably members of two families. Furthermore, the individuals buried in the northern group were taller than their counterparts in the western group, who were in turn taller than those buried at small sites elsewhere in the canyon (Akins 1986:136; Stodder 1989:184–185). Individuals buried at small sites also exhibited more indications of iron-deficiency anemia. Altogether, these findings suggest that the individuals buried at Pueblo Bonito had a better diet than those buried at small sites (Akins 2003:100; Nelson et al. 1994:89, 97; Stodder 1989:79).

Grave good comparisons have demonstrated that these health differences can be attributed to the relative status of the different populations. Nancy Akins (1986:131–133, 2003:102–104) has documented a three-tier social hierarchy whose uppermost tier was represented by Pueblo Bonito's northern burial room group (Akins 1986:131–133, 2003:102–104). Two adult males in this group were interred with thousands of artifacts, most notably turquoise beads and other jewelry, as well as such rare and valuable objects as shell inlaid with turquoise, a shell trumpet, and a turquoise-covered cylindrical basket filled with turquoise and shell beads (Akins 1986:117, 163; Pepper 1909, 1920:163–177). Altogether, the burials in the northern burial room group contained roughly 17 times more artifacts than did those in the western burial group, which constituted the intermediate tier in the hierarchy (Neitzel 2003b: Figure 9.2). The lowest level consisted of burials from various small sites in the canyon. Comparisons of how old individuals were when they died with the kinds and quantities of artifacts that were buried with them indicate that status was ascribed at

Jill E. Neitzel

Pueblo Bonito and achieved at village sites (Akins 1986:132–133, 2003:102–104).

Mortuary analyses have also revealed some sort of organizational change at Pueblo Bonito. During the 130 years when the two burial room groups were actively used, the sex ratios in both groups shifted from predominantly male to female (Akins 1986:161–163; Neitzel 2000). The significance of this shift is not yet fully understood. Peter Peregrine (2001) has suggested that it reflects a transition to matrilineal descent and matrilocal residence, but this hypothesis has not been supported by recent biological analyses (Schillaci and Stojanowksi 2003).

Other analyses have shown that the individuals in Pueblo Bonito's two burial room groups are more closely related to each other than they are to the human remains from other canyon sites (Akins 2003:101). Interestingly, Pueblo Bonito's two groups are most similar to remains from different sites (Akins 1986:75). The northern group's remains are most similar to those from a site near Fajada Butte, whereas the western group's remains are most similar to those from the small site Bc59. These patterns suggest that Pueblo Bonito's two families may have had lineage or clan connections with the inhabitants of different small sites.

At an even larger spatial scale, the historical Puebloan populations with which Pueblo Bonito's two burial groups are most similar also differ (Schillaci, Ozolins, and Windes 2001). Individuals in the northern group most closely resemble individuals from two ancestral Zuni sites and one Hopi site, whereas those from the western group most closely resemble individuals from sites in the Rio Grande Valley. Michael Schillaci and his colleages (2001:142) have interpreted these associations as indicating that Pueblo Bonito's two families or clans were endogamous and that they traveled in different directions when the site was abandoned.

Population

In comparison with Pueblo Bonito's function and organization, contextual comparisons reveal less about the structure's population. For example, although the number of individuals interred within the structure is consistent with low population estimates, the burials themselves provide no definitive answer about the size of the resident population

(Akins 2003:104). Similarly, the burials say little about the numbers of pilgrims who may have gathered periodically at the site. When compared with human remains from five other major sites in the northern Southwest, Pueblo Bonito's crania were the least similar to the others (Lumpkins 1984:91). Based on the internal homogeneity and external distinctiveness of Pueblo Bonito's human remains, Nancy Akins (2003:105) concluded that "if there were pilgrims, and if any died while at Pueblo Bonito, ... they were not buried there."

Comparisons with other canyon great houses suggest that the view of Pueblo Bonito as never housing more than several hundred people should be qualified in two ways. First, Pueblo Bonito was not a settlement in and of itself. Rather, it was one structure, albeit the largest and most important, in a broader community whose boundaries have been vigorously debated by Chacoan archaeologists. At a minimum, this community encompassed Pueblo Bonito and its four closest great house neighbors, which together are referred to as the Pueblo Bonito complex or downtown Chaco (see Figure 9.2; Ashmore, Chapter 7; Stein et al., Chapter 8; Holley and Lekson 1999:40). Others argue that this community, which Lekson (in Holley and Lekson 1999:39) has called a proto-urban settlement, was even larger, including additional great houses (Neitzel 1989a:513) or perhaps the entire canyon and beyond (Lekson 1999:12; Wilcox 1999:130).

Depending on how its boundaries are defined, the population of this broader community may have been anywhere between 2,000 and 6,000 people (Neitzel 2003:148; for an even higher estimate, see Wilcox 1993). Pueblo Bonito's residents constituted only a small fraction of this total. Nevertheless, settlement pattern and burial analyses have shown that these people were the most powerful in Chacoan society and that their home was the most important place in the northern Southwest. Thus, the fact that Pueblo Bonito itself did not have many residents is not a reflection on the structure's preeminent role.

FUTURE RESEARCH DIRECTIONS

Architectural analyses have extensively documented Pueblo Bonito, dated its major construction stages, and provided insights into the structure's

141

function, the organization of the society that built and used it, and the size of its resident population. An even fuller understanding is achieved when the results of these investigations are interpreted with reference to the building's broader context. All of this knowledge raises the question of whether there are any aspects of Pueblo Bonito's architecture that remain to be studied. To answer this question, I queried a panel of 20 archaeologists who had previously conducted architectural research at the site. The list of their responses is surprisingly long.

No Excavations

Given the National Park Service's policy of site preservation, the future studies that are the most feasible are those requiring no further excavations. The list of suggestions is quite diverse, with the primary interests being Pueblo Bonito's appearance, construction and design, and function.

APPEARANCE

Richard Friedman, John Stein, and Karen Kievit want to do a complete, three-dimensional laser scan of Pueblo Bonito as it is today. Such a scan would provide an accurate model of the building, showing all floor levels, doors, windows, and other visible features. This information would have both practical and research value. As a management tool, the model would enable the National Park Service to closely monitor future changes in the building's condition. Researchers could use the model to gain insight into Pueblo Bonito's various components and how they "interact" with one another. For example, Karen Kievit suggests that a three-dimensional scan could help refine previous moment-in-time reconstructions (e.g., Kievit 1998; Stein et al. 2003). The computerized stage-by-stage models could then be used to examine the building from different viewing angles, both inside and outside, and to add individuals and groups of people at different places within the building (e.g., in open spaces, on roofs). These manipulations could provide new insights into Pueblo Bonito's appearance and also reveal where and at what distance people could have been visible within the structure's landscape.

Another perspective on Pueblo Bonito's appearance might be achieved by consulting Pueblo ethnographies and living descendants. According to Karen Kievit, a full understanding of architecture requires an appreciation of its significance for the humans who create and occupy it (see Saile 1990:57). In the absence of living Chacoan informants, she proposes two approaches. First, the available chronicles of Pueblo culture should be reexamined for what they say about architecture; and second, living descendants should be asked to "see and read" Pueblo Bonito as it has been reconstructed. Kievit recognizes the difficulties of relying on ethnographic analogy (see Cordell 1992:5); but she also thinks that ethnographies and living descendants might reveal alternative views of Pueblo Bonito's architecture and of the visual importance of its various components.

One gap in our understanding of Pueblo Bonito's appearance concerns the addition that was constructed directly behind the building's north wall and was buried in 1941 by the collapse of Threatening Rock. Whereas John Stein and his colleagues (2003: Figure 4.22) have dated this addition to 1115–1250, Gwinn Vivian thinks that it was erected earlier. Given the enormity of the covering debris, only archival sources can reasonably be used to investigate what lies beneath. Vivian suggests that a reexamination of a short report by John Keur (1933) might be informative. Another possibility proposed by Stephen Lekson is to investigate the rumored existence of a model of Pueblo Bonito purportedly produced by the WPA and used as an exhibit backdrop at the American Museum of Natural History. Such a model, if it ever existed, could provide a record of what was covered when Threatening Rock collapsed. Lekson would also like to systematically reexamine archival photographs of the northern addition as well as of Pueblo Bonito's two mounds. According to him, old photographs offer a potentially useful means of reconstructing those portions of the structure that were destroyed, rebuilt, or stabilized (or in the case of the mounds, plowed and trenched) during the historical period.

CONSTRUCTION AND DESIGN

Several researchers suggested Pueblo Bonito's construction and design as topics for future research. One set of studies concerns the building's raw materials. Anna Sofaer would like practical-minded archaeologists and builders of today to investigate the logistics of obtaining and processing building materials such as stone, timber, and adobe and then to theorize and test the methods that the Chacoans employed to erect and maintain this four-story structure.

Stephen Durand is especially interested in the sources of the stones used in Pueblo Bonito's walls. Determining whether they were quarried from a few nearby locations or obtained from throughout the canyon has implications for how the building's construction was organized. According to Durand, a related issue for further study is why a change in raw material occurred with McElmo style masonry. Earlier styles (Judd's I–IV) involved well-consolidated, bedded sandstone quarried somewhere on the mesa tops. The later, McElmo style was technically similar to its predecessors (Lekson 1986:17) but was characterized by a shift to massive sandstone from other sources. Durand states that alternative explanations for this style shift—including his own view that it was due to a depletion of available stone—need to be tested.

Michael Marshall identifies another unanswered question about Pueblo Bonito's masonry—whether it was meant to be seen. He suggests that at least some of the building's stonework was plastered with adobe and/or painted (also see Metcalf 2003:78). If future research demonstrates that significant portions of Pueblo Bonito's core-and-veneer walls were not visible, then archaeologists would need to reconsider long-held assumptions about the social significance of Chacoan masonry and its contribution to the appearance of Pueblo Bonito and other great houses.

John Stein proposes other materials as deserving further study. He would like to document how extensively adobe was used in constructing Pueblo Bonito's pavements, mounds, and other features and to investigate the use of layers of clean sand and of purposeful fill containing trash. Such fill was deliberately deposited in some interior rooms and in the northeast foundation complex, prompting Stein to wonder whether it may have had symbolic meaning.

For another perspective on Pueblo Bonito's construction, Marshall would like to quantify various aspects of its resulting form. One of his proposed projects is to continue Dee Hudson's (1972) search for standard units of measurement, noting that such an endeavor would benefit from consultations with mathematicians. Marshall wants to determine whether there are regularities in the sizes of the building's different components, such as its great kivas, small kivas, and rooms with different functions.

Another set of measurements proposed by Marshall involves comparisons of the volume of Pueblo Bonito's mass with that of its enclosed space. He characterizes the magnitude of the building's construction materials as immense, including the core and veneer of walls, the fill between kivas and their enclosures, and the fill above dome-shaped kiva roofs to make them flat. Marshall would like to compare the total volume of these materials to the total volume of the resulting enclosed space through time and in the building's different parts. The results would indicate whether construction during various stages was intended primarily for usable interior space or for an impressive exterior appearance.

To obtain further insights into Pueblo Bonito's design, Phillip Tuwaletstiwa wants to see more analyses of the structure's alignments, spatial patterns, and their embedded meanings. He thinks that additional astronomical alignments may be discovered, especially ones related to the lunar cycle. Tuwaletstiwa would also like the search for patterns and encoded symbolic meanings to be expanded beyond the building's floor plan to consider its vertical dimension as well. In addition he proposes further analyses of the connections between Pueblo Bonito's disparate elements to see how they integrate with one another to form a cultural landscape (e.g., the pine tree and the huge great kiva to the north of it). Tuwaletstiwa observes that some profoundly meaningful patterns may be subtle, noting the possible presence of a "golden section" formed by a square drawn around the structure's north-south wall and a rectangle drawn around the entire structure.

FUNCTION

The studies proposed by Marshall of Pueblo Bonito's volume and by Tuwaletstiwa of its alignments and spatial patterns could both contribute to a greater understanding of Pueblo Bonito's function. Other archaeologists advocate investigations

143

of particular structural features to determine their purpose. Wendy Bustard and Phil Tuwaletstiwa both think that proposed interpretations of Pueblo Bonito's big, empty rooms should be systematically evaluated. Bustard has interpreted their lack of features as indicating a possible storage function. In her view a worthwhile approach would be a cross-cultural study to see how and when other societies spend considerable effort on constructing empty space. Tuwaletstiwa, noting the rooms' honeycomb arrangement, describes them as dark, unventilated, and consequently unusable for cooking and other activities of daily life. He hypothesizes that the rooms' purpose was structural, serving to increase Pueblo Bonito's height and thus give it a more imposing exterior appearance.

Joan Mathien highlights the need for archival research to document another aspect of Pueblo Bonito's rooms—the numbers of hearths and other floor and wall features excavated by the Hyde Expedition. As noted previously, Jonathan Reyman (1987, 1989) has asserted that the project's field notes mention more hearths than were reported by Pepper (1920). Mathien would like to see that data published along with any other information that could be gleaned from field notes about features, especially those found in fall from upper story rooms. This information would not only clarify how Pueblo Bonito's function changed through time, it would also be useful for deriving more precise population estimates for each construction stage.

Inspired by Patty Crown and Chip Wills's (2003) work on remodeled kivas, Mike Marshall thinks that evidence of periodicity should be sought in the archival records of other features, such as modified rooms, superimposed fireplaces, and layered plaster. He would like to document the distribution of such evidence and then to address questions of frequency, intervals, and whether the periodicity was rhythmic or arrhythmic. According to Marshall, investigations of periodicity could offer clues as to the kinds of ceremonies that occurred at Pueblo Bonito, particularly those marking calendrical time.

Further Excavations

The suggested architectural studies that would require at least some further excavation at Pueblo Bonito are less feasible than nondestructive studies using photography or archival research given the National Park Service's site preservation policy. Nevertheless, the list compiled from my panel identifies important issues that targeted excavations could help resolve. These issues are concerned mainly with chronology and some of the structure's most notable features.

Basketmaker and Pueblo I structures: Both Ruth Van Dyke and Tom Windes would like to excavate Pueblo Bonito's earliest construction in order to date it more precisely and to understand its function more fully. Van Dyke is particularly interested in the pithouses reported by Judd (1964:22, 57, Figure 7) as lying beneath the plaza. She wonders whether these pithouses might be the remains of a Basketmaker community, noting that the Peñasco Blanco great house was sited in part to reference an earlier Basketmaker community.

Both Windes and Tuwaletstiwa think that Pueblo Bonito's initial Pueblo I roomblock should be reexcavated. Windes would like to examine the features in the rooms around Room 6, and Tuwaletstiwa would like to do the same for Room 28 and the four rooms comprising the adjacent burial room group. Both wonder whether these early rooms represent classic Pueblo I habitations or were part of a special use area from the start. Windes notes that documentation and comparison of the features in all early rooms would contribute to a better understanding of Pueblo Bonito's initial function.

Pithouses and Kivas: Both Van Dyke and Windes advocate investigations of the pithouses associated with Pueblo Bonito's initial Pueblo I roomblock. Windes is curious about how their spatial patterning compares with the layout of other Pueblo I communities, such as McPhee village. Van Dyke and Lekson would like to excavate the early, oversize pithouses, most notably the one in front of Old Bonito and below Kiva 2c, which both think may be a great kiva. According to Lekson, the enormous great kiva in the southwest plaza should also be excavated. Lekson thinks that this great kiva was the largest in the Chaco region, and Tuwaletstiwa suspects that it was related in some way to the pine tree. Van Dyke also notes the need for further investigations to determine exactly how many great kivas were present at Pueblo Bonito and what their construction sequences were. This latter information could help test John Stein's claim that great kiva construction occurred sequentially in a spiral pattern around Pueblo Bonito's plaza (Stein et al. 1997, 2003).

Mounds: Several researchers identify Pueblo Bonito's mounds as needing further study. Although the National Park Service's official policy is site preservation, Chip Wills has received permission to reexcavate trenches that Judd (1964) dug through the mounds. This project should help determine whether the mounds grew as a result of incremental trash deposition or one or more deliberate construction episodes. Evidence of deliberate construction would support the hypothesis, proposed by both Marshall and Tuwaletstiwa, that a primary concern in Pueblo Bonito's construction was creating mass for an impressive exterior appearance. Such evidence is also necessary for evaluating Stein's assertion that the mounds were "platforms" with structures on their tops (Stein et al. 2003:52). Stein and Marshall wonder whether the mounds' stratigraphy will reveal layers of adobe that could provide information on periodicity.

Foundation Complex: A perplexing question about Pueblo Bonito's architecture is the purpose of the northeast foundation complex. Stephen Plog would like to reexcavate the complex to determine whether it constitutes the foundations for unfinished construction or represents something else. Tuwaletstiwa suggests that the complex may be Pueblo Bonito's shadow image and that it could symbolize the top of the underworld.

Hillside Ruin: Van Dyke would like to see further excavations at Hillside Ruin, which is located immediately north of the foundation complex. This project would reveal whether the ruin is the remains of a 20- to 30-room pueblo, as described by Windes (2003:30–31), or a complex of platforms, as described by Stein and his colleagues (2003:55–56). According to Gwinn Vivian, excavations could also help clarify Hillside Ruin's temporal and spatial relationships to both Pueblo Bonito proper and the north addition. From a broader perspective, Van Dyke notes that further investigations at Hillside Ruin would contribute to a better understanding of McElmo-style architecture throughout the canyon.

Reuse: Mike Marshall proposes targeted excavations to investigate the timing and nature of Pueblo Bonito's reuse after abandonment. Reuse could be ceremonial, as indicated by repairs and late ceramics in kivas, or secular, as indicated by residential construction. The relative timing of these two types of reuse, either simultaneous or sequential, is important for understanding Pueblo Bonito's postabandonment role as a sacred place (Windes 2003:29–30).

The Broader Context

Some members of my panel believe that a fuller understanding of Pueblo Bonito's architecture requires comparisons with data collected from other Chacoan sites. The suggested "other site" projects that require no excavation are concerned primarily with cultural landscapes and alignments. The suggested excavation projects, which again are less feasible owing to preservation concerns, seek to broaden the availability of subsurface data from different kinds of settlements.

Landscapes and Alignments: Tuwaletstiwa would like to see more studies of how natural and constructed features were integrated to form Pueblo Bonito's cultural landscape. Examples of natural features include Fajada Butte, Threatening Rock, the pine tree, a cave to the north of Pueblo Bonito, and various rock formations associated with other great houses (see A. Marshall 2003:12–13). Examples of constructed features include other canyon great houses, roads, mounds, berms, ramps, scaffolds, staircases, and petroglyphs. Tuwaletstiwa describes the constructed features as having ceremonial functions and characterizes the cultural landscape formed by them and by natural features as being imbued with sacred meanings.

According to Tuwaletstiwa, one aspect of Pueblo Bonito's cultural landscape that deserves further study is the astronomical alignments within and between great houses (also see Sofaer, Chapter 9, this volume). The potential of such research is highlighted by the previously documented links between Pueblo Bonito, the Fajada Butte spiral petroglyph, which includes an image of Pueblo Bonito, and the solar and lunar events associated with both (see Farmer 2003). Lunar alignments are of particular interest to Tuwaletstiwa because, unlike solar alignments, they are not obviously related to agriculture, and because they rarely occur in prehistoric architecture. He notes that intra- and intersite lunar alignments have been documented at other great houses and at Fajada Butte (Malville, Eddy, and Ambruster 1991; Sofaer 1997; Sofaer, Sinclair, and Doggett 1982) and proposes that a systematic search for such alignments be undertaken to determine how extensively they occur.

One previously documented set of lunar alignments raises additional questions that Tuwaletstiwa would like to see studied. He describes how the three earliest canyon great houses exhibit a double alignment with the lunar standstill: Pueblo Bonito and Una Vida align with the southernmost extension of moonrise, and Pueblo Bonito and Peñasco Blanco align with the southernmost extension of moonset. Apparently, the three structures were built together according to a plan that was based on sophisticated astronomical knowledge and that probably had religious significance. This coordinated construction raises the question of who developed and implemented it. Were they indigenous Chacoan farmers? Or outsiders, such as the Toltecs, as proposed by Tuwaltetstiwa? These questions can only be answered by searching for astronomical alignments at earlier sites and by continuing to evaluate the evidence for a Mesoamerican presence in the canyon (e.g., McGuire 1980; Cobb, Maymon, and McGuire 1999).

Dennis Doxtater is also interested in further studies of the alignments and spatial patterns at Chacoan sites. According to him, the cardinally oriented great houses in Chaco Canyon comprise a design set that represents the Chacoan world. He also thinks that Canyon de Chelly in northeastern Arizona is Chaco Canyon's "nearly invisible twin." Doxtater proposes linking these ideas in a multiscalar analysis that would investigate whether Pueblo Bonito's floor plan and cross-section depict a microcosm or homolog of his diagram of the De Chelly cosmos (see Doxtater 2002, 2003a, 2003b).

More excavations: A recurring lament in discussions of the broader context of Pueblo Bonito's architecture is the paucity of excavation data from other Chacoan sites. Such data could provide a comparative framework for interpreting Pueblo Bonito's various features as well as its overall function. More excavations would also help alleviate a problem noted by Wills—the dualism between Pueblo Bonito and other great houses and between great houses and small sites that currently pervades Chacoan studies. At present, only one canyon great house, Pueblo Alto, has been excavated using contemporary standards (Windes 1987). Nominations for the next great house to be excavated include Hungo Pavi and Peñasco Blanco by Wendy Bustard and Wijiji by Stephen Durand. Barbara Mills would also like to see small sites added to the list, and Karen Kievit thinks that excavations should be conducted at great houses located outside the canyon as well.

A variety of comparisons could be done with excavation data from additional sites. Mills would like to compare Pueblo Bonito's room and kiva features with those at other great houses and small sites. Wesley Bernardini is especially interested in how the initial construction of Pueblo Bonito and other canyon great houses compares in layout, room sizes and features, and kivas. Wendy Bustard and Mike Marshall want to examine the great kivas and other features at additional great houses to determine whether the ritual renewal documented by Crown and Wills (2003) for Pueblo Bonito occurred elsewhere. Marshall also suggests extending the search for standard units of measurement to other great houses. Another proposal by Bernadini is to compare the excavation data from the mounds at Pueblo Bonito, Pueblo Alto (Windes 1987), and other great houses. Gwinn Vivian wants to compare the "envelope" of rooms backing Pueblo Bonito (Lekson's Stage II) with those at Peñasco Blanco, Chetro Ketl, and other great houses. Finally, Anne Marshall would like three-dimensional models to be made of additional great houses, adding to those by John Stein and his colleagues (2003, and see Chapter 8, this volume), Karen Kievit (1998), and John Kantner (2003).

An Approach to Avoid
While all of the studies proposed by my panel constitute productive avenues for future research, there is one widely used approach that I think should be avoided. When this typological approach was first employed in the 1970s, it transformed the study of Chacoan archaeology. At that time the conventional wisdom about how the Chacoans were organized was derived primarily from ethnographic analogy, resulting in the conclusion that they were egalitarian (Vivian 1970). The advent of

Jill E. Neitzel

the typological approach prompted a systematic review of the available archaeological evidence, which indicated that the Chacoans should instead be categorized as a ranked society or chiefdom (Grebinger 1973; Martin and Plog 1973:270–271). This conclusion laid the groundwork for much of the research by the National Park Service's Chaco Project (e.g., Hayes, Brugge, and Judge 1981; Judge and Schelberg 1984).

The original designation of Chaco as a ranked society or chiefdom was based primarily on the realization that the presence of contemporaneous "town" and "village" sites and the association of irrigation systems and elaborate burials with the towns were manifestations of an organizational hierarchy (Grebinger 1973). Although the "chiefdom" label was for a variety of reasons never widely adopted by Chacoan archaeologists, it had long-term consequences for their research. For example, it led many investigators to assume that redistribution, a key trait in the traditional definition of chiefdoms (Service 1962), was the basis of the Chacoan economy (Judge 1979). This assumption has pervaded Chacoan research over the past two decades but has never been systematically tested, even as ethnographers and archaeologists working in other areas have documented that chiefdoms do not always have redistributive economies (e.g., Earle 1977; Helms 1979; Taylor 1975).

Although the typological approach continues to dominate Chacoan research, I think that it has outlived its usefulness. In recent years it has been the source of endless and ultimately fruitless debates about labels that have not increased our understanding of either Pueblo Bonito or Chacoan society. Most long-standing and current discussions of such terms as complexity, regional system, polity, rituality, town, ceremonial center, and corporate versus network leadership strategies have been "is it or is it not?" arguments about classification. Although most of these typological debates have been concerned with broader units of analysis (e.g., downtown Chaco, the canyon, or Chacoan society as a whole), they have affected interpretations of Pueblo Bonito and its architecture in several ways. Most significantly, the typological approach has been used to interpret Pueblo Bonito's architecture, as illustrated by the ongoing either/or arguments about whether the building

was a residence or a ceremonial center. Also, typological debates at broader scales have impacted the kinds of interpretations proposed for Pueblo Bonito's architecture. For example, the idea that Pueblo Bonito was a ceremonial center has its roots not just in architectural data and other evidence from the structure itself but also in more general discussions about redistribution, which is a legacy of the "chiefdom" label.

Use of the term *ceremonial center* exemplifies how the typological approach represents an intellectual dead end for future research on Pueblo Bonito's architecture. As Stein and his colleagues (2003:59) have noted, the meaning of the label is vague and ambiguous. Furthermore, its usage has been primarily classificatory, as a contrasting category for residential sites. This is a false contrast for Pueblo Bonito, which had multiple, interrelated functions as an elite residence, a place of ceremonies, a storage facility, and some sort of trading center. Recently, Colin Renfrew (2001) characterized Chaco Canyon, with Pueblo Bonito at its heart, as a Location of High Devotion, which seems to be another way of saying ceremonial center. To his credit, Renfrew explicitly lists what he means by his label—a place where key rituals were conducted by elite religious specialists and were attended by large numbers of religious pilgrims. But he also acknowledges that this designation fails to convey that the canyon, and by implication Pueblo Bonito, probably had secular functions as well (Renfrew 2001:20).

Future research on Pueblo Bonito's architecture needs to move beyond debates about labels. To paraphrase Ben Nelson (1995), we need to worry less about what we call the structure and more about documenting the range of activities represented in the archaeological record, how they changed through time, and how they interacted to produce what was undoubtedly a complex and vibrant social milieu. Future studies should be directed at investigating the nature of this complexity rather than trying to pigeonhole it into a typological category. So, for example, instead of obsessing about whether Pueblo Bonito was primarily a ceremonial center or a residence, archaeologists should direct their efforts toward elucidating the various kinds of rituals that were conducted at the site, when and where within the structure they

147

occurred, who was involved, how the various ceremonies changed through time, and how they were integrated with one another as well as with the structure's other functions. The same kinds of questions can be asked about Pueblo Bonito's role as a residence, a storage facility, and a trading center. Assumptions about redistribution and pilgrimages should not just be asserted but should be systematically evaluated in the same way. If archaeologists can avoid typological debates as they test assumptions and investigate the numerous research questions proposed by my panel, then future research on Pueblo Bonito's architecture will most certainly continue to add to our understanding of the people who built and used this magnificent edifice.

Conclusion

Pueblo Bonito is a structure that overwhelms. With its enormous size, complex design, and fine masonry, the building, even in ruin, clearly represents an impressive engineering and aesthetic feat. More than a century of archaeological research has made Pueblo Bonito the most thoroughly excavated and intensively analyzed large site in the American Southwest. Much of this research has focused on the building's architecture. Initial architectural studies emphasized basic documentation—description, mapping, and defining a chronology, topics that received their most complete treatment in Neil Judd's (1964) landmark study. The findings presented in this seminal work continue to be evaluated today as investigators strive to document more precisely the dates and boundaries of each successive construction episode and to reconstruct what the entire building looked like after each project was completed.

As these efforts at mapping and dating continue, the dominant interests in current architectural analyses have shifted to a concern with social and behavioral issues—what Pueblo Bonito's function was, how the people who built and used the structure were organized, and how many people lived within the building. Efforts to answer these questions have relied on intensive analyses of various aspects of Pueblo Bonito's architecture and on interpreting the results of these studies with reference to their broader context, in comparison either

with Pueblo Bonito's location, the characteristics of other great houses, or the results of mortuary and artifact analyses done at Pueblo Bonito and other Chacoan sites. Taken together, the results of these various studies have produced a portrait of Pueblo Bonito that the site's original excavators could never have imagined possible.

Despite all that has been learned about Pueblo Bonito's architecture, there is more research to be done, as evidenced by the many projects suggested by my panel. Given the National Park Service's policy of preservation, the most feasible studies are those that require no further excavations and are concerned primarily with issues related to Pueblo Bonito's appearance, construction, design, and function. Projects that could be undertaken if further excavations at Pueblo Bonito were permitted focus on the dates and other characteristics of the building's most notable features. Finally, data from other Chacoan sites, both large and small, would help archaeologists to interpret Pueblo Bonito's architecture within its broader context.

Together, all of these suggestions promise a productive future for continued research on Pueblo Bonito's architecture. They also illustrate an enduring characteristic of Chacoan studies in general—one study inevitably leads to another, requiring different kinds of data collected in different ways and at different spatial scales. So, for example, while the question of when Pueblo Bonito's great kivas were built can be addressed to some extent by reexamining data collected by Judd (1964), a more complete answer would require state-of-the-art excavations of the site's still-buried great kivas. The results of such excavations would in turn beg temporal comparisons with other kinds of construction at the site and with other aspects of Pueblo Bonito's design, such as its astronomical alignments. The list of related issues could go on and on both at Pueblo Bonito and at larger spatial scales. A similar cascade of questions could be enumerated for the other research topics proposed by my panel of experts.

Many on my panel acknowledge a conundrum underlying their various proposals for future research on Pueblo Bonito's architecture. While they praise the National Park Service's policy of preservation, they also advocate further excavations of the structure. In their view, limited excavations with specific objectives offer a way to balance the seemingly contradictory goals of preserving Pueblo Bonito and learning more about the structure and the people who built and used it.

One cautionary message is that future studies of Pueblo Bonito's architecture should not get bogged down in discussions of typology. The lesson to be learned from previous struggles with terminology is that trying to find the right label is frustrating and ultimately unproductive. Arguments about whether Pueblo Bonito fits into one category or another ultimately lead nowhere, and they distract us from what may be the structure's most important characteristic—its complexity. This structure does not match contemporary, ethnographic, and historical analogs, and this lack of fit, which has been the source of the most heated debates in Chacoan archaeology, is ultimately what makes Pueblo Bonito such a significant site.

The alternative to the classificatory debates inherent in our search for the best labels is to focus instead on elucidating and comparing different aspects of Pueblo Bonito's architecture and how they changed through time. The results should in turn be interpreted with reference to the architecture of other Chacoan sites and to the burials and artifacts from Pueblo Bonito and elsewhere. This future research will not only add to our understanding of Pueblo Bonito and its role in Chacoan society, it will also provide a broader appreciation of the range of social forms that existed in the past.

Acknowledgments

Any archaeologist who investigates Pueblo Bonito is indebted to George Pepper and Neil Judd, whose excavations provided the foundation for all that we presently know about the site. In the years since their seminal work, research on Pueblo Bonito has become a collaborative endeavor involving numerous investigators. Much of the research summarized in this chapter was done by contributors to *Pueblo Bonito: Center of the Chacoan World*, which I edited for Smithsonian Institution Press. The volume's contributors are Nancy Akins, Wendy Bustard, James Farmer, Dabney Ford, Richard Friedman, Anne Marshall, Joan Mathien, Mary Pat Metcalf, John Stein, Tom Windes, and myself. Wendy Bustard, Richard Friedman, Anne Marshall, Joan Mathien, John Stein, and Tom Windes also generously shared with me their thoughts about the kinds of architectural studies that could be conducted at Pueblo Bonito in the future. Additional projects were suggested by Wesley Bernardini, Ruth Van Dyke, Dennis Doxtater, Stephen Durand, Karen Kievit, Steve Lekson, Mike Marshall, Barbara Mills, Steve Plog, Anna Sofaer, Phil Tuwaletstiwa, Gwinn Vivian, and Chip Wills. Tom Rocek read an earlier draft of this paper and provided useful suggestions for improvement. Robert Schultz drafted Figure 5.7. My heartfelt thanks to all, and my apologies if I have misrepresented any of their suggestions.

Notes

1. In the remainder of this chapter Lekson's (1986) dates will be used for all stages except Stage 1, whose beginning date is modified based on Windes and Ford (1996).

2. Judd's estimate that Pueblo Bonito had 1,000 residents is stated in somewhat different ways in his two major publications on the site. In his material culture volume, Judd (1954:325) reported that the number of occupants was more than 1,000. In his architecture volume, Judd (1964:22) said that the building was occupied by "possibly 1,000 individuals."

3. For a discussion of how this framed view was not fully achieved, see A. Marshall 2003:12.

References

Adler, Michael A.

1989   Ritual Facilities and Social Integration in Nonranked Societies. In *The Architecture of Social Organization in Prehistoric Pueblos*, edited by William D. Lipe and Michelle Hegmon, pp. 35–52. Crow Canyon Archaeological Center Occasional Paper 1. Cortez.

1993   Why Is a Kiva? New Interpretations of Prehistoric Social Integrative Architecture in the Northern Rio Grande Region of New Mexico. *Journal of Anthropological Research* 49:319–346.

Akins, Nancy J.

1986   *A Biocultural Approach to Human Burials from Chaco Canyon, New Mexico*. Reports of the Chaco Center 9. Division of Cultural Research, National Park Service, Santa Fe.

2003   The Burials of Pueblo Bonito. In *Pueblo Bonito: Center of the Chacoan World*, edited by Jill E. Neitzel, pp. 94–106. Smithsonian Books, Washington, DC.

Bernadini, Wesley

1999   Reassessing the Scale of Social Action at Pueblo Bonito. *Kiva* 64:447–470.

Betancourt, Julio L., Jeffrey S. Dean, and Herbert M. Hull
1986   Prehistoric Long-Distance Transport of Construction Beams, Chaco Canyon, New Mexico. *American Antiquity* 51:370–375.

Bustard, Wendy
2003   Pueblo Bonito: When a House Is Not a Home. In *Pueblo Bonito: Center of the Chacoan World*, edited by Jill E. Neitzel, pp. 80–93. Smithsonian Books, Washington, DC.

Cameron, Catherine M.
1984   A Regional View of Chipped Stone Raw Material Use in Chaco Canyon. In *Recent Research on Chaco Prehistory*, edited by W. James Judge and John D. Schelberg, pp. 137–152. Reports of the Chaco Center 8. Division of Cultural Research, National Park Service, Albuquerque.
2001   Pink Chert, Projectile Points, and the Chacoan Regional System. *American Antiquity* 66:79–102.

Cobb, Charles R., Jeffrey Maymon, and Randall H. McGuire
1999   Feathered, Horned, and Antlered Serpents: Mesoamerican Connections with the Southwest and Southeast. In *Great Towns and Regional Polities in the Prehistoric Southwest and Southeast*, edited by Jill E. Neitzel, pp. 165–181. University of New Mexico Press, Albuquerque.

Cooper, Laurel M.
1995   Space Syntax Analysis of Chacoan Great Houses. Unpublished Ph.D. dissertation, Department of Anthropology, University of Arizona, Tucson.

Cordell, Linda S.
1992   The Nature of Explanation in Archaeology: A Position Statement. In *Understanding Complexity in the Prehistoric Southwest*, edited by George J. Gumerman and Murray Gell-Mann, pp. 1–13. SFI Studies in the Sciences of Complexity, Proceedings 14. Addison-Wesley, Reading, MA.

Crown, Patricia L., and W. H. Wills
2003   Modifying Pottery and Kivas at Chaco: Pentimento, Restoration, or Renewal? *American Antiquity* 68:511–532

Dean, Jeffrey S., and Richard L. Warren
1983   Dendrochronology. In *The Architecture and Dendrochronology of Chetro Ketl, Chaco Canyon, New Mexico*, edited by Stephen H. Lekson, pp. 105–240. Reports of the Chaco Center 6. Division of Cultural Research, National Park Service, Albuquerque.

Doxtater, Dennis
2002   A Hypothetical Layout of Chaco Canyon Structures via Large-Scale Alignments between Significant Natural Features. *Kiva* 68:23–48.
2003a   Parallel Universes on the Colorado Plateau: Indications of Chacoan Integration of an Earlier Anasazi Focus at Canyon de Chelly. *Journal of the Southwest* 45(Spring/Summer):33–62.

2003b   The Sacred Anasazi Site of Aztec in the Larger De Chellian-Chacoan Georitual Landscape. Paper presented at the 51st Congreso Internacional de Americanistas, Santiago, Chile.

Doyel, David E., Cory D. Breternitz, and Michael P. Marshall
1984   Chacoan Community Structure: Bis sa'ani and the Chaco Halo. In *Recent Research on Chaco Prehistory*, edited by W. James Judge and John D. Schelberg, pp. 37–54. Reports of the Chaco Center 8. Division of Cultural Research, National Park Service, Albuquerque.

Drager, Dwight L.
1976   Anasazi Population Estimates with the Aid of Data Derived from Photogrammetric Maps. In *Remote Sensing Experiments in Cultural Resource Studies*, edited by Thomas R. Lyons, pp. 151–171. Reports of the Chaco Center 1. Division of Cultural Research, National Park Service, Albuquerque.

Earle, Timothy K.
1977   A Reappraisal of Redistribution: Complex Hawaiian Chiefdoms. In *Exchange Systems in Prehistory*, edited by Timothy K. Earle and Jonathan E. Ericson, pp. 213–229. Academic Press, New York.

Farmer, James D.
2003   Astronomy and Ritual at Chaco Canyon. In *Pueblo Bonito: Center of the Chacoan World*, edited by Jill E. Neitzel, pp. 61–71. Smithsonian Books, Washington, DC.

Fritz, John M.
1978   Paleopsychology Today: Ideational Systems and Human Adaptation in Prehistory. In *Social Archaeology: Beyond Subsistence and Dating*, edited by Charles L. Redman, Mary Jane Berman, Edward V. Curtain, William T. Langhorn, Nina M. Versaggi, and Jeffrey C. Wanser, pp. 37–59. Academic Press, New York.
1987   Chaco Canyon and Vijayanagara: Proposing Spatial Meaning in Two Societies. In *Mirror and Metaphor: Material and Social Constructions of Reality*, edited by Daniel W. Ingersoll and Gordon Bronitsky, pp. 313–348. University Press of America, Lanham, MD.

Grebinger, Paul
1973   Prehistoric Social Organization in Chaco Canyon, New Mexico: An Alternative Reconstruction. *Kiva* 39:3–23.

Hayes, Alden C., David M. Brugge, and W. James Judge
1981   *Archaeological Surveys of Chaco Canyon.* Publications in Archaeology 18A, Chaco Canyon Studies. National Park Service, Washington, DC.

Helms, Mary W.
1979   *Ancient Panama: Chiefs in Search of Power.* University of Texas Press, Austin.

150

Hine, Robert V.

1962 *Edward Kern and American Expansion.* Yale University Press, New Haven.

Holley, George R., and Stephen H. Lekson

1999 Comparing Southwestern and Southeastern Great Towns. In *Great Towns and Regional Polities in the Prehistoric American Southwest and Southeast*, edited by Jill E. Neitzel, pp. 39–43. University of New Mexico Press, Albuquerque.

Hudson, Dee T.

1972 Anasazi Measurement Systems at Chaco Canyon, New Mexico. *Kiva* 38:27–42.

Jackson, William H.

1878 Report on the Ancient Ruins Examined in 1875 and 1877. In *Tenth Annual Report of the United States Geological and Geographical Survey of the Territories*, pp. 411–430. U.S. Government Printing Office, Washington, DC.

Jordan, Gretchen

2002 Political Integration and Pilgrimage in Middle Range Societies: A Test Case in Chaco Canyon, New Mexico. Unpublished Ph.D. dissertation, Department of Anthropology, University of Colorado, Boulder.

Judd, Neil M.

1925 Everyday Life in Pueblo Bonito. *National Geographic* 48:227–262.

1954 *The Material Culture of Pueblo Bonito.* Smithsonian Miscellaneous Collections 124. Washington, DC.

1964 *The Architecture of Pueblo Bonito.* Smithsonian Miscellaneous Collections 147(1). Smithsonian Institution, Washington, DC.

Judge, W. James

1979 The Development of a Complex Ecosystem in the Chaco Basin, New Mexico. In *Proceedings of the First Conference on Scientific Research in the National Parks*, 2, edited by R. M. Linn, pp. 901–906. National Park Service Transactions and Proceedings 5. Washington, DC.

1989 Chaco Canyon–San Juan Basin. In *Dynamics of Southwest Prehistory*, edited by Linda S. Cordell and George J. Gumerman, pp. 209–261. School of American Research Press, Santa Fe.

Judge, W. James, and John D. Schelberg, eds.

1984 *Recent Research on Chaco Prehistory.* Reports of the Chaco Center 8. Division of Cultural Research, National Park Service, Albuquerque.

Kantner, John

2003 The Chacoan World Database. <http://sipapu.gsu.edu/chacoworld.html>.

Keur, John Y.

1933 A Study of Primitive Indian Engineering Methods Pertaining to Threatening Rock. Ms. on file, NPS Chaco Archives, University of New Mexico, Albuquerque.

Keivit, Karen

1998 Seeing and Reading Chaco Architecture at 1100. Unpublished Ph.D. dissertation, Department of Anthropology, University of Colorado, Boulder.

Lekson, Stephen H.

1984 Standing Architecture at Chaco Canyon and the Interpretation of Local and Regional Organization. In *Recent Research on Chaco Prehistory*, edited by W. James Judge and John D. Schelberg, pp. 55–73. Reports of the Chaco Center 8. Division of Cultural Research, National Park Service, Albuquerque.

1986 *Great Pueblo Architecture of Chaco Canyon, New Mexico.* University of New Mexico Press, Albuquerque.

1988 The Idea of the Kiva in Anasazi Archaeology. *Kiva* 53:213–234.

1991 Settlement Patterns and the Chaco Region. In *Chaco and Hohokam: Regional Systems in the American Southwest*, edited by Patricia L. Crown and W. James Judge, pp. 31–55. School of American Research Press, Santa Fe.

1997 Points, Knives, and Drills of Chaco Canyon. In *Ceramics, Lithics, and Ornaments of Chaco Canyon: Analyses of Artifacts from the Chaco Project, 1971–1978*, edited by F. Joan Mathien, pp. 659–697. Publications in Archaeology 18G, Chaco Canyon Series. National Park Service, Santa Fe.

1999 Great Towns in the Southwest. In *Great Towns and Regional Polities in the Prehistoric American Southwest and Southeast*, edited by Jill E. Neitzel, pp. 3–21. University of New Mexico Press, Albuquerque.

Lumpkins, William

1984 Reflections on Chacoan Architecture. In *New Light on Chaco Canyon*, edited by David Grant Noble, pp. 19–24. School of American Research Press, Santa Fe.

Malville, J. McKim, Frank W. Eddy, and Carol Ambruster

1991 Moonrise at Chimney Rock. *Archaeoastronomy* (Supplement to the *Journal for the History of Astronomy*) 1b:s34–s50.

Marshall, Anne Lawson

2003 The Siting of Pueblo Bonito. In *Pueblo Bonito: Center of the Chacoan World*, edited by Jill E. Neitzel, pp. 10–13. Smithsonian Books, Washington, DC.

Marshall, Michael P., John R. Stein, Richard W. Loose, and Judith E. Novotny

1979 *Anasazi Communities of the San Juan Basin.* Public Service Company of New Mexico, Albuquerque, and the New Mexico Historic Preservation Bureau, Santa Fe.

Martin, Debra L., Nancy J. Akins, Alan H. Goodman, H. Wolcott Toll, and Alan C. Swedlund

2001 *Harmony and Discord: Bioarchaeology of the La Plata Valley.* Laboratory of Anthropology

Notes 242. Office of Archaeological Studies, Museum of New Mexico, Santa Fe.

Martin, Paul S., and Fred Plog
1973   *The Archaeology of Arizona.* Doubleday/Natural History Press, Garden City, NY.

Mathien, Frances Joan
2003   Artifacts from Pueblo Bonito: One Hundred Years of Interpretation. In *Pueblo Bonito: Center of the Chacoan World*, edited by Jill E. Neitzel, pp.127–142. Smithsonian Books, Washington, DC.

McGuire, Randall H.
1980   The Mesoamerican Connection in the Southwest. *Kiva* 46:30–38.

Metcalf, Mary Pat
1997   Civic Spaces: Prehistoric Political Organization in the Northern Southwest, 1100–1300. Unpublished Ph.D. dissertation, Department of Anthropology, University of Virginia, Charlottesville.
2003   Construction Labor at Pueblo Bonito. In *Pueblo Bonito: Center of the Chacoan World*, edited by Jill E. Neitzel, pp. 72–79. Smithsonian Books, Washington, DC.

Neitzel, Jill E.
1989a The Chacoan Regional System: Interpreting the Evidence for Sociopolitical Complexity. In *The Sociopolitical Structure of Prehistoric Southwestern Societies*, edited by Steadman Upham, Kent G. Lightfoot, and Roberta A. Jewett, pp. 509–556. Westview Press, Boulder.
1989b Regional Exchange Networks in the American Southwest: A Comparative Analysis of Long-Distance Trade. In *The Sociopolitical Structure of Prehistoric Southwestern Societies*, edited by Steadman Upham, Kent G. Lightfoot, and Roberta A. Jewett, pp. 149–295. Westview Press, Boulder.
1994   Boundary Dynamics in the Chacoan Regional System. In *The Ancient Southwestern Community: Models and Methods for the Study of Prehistoric Social Organization*, edited by W. H. Wills and Robert D. Leonard, pp. 209–240. University of New Mexico Press, Albuquerque.
2000   Gender Hierarchies: A Comparative Analysis of Mortuary Data. In *Women and Men in the Prehispanic Southwest: Labor, Power, and Prestige*, edited by Patricia L. Crown, pp. 137–168. School of American Research Press, Santa Fe.
2003a Three Questions about Pueblo Bonito. In *Pueblo Bonito: Center of the Chacoan World*, edited by Jill E. Neitzel, pp. 1–9. Smithsonian Books, Washington, DC.
2003b Artifact Distributions at Pueblo Bonito. In *Pueblo Bonito: Center of the Chacoan World*, edited by Jill E. Neitzel, pp. 107–126. Smithsonian Books, Washington, DC.

2003c The Organization, Function, and Population of Pueblo Bonito. In *Pueblo Bonito: Center of the Chacoan World*, edited by Jill E. Neitzel, pp. 143–149. Smithsonian Books, Washington, DC.

Neitzel, Jill E., ed.
2003   *Pueblo Bonito: Center of the Chacoan World.* Smithsonian Books, Washington, DC.

Neitzel, Jill E., and Ronald L. Bishop
1990   Neutron Activation of Dogoszhi-Style Ceramics: Production and Exchange in the Chacoan Regional System. *Kiva* 56:67–85.

Nelson, Ben A.
1995   Complexity, Hierarchy, and Scale: A Controlled Comparison between Chaco Canyon, New Mexico, and La Quemada, Zacatecas. *American Antiquity* 60:597–618.

Nelson, Ben A., Debra L. Martin, Alan C. Swedlund, Paul R. Fish, and George J. Armelagos
1994   Studies in Disruption and Health in the Prehistoric American Southwest. In *Understanding Complexity in the Prehistoric Southwest*, edited by George J. Gumerman and Murray Gell-Mann, pp. 59–112. SFI Studies in the Sciences of Complexity, Proceedings vol. 16. Addison-Wesley, Reading, MA.

Pepper, George H.
1905   Ceremonial Objects and Ornaments from Pueblo Bonito, New Mexico. *American Anthropologist* n.s. 7:183–197.
1909   The Exploration of a Burial Room in Pueblo Bonito, New Mexico. In *Anthropological Essays: Putnam Anniversary Volume*, pp. 196–252. G. E. Steckert, New York.
1920   *Pueblo Bonito.* Anthropological Papers of the American Museum of Natural History 27. New York.

Peregrine, Peter N.
2001   Matrilocality, Corporate Strategy, and the Organization of Production in the Chacoan World. *American Antiquity* 66:36–46.

Powers, Robert P.
1984   Regional Interaction in the San Juan Basin: The Chacoan Outlier System. In *Recent Research on Chaco Prehistory*, edited by W. James Judge and John D. Schelberg, pp. 23–36. Reports of the Chaco Center 8. Division of Cultural Research, National Park Service, Albuquerque.

Powers, Robert P., William B. Gillespie, and Stephen H. Lekson
1983   *The Outlier Survey: A Regional View of Settlement in the San Juan Basin.* Reports of the Chaco Center 3. Division of Cultural Research, National Park Service, Albuquerque.

Renfrew, Colin
2001   Production and Consumption in a Sacred Economy: The Material Correlates of High Devotional Expression at Chaco Canyon. *American Antiquity* 66:14–25.

Jill E. Neitzel

Reyman, Jonathan E.

1976 Astronomy, Architecture, and Adaptation at Pueblo Bonito. *Science* 193(4257):957–962.

1987 Review of Recent Research on Chaco Prehistory. *Kiva* 52:147–151.

1989 The History of Archaeology and the Archaeological History of Chaco Canyon, New Mexico. In *Tracing Archaeology's Past, The Historiography of Archaeology*, edited by Andrew L. Christenson, pp. 41–51. Southern Illinois University, Carbondale and Edwardsville.

Saile, David G.

1990 Understanding the Development of Pueblo Architecture. In *Pueblo Style and Regional Architecture*, edited by Nicholas C. Markovich, Wolfgang F. E. Preiser, and Fred G. Sturm, pp. 49–63. Van Nostrand Reinhold, New York.

Schelberg, John D.

1984 Analogy, Complexity, and Regionally Based Perspectives. In *Recent Research on Chaco Prehistory*, edited by W. James Judge and John D. Schelberg, pp. 5–21. Reports of the Chaco Center 8. Division of Cultural Research, National Park Service, Albuquerque.

Schillaci, Michael A., and Christopher M. Stojanowski

2003 Postmarital Residence and Biological Variation at Pueblo Bonito. *American Journal of Physical Anthropology* 120:1–15.

Schillaci, Michael A., Erik G. Ozolins, and Thomas C. Windes

2001 Multivariate Assessment of Biological Relationships among Prehistoric Southwestern Amerindian Populations. In *Following Through: Papers in Honor of Phyllis S. Davis*, edited by Regge N. Wiseman, Thomas C. O'Laughlin, and Cordelia T. Snow, pp 113–149. Papers of the Archaeological Society of New Mexico 27. Albuquerque.

Service, Elman

1962 *Primitive Social Organization*. Random House, New York.

Simpson, James H.

1850 *Journal of a Military Reconnaissance from Santa Fe, New Mexico, to the Navajo Country in 1949*. U.S. Senate Executive Document 64. Thirty-First Congress, First Session. Washington, DC.

Snow, David H.

1973 Prehistoric Southwestern Turquoise Industry. *El Palacio* 79:33–51.

Sofaer, Anna

1997 The Primary Architecture of the Chacoan Culture: A Cosmological Expression. In *Anasazi Architecture and American Design*, edited by Baker H. Morrow and V. B. Price, pp. 88–130. University of New Mexico Press, Albuquerque.

Sofaer, Anna, Rolf Sinclair, and LeRoy Doggett

1982 Lunar Markings on Fajada Butte, Chaco Canyon, New Mexico. In *Archaeoastronomy in the New World*, edited by Anthony F. Aveni, pp. 169–181. Cambridge University Press, Cambridge.

Stein, John R., and Stephen H. Lekson

1992 Anasazi Ritual Landscapes. In *Anasazi Regional Organization and the Chaco System*, edited by David E. Doyel, pp. 87–100. Maxwell Museum of Anthropology, Anthropological Papers 5. University of New Mexico, Albuquerque.

Stein, John R., Dabney Ford, and Richard Friedman

2003 Reconstructing Pueblo Bonito. In *Pueblo Bonito: Center of the Chacoan World*, edited by Jill E. Neitzel, pp 33–60. Smithsonian Books, Washington, DC.

Stein, John R., Judith E. Suiter, and Dabney Ford

1997 High Noon in Old Bonito: Sun, Shadow and the Geometry of the Chaco Complex. In *Anasazi Architecture and American Design*, edited by Baker H. Morrow and V. B. Price, pp. 133–148. University of New Mexico Press, Albuquerque.

Stodder, Ann L.W.

1989 Bioarchaeological Research in the Basin and Range Region. In *Human Adaptations and Cultural Changes in the Greater Southwest: An Overview of Archaeological Resources in the Basin and Range Province*, by A. H. Simons, Ann L.W. Stodder, D. D. Dykeman, and P. A. Hicks, pp. 167–190. Arkansas Archaeological Survey Research Series 32. Wrightsville.

Taylor, Donna

1975 Some Locational Aspects of Middle-Range Hierarchical Societies. Unpublished Ph.D. dissertation, Department of Anthropology, City University of New York.

Toll, H. Wolcott

1985 Pottery Production, Public Architecture, and the Chaco Anasazi System. Unpublished Ph.D. dissertation, Department of Anthropology, University of Colorado, Boulder.

Toll, H. Wolcott, and Peter J. McKenna

1997 Chaco Ceramics. In *Ceramics, Lithics, and Ornaments of Chaco Canyon: Analyses of Artifacts from the Chaco Project, 1971–1978*, edited by F. Joan Mathien, and Thomas C. Windes, pp. 19–230. Publications in Archaeology 18F, Chaco Canyon Studies. National Park Service, Santa Fe.

Turner, Christy G. II, and Jacqueline A.Turner

1999 *Man Corn: Cannibalism and Violence in the Prehistoric American Southwest*. University of Utah Press, Salt Lake City.

Vivian, R. Gordon, and Paul Reiter

1960 *The Great Kivas of Chaco Canyon and Their Relationships*. School of American Research and Museum of New Mexico Monographs 22. Santa Fe.

Vivian, R. Gwinn

1970   An Inquiry into Prehistoric Social Organization, Chaco Canyon, New Mexico. In *Reconstructing Pueblo Societies*, edited by William A. Longacre, pp. 59–83. University of New Mexico Press, Albuquerque.

Wilcox, David R.

1993   The Evolution of the Chacoan Polity. In *The Chimney Rock Symposium*, edited by J. McKim Malville and Gary Matlock. Rocky Mountain Forest and Ranger Experiment Station, USDA Forest Service, Ft. Collins, Colorado.

1999   A Peregrine View of Macroregional Systems in the North American Southwest, 750–1250. In *Great Towns and Regional Polities in the Prehistoric American Southwest and Southeast*, edited by Jill E. Neitzel, pp. 115–141. University of New Mexico Press, Albuquerque.

Williamson, Ray A.

1977   Archaeoastronomy at Pueblo Bonito. *Science* 197(4304):618–619.

1978   Pueblo Bonito and the Sun. *Archaeoastronomy* 1(2):5–7.

1987a   *Living the Sky: The Cosmos of the American Indians.* University of Oklahoma Press, Norman.

1987b   Light and Shadow, Ritual, and Astronomy in Anasazi Structure. In *Astronomy and Ceremony in the Prehistoric Southwest*, edited by John B. Carlson and W. James Judge, pp. 99–119. Maxwell Museum of Anthropology, Anthropological Papers 2. University of New Mexico, Albuquerque.

Windes, Thomas C.

1984   A New Look at Population in Chaco Canyon. In *Recent Research on Chaco Prehistory*, edited by W. James Judge and John D. Schelberg, pp. 75–87. Reports of the Chaco Center 8. Division of Cultural Research, National Park Service, Albuquerque.

1987   *Investigations at the Pueblo Alto Complex, Chaco Canyon, New Mexico, 1975–1979.* Publications in Archaeology 18F, Chaco Canyon Studies. National Park Service, Santa Fe.

2003   This Old House: Construction and Abandonment at Pueblo Bonito. In *Pueblo Bonito: Center of the Chacoan World*, edited by Jill E. Neitzel, pp. 14–32. Smithsonian Books, Washington, DC.

Windes, Thomas C., and Dabney Ford

1996   The Chaco Wood Project: The Chronometric Reappraisal of Pueblo Bonito. *American Antiquity* 61:295–310.

Windes, Thomas C., and Peter J. McKenna

2001   Going against the Grain: Wood Production in Chacoan Society. *American Antiquity* 66:119–140.

Zeilik, Michael

1984   Archaeoastronomy at Chaco Canyon. In *New Light on Chaco Canyon*, edited by David G. Noble, pp. 65–72. School of American Research Press, Santa Fe.

1986   Keeping a Seasonal Calendar at Pueblo Bonito. *Archaeoastronomy* 9(1–4):79–87.

1987   Anticipation in Ceremony: The Readiness Is All. In *Astronomy and Ceremony in the Prehistoric Southwest*, edited by John B. Carlson and W. James Judge, pp. 25–42. Maxwell Museum of Anthropology, Anthropological Papers 2. Albuquerque.

Jill E. Neitzel

6

The Changing Faces
of Chetro Ketl

Stephen H. Lekson

Thomas C. Windes

Patricia Fournier

CHETRO KETL WAS EITHER THE LARGEST or the second largest building in Chaco, after Pueblo Bonito. Some archaeologists thought Bonito bigger; others favored Chetro Ketl. Its construction (990 to 1115) began almost a century later than Pueblo Bonito's, but Chetro Ketl soon rivaled its older neighbor as the architectural focus of "downtown" Chaco. Rivalries between the excavators of Pueblo Bonito and Chetro Ketl shaped the history of research at Chaco. Edgar Hewett excavated about two-thirds of Chetro Ketl's 400 rooms in 1920–1921 and 1929–1937. He actively promoted his Chetro Ketl over Neil Judd's nearby Pueblo Bonito. Translating the name "Pueblo Bonito" as "beautiful town," Hewett sniffed: "It may be doubted if in the great days of Chaco it [Pueblo Bonito] was distinguished among its neighbors for its beauty. Several others probably surpassed it in this respect" (1936:32), leaving little doubt that (in his eye) Chetro Ketl set the tone for great house glamour. We feel that Pueblo Bonito was, in fact, the "heart" of Chaco Canyon (age before beauty?), but Chetro Ketl was a close second, and a very interesting building on its own merits.

In this chapter, we briefly describe the site; review the history of research; present a revised version of its construction sequence; discuss, at some length, how Chetro Ketl looked, from various viewpoints (see Kievit 1998); and conclude

with some remarks on the changing form of Chetro Ketl, and the implications for understanding Chaco Canyon.

Chetro Ketl is an immense D about 140 m by 85 m (Figures 6.1 and 6.2). The "D" was not oriented to the cardinal directions (as discussed below); nevertheless, for ease of description, we will use conventional directions, with the long, straight rear of the D being nominal north and the bowed curve of the D being south.

The center of the D was an elevated, enclosed plaza. The plaza was surrounded on the east and west by wings of rooms (each three rooms deep); on the north by a long north wall (again three rooms deep) with a massive, central roomblock projecting out into the plaza; and on the south by enclosing walls. The wings were probably two or three stories tall, terracing down to a single story of plaza-facing rooms; the rear wall reached up to five stories, but (as we shall see) two of those stories were "buried" below grade. There were about 400 rectangular rooms, with two major round rooms ("kivas") in the west wing, three round rooms and a "tower kiva" in the central roomblock, and no round rooms in the east wing. Several round rooms were subsequently added to the east wing—we believe late in, or even after, the Bonito phase. A huge great kiva occupied the southeast corner of the plaza; a smaller one (the Court Kiva) sat in a

FIGURE 6.1. Chetro Ketl from the west. (Photograph by S. H. Lekson)

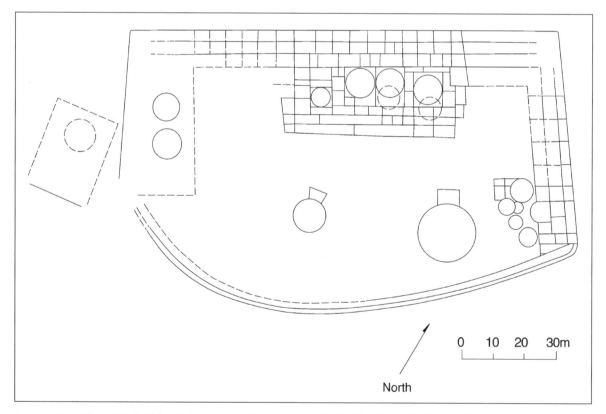

FIGURE 6.2. Chetro Ketl. (After Lekson 1983: Figure 4.39; redrafted by David Underwood)

Lekson, Windes, and Fournier

corresponding position in the south-central plaza. Other features included a huge mound, much plundered and excavated, outside the southeast corner of the building and, beyond that, a contentious feature called the "Chetro Ketl field" (see Stein and others, Chapter 8, this volume, for additional discussion). Other structures along the canyon wall behind Chetro Ketl, such as Talus Unit, which can also be considered part of its larger design, are more fully described below.

HISTORY OF RESEARCH

Chetro Ketl was excavated by Edgar Hewett, director of the Museum of New Mexico, the School of American Research, and founder and chair of the anthropology department at the University of New Mexico. Work began in 1920–1921, ceased for seven years (while Neil Judd worked in the canyon), and then resumed from 1929 to 1937. Hewett was not noted for his field archaeology, laboratory analysis, or technical writing, but his staff included archaeologists who were skilled at all these things. Several aspects of the work at Chetro Ketl were well reported in theses and dissertations (Hawley 1934; Miller 1937; Reiter 1933, among others) and monographs (Vivian and Reiter 1960), but no comprehensive report ever appeared describing Hewett's extensive excavations and stabilization of the east wing and central roomblock. In 1947, a catastrophic flood toppled the tallest sections of the rear wall, leading to important salvage excavations in the northwest section of the central roomblock (Vivian, Dodge, and Harman 1978). The Chaco Project attempted to gather and summarize the surviving field notes and sponsored the sampling of architectural wood (beams, lintels, etc.) for dating (Lekson, ed. 1983). Windes subsequently sampled many more of these elements (reported below).

CONSTRUCTION SEQUENCE

The sequence of construction is presented here mainly through figures. The basic sequence closely follows that developed previously (Lekson, ed. 1983; Lekson 1984:152–192), with some fine-tuning from 327 new dates obtained by Windes from the 1,910 wood elements documented in situ

at the site (as of January 2004) along with another 398 specimens remaining from the 1947 flood and stored in an old park bunker, 117 charcoal specimens that Hawley recovered from the trash mound, and at least 200 more flood elements reused for stabilization in other canyon great houses (Casa Rinconada, Hungo Pavi, Kin Bineola, Kin Kletso, Peñasco Blanco, Pueblo del Arroyo, Talus Unit, and possibly others)—a total of about 2,625 elements. Approximately 1,941 of them have been sampled. Documentation of the in situ Chetro Ketl wood took place primarily between 1990 and 1996, with a few later additions. Although it is difficult to be precise about numbers, given the cutting (e.g., duplication) of elements for stabilization, missing specimens no longer in situ, and myriad other problems, wood and charcoal from Chetro Ketl have yielded about 1,285 tree-ring dates. This total is more than for any other great house, except perhaps Aztec's West Ruin, but it still fails to provide good chronometric data for some building episodes, particularly during the initial and late constructions, for the west wing and the arc of rooms bordering the south side of the plaza ("the moat rooms"), for many kivas, and for the uppermost stories. Dates from in situ elements at Chetro Ketl are also much less straightforward than at other great houses because of the extensive reuse of beams by the NPS and the frequent prehistoric reuse of timbers on a scale not duplicated at other sites. Finally, stabilization introduced about 119 modern elements into Chetro Ketl, but these are not included in the totals reported here.

With these caveats in mind, the 1,285 dated elements suggest that Chetro Ketl was built between about 990/1000 and 1112, with subsequent minor additions and modifications after the Bonito phase. Only glimpses of the earliest structure have been observed under the massive buildings raised in the early to mid-1000s. A few dates associated with the subterranean room under Room 92 in this early building, and others scattered among later construction episodes in the nearby central roomblock, indicate that an early linear roomblock, which underlies the central row of rooms in the central roomblock, was built about 990/1000. Massive remodeling episodes and additions in the 1030s through the 1060s (Figure 6.3) gave form to the present configuration. Although by the 1070s

157

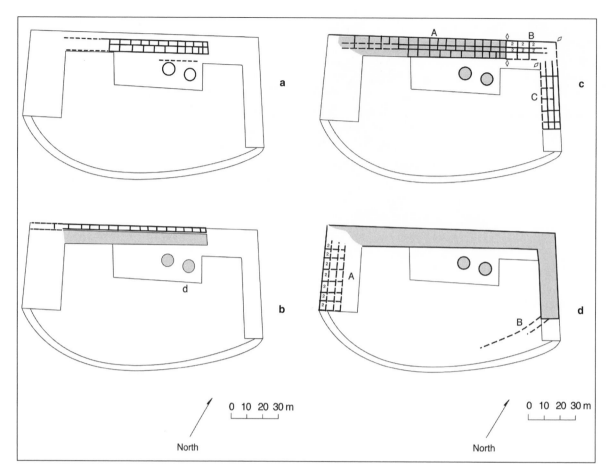

FIGURE 6.3. Chetro Ketl construction sequence: (a) 1035–1040, (b) 1045–1050, (c)1050–1055, (d) 1050? –1075?. (After Lekson 1983: Figure 4.41; redrafted by David Underwood)

the architectural mass of Chetro Ketl was well-defined, tweaking of the general form in smaller but still substantial episodes of construction continued, culminating in the addition of the colonnaded rooms, the last remodeling of the Kiva G complex in 1112, and, perhaps, the reconfiguration of the Court Kiva into a great kiva (Figure 6.3).

POINTS OF VIEW

Great houses were built to be seen (for further discussion, see Stein and others, Chapter 8, this volume). Chetro Ketl could be seen, in fact or in imagination, from countless points of view. Even, perhaps, from below: Pueblos (the people) and pueblos (the architectural form) emerged from an underworld (cosmological and literal), and aspects of Chetro Ketl might be seen as rising or emerging from below (see discussion of plaza levels, below).

Topography, architecture, and convenience suggest four "points of view" for thinking about Chetro Ketl: front, back, inside, and outside. *Front* refers to views from the south or southeast of the building. *Back* will be used here for ground-level views from the north and northwest. *Inside* refers to within the plaza. *Outside* removes the viewer from the plane of the building, to the cliffs above Chetro Ketl.[1]

Roads directed people's paths through Chaco, and directed/selected their views of its monuments (Kievit 1998). We have some sense of the road network around and between Pueblo Alto and Pueblo Bonito, but less certainty about Chetro Ketl's (Stein et al., Chapter 8, this volume; Windes 1987; Kievit 1998). Extrapolating from the dense road networks around Bonito and Alto, we can be confident that views of Chetro Ketl were aligned by roads, as well as being sure of at least a few "outside," cliff-top view points, but we cannot (or currently do not)

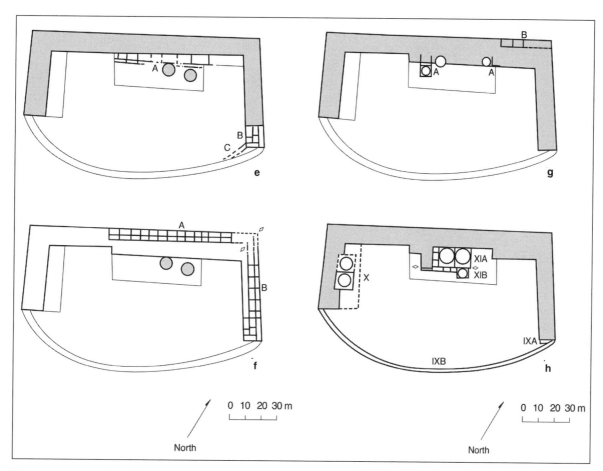

FIGURE 6.3. (cont'd.). Chetro Ketl construction sequence: (e) 1050–1060, (f) 1060–1070, (g) 1070–1075, (h) 1075–1115. (After Lekson 1983: Figure 4.41; redrafted by David Underwood)

know road routes on the ground level around Chetro Ketl. Road access at the cliff behind Chetro Ketl is reasonably well known, but major disturbances of the floodplain in front (i.e., south and southeast) of the building prevent any confident reconstruction of road routes on the ground.

Front

From the front, viewers saw the elevated plaza and its enclosing walls. Outside the building, to the east, were the mound(s) and the "Chetro Ketl field." Both mound and field are matters of much debate (Stein et al., Chapter 8, this volume; Vivian 1974, 1992). Outside Chetro Ketl to the west was an appended structure, never excavated, which has been interpreted in several ways; we mapped it as an associated "McElmo" building, but with little confidence (Lekson, ed. 1983). This, too, we decline to discuss here, avoiding additional unfounded

notions in an already heady mix of interpretations. Thus, our "front" view of Chetro Ketl looks resolutely north from the untrammeled valley floor, unobscured by mounds, "fields," and "McElmo" additions.

ELEVATED PLAZA

A singular fact of Chetro Ketl, which cannot fail to strike modern visitors, is the elevation of its plaza above the valley floor (Figure 6.4). Today, visitors walk a level path through the south-facing walls into the plaza of Pueblo Bonito, and plaza levels at other great houses are approximately on the same level as their surrounding terrain. But at Chetro Ketl, the visitor climbs more than 1.75 m up to the plaza and can look back down onto the floodplain below. Whatever their actual stratigraphy and architectural history, other great house plazas appear level; Chetro Ketl's appears dramatically

159

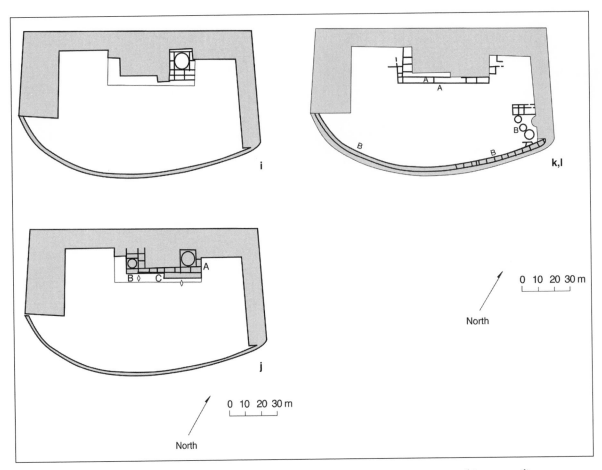

FIGURE 6.3. (cont'd.). Chetro Ketl construction sequence: (i) 1090–1095, (j) 1095–1105, (k) 1105+, (l) 1105+. (After Lekson 1983: Figure 4.41; redrafted by David Underwood)

elevated. The difference is marked and almost certainly designed. (Pueblo Alto may share this characteristic, but less markedly; if so, it is intriguing that Pueblo Alto's plaza walls also resembled Cheto Ketl's, described below.)

The current ground surface of the plaza approximates the uppermost or last plaza level of Chetro Ketl; we know this from the exposure of wall foundations on plaza-facing walls (for example, the Colonnade, discussed below).

Pueblo plazas rise through time; their stratification is the result of natural and cultural deposition, compacted through use and periodic maintenance. Chetro Ketl may have been different: the scant notes from excavation suggest that the plaza rose in two (or a very few) major events (Lekson 1983:47); that is, they were constructed. Plaza construction, rather than accretion, is supported (logically and structurally) by the enclosing walls.

The plaza walls (the "moat," discussed below) did several things, architecturally, but one thing they did was enclose space, making it possible to purposefully raise the plaza level. That is, the plaza was raised within an architectural structure.

We have limited data on other great house plazas. Judd trenched Pueblo Bonito's, several times, but the most useful published information is limited to a single profile (Judd 1964: Figure 7) of a cut through the west plaza. This trench hit two great kivas, a great deal of miscellaneous architecture, and a deep stratigraphic jumble, but a 30-foot stretch of (apparently) preserved plaza stratigraphy is shown between stations 335 and 365 (Kiva Q). About five major plaza depositional events (more than 3 vertical meters) are indicated as thick, horizontal strata. This profile supports (or at least does not contradict) suggestions in the few surviving Chetro Ketl field notes that the

Lekson, Windes, and Fournier

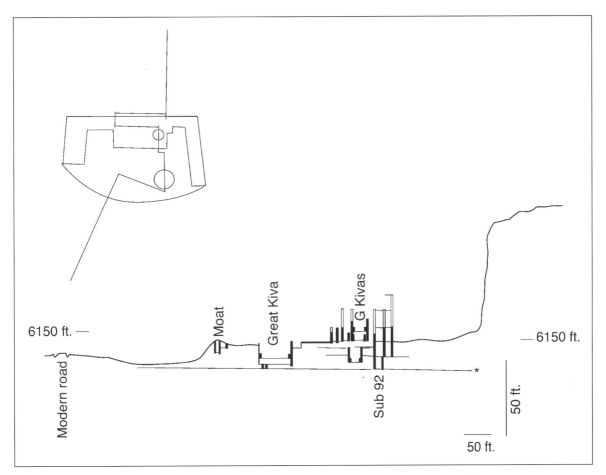

FIGURE 6.4. Schematic, composite profile of Chetro Ketl, from cliffs (right) to modern road (left). (Profile locations indicated above.) Vertical exaggeration 2.5. Star indicates probable valley floor at time of initial construction, as indicted by floor level of "Sub 92." Masonry walls in black, projected upper story walls in white. (Field data from S. H. Lekson and T. C. Windes; redrafted by David Underwood)

Chetro Ketl plaza rose in relatively few major events, rather than myriad smaller accretions. The only other modern excavation of a Chaco great house plaza, at Pueblo Alto, revealed a situation somewhat different than at Chetro Ketl and Pueblo Bonito: at Pueblo Alto, thin deposits covered the underlying bedrock in most of the plaza, but deposits in front of living rooms were much thicker, paved clay surfaces (Windes 1987:453).

The situation at Pueblo Alto suggests that plazas could be and were maintained: cleared, kept clean, probably swept. That is, casual accumulation was not a necessary aspect of Chacoan plazas. This should not surprise us, given the rigidity of Chacoan forms and the evident ability to deploy large labor forces in its construction. Some public surfaces (such as roads) were apparently maintained

at grade by labor-intensive clearing and leveling. Although gradual accretion may have played a role in the elevation of Chetro Ketl's plaza, evidence for road maintenance and a clear plaza at Pueblo Alto suggests that Chacoans could have kept the plaza at its original grade *had they chosen to do so*; that is, they had the organization and techniques to maintain plaza surfaces at construction grade, or to build and construct elevated plazas. We believe that the elevated plaza at Chetro Ketl resulted from purposeful, planned construction event(s).

THE "MOAT"
The exterior edges of the plaza were defined by two closely spaced, parallel walls that arc across the front of the building (Figure 6.2). Excavators referred to these walls as "the moat" because,

161

when they excavated the interior fill, the result was a long, narrow, trench-like space, apparently below the present (and last) plaza surface. Indeed, the floor level of the moat was well below the last plaza surface, which had been raised within the structural confines of the moat itself. Rooms were appended to the interior (plaza side) of the moat, and their floors were higher than the floors of the moat itself. That is, they were added after construction of the moat and elevation of the plaza level.

The moat was excavated and exposed only at its eastern end, and the articulation of moat, rooms, and the south end of the east wing of Chetro Ketl is visually arresting but architecturally confusing (Lekson 1983: Figure II.1). One of the first areas excavated at Chetro Ketl (in 1920), it has subsequently suffered most from well-intentioned stabilization and repair. It is almost impossible, now, to determine the construction sequence: Our best guess is that the moat articulated with the original ground floor of the east wing (currently a story below the plaza, but still well above the valley floor). The moat was plastered inside and out, and a smooth, featureless floor ran between its walls. There were no cross-walls in the excavated portion. We believe but cannot prove that the moat was roofed. As originally built, perhaps about 1070, it must have been a freestanding structure: a long, narrow, curving, hall-like room with no evident doors or openings to either the plaza or the valley floor. When the plaza was raised to the moat's roof level, the moat was filled, apparently with clean fill.

What was the moat? We have no idea. Clearly, it was not a normal domestic or habitation feature. The space was barely wide enough for a person to pass through, much less live in. The moat would have allowed unobserved movement between the east and west wings (until it was filled). It is worth noting that small tunnels between kivas, roomblocks, and towers were not uncommon at later, Pueblo III "unit pueblos" in the Northern San Juan region (but not elsewhere and not at Chaco small sites); perhaps those tunnels recall, on small, domestic scales, the monumental enclosed passages of the moat and features like it at other Chaco great houses (e.g., Pueblo Alto). But this is only conjecture.

From the front of Chetro Ketl, the moat would have presented a long, blank, curving wall. We do not know if there was an opening or gate in the unexcavated two-thirds of the moat; we think there probably was. We believe that the moat would have impeded, and probably blocked, a view (from the front) of the plaza and all but the tallest walls of the central block as they stood at the time of the moat's construction. As the central block rose upward, more would have been visible from the front of Chetro Ketl.

When the plaza surface was raised, probably after 1070, the moat was filled and changed from standing structure to retaining wall. A new plaza-enclosing structure was built: a row of small, rectangular, single-story rooms (with floors at or near the roof level of the moat) with doors opening onto the plaza. It appears that the exterior walls of these new rooms were built up from the top of the interior (plaza-facing) wall of the moat. If left exposed, the moat would have formed a filled sub-story below the row of rooms that replaced it, with a narrow exterior ledge or terrace running along the exterior of the new row of rooms created by the filled space between the plaza-facing and exterior walls of the older structure. This ledge would have been about the same width as the balconies on the rear wall of Chetro Ketl (discussed below) and may represent a similar, raised exterior walkway.

Back

The rear wall of Chetro Ketl offers one of the most dramatic views in Chaco Canyon. We suspect that most visitors to Chaco have taken photos looking down that long, tall rear wall. While the "business end" of Chetro Ketl was the plaza, the rear wall was perhaps the most monumental aspect of the building. The original rear wall of Chetro Ketl is 4.5 m in height and extends an additional 4 m below the graveled path modern visitors follow along the back of the building (Figure 6.4). That is, the first Chetro Ketl, built about 990/1000, was almost two stories below the present ground surface! This construction is known only from a few exposures below the lower floors of later construction: wall segments here and there, which approximately parallel the later rear walls.

Sofaer (Chapter 9, this volume) and her colleagues argue that the rear wall was closely aligned to the lunar standstill. Others point out that the wall roughly parallels the canyon walls, which run relatively straight behind the building. The building clearly faces and parallels the canyon wall; that is, the canyon wall was "part" of Chetro Ketl (discussed below), so this argument may have merit. As Knowles (1974), Windes (1987), and others point out for Pueblo Bonito, Chetro Ketl also takes advantage of the passive solar properties of the cliffs—no small matter in the cool months at Chaco, when you can really feel the difference. Interestingly, only Pueblo Bonito and Chetro Ketl take advantage of this property; other great houses don't (with the possible exception of Hungo Pavi—does this signify winter or year-round use of some structures, and not others?).

The precise siting of Chetro Ketl may have been determined by a larger plan for the canyon; specifically, its placement symmetrical to Pueblo Bonito across a north-south master axis (Fritz 1978). If the placement of Chetro Ketl were fixed by larger design considerations, and if the building was intended to address and incorporate the canyon walls, then the parallel alignments of canyon and rear wall make sense. But we also welcome the happy possibility that both lunar astronomy and canyon form converged in a design decision doubly charged with symbolism: both lunar and canyon orientations may have been important and simultaneously answered by the alignment of Chetro Ketl's rear wall.

Once that decision was made, subsequent construction followed it closely. The earliest construction (about 990/1000) was filled in (and the plaza elevated) as a platform for a second rear wall (about 1040); that too was "buried" (but left unfilled) by raising the plaza inside the building and, importantly, raising the surface outside the building's back or rear wall. That construction thus became a "basement" or below-grade floor level, supporting additional stories added above. The third rear wall (about 1050) consists of a row of rooms added to the exterior of the building, thus moving the rear wall about 4.5 m closer to the canyon wall. This construction was in a sense self-contained, directly congruent to but structurally independent from the older rear wall. Thus, there is a stout "double" wall (a new wall built directly against the older wall). Subsequent, planned additions were probably upward extensions: upper stories built on lower walls designed

(in their width) to support higher walls. We cannot date this highest construction, and it may have been part of a single construction event.

It is possible that, until about 1050 or later, the central block did not articulate with the east wing; that is, there may have been an open area where the northeast corner of the building now stands (or, more correctly, where that corner is now projected; it is obscured by Edgar Hewett's fill piles). While unusual, this situation would not have been unique: Chetro Ketl at this point may have resembled the much later building called Aztec East, at Aztec Ruins. After 1050, we think, the rear wall of the central block was extended to the east on precisely the same alignment by adding about one-quarter to one-third of its original length. It seems likely that the possible plaza-enclosing walls exposed in excavations of the Great Kiva and clearly predating the moat were constructed about this time.

Additional stories were added over both old and new rear walls. The highest standing remnants, which vanished when a flood wreaked havoc on Chetro Ketl in 1947, stood over the juncture of the old central block and its eastward extension. Counting back to the long-buried original Chetro Ketl, the highest-standing portions of the rear wall rose five stories (with hints of a sixth) over the original valley bottom. But the ground surface behind Chetro Ketl was probably no longer at that original level; it too rose, perhaps as planned construction matching the elevation of the plaza, perhaps as a natural process, or (most likely) a combination of both natural and architectural operations. Our interpretations are hampered by a lack of deep excavation between Chetro Ketl's rear wall and the living walls of the canyon. (Hewett dug such a trench, but all records are lost.) A deep trench and some intelligent geoarchaeology would go a long way to resolving a number of Chetro Ketl conundrums. However it happened, the ground surface (which was almost certainly architectural) at Chetro Ketl's back or rear rose up to the top of the second rear wall's first story. Other structures, discussed below, were built on this elevated surface; thus the high level of the ground surface behind Chetro Ketl does not postdate the later construction events of the building's rear wall.

163

The rear wall of Chetro Ketl, in its final config-uration, resembled a straightened version of Pueblo Bonito's: several stories tall, with a reced-ing upward slope ("battered" but not terraced). The level of each story was marked by lines of vigas, squared off at the wall surface; by small, square vent openings (two per room, placed high in the corners of each room's exterior wall); by small, raised-sill "storage" doors, filled with masonry matching that of the wall fabric; and by projecting cantilevered beams that once supported balconies. (Similar features were present at Pueblo Bonito, Pueblo del Arroyo, and probably at other mid-eleventh-century great houses.)

Balconies were a major element of the rear wall. They are gone today, represented only by empty beam sockets and the long, narrow "grooves" left by decades of stabilization. Based on surviving examples at Chaco great houses (Pueblo del Arroyo, photographed in the nineteenth century) and later Mesa Verde cliff-dwellings, balconies were narrow, probably less than a meter wide, sup-ported on short, projecting beams. They were con-structed much like the interior upper floors were: primary beams (cantilevered), smaller secondary beams, closing material, and a thin layer of dirt and clay. Presumably the wooden structural ele-ments were lashed in place, but how the balconies were finished along their exterior edges, to hold in the dirt and clay, is a mystery. These balconies were built during wall construction; hence the "grooves" representing the intrusion of closing material and earth surfaces into the wall fabric.

The balconies were "original equipment" and obviously would have aided in construction of upper story walls. They gave masons a place to stand when building the rear wall. But they con-tinued to have purposes after construction: they were access routes along the back or exterior of each story, providing a walkway around the out-side of the building on the second and third (and possibly even fourth) stories. This may represent a warehouse technology, to allow passage around sealed, interior storage rooms. Shade from bal-conies might also have served to cool the rear wall and the rooms behind it during summer.

Balconies would have greatly altered the appear-ance of the rear wall. Whereas today we see a sheer, tall face, with finely detailed masonry and an elegant batter, the balconies would have broken that face into clear vertical segments and could well have further disrupted the clean lines we see today with stacked objects, busy people, and other clutter of a living building. Chaco is Chaco, and our imagina-tions should not be bound to the quotidian: other possibilities for balconies include display of objects, ritual or sumptuary, visible but safely elevated above the ground, and (as suggested by Randall Morrison for Chetro Ketl) performance areas uti-lizing the observation sites and the remarkable acoustics of the canyon walls. In any event, Chetro Ketl's rear wall with its balconies would look very different than the wall looks today, in ruin or in graphic reconstruction.

Inside

The plaza of Chetro Ketl was almost certainly the focus of the building: its design, its function, and perhaps its very idea. Surprisingly (or, perhaps, mercifully) archaeologists at Chaco tended to neglect plazas in favor of rooms and kivas, but Hewett in his first fieldwork at Chetro Ketl set an example prescient at its time and subsequently ignored: he measured off a large square area in the southeast corner of the plaza, including the Great Kiva and the end of the east wing, and excavated across that entire surface, including the plaza. His subsequent work ignored the plaza, beyond obvi-ous great kivas. Thus a remarkable number of plaza features are visible today in the southeast corner of the plaza, but not elsewhere at the ruin. In this section, we will briefly revisit the elevation of the plaza, discuss the presence and significance of plaza "kivas," consider Chetro Ketl's great kivas, and address the changing nature of the plaza-facing walls of the central block.

PLAZA SURFACES

As discussed above, the present plaza level at Chetro Ketl approximates the final prehistoric level, at least as indicated by final construction of plaza-facing walls (see Colonnade, below). Much of the elevated plaza may be natural, presumably eolian, deposits, but we believe that the majority of the plaza repre-sents cultural—and, more accurately, architec-tural—fill. If so, the elevated plaza represents a remarkable amount of fill; at least 12,000 m^3 of earth, and probably twice that amount, in several major events spaced over a century. Think of piling fill 2 m deep or more over a soccer field. (Earth-moving on this scale has never been considered in labor estimates for Chaco architecture, and it should be; Chetro Ketl was not unique.) As the plaza rose in smaller increments, the building rose too, in larger increments: this is clearest in the central block (Figure 6.4). "Old Bonito" may have been buried by gradual accretion, but we believe that plaza and roomblocks rose during larger additions at Chetro Ketl.

"KIVAS" (ROUND ROOMS)

The raising of the plaza provided sites for plaza "kivas"—that is, round rooms excavated into plazas, below grade. Below-grade plaza kivas were the earliest form at many canyon great houses (e.g., Pueblo Bonito, Pueblo Alto, Talus Unit). They were later joined or replaced by round rooms built above-grade within roomblocks. These are variously and inelegantly described as "elevated," "blocked-in," or "enclosed" kivas. (We will revisit them from "Outside" Chetro Ketl, below.) Plaza kivas begin and perhaps end the architectural story of Chetro Ketl. Although Hewett plumbed the building's depths, spectacularly and dangerously in the Kiva G complex (Figure 6.2), he did not reach deep enough to expose the kivas of the first Chetro Ketl (990 to 1000); these structures, if they exist, would have been excavated into the original valley surface (which presumably had been leveled for construction). The tops of their walls would thus be 4.8 m below the present plaza, and their floors could be as deep as 8 m. The earliest known plaza kiva at Chetro Ketl is Kiva G-5; the tops of its walls, presumably indicating plaza level, are more than 1.5 m *above* the base level of the original roomblock walls. G-5 was built after the plaza had risen more than a meter. Hints of other round room floors in the Kiva G complex indicate later, higher plazas; around 1050/1060, however, round rooms began to be built not into the plaza, but raised up in the roomblock. (We consider these elevated round rooms below.) We think that few plaza "kivas" were built after about 1050/1060, but they reappear later: when Hewett excavated the southeastern portion of the plaza, he exposed a remarkable number of small kivas at the highest or near-highest plaza level, presumably built in the

1100s (one of these structures had been used as a dump, with trash dominated by Chaco-McElmo Black-on-white) (Figures 6.2 and 6.3). These very late plaza "kivas" are troublesome. We do not know if other examples exist. We are reasonably certain they did not along the final, plaza-facing walls of the central roomblock (i.e., the colonnade), but similar small, round rooms may have ringed the east and west edges of the plaza. We simply do not know. We believe that these round rooms represent the late restructuring of great houses, signaled by the intrusion of small round rooms into existing rectangular rooms (unlike the construction of Chacoan elevated round rooms, built into designed enclosures); Windes interprets this architectural intrusion as people establishing basically small-house occupations within the fabric of the great house. Absent deep excavations in Chetro Ketl's plaza, we cannot know if the round rooms evident in the southeast plaza were late intrusions, or the last in a long series of below-grade round rooms known as plaza "kivas."

GREAT KIVAS

The Great Kiva in Chetro Ketl's plaza had substantial time (and real) depth (Vivian and Reiter 1960). Although their accounts are far from clear, Hewett and his colleagues interpreted its stratigraphy as representing at least two great kivas, superimposed. But it appears more likely that the presently observable structures represent an earlier, lower great kiva substantially remodeled and raised, with a higher floor and extended walls, presumably coordinated with a plaza raising event. It seems unlikely that there are more great kivas below these two; fragments of possible plaza-enclosing walls were exposed below the lowest floor of the great kivas. Other great kivas may have been present, presumably to the north (following the complex history of great kivas at Pueblo Bonito). There certainly was a second great kiva, the so-called Court Kiva, about 30 m west of the currently open Great Kiva. The Court Kiva is curious on several counts: it began as a very large, subterranean, Chaco-style kiva (identical to "enclosed" or "elevated" kivas), built from a high (if not the highest) plaza surface. The placement of this Chaco-style kiva is perplexingly removed from the central roomblock. The Court Kiva sits in no clear

165

association with any rooms or suites (in contrast to elevated kivas, discussed below). Its position is in some ways complementary to the much larger, open Great Kiva (which was surely in place prior to construction of the Court Kiva): at similar distance from the two plaza-facing corners of the central block (Figure 6.2). Intriguingly, the Court Kiva was subsequently modified into a great kiva, or at least the distinctive floor features of a great kiva were superimposed on those of the existing Chaco-style kiva. This was probably late in Chetro Ketl's history, perhaps in the late 1090s or early 1100s.

The alignment of the great kiva features in the Court Kiva deviates from those of the larger great kiva. The Great Kiva symmetries are not cardinal, but address instead the axes of the building's rear wall and the canyon wall. The Court Kiva, however, when converted to a great kiva, faces both north and directly toward the colonnade. The Court Kiva was transformed into a traditionally aligned great kiva; a fanciful interpretation might make this conversion an assertion of traditional architectural form literally displayed against the novelty of the colonnade—and whatever that exotic feature represented.

THE COLONNADE

The colonnade (Figure 6.5) was the last plaza-facing wall of the central roomblock, and it surely dominated the plaza. We do not know what the

FIGURE 6.5. Chetro Ketl colonnade (Photograph by S. H. Lekson)

earlier walls of the central roomblock looked like; they were not exposed in deep excavations. Perhaps they too were colonnades, but probably not. The colonnade was not the last plaza construction: apparently, sometime after the colonnade was built, the openings were filled in with crude masonry and a row of rooms was built outside (i.e., on the plaza side). These rooms did not survive, presumably because their masonry was insubstantial (the foundations or base course are still visible). In our opinion the Chetro Ketl colonnade was unique; rumors of a comparable feature at Bc 51 are not convincing, admittedly at many years' remove.

Whether unique to Chetro Ketl or to Chaco, no comparable features are known from other Anasazi sites. Colonnades very like Chetro Ketl's were prominent at Paquimé, far to the south, and Lekson (1999) holds out hopes for a similar feature in the unexcavated portions of Aztec Ruins (especially Aztec North), but Chetro Ketl's colonnade currently stands alone in Anasazi building. Because of the historical importance of the colonnade in interpretations of the Bonito phase, we devote considerable space to it here.

Hewett (1936:65) recognized the colonnade as "an architectural feature found nowhere else in America north of Aztec Mexico," an interpretation made more emphatically by Edward Ferdon (1955) in *A Trial Survey of Mexican-Southwestern Architectural Parallels*. Subsequent archaeologists and visitors have accepted a vague Mexican inspiration for the colonnade, but Mexico is a big place with a long history. Nelson (2000, 2005) notes that colonnades have separate histories in various parts of Mexico. Di Peso (1974), Lister (1978), and Hayes (1981) sought the source in Tula, but (as we shall see) this derivation seems unlikely. The colonnade is potentially a very important feature, as provocative as an I-shaped ballcourt or an Iroquois longhouse, had either been found at Chaco. Therefore, an extended discussion of its provenance seems warranted. We review here several models for understanding Chetro Ketl's colonnade.

Much has been discussed concerning the similarities in architectural features between Tula and Chaco Canyon, and particularly the colonnade, since Ferdon (1955) suggested that Toltecs or people influenced by them introduced new traits into the Southwest through pochteca-like merchants. This statement as well as different commodities and conceptions found in the Southwest whose origin is assumed to be "Mesoamerican," most of which are questionable (Lekson, 1983; McGuire 1980:10), led to the elaboration of different models based on one or more interaction dimensions: the exchange of information, the exchange of material goods, sociopolitical relations, or the movement of people (Hegmon et al. 2000:4).

The isolationist model rejects the possibility that interaction with Mesoamerica affected Southwestern developments (as discussed by Frisbie 1983:216; see also Judge 1989, 1991). The rejection of direct connections assumes that ideas and goods move by indirect and nondependent exchange (e.g., Nelson 2000:318, 2006).

In the Southwest, an early Mesoamerican influence in the Hohokam Pioneer period of southern Arizona has been suggested as having occurred through an unregulated diffusion process. A later intrusion by the Hohokam during the Colonial period (now dated to ca. 750–900; Doyel and Fish 2000:5) came via the west Mexican coast, apparently as a well-planned pochteca entry, with developed colonies and trading posts (Schroeder 1981:45, 49, 51; Haury 1976:343–348). The Hohokam as trade-merchants could then have introduced Mesoamerican traits to Chaco (Schroeder 1981). In this model, interaction was mediated through the Hohokam, who transmitted ideas and commodities from Mesoamerica through northwestern Mexico.

The pochteca model proposed that groups of specialized traders from Mesoamerica intervened directly in Chaco, controlling cultural developments through political-economic influences (Kelley 1966; Kelley and Kelley 1975; Lister 1978). Wallerstein's world-systems model was adopted to interpret pochetca political-economic relationships between Mesoamerica and the Southwest (e.g., Braniff 1994; Di Peso 1974, 1983). The social relations involved in political-economic exchanges are the result of dependency relations as an imperial strategy from the core impacts the periphery, integrating the periphery as a frontier. In this model, Chacoan "great houses" may be viewed as emporia designed for turquoise procurement and distribution on the northern frontier of the Mesoamerican world economy (e.g., Weigand and Harbottle 1993). The boundaries of the system are

those of Greater Mesoamerica extending its domain to the American Southwest.

After the demise of Teotihuacan around AD 600, rearrangements of power structures at the core resulted in warfare and the formation of new polities on the periphery. These pressures may have affected developments in the Southwest with the aggregation and adoption of Mesoamerican practices (Nelson 2000). This model views violence as a form of sociopolitical interaction. Another model considered war as well as long-distance trade and mining as the factors that led to the integration of the Southwest into a symbiotic interaction sphere, as part of a Mesoamerican "world economy" (Weigand 2001:39; see also Kelley 1995; Pailes and Whitecotton 1979).

The pochteca model has been criticized because the data are insufficient to support it (e.g., Cordell 1984; McGuire 1980; Mathien 1986; Vivian 1970). The connection between Mesoamerica and the Southwest was indirect, through exchange with North and West Mexico with the articulation of different regional alliances (Cobb et al. 1999; McGuire 1980; Upham 1986). Interaction was mediated by northwestern Mexico and included the exchange of information and goods both from this region and from the core, with no direct political-economic influence on Southwestern developments.

Nevertheless, parallels between Mesoamerican and Chacoan architecture still haunt scholars. These similarities and their meaning are not easily explained (Cobb et al. 1999:170; Lekson 1983, 2000; Weigand 2001:58). As noted above, the Chetro Ketl colonnade is one of these similarities.

From our perspective, the analogy between the impressive colonnaded halls with round columns and rectangular pilasters found in Tula and the modest colonnaded hall with pilaster-like features in Chetro Ketl remains valid. The parallels in certain aspects of architecture at Tula and Chaco Canyon, particularly the unique colonnade at Chetro Ketl, are probably attributable to the adoption of Mesoamerican symbols propitiated by the flow of ideas carried by merchants, which were modified for the Southwest situation (e.g., Bey and Ringle 2000; Lekson 2000:12–13; Ringle et al. 1998).

During the Early Postclassic period (900–1200), Tula was the first major post-Teotihuacan state system in central Mexico, influencing vast areas of precolumbian Mexico through new, widely shared religious symbols associated with Quetzalcoatl, the feathered or plumed serpent—the god of creation associated with the planet Venus. Like Teotihuacan, Tula may have been a territorial state (e.g., Charlton and Nichols 1997:188, 197).

The city of Tula apparently covered more than 16 km² and had a population that has been estimated at between 32,000 and 60,000 (Diehl 1981:284; Healan et al. 1989:245). The urban architecture exhibits a complex plan with a sunken main plaza; pyramid structures; I-shaped ballcourts; sunken patios; colonnaded halls and vestibules with round columns or square pillars; halls and large rooms with central impluvia and an open area above them; halls, vestibules, and rooms with stone benches, sometimes with altars projecting from them; and walls that surround pyramids.

The main precinct is formed by a monumental platform with sloping sides, which covers more than 1,900,000 m². The religious-administrative area, encompassing about 15,500 m², consists of several major buildings: the Palacio Quemado (Burnt Palace), covering more than 1,500 m², is the most impressive, with 305 columns and pillars (e.g., Patiño 1994:51).

Colonnaded halls and corridors exhibit a careful and harmonic architectural design, as does the general plan of colonnaded buildings. Most colonnaded halls (measuring up to 400 m²) and vestibules apparently were covered with flat roofs built on a base of horizontal beams and sufficiently sloped for drainage. Columns and pilasters may have been constructed using eight or four vertical poles, respectively, covered with small pieces of limestone and clay, and coated with stucco. The room walls as well as columns and pillars supported the roofs, and doorways had wooden lintels (e.g., Acosta 1960:48; Diehl 1989:24; Margáin 1971:65).

By the time Tula attained the zenith of its power, its zone of dominance in Central Mexico may have encompassed more than 25,000 km². Such domination was probably mainly militaristic, involving payment of tribute. This area was integrated economically, politically, socially, and ideologically, although the physical evidence of imperial control over this region is not clear. In addition, Tula's attainment of true preeminence as a center of trade and commerce, and the extent of the trade networks associated with or dominated by the Toltec state, are not clear (e.g., Charlton and Nichols 1997:196–197; Davies 1977:320).

Colonnaded halls with columns or pillars predate Tula. Pilasters have been identified in residential compounds and "palaces" like the Quetzalpapalotl precinct in Teotihuacan (e.g., Cabrera 1998; Morelos 1993), built before 600; therefore they may be part of an old architectural tradition in Central Mexico. Epiclassic settlements such as Plazuelas, Guanajuato (ca. 600–750), have colonnaded halls with wood pilasters at ceremonial-administrative precincts (Castañeda 1998; Juárez 1999).

At Tula we find similarities with northern Mexican architectural columns and pilasters (e.g., Acosta 1956–1957: Map 1; Paredes 1990:120), particularly with those at La Quemada and Alta Vista. The strongest parallels, though, including calendrical orientations, are between Tula and Chichen Itza, a coeval polity located in the Yucatan; the extant archaeological evidence points to direct interaction between Tula and Chichen Itza.

Recent research at La Quemada shows that previous interpretations that this settlement was a Toltec outpost, controlling the redistribution of turquoise from Chaco Canyon to Tula, are not valid. The occupation of the site and the construction of the impressive Hall of Columns date to the late Classic and Epiclassic periods (500–900) based on radiocarbon dates; La Quemada represents the growth of an autonomous polity in the northern periphery, independent of the Mesoamerican core states (Nelson 1997).

Architectural features at Alta Vista include astronomical markers apparently derived from Teotihuacan (Aveni et al. 1982), which evidence information exchange. Some authors believe that Alta Vista was integrated into the influence sphere of Teotihuacan (Kelley 1976), either through colonization or as a result of political and economical pressures (Weigand 1993). The Hall of Columns was built between 200 and 550, probably by the end of this phase if we compare this building with the one at La Quemada. Alta Vista and La Quemada were abandoned around 900 (Gómez-Gastélum 1999).

North of Alta Vista, and after its decline, small settlements like La Ferrería exhibit modest halls of columns and contain evidence that exotic birds were raised, apparently influenced by Casas Grandes as well as interaction with Nayarit and Sinaloa (Guevara 2001:56–57). In Northwest Mexico, sites like El Cuarenta, Jalisco (500–1000), exhibit halls with massive masonry columns (Piña Chan and Taylor 1976:3).

The northern frontier of the Mesoamerican culture area shifted through time. Most researchers include the Pacific Coast of northwest Mexico (Nayarit and Sinaloa) in Mesoamerica after the decline of Teotihuacan (e.g., Braniff 1994; Schöndube 1990). Western Mexico is key to understanding early social interaction between Mesoamerica and the Southwest; recent research in Michoacan shows that ceramic styles developed prior to 350 reached Arizona and became part of the Hohokam design repertoire for the Snaketown phase; the patterns are symbols of complex cosmological systems that may have been widely shared by groups in northwestern Mexico and the American Southwest (Carot 2000:100–101). Probably between 900 and 1150, casual trade between Northwest Mexico and the Southwest was reinforced, accelerated, and formalized through middlemen (McGuire 1980:30).

Several routes that follow natural corridors are proposed for the flow of commodities, ideas, and even for the movement of groups of colonizers; most scholars agree that the main routes were up the coast to Guasave, Sinaloa, and Huatabampo, Sonora, and up the east flanks of the Sierra Madre or through the Great Chichimeca deserts from central Mesoamerica to Durango on the periphery (Braniff 1994:73; McGuire 1980:29). After the decline of Alta Vista around 900, the second route may not have been viable in terms of promoting interaction between the Mesoamerican core and Chaco Canyon.

The Mesoamerica-Chaco connection thus may have been the result of an interaction mechanism of indirect contact between nuclear Mesoamerica and Chaco through northwestern Mexico. Long-distance interaction resulted in the transmission not only of goods but also of ancient Mesoamerican architectural styles as part of a complex ideological scheme that was never successfully integrated in the Chacoan context. The development and dispersion of traits such as colonnaded halls cannot be attributed to the Toltecs.

Chaco Canyon selectively employed prestige symbols from Mesoamerica and northwestern Mexico that were embedded in more complex worldviews. Social interaction may have taken place as an indirect process through long-distance exchange networks, and only a limited number of features associated with these systems were transmitted, without having any drastic impact on the social structure among the Anasazi. A limited number of ideas and stylistic trends were acquired, modified, and integrated in the Southwestern milieu; Mesoamerican patterns, sets of rules, and conceptual regularities did not find their way to Chaco. The evidence suggests that Mesoamerican interests were exclusively directed toward Southwestern goods such as turquoise; Chacoan ideas and conceptions probably did not find their way southward.

A logical alternative, of course, would be the colonnade as an independent invention, totally unrelated to Mexican architecture. Given the number of Mesoamerican objects found at Chaco and strong arguments for the U.S. Southwest being, in some sense, the northwest of ancient Mexico (e.g., Lekson 1999; Nelson 2000), the idea of independent invention seems unlikely and unnecessary.

Thus we conclude that the Chetro Ketl colonnade is a local architectural interpretation of Mexican models, modified to suit local materials and techniques. Note that the "columns" were short and squat: they rose from a standard Chacoan wall about 0.8 m above ground level to a roof about 2.1 m above the plaza level. The openings between columns were more than twice the width of typical rectangular doors, but not much larger than the span of the largest T-shaped doors at Chaco (for example, one in Room 38 at Chetro Ketl), and less than a quarter of the beam span between the pillars of Chetro Ketl's Great Kiva.

The "raised sill" of the colonnade resembles the raised sills of storage doors and separates the Chacoan form from most Mexican examples. We believe that this modification of Mexican models reflects concern with the load-bearing requirements of the columns, problematic foundations for small column footprints (recall the huge sandstone disks beneath great kiva columns), and the likelihood of failure of tall, small-section rectangular piers under uneven loads. They could indeed build freestanding columns that worked well under huge loads: witness the masonry columns beneath great kiva roofs. We suggest, without engineering analysis to back up our suggestion, that great kiva loads, coming from all sides of the column, worked together to stabilize the column, whereas a colonnade was unsupported on its open, plaza-facing side. That is, no forces or loads countered the outward push of heavy roofing. In short, by the early 1100s, Chacoan builders had full command of their materials and techniques, and they probably were wary of building full-height columns in a colonnade.

The colonnade would have been a remarkable architectural statement, possibly the defining form at Chetro Ketl or even at Chaco. It was prominent, even dominating, within the plaza. But it would have been invisible from the front of the building (from the valley bottom) the back of the building, and from outside the building (from the cliffs above). There are two major exceptions to this last statement: stairways across the rincon and across the canyon offered distant, oblique views of the colonnade (Figure 6.6).

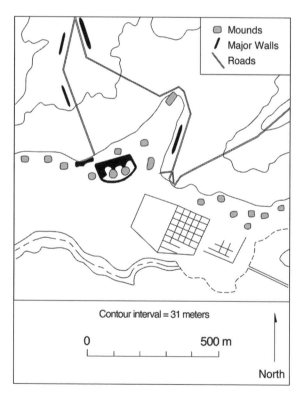

FIGURE 6.6. Chetro Ketl rincon and roads. (After Holley and Lekson 1999: Figure 3.1, redrafted by David Underwood)

Because the alignment of Chetro Ketl's rear wall was almost perpendicular to the southeast-northwest trend of the canyon, the colonnade did not directly face the opposite canyon wall but instead opened up-canyon, out to nothing. We conclude that the colonnade was meant to be seen from inside Chetro Ketl—that is, from within the plaza.

Outside
"Outside" here refers to out, back, and above: the cliff-top views that clearly were part of Chetro Ketl's design. (As noted above, views from the opposite canyon rim, while impressive, were much greater in distance and less direct in angle.) Great houses in and beyond the canyon were designed and sited to see and be seen. Roads and landscape architecture extended the design of great houses to their approaches, channeling traffic and creating viewpoints. Great houses were parts of shaped landscapes, and vice versa.

These aspects of great house design are particularly evident at Cheto Ketl. Roads on the cliffs above the building channeled traffic to particular viewpoints (several are still in use by today's visitors), and then down to specific approaches to the building (Figure 6.6). Chetro Ketl sits to the west of the mouth of a short rincon. Three major stairs led down to Chetro Ketl: due east, across the rincon; at the head of the rincon; and above Talus Unit. The stairway due east across the rincon offered an oblique view of the colonnade and the interior of the plaza from a distance of about 200 m (closer than the cross-canyon stairway, 600 m distant). It is not clear where the road that leads down this stairway begins. It may be connected to the Pueblo Alto–Pueblo Bonito–Chetro Ketl network, but more likely it represents one of three stairways at the end of a road running off to the northeast, away from Pueblo Alto and downtown Chaco (Windes 1987: Figure 5.2). The rincon-head stairway and the Talus Unit complex represent two forks of the Pueblo Alto–Chetro Ketl road, which joined or incorporated the Great North Road (Figure 6.6). The Great North Road enters Chaco through an opening in the massive wall running east from Pueblo Alto and then runs along the east side of Pueblo Alto's mound to an elaborate terrace/stairway, where it is joined by a spur road from Pueblo Alto itself. These combined routes

Lekson, Windes, and Fournier

continue for about 150 m and then fork into two roads, one running to the Chetro Ketl rincon-head stairway and the other to the Talus Unit complex.[2]

The rincon-head stairway is today marked by an impressive earth-filled masonry ramp on the rincon floor and broad stairs cut into the sandstone above. Between the two, a long span must have been crossed by a wooden stairway, now gone. The cliff top at the rincon head does not present a good view of Chetro Ketl: indeed, the building was not directly visible, though this stairway did look out onto the Chetro Ketl mound and the "Chetro Ketl field." The overlook above Talus Unit provided the best viewpoint, above the northwest corner of Chetro Ketl. Talus Unit itself represents a small great house and an elaborate masonry ramp–sandstone stairway complex, which almost certainly included a long wooden stairway, now gone (Lekson 1986). A remarkable solid masonry pier, rising west of the ramp in the middle of the Talus Unit complex, may represent another stairway. It is possible that a third route existed down from the overlook, just east of Talus Unit. This third route is suggested by numerous beam sockets pecked into the sheer cliff face behind the northwest corner of Chetro Ketl. A number of these sockets form horizontal lines 2 or 3 m long, suggesting roof lines at remarkable (even alarming) elevations up the cliff face. These beam sockets are understudied, but they are usually interpreted as a cliff face "pueblo" or masonry structure. We doubt this for two reasons: there is no corresponding rubble beneath the beam sockets, and the lines of beam sockets do not appear to form stories. We suggest, instead, that these beam sockets formed a third stairway at Talus Unit, a stairway made entirely of wood with platforms and stages socketed directly into the cliff face. Thus there were certainly one and perhaps as many as three monumental stairways leading down from the end of the road (the Great North Road?) above Talus Unit. The cliff above Talus Unit was clearly a major viewpoint, where those traveling on the road first saw Chetro Ketl. What did they see?

From the cliff above Talus Unit, the viewer looked down on the northwest corner of Chetro Ketl (this analysis owes much to Karen Kievit's analysis; see Kievit 1998:229–235, and n. 8). The curve of the D shape of the building would be evident, but from this viewpoint the sharp, near-right-angle formed by the straight rear wall and the west wing would be foremost. The west wing would be the closest and most visible part of Chetro Ketl; unfortunately, we know relatively little about this unexcavated portion of the site, beyond the fact that it included two major, elevated round rooms. The rear wall was prominent, but because of the steep angle (the viewer was not directly over the rear wall, but almost), the impact of its height was greatly diminished. It's hard to tell how tall something is from directly or nearly directly overhead. Its length is also foreshortened from this viewpoint.

We will return to the central roomblock below, but for a moment we jump over that complex to the Great Kiva and the southeast corner of the building. Those impressive features would be farthest from the viewer and at a shallow, oblique angle of view, and difficult to comprehend; indeed, the circularity of the Great Kiva is not obvious from the Talus Unit viewpoint.

The complex central roomblock was and is open to view from above Talus Unit. Perhaps as visually important as the two round rooms of the west wing, the central roomblock would have presented an arresting vista dominated by "kivas" (round rooms). These were elevated round rooms, built on the second and third stories of a rectangular mass of rooms. The nearest round room (Kiva N) was a tower kiva: that is, two and perhaps three round chambers built in a column. Its exterior was not round or silo-like; instead it was a rectangular construction with a circular interior roof evident on the uppermost surface. (It is unlikely that the lower round rooms would be evident from the Talus Unit viewpoint, or indeed from the plaza.) West of the tower were two large, Chaco-style round rooms (Kivas I and J), elevated on the first-story level and surrounded on three and perhaps four sides by second-story rooms, thus forming a partially or fully enclosed courtyard or sunken patio in the center of the massive central roomblock. These unusual forms would be very obvious from the Talus Unit viewpoint; as with the colonnade (invisible from the Talus Unit overlook), there was nothing like them elsewhere at Chaco or in the region. Inward-focused patios are, of course, a southern form, known from the Hohokam region and throughout northern Mexico (as well as farther

171

south). North Mexican and Mesoamerican patio forms do not, of course, have "kivas" in the middle of the patios. (Were Kivas I and J a local transformation of southern forms?) Towering over Kivas I and J was the Kiva G complex, the formal antithesis of the sunken patio: Kiva G (in its final form) was an enclosed round room on the third-story level, taller than the tower kiva at the other end of the central roomblock.

Beyond the central roomblock lay the plaza. As noted above, the Great Kiva was visible, but the shallow angle of view made its form uncertain. If it had risen a story above the plaza, like the great kivas reconstructed at Aztec Ruin, it would of course have been more prominent (but it is also difficult to determine the form of the reconstructed great kiva at Aztec from the bluffs behind that site). The Court Kiva, however, was sited to be easily visible from the Talus Unit overlook, facilitated by the absence of structures between the central roomblock and the west wing (Figure 6.2); these two masses are connected by only a few rows of rooms along the back wall. Today, the Court Kiva is backfilled and invisible. At 1100, it might have been more obvious from the Talus Unit overlook than the much larger Great Kiva.

Thus we return to the Court Kiva, a curious structure. As noted above, it was placed far out into the plaza, an apparent spatial complement to the Great Kiva. It also had a curious history: first a Chaco-style kiva, later a great kiva. It was of remarkable size: the Court Kiva was one of the largest Chaco-style kivas and, subsequently, one of the smallest great kivas (Lekson 1984: Figure 3.5). If, as Lekson argues (see below and Chapter 2, this volume) Chacoan "kivas" (round rooms) were in fact residences, the Court Kiva by its conspicuous size and placement may have been the residence of a family or group of central importance to Chetro Ketl. Its subsequent conversion to a great kiva is intriguing and suggestive, but we have speculated more than enough without following that tantalizing lead.

The Changing Faces of Chetro Ketl

Like all the largest great houses, Chetro Ketl changed through time. We are uncertain of its initial configuration (did the original Chetro Ketl have wings, or plaza-enclosing walls?), but that plan apparently determined the orientation and perhaps the form of subsequent building episodes. The original rear wall probably fixed the orientation of subsequent rear walls (and, by extension, the central roomblock). There may have been early east and west wings, too: there are hints, in walls observed below the Great Kiva, of plaza-enclosing walls long before the moat, parallel in form but smaller in extent. The rebuilding of the Great Kiva indicates its location was fixed sometime after those earlier enclosing walls, and then maintained in place. Compared with Pueblo Bonito, Chetro Ketl's plan unfolded in a relatively steady progression. Or so it seems: perhaps its shorter construction history (by a century), and the less extensive excavations, give Chetro Ketl a false picture of architectural simplicity.

Hewett was not Neil Judd's equal as an excavator. Judd's work at Pueblo Bonito revealed significant razing and rebuilding, sometimes on plans and orientations quite different from preceding construction. Chetro Ketl evidences less of that large-scale dithering: its form appears to have simply enlarged, in stages, upon an initial design. However, we cannot be sure of this conclusion: Hewett seldom plumbed the depths of the site, and where he did, earlier walls were often found. (Most paralleled or prefigured later construction.) Conversely, Judd never took apart a complex, above-grade kiva construction, as Hewett and his colleagues did with Kiva G (Miller 1937). The daring of that excavation is unequalled in Chacoan archaeology. (Visit Kiva G, today, and think what OSHA would have said.)

The Kiva G complex looms large in recent discussions of Chacoan "kivas" (Crown and Wills 2003). The Kiva G complex is the most conspicuous example of the in-place rebuilding of Chetro Ketl's round rooms (note also the Court Kiva and Great Kiva). As noted above, Hewett's excavation strategies may be to blame for the lack of evidence for rebuilding at other kivas: Hewett often stopped digging at the uppermost floor, so lower, earlier structures (if present) were not exposed. Crown and Wills attribute "kiva" reconstruction to "ritual renewal" comparable to rebuilding of Shinto shrines every twenty years, or refacing of Mesoamerican pyramids on a longer ritual cycle

(Crown and Wills 2003:525). This intriguing argument begins with the assumption that kivas were, fundamentally, ritual structures. Crown and Wills wisely distance their argument from the prevailing popular view of kivas as churches—a Park Service metaphor, not theirs; they see kivas, great and small, as "communal buildings in which ritual took place" (Crown and Wills 2003:518). Repeated rebuilding thus reflects requirements for ritual renewal by the user group, which varied from structure to structure.

The modification and rebuilding of Chaco round rooms may be evidence of habitation: as Crown and Wills note, small Chaco "kivas" were modified and rebuilt far more often than rectangular rooms. Rectangular living rooms were sometimes modified but seldom rebuilt, unless the addition of new stories or roomblocks constitutes rebuilding. Lekson has used this same evidence (of intensive rebuilding and remodeling) to argue that "kivas" were domiciles: more architectural effort was expended on the family home than on areas used for storage or other great house functions. Lekson (1984, 1988, 1989, and Chapter 2, this volume) argues that small Chaco and Mesa Verde "kivas" were not ritual structures (that is, the earliest examples of Pueblo kivas), but instead the last of a centuries-long tradition of pithouse dwellings. The argument is too long to repeat here, but Anasazi "kivas" may be seen as analogous (but not necessarily historically connected) to Navajo hogans: traditional house forms in which much family and individually oriented ceremony indeed takes place, but fundamentally *houses*. At Yellow Jacket, the largest Mesa Verde site, there is one "kiva" for every three above-ground rooms (Kuckelman 2003); the "user group" in that case is almost certainly a single family. If this was the case at Pueblo III sites in the Mesa Verde area, why should we believe anything different of Pueblo II "kivas" at Chaco? The room-to-kiva ratios differ wildly, but surely this reflects more on the unusual nature of great houses than on the pithouse-"kivas." (In this argument, great kivas are seen as "communal buildings in which rituals took place," and the historical precursors of modern Pueblo forms.)

Lekson believes "kivas" at small sites were residences and, at great houses, elite residences—conspicuous and expensive housing. Building big, flashy houses would have posed a problem for emerging elites at Chaco: If homes are traditionally below grade, how do you make one conspicuous? Elevate it, get it out of the ground and up where it can be seen. The Kiva G complex, ending with a third-story "kiva," is a remarkable example. But even elevated, enclosed kivas are not obvious from ground level; the viewer sees the rectangular exterior walls, not the house form itself.

Windes does not discount the possibility that "kivas" were used in part as habitations, but he does not believe that they were "living rooms" in the traditional sense. Rectangular, surface living rooms are in fact found in great houses, but given the differences in location, shape, floor features, and artifacts, we must ask what roles these two very different types of structures took. In addition, Windes believes that the small kivas represent part of the triad of structures associated with basic domestic units, as found in small sites and tucked away in the corners of great houses during the last occupations, but that the very large "court" kivas, later shifted in location from the plazas to the roomblocks, are specific to Chaco great houses and represent some activity beyond mere domestic use; in fact, their very size, sometimes with the feature attributes of great kivas, would place them as great kivas anywhere else outside the confines of the great house.

Presumably, Chacoan viewers had keys to denote "kiva" versus non-kiva spaces: distinctive ladders, for example. But the most spectacular architectural message would be seen from above: the circular "kiva" wall within the rectangular enclosure. This view of Chetro Ketl was offered, most effectively, from the Talus Unit overlook. It seems possible that the road was routed to allow people moving in-canyon on the North Road to see, and appreciate, the spectacular size, elevation, and monumentality of Chetro Ketl's Kivas I, J, and G, and the two (unexcavated) kivas of the west wing. (There were no major round rooms in the east wing, a fact perhaps of significance for the routing of the road to Talus Unit.) Consider, also, the very large Court Kiva: as noted above, it was particularly visible from the Talus Unit overlook.

Given the multiple possible routes for entering the canyon (three at Chetro Ketl alone, and several more were practical but unbuilt), Chaco planners had choices to make about road routes and labor investment in ramps, stone stairs, and wooden stairways. It appears that of Chetro Ketl's three routes, Talus Unit was the most complex, with perhaps three monumental stairways running from the overlook down to Chetro Ketl. (It was also the most direct route from Pueblo Alto to Chetro Ketl, but arguments of simple efficiency are probably misplaced at Chaco.)

We suggest that the basic plan of Chetro Ketl was fixed by about 1030 and that road alignments were planned or adjusted later, to direct travelers on the North Road to particular views of the great building. Those views emphasized some aspects of Chetro Ketl over others: the Talus Unit overlook is not optimal for seeing the rear wall, the elevated plaza, the Great Kiva, or the colonnade, but the major kivas were spectacularly visible. If these were important people's homes, incoming visitors knew their number and scale long before reaching the canyon floor.

Conversely, these structures and much else (for example, the colonnade) were not visible from the canyon floor (i.e., from the "front" of Chetro Ketl). The elevated plaza made Chetro Ketl itself difficult to see from mid canyon. The elevation of Chetro Ketl's plaza is clearly a strong architectural signal, but what is it telling us? The enormous labor required would have made it possible to build over and upwards from earlier structures, but we believe that the elevation of the building itself above the valley bottom was the goal. A simple explanation for raising the building might be to avoid floods. It is unlikely that the Chaco Wash ever jumped its banks to threaten great houses; however, some Bonito phase structures were in fact completely buried by stream deposits (Judd 1954: Plate 4 lower; 1964: Plate XX). (Note that Chetro Ketl's disastrous flood in 1947 came from its own rincon, not from the Chaco Wash.) It is possible that Chetro Ketl was raised for practical reasons, but we suspect there was more involved, such as rituals of renewal or expressions of power. The old building was buried and a new building rose on its site, not tell-like but *directly* on the walls of what came before. There is much in Crown and Wills's suggestions of renewal: are parallels in great houses to be found Mesoamerican architecture, in the ritual refacing of pyramids?

But they are also, we think, expressions of power: Chetro Ketl displayed its power to travelers on the North Road (and those on the road from Tsin Kletsin, on the valley rim opposite), but denied that view to those on the valley bottom. Because the plaza was elevated, the building was difficult to see from the canyon floor and from habitations on the opposite side of the canyon. We think that was a design choice (constrained by landscape and prior history): Chetro Ketl did not need or want to expose its structure to southside riffraff, who presumably knew their place in Chacoan society, but its monumental plan was literally an open book for road-travelers from the north. Perhaps the southsiders walked the roads; perhaps they even lived in the great houses (Windes 1987, 1993); but Lekson believes that great houses and small sites represent different social strata, and roads extend great houses' reach in a regional architecture, layering power over larger landscapes. Architectural expressions of power were manifested in the changing forms and structured views of Chetro Ketl.

NOTES

1. We avoid views from west (Pueblo Bonito) and east (stairway across the rincon, east of Chetro Ketl) not because they were not important, but because uncertainties about the nature of the large masonry structure appended to the west side of Chetro Ketl make the Pueblo Bonito view uncertain, and the original nature of the Chetro Ketl mound (the foreground of the east rincon stairway) is hotly debated. Moreover, following Kievit 1998, we limit our cliff-top viewpoint to the end of the road above Talus Unit, although closer views were available along the cliff rim to the east. From the Talus Unit overlook, as Kievit notes, Pueblo Bonito is not visible: this location above Talus Unit is probably the westernmost point on the canyon rim behind Chetro Ketl where this happens: travel further west along the rim and Pueblo Bonito comes into view. The route of the road to this point was probably not an accident.

2. The Talus Unit complex and the rincon-head ramp are perhaps the most monumental stairways entering downtown Chaco. It would be possible to argue that the North Road runs down the Talus Unit complex and the rincon-head ramp to Chetro Ketl, and that the North Road is therefore associated with Chetro Ketl and

other large sites east of the "Fritz line" separating the east and west halves of downtown Chaco (Fritz 1978). Consider the half-dozen largest buildings at Chaco in relation to this line. To the west are Pueblo Bonito, which was not directly connected to the North Road, and Peñasco Blanco, which had clear road connections to the west. Both of these major buildings shared the ancient, curved form, reminiscent of Pueblo I villages. Also to the west are some of the largest, late "McElmo" structures: Kin Kletso, the massive "McElmo" blocks of the north and south wings of Pueblo del Arroyo, and New Alto. East of the Fritz line are several very large, conspicuously rectangular, L or [-shaped buildings: Chetro Ketl, Hungo Pavi, and (less certainly) Una Vida. Una Vida, alone of the three early Bonito phase sites, abandoned the curved form and became a rectangular or subrectangular L. Pueblo Alto straddles the Fritz axis but clearly falls in the [-shaped group. Chetro Ketl and Aztec Ruins are formally quite similar (as noted above), and many archaeologists have noted the nearly identical forms of Hungo Pavi and Salmon Ruins. Might Chetro Ketl and Hungo Pavi (and perhaps other major buildings east of the line) have been associated with the North Road, and in some sense historically connected with the later buildings at the North Road's other end, Salmon and Aztec Ruins? Many objections can be raised to this line of speculation, but we offer it here because it may prove a useful basis for future thinking about the North Road and its implications for downtown Chaco.

REFERENCES

Acosta, Jorge R.
1956–   Interpretación de algunos datos obtenidos en
1957   Tula relativos a la época tolteca. *Revista Mexicana de Estudios Antropológicos* 14:75–160. Sociedad Mexicana de Antropología, México.
1960   Las exploraciones arqueológicas en Tula, Hgo., durante la XI temporada, 1955. *Anales del Instituto Nacional de Antropología e Historia* XI:39–72. México.

Aveni, Anthony F., Horst Hatung, and J. Charles Kelley
1982   Alta Vista (Chalchihuites): Astronomical Implications of a Mesoamerican Ceremonial Outpost at the Tropic of Cancer. *American Antiquity* 47:316–335.

Bey, George J. III, and William M. Ringle
2000   From the Bottom Up: The Tingle and Nature of the Tula-Chichen Exchange. Paper presented at the Colloquium "Rethinking Tula, Tollan, and Chichen Itzá," Dumbarton Oaks, Washington, DC.

Braniff, Beatriz
1994   The Mesoamerican Northern Frontier and the Gran Chichimeca. In *Culture and Contact: Charles C. Di Peso´s Gran Chichimeca*, edited by Anne I. Woosley and John C. Ravesloot, pp. 65–82. University of New Mexico Press, Albuquerque.

Cabrera, Rubén
1998   El urbanismo y la arquitectura en La Ventilla. Un barrio en la ciudad de Teotihuacan. In *Antropología e Historia del Occidente de México. XXIV Mesa Redonda de la Sociedad Mexicana de Antropología*, vol. 3, pp. 1523–1547. Sociedad Mexicana de Antropología, México.

Carot, Patricia
2000   Las Rutas del Desierto: de Michoacán a Arizona. In *Nómadas y Sedentarios en el Norte de México, Homenaje a Beatriz Braniff*, edited by Marie-Areti Hers, José L. Mirafuentes, M. Dolores Soto, and Miguel Vallebueno, pp. 91–112. Universidad Nacional Autónoma de México, México.

Castañeda, Carlos
1998   Elementos para la discusión de una relación de frontera: la arquitectura de Plazuelas. In *Antropología e Historia del Occidente de México. XXIV Mesa Redonda de la Sociedad Mexicana de Antropología*, vol. 2, pp. 879–889. Sociedad Mexicana de Antropología, México.

Charlton, Thomas H., and Deborah L. Nichols
1997   Diachronic Studies of City-States: Permutations on a Theme. Central Mexico from 1700 BC to AD 1600. In *The Archaeology of City-States: Cross-Cultural Approaches*, edited by D. L. Nichols and T. H. Charlton, pp. 167–207. Smithsonian Institution Press, Washington, DC.

Cobb, Charles, Jeffrey Maymon, and Randall H. McGuire
1999   Feathered, Horned, and Antlered Serpents: Mesoamerican Connections with Southwest and Southeast. In *Great Towns and Regional Polities in the Prehistoric American Southwest and Southeast*, edited by Jill E. Neitzel, pp. 165–181. Amerind Foundation, Dragoon, AZ, and University of New Mexico Press, Albuquerque.

Cordell, Linda S.
1984   *Prehistory of the Southwest*. Academic Press, New York.

Crown, Patricia, and W. H. Wills
2003   Modifying Pottery and Kivas at Chaco: Pentimento, Restoration or Renewal? *American Antiquity* 68:511–532.

Davies, Nigel
1977   *The Toltecs until the Fall of Tula*. University of Oklahoma Press, Norman.

175

Di Peso, Charles C.

1974 *Casas Grandes: A Fallen Trading Center of the Gran Chichimeca*, vol. 2. Amerind Foundation, Dragoon, and Northland Press, Flagstaff.

1983 The Northern Sector of the Mesoamerican World System. In *Forgotten Places and Things: Archaeological Perspectives on American History*, edited by Albert E. Ward, pp. 11–22. Contributions to Anthropological Studies 3. Center for Anthropological Research, Albuquerque.

Diehl, Richard A.

1981 Tula. In *Archaeology: Supplement to the Handbook of Middle American Indians*, vol. 1, edited by J. A Sabloff, pp. 272–295. University of Texas Press, Austin.

1989 Previous Investigations at Tula. In *Tula of the Toltecs: Excavations and Survey*, edited by D. M. Healan, pp. 13–33. University of Iowa Press, Iowa City.

Doyel, David E., and Suzanne K. Fish

2000 Prehistoric Villages and Communities in the Arizona Desert. In *The Hohokam Village Revisited*, edited by Davie E. Doyel, Suzanne K. Fish, and Paul R. Fish, pp. 1–35. Southwestern and Rocky Mountain Division of the American Association for the Advancement of Science, Boulder.

Ferdon, Edwin N., Jr.

1955 *A Trial Survey of Mexican-Southwestern Architectural Parallels*. School of American Research and Museum of New Mexico, Santa Fe.

Frisbie, Theodore R.

1983 Anasazi-Mesoamerican Relationship: From the Bowels of the Earth and Beyond. In *Proceedings of the Anasazi Symposium 1981*, edited by J. E. Smith, pp. 215–227. Mesa Verde Museum Association, Cortez, CO.

Fritz, John M.

1978 Paleopsychology Today: Ideational Systems and Human Adapation in Prehistory. In *Social Archaeology*, edited by Charles L. Redman et al., pp. 37–59. Academic Press, New York.

Gómez Gastélum, Luis

1999 Identidad regional e interacción en el noroeste mexicano. Unpublished M.A. thesis, Escuela Nacional de Antropología e Historia, México DF.

Guevara, Arturo

2001 La Ferrería, Durango. *Arqueología Mexicana* IX(51):54–57.

Hawley, Florence Hawley

1934 *The Significance of the Dated Prehistory of Chetro Ketl*. University of New Mexico Bulletin, Monograph Series 1(1). University of New Mexico Press, Albuquerque.

Hayes, Alden C.

1981 A Survey of Chaco Canyon Archaeology. In *Archaeological Surveys of Chaco Canyon*, by Alden C. Hayes, W. James Judge, and David M. Brugge, pp. 1–68. Publications in Archaeology 18A. National Park Service, Washington, DC.

Healan, Dan M., Robert H. Cobean, and Richard A. Diehl

1989 Synthesis and Conclusions. In *Tula of the Toltecs: Excavations and Survey*, edited by D. M. Healan, pp. 239–251. University of Iowa Press, Iowa City.

Hegmon, Michelle, Kelley Hays-Gilpin, Randall H. McGuire, Alison E. Rautman, and Sarah H. Schlanger

2000 Changing Perceptions of Regional Interaction in the Prehistoric Southwest. In *The Archaeology of Regional Interaction: Religion, Warfare, and Exchange across the America Southwest and Beyond*, edited by Michelle Hegmon, pp. 1–21. University Press of Colorado, Boulder.

Hewett, Edgar L.

1936 *The Chaco Canyon and Its Monuments*. University of New Mexico Press, Albuquerque.

Holley, George R., and Stephen H. Lekson

1999 Comparing Southwestern and Southeastern Great Towns. In *Great Towns and Regional Polities*, edited by Jill E. Neitzel, pp. 39–43. University of New Mexico Press, Albuquerque.

Juárez, Daniel

1999 Exploraciones en San Juan el Alto, municipio de Pénjamo, Guanajuato. *Arqueología* 22:41–68. Instituto Nacional de Antropología e Historia, México.

Judd, Neil M.

1954 *The Material Culture of Pueblo Bonito*. Smithsonian Miscellaneous Collections 124. Smithsonian Institution, Washington, DC.

1964 *The Architecture of Pueblo Bonito*. Smithsonian Miscellaneous Collections 147(1). Smithsonian Institution, Washington, DC.

Judge, W. James

1989 Chaco Canyon–San Juan Basin. In *Dynamics of Southwest Prehistory*, edited by Linda S. Cordell and George J. Gumerman, pp. 209–262. Smithsonian Institution Press, Washington, DC.

1991 Chaco: Current Views of Prehistory and the Regional System. In *Chaco and Hohokam*, edited by Patricia L. Crown and W. James Judge, pp. 11–30. School of American Research Press, Santa Fe.

Kelley, J. Charles

1966 Mesoamerica and the Southwestern United States. *Handbook of Middle American Indians* 4:95–110. University of Texas Press, Austin.

1976 Alta Vista: Outpost of Mesoamerican Empire on the Tropic of Cancer. *Las Fronteras de Mesoamerica: XIV Mesa Redonda de la Sociedad Mexicana de Antropología* 1:21–40. México DF.

1995 Trade Goods, Traders and Status in Northwestern Greater Mesoamerica. In *The Gran Chichimeca:*

Essays on the Archaeology and Ethnohistory of Northern Mesoamerica, edited by Jonathan E. Reyman, pp. 102–145. Avebury, Aldershot, UK.

Kelley, J. Charles, and Ellen A. Kelley

1975   An Alternative Hypothesis for the Explanation of Anasazi Culture History. In *Collected Papers in Honor of Florence Hawley Ellis*, edited by Theodore R. Frisbie, pp. 178–223. Hooper Publishing, Norman, OK.

Kievit, Karen A.

1998   *Seeing and Reading Chaco Architecture at* AD *1100*. Ph.D. Dissertation, University of Colorado, Boulder.

Knowles, Ralph L.

1974   *Energy and Form: An Ecological Approach to Urban Growth*. MIT Press, Cambridge, MA.

Kuckelman, Kristin A., ed.

2003   *The Archaeology of Yellow Jacket Pueblo (Site 5MT5): Excavations at a Large Community Center in Southwestern Colorado* [HTML Title]. Available: http://www.crowcanyon.org/ yellowjacket.

Lekson, Stephen H.

1983   Chacoan Architecture in Continental Context. In *Proceedings of the Anasazi Symposium 1981*, edited by Jack E. Smith, pp. 183–206. Mesa Verde Museum Association, Mesa Verde.

1984   *Great Pueblo Architecture of Chaco Canyon, New Mexico*. Publications in Archaeology 18B. National Park Service, Albuquerque.

1986   The Architecture of Talus Unit, Chaco Canyon, New Mexico. In *Prehistory and History*, edited by Nancy Fox, pp 43–59. Papers of the Archaeological Society of New Mexico 11. Ancient City Press, Santa Fe.

1988   The Idea of the Kiva in Anasazi Archaeology. *Kiva* 53:213–234.

1989   Kivas? In *The Architecture of Social Integration in the Prehistoric Pueblos*, edited by William Lipe and Michelle Hegmon, pp. 161–167. Occasional Publication 1. Crow Canyon Archaeological Center, Cortez.

1999   *Chaco Meridian: Centers of Political Power in the Ancient Southwest*. Altamira, Walnut Creek, CA.

2000   Ancient Chaco's New History. *Archaeology Southwest* 14(1):12–14.

Lekson, Stephen H., ed.

1983   *The Architecture and Dendrochronology of Chetro Ketl, Chaco Canyon, New Mexico*. Reports of the Chaco Center 6. National Park Service, Albuquerque.

Lister, Robert H.

1978   Mesoamerican Influence at Chaco Canyon, New Mexico. In *Across the Chichimec Sea: Papers in Honor of J. Charles Kelley*, edited by Carroll L. Riley and Basil C. Hedrick, pp. 233–241. Southern Illinois University Press, Carbondale.

McGuire, Randall H.

1980   The Mesoamerican Connection in the Southwest. *Kiva* 46(1–2):3–33.

Margáin, Carlos R.

1971   Pre-Columbian Architecture of Central Mexico. In *Archaeology of Northern Mesoamerica: Supplement to the Handbook of Middle American Indians*, vol. 10, edited by G. F. Ekholm, pp. 45–91. University of Texas Press, Austin.

Mathien, Frances Joan

1986   External Contact and the Chaco Anasazi. In *Ripples in the Chichimec Sea: New Considerations of Southwestern-Mesoamerican Interactions*, edited by Frances Joan Mathien and Randall H. McGuire, pp. 220–242. Southern Illinois University Press, Carbondale.

Miller, James Marshall

1937   *The G Kivas of Chetro Ketl*. M.A. thesis, Department of Architecture, University of Southern California, Los Angeles.

Morelos, Noel

1993   *Procesos de producción de espacios y estructuras en Teotihuacan. Colección Científica 274*. Instituto Nacional de Antropología e Historia, México DF.

Nelson, Ben A.

1995   Complexity, Hierarchy, and Scale: A Controlled Comparison between Chaco Canyon, New Mexico, and La Quemada, Zacatecas. *American Antiquity* 60:597–618.

1997   Chronology and Stratigraphy at La Quemada, Zacatecas, Mexico. *Journal of Field Archaeology* 24:85–109.

2000   Aggregation, Warfare, and the Spread of the Mesoamerican Tradition. In *The Archaeology of Regional Interaction: Religion, Warfare, and Exchange across the American Southwest and Beyond*, edited by Michelle Hegmon, pp. 317–337. University Press of Colorado, Boulder.

2006   Mesoamerican Objects and Symbols in Chaco Canyon Contexts. In *The Archaeology of Chaco Canyon: An 11th Century Pueblo Regional Center*, edited by Stephen H. Lekson, pp. 339–371. School of American Research Press, Santa Fe.

Pailes, Richard A., and Joseph W. Whitecotton

1979   The Greater Southwest and the Mesoamerican "World" System: An Exploratory Model of Frontier Relationships. In *The Frontier: Comparative Studies*, edited by W. W. Savage and S. I. Thompson, pp. 105–121. University of Oklahoma Press, Norman.

Paredes, Blanca

1990   *Unidades habitacionales en Tula*, Hidalgo. Colección Científica 210. Instituto Nacional de Antropología e Historia, México.

Patiño, Hector

1994　Tula en números. *Arqueología Mexicana* II(7):51. México.

Piña Chan, Román, and Joan Taylor

1976　Cortas Excavaciones en el Cuarenta, Jalisco. *Boletín del Departamento de Monumentos Prehispánicos* 1:1–14. México.

Reiter, Paul

1933　*The Ancient Pueblo of Chetro Ketl.* M.A. thesis, University of New Mexico, Albuquerque.

Ringle, William M., Tomás Gallareta Negrón, and George J. Bey III

1998　The Return of Quetzalcoatl: Evidence for the Spread of a World Religion during the Epiclassic Period. *Ancient Mesoamerica* 9:183–232.

Schöndube, Otto

1990　El occidente de México, ¿marginal a Mesoamérica? In *La validez teórica del concepto de Mesoamérica: XIX Mesa Redonda de la Sociedad Mexicana de Antropología*, pp. 129–134. Colección Científica 198. Instituto Nacional de Antropología e Historia, México.

Schroeder, Albert H.

1981　How Far Can a Pochteca Leap without Leaving Footprints? In *Collected Papers in Honor of Erick Kellerman Reed*, edited by Albert H. Schroeder, pp. 43–64. Papers of the Archaeological Society of New Mexico 6. Albuquerque.

Upham, Steadman

1986　Imperialists, Isolationists, World Systems and Political Realities: Perspectives on Mesoamerican-Southwestern Interaction. In *Ripples in the Chichimec Sea: New Considerations of Southwestern-Mesoamerican Interactions*, edited by Frances Joan Mathien and Randall H. McGuire, pp. 205–219. Southern Illinois University Press, Carbondale.

Vivian, Gordon R., and Paul Reiter

1960　*The Great Kivas of Chaco Canyon and Their Relationships.* School of American Research and Musem of New Mexico Monographs 22. Santa Fe.

Vivian, R. Gwinn

1970　*Aspects of Prehistoric Society in Chaco Canyon, New Mexico.* Ph.D. Dissertation, Department of Anthropology, University of Arizona, Tucson.

1974　Conservation and Diversion: Water Control Systems in the Anasazi Southwest. In *Irrigation's Impact on Society*, edited by Theodore Downing and McGuire Gibson, pp. 95–112. Anthropological Papers 25. University of Arizona Press, Tucson.

1992　Chaco Water Use and Managerial Decision Making. In *Anasazi Regional Organization and the Chaco System*, edited by David E. Doyel, pp. 45–57. Anthropological Papers 5. Maxwell Museum of Anthropology, University of New Mexico, Albuquerque.

Vivian, R. Gwinn, Dulce N. Dodge, and Gayle H. Harman

1978　*Wooden Ritual Artifacts from Chaco Canyon, New Mexico.* Anthropological Papers 32. University of Arizona Press, Tucson.

Weigand, Phil C.

1993　*Evolución de una civilización prehispánica.* El Colegio de Michoacán, México.

2001　El norte mesoamericano. *Arqueología Mexicana* IX(51):34–39.

Weigand, Phil C., and Garman Harbottle

1993　The Role of Turquoise in the Ancient Mesoamerican Trade Structure. In *The American Southwest and Mesoamerica*, edited by J. E. Ericson and T. G. Baugh, pp. 159–178. Plenum Press, New York.

Windes, Thomas C.

1987　*Investigations at the Pueblo Alto Complex, Chaco Canyon, New Mexico 1975–1979.* Publications in Archaeology 18F. National Park Service, Santa Fe.

1993　*The Spadefoot Toad Site: Investigations at 29SJ629, Chaco Canyon, New Mexico.* Reports of the Chaco Center 12. National Park Service, Santa Fe.

7

Building Social History at Pueblo Bonito

Footnotes to a Biography of Place

Wendy Ashmore

Briefly stated, then, and in words written on the spot, one cannot view the remains of Pueblo Bonito for long without becoming aware that the place has had an exceptionally long and interesting history (Nelson 1996 [1920]:388).

If a nucleus is to be found anywhere about the village it lies among the cluster of relatively small, crowded structures at the top of the crescent since larger rooms curve east and west. The quantity and diversity of ceremonial paraphernalia stored in some of those small rooms suggest an importance in the community quite out of proportion to their size. And four of them had come eventually to be used for burials—priesthood burials if one may judge from the wealth of accompanying ornaments (Judd 1964:58).

Much of our sense of cultural continuity in great houses such as Pueblo Bonito arises from our interpretation of activities on the basis of material culture from a common architectural space. But this use of space, whether it reflects continuity or discontinuity in time and culture, masks activities, possible temporal breaks, and differences in cultural orientation by inhabitants adapting to an already present, massively built architectural environment resistant to normal deterioration (Windes 2003:32).

THE MOST EXTENSIVELY EXCAVATED and intensively studied construction complex in the core of

Chaco Canyon, Pueblo Bonito has yielded an intricate record of architectural growth and modification. Planning and conscious design are frequently inferred, embodied in multiple construction stages. Astronomical alignments and landscape reference are widely thought to figure in architectural form throughout the building's history.

The first two statements in the epigram capture some of this sense of the building's architectural complexity; the third is a sobering caution about interpreting the quite evident complexity. That is, despite perceived consistencies of design through time, growth was discontinuous and far from linear. Characterized alternately by building spurts, periods of minor modification, episodes of internal reworking, localized room abandonment, and times seemingly only of maintenance, the intricate construction history at Pueblo Bonito suggests that the architecture cumulatively charts important developments in the social order of its builders. This essay explores potential social implications of select aspects of architectural change and stasis at Pueblo Bonito between the early ninth and midtwelfth centuries, with special focus on the treatment of the earliest roomblock. In particular, the enduring but shifting attention given to the northern sector suggests establishment there of an *axis mundi*, perhaps for the Chacoan world as a whole.

ENCOUNTERING PUEBLO BONITO

Major excavations in the 1890s and 1920s not only yielded primary architectural data but also kindled still-burning questions of just what Pueblo Bonito was, for whom, at what times (e.g., Judd 1964, 1981; Neitzel 2003 and Chapter 5, this volume; Pepper 1996 [1920]) (Figures 7.1 and 7.2). Although ambiguities from the initial field projects hamper resolution of some issues, new theoretical models and expanding analyses of material evidence suggest broad outlines of how Chaco society was organized and the roles that Pueblo Bonito played in that society, as a focus for residence, exchange, and—especially—ritual. While architecture retains a fundamental interpretive role, scrutiny of all available evidence remains essential for understanding social practices embodied in the building.

In recent years, multiple authors steeped in Chacoan studies have written critically discerning biographies of Pueblo Bonito as a building, in which Lekson's seven construction stages and their subdivisions are common points of reference (e.g., Bustard 1996; Cooper 1995; Durand 1992; Lekson 1986, 1999; Metcalf 1997; Stein, Suiter, and Ford 1997; Wills 2000; Windes and Ford 1992, 1996; but see Neitzel 2003 and Chapter 5, this volume; Windes 2003). In these volumes' various chapters, the same authors bring diverse theoretical perspectives and different specific evidence to bear in drawing perceptive insights about social implications of the building's life history.

I encounter Pueblo Bonito and its immense interpretive literature as an outsider, an archaeologist who mostly explores the space and architecture of the ancient Maya and their neighbors, far to the south of the Chaco world. Despite marked differences in Maya and Chacoan societies and cultures, seeming parallels in treatment of architecture and space invite comment. Some of these involve spatial principles, discussed below, that may have been shared among many indigenous societies of the New World (e.g., Ashmore 1991; Gillespie 1991; Hall 1997; Townsend 1992). Equally pertinent for this essay, however, are acts of creating and modifying architectural space, acts whose traces at Pueblo Bonito appear to exemplify social practices that have been identified widely in the world, both in antiquity and today (e.g., Hall 1966; Low 2000). These acts highlight movements, whether as ritual dance, procession, or everyday transit, accentuated by ambient sights, sounds, and aromas, and collectively endowing architecture and landscapes with meaning and memory (e.g., Basso 1996; Bradley 1993; Ortiz 1994; Scully 1989; Vogt 1992).

Gratefully acknowledging the crucial contributions of Chaco colleagues, in print and in generous conversations, I offer an outsider's view on a very few aspects of Pueblo Bonito's richly textured life history, and on some possible social implications of architectural stasis and change. In so doing, I join those who regard architecture and landscape as social history and look to indications of the social practices that were followed in creating that history

FIGURE 7.1. The northwest sector of Pueblo Bonito during Pepper's excavations. (Pepper 1920: Figure 4, Courtesy of American Museum of Natural History, AMNH 412024; Chaco Culture National Historical Park, Chaco Archives CHCU 104414)

180

Wendy Ashmore

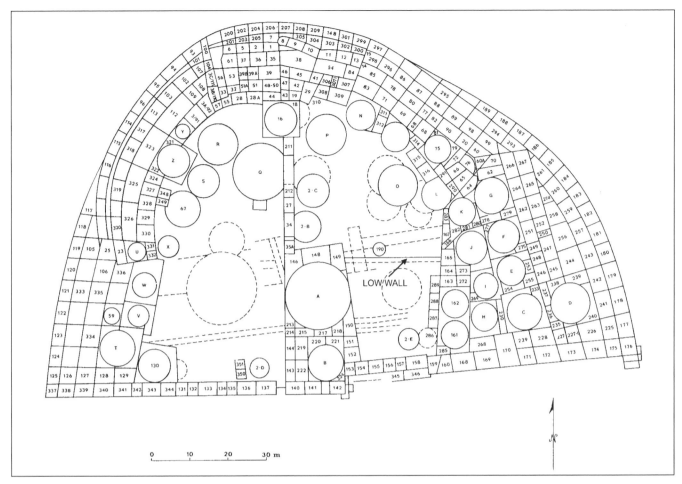

FIGURE 7.2. Plan of Pueblo Bonito rooms, showing the low wall discussed in this chapter. (After Lekson 1986:111, Figure 4.17)

at Pueblo Bonito. Specifically, the essay considers the following distinct but interrelated topics, with comments offered here as footnotes to Pueblo Bonito's ongoing biography: establishing the pueblo; plans and designs; symmetry and asymmetry; and civic, public, and devotional space.

ESTABLISHING THE PUEBLO

Broad outlines of the founding sequence are relatively well known. The footnote here is a matter of emphasis, urging recognition of the significance of location of the earliest portions of the pueblo and of practices that might have sustained its importance. A quick review of the founding history sets the stage.

Stratigraphically, we know that pithouses underlie parts of what became Pueblo Bonito (Judd 1964;

Lekson 1986 and Chapter 2, this volume), and in Judd's view (1964:57) they had been forgotten when the pueblo was established (but see Neitzel, Chapter 5, this volume). Similarly, it is well established that the earliest pueblo roomblocks are in the northern part of the building. Combined evidence from abutment stratigraphy and dendrochronology leads Windes and Ford to identify the earliest as Rooms 1-2-5-6-35-36-37-61, part of Lekson's Stage IB (Figure 7.3), erected probably before 860 (Windes 2003:20–21; Windes and Ford 1992, 1996). Although these and other "big-room suites" are likely to have been storage facilities instead of living rooms, they are contiguous with habitation suites (Windes and Ford 1992:79–80; cf. Metcalf 1997:340; Vivian 1990; Wills 2000:32).

Applications of Hillier and Hanson's (1984) space syntax method—which measures room

181

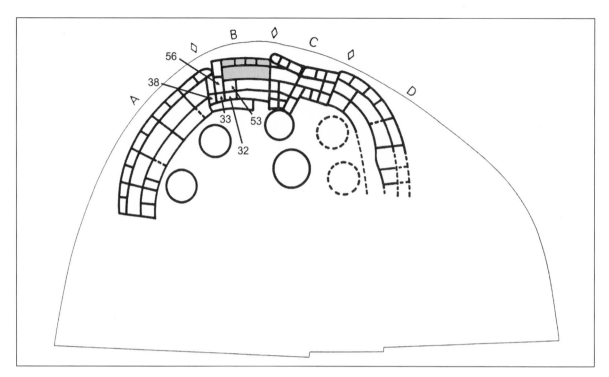

FIGURE 7.3. Plan of Pueblo Bonito showing location of Stage I rooms. Diamonds along upper perimeter show divisions between letter-designated substages (A–D). Early rooms mentioned in text are labeled; shaded area in IB designates Rooms 1, 2, 5, 6, 35, 36, 37, and 61, collectively. (After Lekson 1986:114, Figure 4.20a)

accessibility, segregation, and integration—yield intriguing observations on early growth. Bustard, for example, describes rooms in the initial two-row suites as all being no more than two steps removed from outdoor (plaza) access, but she sees that arrangement as "undoubtedly fleeting" (1996:90). It was the earliest roomblock complex (Lekson's Stage IB) that was most immediately and dramatically affected. By the time construction of what Lekson defines as Stage I was completed, rooms in the IB set were more segregated both internally and from what became the west court than were their neighbors to the west (Lekson's Stage IA). Cooper (1995:170) observes that the most integrated space in that earlier set was the front row of the original big-room suite, Rooms 35-36-37-61, while the most segregated were two adjacent (but not connecting) rooms, 33 and 56, which Windes and Ford (1996) identified as later additions. In subsequent centuries, this pair was the site of interment of some of the few burials that have been discovered at Pueblo Bonito, including the extraordinarily bejeweled males in Room 33 (see below; Akins and Schelberg 1984; Judd 1964:58; Mathien 1997, 2001; Pepper

1909). Judd's statement captures this in the epigram, based on his observations from the 1920s.

More than one observer has recognized that this and neighboring north-sector roomblocks remained accessible and were *not* buried under masses of subsequent construction (e.g., Judd 1964:66; Stein, Suiter, and Ford 1997:136; Windes 2003). Indeed, Windes and Ford (1992:77) cite this preservation as characteristic of the early cores of Chacoan pueblos that became great houses. They add that at Pueblo Bonito specifically, "Some of the latest repair/remodeling dates came from around this core, which served as a pivotal point for subsequent construction. The continued importance of the core is also attested to by the quantities of status goods and individuals found in and adjacent to it" (1992:77). And they "are tempted to argue that the location of the Pueblo I [i.e., ninth-century] houses, which were incorporated, not demolished, into the later AD 900s architecture, provided continuity of the societal organization that gave rise to the AD 900s Early Bonito phase and the great houses" (1992:83).

Perhaps similarly, I am tempted to add a footnote *underscoring* the fundamental importance of these early houses, *and their location*, to suggest that they materialized social continuity, providing a strong anchor for social memory throughout Pueblo Bonito's history. The placement of Burials 13 and 14 in Room 33 (before 1040; Mathien 2001:114)—together with their elaborate turquoise bracelets and anklets, thousands of pieces of turquoise and shell, multiple flutes, and "staves or sticks of 'ceremonial' significance" (Fritz 1978:53)—is eloquent testimony to the significance of the north sector for ritual activities, as are coeval and later activities in three other burial rooms (32, 53, 56) and unique arrays of more than 100 late-eleventh-century cylinders and myriad other vessels and objects cached in Room 28 (Judd 1981:22–26; Windes 2003:25); the "mass" of ceremonial sticks and more than 49 arrows in Room 32; and the 12 macaws and 4 blue jays sheltered (plus two macaws interred) in Room 38 (Pepper 1909, 1996). As important is the fact that all of these interments or caches represent ritual behavior enacted out of general view, and limited in access. (Whether they were therefore "private" acts is a question discussed later.)

Concealment, secrecy, and cyclical understanding figure importantly in inferences that are drawn from this point. For that reason, it is critical to include more explicit allusion to the ancient people in Pueblo Bonito, whether present as residents or visitors, and consideration of their possibilities for assembly, isolation, and movement within the building and the adjoining open space. That is, as noted earlier, places become meaningful in people's remembered experience of them, either directly or through being informed of the sights, sounds, textures, and aromas. One need not adopt a phenomenological perspective to reinstall people into those places (e.g., Thomas 1993; cf. Bradley 1993; Renfrew 2001a:16). What *is* needed, however, is more complex acknowledgment of experiential options than we as archaeologists customarily include. Such acknowledgment is exemplified, for example, in Metcalf's (1997) insightful, primarily quantitative analysis of ancient Pueblo civic space and political leadership. Toward the end, she urges future development of a "visibility index." Such an index would reconstruct lines of sight, acknowledging wall height and doorway location, to "determine how visible entrances to spaces were" and, from that, how tightly controlled entry could have been

(Metcalf 1997:278). Cooper calls attention to the importance of light and visibility in a different way: "The ruins as they stand now are filled with light, but one can imagine how difficult path-finding [within roomblocks] must have been with only the aid of torches and the occasional shaft of sunlight" (Cooper 1995:160). Tringham (1994) points to the efficacy of perspective views for helping repopulate ancient spaces, to augment the precise (but socially vacant) scaled plan-and-profile records on which we rely (see also Kievet 1998). Two published instances for Pueblo Bonito are reproduced here as Figures 7.4 and 7.5. Notwithstanding whatever artistic license is involved in either image, the scenes give a clearer sense of human scale and the possibilities for action and experience.

From that social perspective, I draw on Fritz's (1978) interpretations (discussed further below) to suggest that this *northern position of concealment* at Pueblo Bonito links the cited burials and cached (or stored?) ritual paraphernalia to the northern room and associated "subfloor feature" of Casa Rinconada, the starting place from which ritual performers were once seen to have emerged into the great kiva assembly space. That is, I speculate that both northern locales were *understood* as places of emergence or return, known to people in the pueblo but, for most, with origins and destinations concealed from active view (see also Stein et al., Chapter 8, this volume).

In that regard, the position at the *north* end of the axis of symmetry (for Pueblo Bonito, Casa Rinconada, Chaco Canyon, or possibly a wider area) reminds me of the importance of north as an evident destination of pilgrimage or procession in the Chaco world (Sofaer et al. 1989; cf. Cooper 1995:154–155), perhaps a place of emergence linked to *shipap* (e.g., Marshall 1997; Ortiz 1969 [for Tewa]; Snead and Preucel 1999 [for Keres]) and, metaphorically, ancestry, and part of an axis connecting worldviews in multiple indigenous societies of the Americas (Ashmore 1989; Lekson 1999). For the Classic Maya, I believe it to have anchored an axis of human ancestry and of cosmic creation: the axis as a whole is a horizontal translation of the vertical connection between earth and sky, and represents the world tree, the *axis mundi* linking the layers of the cosmos (Ashmore 1989, 2005; Eliade 1959; Freidel, Schele, and Parker

FIGURE 7.4. Looking northwest across Pueblo Bonito plaza at around 1050. (Judd 1964: Plate 8; courtesy of National Geographic Society, Picture ID 57360 from the National Geographic Image Collection)

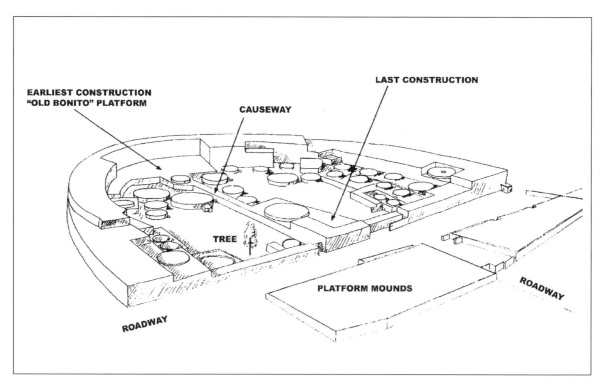

FIGURE 7.5. Perspective reconstruction view of Pueblo Bonito from southwest, including tree location and earthen mounds. (Adapted from Townsend 1986 by Stein et al. 1997: Figure 9.6, courtesy of the authors and University of New Mexico Press)

Wendy Ashmore

1993). Others, notably Doxtater (1991) and Marshall (1997), have applied Eliade's concepts of *axis mundi*, cardinal axes, and centers to inferences of Chacoan worldview, and it seems possible that the north-south axis of human ancestry and of cosmic creation of the sort inferred for the Maya may pertain here as well (e.g., Sofaer et al. 1989:373, citing multiple sources; cf. Van Dyke, Chapter 4, this volume).

Although Doxtater (1991) cautions that the orienting axes of Pueblo worldview today are multiple, changing, and frequently *not* cardinal, Lekson and others have argued that the north-south "meridian was the major defining axis of Chaco" (Lekson 1999:82; also see Fritz 1978). Moreover, Lekson points out that

> north was not important to daily, seasonal, or annual life. The time scales of calendar, economic year, and ritual cycles were measured by the movements of the sun, along the eastern and western horizons. Sun, moon, and stars were constantly but erratically wandering; those celestial orbs were anything but fixed.
>
> North, however, was a fixed point—though at 1100, a void (Polaris was off the mark)—around which the heavens revolved. Indeed, North was the *only* fixed direction....
>
> ...Pueblo people call north "the heart of the sky."... Everyone knew north—everyone could see the stars revolve around the Heart of the Sky. When charged with meaning, north was especially potent because it was manifest and knowable: You could see it, even if you could not understand it (Lekson 1999:86, emphasis in original).

I would suggest, further, that the attributes of constancy and void (or perhaps more properly, concealment) might have been components of a concept of north at Pueblo Bonito, and of linking the building's day-to-day life with its increasingly distant founding. That is, even as time and generations separated residents and visitors from the building's founders, occupation and use of the northern sector rooms continued, and continued so emphatically that multiple authors comment on it, as cited earlier. I would suggest that the attention constitutes recognition, transmitted across generations, of where this important building was

founded, and by extension, a place where connection to the founders could be commemorated. The importance of such places as materializing corporate social memory of ancestry has been inferred in multiple and varied cultural contexts (e.g., Barrett 1999; Bradley 1987; Gillespie 2000; R. Joyce 2000). By the time of the impressive interments and caching described above, the memory of founding and ancestry would have been well in place. Even localized intervals of disuse (e.g., Judd 1964:78) did not erase materialized memory. The north sector as a whole was a constant in Pueblo Bonito life. And hidden ritual activity was what commemorated its significance.

All *interments* are, by definition, concealed, but I would highlight that, of the many rooms that had gone into disuse—some of which had become receptacles for what we consider refuse (e.g., Judd 1981:21–22, Figure 3)—the chamber selected for interment of Burials 13 and 14 was one of the most inaccessible rooms in the northern sector (Cooper 1995; Judd 1964:64). Although certainly other burials were placed elsewhere in the west and north sectors of the pueblo (Akins and Schelberg 1984), and bioanthropological analyses suggest that the individuals in different sectors came from distinct populations (Mathien 2001:104), I suspect that additional factors could be involved, beyond the group from which the decedents had come. Inasmuch as the preceding speculations rest partly on arguments concerning symmetry, and partly on change in public and devotional space (especially with regard to secrecy and to access to esoteric knowledge), I return to the subject under those topics, below.

PLANS AND DESIGNS

Many have inferred quite deliberate decisions in site selection and Pueblo Bonito's subsequent architectural form, recognizing that these ideas were perpetually under reconsideration, and periodically were significantly rethought, by the successive generations of builders. The evidence for multiple pivotal points when builders clearly revisited Pueblo Bonito's architectural layout has stimulated extended discussion—prominently including site location and possible cosmological symbolism of the layout, and the eleventh-century bursts of construction activity. What *social* roles did orientation play? When was orientation established? And how consistently did it hold?

Site Selection and Plan at Founding
Although ecological and economic factors figure in discussions about site selection (e.g., Crown and Judge 1990:293–294; Judge 1984:4, 1989: 218–219, 234, 238; cf. Windes, Chapter 3, this volume), at least as frequent—if not more so—are allusions to belief, ritual, and worldview. Such ascription seems in keeping with Pueblo Bonito's commonly identified ritual focus (e.g., Cameron and Toll 2001:13; Judge 1989:237), including most recently its designation by Renfrew (2001b) as a Location of High Devotional Expression (LHDE). Less readily expected, perhaps, is the frequency with which those ideas on site selection implicate a north-south axis for the pueblo, finding it expressed in site layout from founding forward through its lifespan.

Fritz's (1978) early expression about such matters embeds location of Pueblo Bonito and Chetro Ketl—and other canyon sites, as we know them *in their final form*—within a canyon-wide mapping of social and cosmological structure, with those two buildings as central anchors in symmetrical distributions of "equivalent" great houses along the east-west extent of the canyon. Social and ideational asymmetry, inequality, and complementarity defined positions (or poles) of a north-south dimension (also see next section, and Neitzel, Chapter 5, this volume). As Redman summarizes key implications of Fritz's argument:

> This carefully planned and controlled architectural construction had two effects: first, only those with access to this special knowledge could design the construction of important buildings; and second, while living or performing rituals in these buildings the inhabitants would be forced to *follow certain pathways and see certain vistas, all of which contributed to a prearranged effect.* Fritz hypothesizes that the impact of these orientations is to provide a parallel on the ground to the cosmological divisions in the universe, and thereby to reinforce the class distinction between the two major divisions in the population (1990:280–281, emphasis added; see also Fritz 1987).

The latter distinctions of class are debated (e.g., Metcalf 1997; Vivian 1990); I return below to cosmology and people's experience of it.

Exploring possible relations with astronomical phenomena, Sofaer (1997, and Chapter 9, this volume; Sofaer et al. 1989) is quite explicit about cardinal solar alignments that pervade Pueblo Bonito architecture, especially the terminal elements most susceptible to azimuth measurements. Pueblo Bonito is one of three major local buildings with such cardinal emphases—the others being Pueblo Alto and Tsin Kletzin, atop mesas, respectively north and south of the canyon—but the only one with a strong north-south axis in a central spine wall. As she notes,

> each day at meridian passage of the sun, the midwall which approximately divides the massive structure of Pueblo Bonito casts no shadow. Similarly, the middle of the sun's yearly passage is marked at Pueblo Bonito as the equinox sun is seen rising and setting closely in line with the western half of its southern wall. Thus the middle of the sun's daily and yearly journeys are visible in alignment with the major features of this building which is at the middle of the Chacoan world (Sofaer 1997:116).

Whereas both Sofaer and Fritz interpret the final form of the pueblo, other analysts look more specifically at its initial roomblock, to which we can then seek to link the later architecture. Pueblo Bonito was certainly not the only early great house in Chaco Canyon, and matters of orientation and location can be addressed for any and all (Lekson, Chapter 2, this volume; Sofaer, Chapter 9, this volume; Windes, Chapter 3, this volume). Pueblo Bonito did, however, acquire a special standing among Chacoan structures (e.g., Neitzel, Chapter 5, this volume). With regard to its site location, Doxtater views Pueblo Bonito as central to a trio of incipient great houses (with Una Vida and Peñasco Blanco) defining a northwest-southeast axis in the canyon, and establishing, in Eliade's terms, a ritual "middle place" in the Chacoan world (Doxtater 1991:169–170; cf. Neitzel, Chapter 5, this volume; Windes, Chapter 3, this volume). Fowler and Stein take a parallel view as to deliberate planning at the time of founding, asserting that

The architectural characteristics of the site suggest that it was intended to be a special building (a great house) from the onset. Ultimately, the great size of the building was the result of planned, large-scale construction events. After three centuries of development, the massive twelfth-century envelope faithfully reflects the original ninth-century plan (Fowler and Stein 1992:101).

Going further, Stein, Suiter, and Ford (1997; also see Stein et al., Chapter 8, this volume) suggest that the Stage I roomblock *location* related *specifically* to the position of a lone ponderosa pine, which they interpret as a gnomon for establishing the true north-south azimuth from the shadow cast by the sun at midday (see also Neitzel, Chapter 5, this volume). Frequently omitted from published plans of the pueblo, the pine was discovered by Judd (1981:3, Plate 2) and had begun growing there no later than 732 (Stein, Suiter, and Ford 1997:144–145). If this solitary shaft was the first marker of solar phenomena for the pueblo, its ultimate architectural successor was the spine wall of Lekson's Stage VII, likely built late in the eleventh century (Lekson 1986:141–142, 1999: 131; Judd 1964: Figures 4 and 5). The wall marks the north-south axis of the final building form, established within a generation or so after the tree died, probably between 1020 and 1059 (Stein, Suiter, and Ford 1997:145). Like the tree, the wall engages the sun's passage, but in this case by inscribing a line briefly with an *absence*, void, or concealment of shadow, over a length that simultaneously reunites the two plazas visually by filling them with light. It would have complemented and contrasted starkly with the dimness of adjacent interior spaces (e.g., Cooper 1995:160). One might also consider this phenomenon the daytime, solar counterpart to the void in the night sky that Lekson describes—an expanse of light symmetrical and complementary to an expanse of darkness (cf. Urton 1981). The next section examines further the possibility and implications of such symmetry and complementarity in time and space.

Perhaps relevant here is Zeilik's review of evidence for solar observations in ancient Pueblo society. In considering instances involving light and shadow phenomena, he suggests that they served less as precise calendric markers than as visual *hierophanies*, Eliade's term for manifestations of the sacred (Zeilik 1989:155–156; cf. Aveni 2001:306). The shadow-casting pine tree and, later, the north-south spine wall would serve equally effectively, but one might consider the latter as a somewhat more formal (more emphatic?) display, to which those within the bounds of the two courts of the plaza or on the roofs of its flanking structures would have collective but exclusive access. This uniquely architecturally choreographed solar marking of the north-south axis could thus have provided daily commemoration of Pueblo Bonito *and its plaza* as the "middle place" in the Chaco world.

Moreover, the rooms along the wall seem plausible, from their contents, as settings for activities associated with preparation for and enactment of ritual, centered on the kivas (Q and A, plus 2B, 2C, and B) and adjacent plaza areas that flank the line on the northwest and southeast (Judd 1964, 1981: Plate 31; Pepper 1996). Access between the two courts was kept open at the midpoint of the wall by a passage between Rooms 34 and 35a (Judd 1964:134). I take this up again below with respect to social aspects of symmetry and asymmetry in the building's layout.

Eleventh-Century Construction Activity
The pronounced building spurts of the mid- and late-eleventh century, in and beyond Pueblo Bonito and other great houses, have elicited distinct interpretations from different authors. Climate and demography are examined as factors, perhaps cyclical in occurrence, but increasingly one encounters reference to ritual and its *social cycles* as choreographing construction.

Whereas Stuart (1997:50) likens the "orgy of activity" to 1930s public works in a time of regional economic stress, Wills suggests that, for Chaco, the attendant scale of tree harvesting is a clue to social strategies, perhaps magnified but probably not sparked by new economic conditions. That is, "trees and tree harvesting were symbolic of a connection between distant montane collection areas and great house architecture, perhaps one that expressed some degree of corporate affiliation by association with upland zones" (Wills 2000:35). He further suggests that harvesting was "very likely part of a *calendric cycle of community activity*," whose rhythms were choreographed via the astronomical (particularly lunar) cycles registered in some buildings (2000:35, emphasis added). For him, the volume of activity is thus a barometer of long-term strategies of social integration within the canyon, involving ritual cycles expressed in the buildings themselves in multiple ways.

Windes and McKenna (2001) document the complex sequence of wood production activities, and drawing from Renfrew's cross-cultural parallels for LHDE, they suggest (in contrast with Stuart and as an alternative to Wills) that perhaps the wood was procured, prepared, and transported by people from the timber source zone in the Chuska Valley, as part of what Renfrew (2001b:22) calls the "sacred economy" (see also English et al. 2001). Windes and McKenna note the coincidence of amplified linkage to the Chuska Valley (as sources for Narbona Pass chert and pottery, as well as timber) with the "rise of fairly new communities" there (2001:136). With regard to social mechanisms of connection, Toll (2001:69) quotes Stoltman's assertion that "periodic 'rites of intensification' are a parsimonious explanation for movement of goods from the Chuska Valley to Chaco Canyon."

The overall impression one takes from these interpretations is that cyclical ritual actions seem likely to have shaped construction in Chaco Canyon great houses. If so, their role in Pueblo Bonito is less strong than is solar observation in shaping the *layout* of the building. The other cycles, however, while registered materially in orientations and forms only beyond Pueblo Bonito itself, may be manifest nonetheless in the *timing* of that building's constructions.

Symmetry, Asymmetry, and Complementarity

The foregoing leads to further consideration of the merging of time and space in the form of the pueblo and of social life within it (e.g., Ortiz 1994).

Much has been written about constructional geometry at Pueblo Bonito, and especially the question of *symmetry* in architectural layout. Some authors emphasize the balance of components and their distribution on either side of the spine wall (e.g., Fritz 1978; Doxtater 1991:171–172) and

write of symmetry and complementarity in design. Others highlight, instead, the distinctions and *asymmetries* between the two "halves" in spatial organization, in the break in azimuth along the final south wall (e.g., Doxtater 1991:172; Sofaer 1997, and Chapter 9, this volume), and especially with respect to specific room forms, construction scales, and access integration (e.g., Bustard 1996; Cooper 1995:275–276; Wills 2000:36). These authors write of asymmetry in layout, but still complementarity and balance—particularly with regard to what they identify (on additional grounds) as distinct social groups within the pueblo (e.g., Akins and Schelberg 1984; Mathien 1997, 2001; Stuart 1997; Windes and Ford 1996).

Stein, Suiter, and Ford (1997) also identify symmetry and complementarity, but they do so in a manner that integrates spatial relations with *time*, possibly cyclical time. In particular, they point to multiple geometrical aspects of Pueblo Bonito's final plan, and of sight-line and transit links beyond the building itself. In tacit agreement with others (e.g., Doxtater 1991; Farmer 2003; Sofaer 1997, and Chapter 9, this volume), their discussion and the alignment illustrations they provide imply a far more complex array of geometries than simply those involving cardinal directions. Within the pueblo, however, the cardinal axis of symmetry retains most influence. Along that axis, the "reversed geometrical relationship of the early and late sections of the building suggest[s] the completion of a calendrical cycle, *and the closure or ritual retirement of the structure*" (Stein, Suiter, and Ford 1997:138, emphasis added; cf. Farmer 2003; Fowler and Stein 1992). Illustrating the cited reversal graphically (reproduced here as Figure 7.6), Stein and his coauthors highlight the complementary positions of earliest and latest construction and what Fritz (1978) calls the "bifold rotational symmetry," along the axis, of the "early (Kiva Q) and late (Kiva A) great kivas" (Stein, Suiter, and Ford 1997:139). From this implicitly temporal dimension of symmetry and complementarity, I am reminded here of the earlier suggestion that a north-south dimension aligns ideas of ancestry and origins, of emergence and departure.

I would suggest that time is embedded in additional ways, in the same axial dimension and particularly its northern terminus, and was recognized

Wendy Ashmore

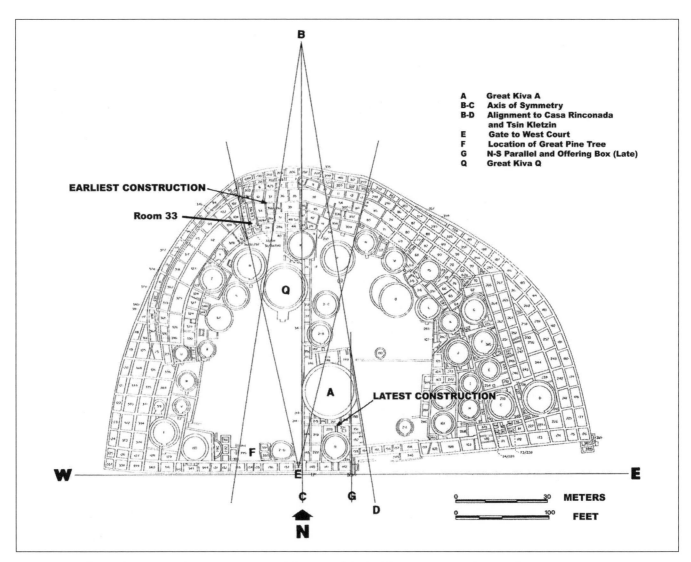

FIGURE 7.6. Plan with position of tree, Room 33, and features of the building's geometry. (Stein et al. 1997: Figure 9.5, courtesy of the authors and University of New Mexico Press)

as such by ancient observers via multiple, cyclically occurring and mutually complementary phenomena. The allusion here is to the voids, absences, and concealments cited earlier, as inscribed within Pueblo Bonito by the sun at midday, and at night by rotation of the stars around an empty northern sector in the sky. Although my knowledge of Puebloan beliefs remains limited, I am reminded of a discussion about a different Native American society that may be apposite in this context. Among Quechuan-speaking people of Misminay, Peru, Urton describes how the night sky maps locales mirroring counterparts on earth. The earthly Vilcanota River, for example,

is the major artery for the movement of water collected from the smaller tributaries of the earth back to the cosmic sea, from where it is taken up into the sky within the Milky Way and recycled through the universe. The Milky Way is itself thought to be the celestial reflection of the Vilcanota River (Urton 1981:38).

The relevance for inferences about Chaco is what seem to be, in the latter case, cyclically complementary, and sometimes quietly dramatic, manifestations of the importance of north and a north-south axis. Pueblo Bonito's apparent uniqueness in manifesting both halves of this fundamental

189

daily cycle would seem to reinforce its often-inferred standing as "middle place" of the Chacoan world.

PUBLIC SPACE AND DEVOTIONAL SPACE

The preceding assertion about daily cycles leads to matters of observation and access in Pueblo Bonito, especially to questions of what constitutes civic, public, and devotional space for such observation. Much discussion of the latter in Chacoan great houses already exists. My footnote considers what materializes concern with secrecy, what constitutes openness, and symmetries and complementarity in the location of what appear to be mutually distinctive ritual observances—either secret or open in their conduct.

To begin, I return to Figures 7.4 and 7.5, and to the importance of acknowledging the three-dimensional nature of the pueblo, as do Stein, Suiter, and Ford (see also Kievet 1998; Lekson, Windes, and Fournier, Chapter 6, this volume; Stein et al., Chapter 8, this volume). It is by moving through the architectural spaces, between enclosed and open places, and from plaza level to rooftop, that a visitor (or a resident) can witness *and be reminded of* the meaning of the place. Alternate observation points recall different pieces in the mosaic of social memory—knowledge—about the place as a whole. Some reminders are subtle, perhaps outside active consciousness. But ritual events and hierophanies punctuate the subtle with more pointed display, especially with regard to who may or may not witness or participate in the events.

As many have pointed out (e.g., Metcalf 1997; Redman 1990), secrecy and invisibility facilitate social control of ritual knowledge. Architecturally, discussion focuses on presence or absence of doors and other access features, and of physical features that either encourage or impede access. Some features, of course, from low walls to sequences of unaligned doorways, can channel movement and sight without preventing them (e.g., Richards 1990; Tringham 1994). Less often discussed archaeologically are ephemeral, nonmaterial factors, such as taboos and other verbal proscriptions about who is entitled to enter a particular place, and when, or about potential temporal fluctuation in its sanctity or openness. Drawing a comparison from modern

Maya villages, even *materially unbroken* and ordinarily unrestricted outdoor space within a household compound can acquire *temporarily exclusive* access while first the men of the household and then the women make necessary preparations for hosting a neighborhood or community feast (Robin 1999, 2002). Nonmaterial restrictions can be as effective as material ones. At Pueblo Bonito, such oral or transitory restrictions are plausible, even though they are not archaeologically demonstrable.

In light of the foregoing, how certain are we about interpreting such ambiguous material access controls as *partial* walls and *narrow* passages? Great attention has been given to Pueblo Bonito's most obtrusive material references to secrecy and access control, the walls that enclose and divide the civic plaza, and the walls and roofs that envelop kivas (for debates concerning identification of "kivas" see Lekson 1989; Lekson, Windes, and Fournier, Chapter 6, this volume; Metcalf 1997). I focus here on plazas.

Metcalf (1997:278–279) cites modern Pueblo authors Ed Ladd, Rina Swentzell, and Alfonso Ortiz as to the importance of a pueblo plaza as center, earth navel, and "middle place" (cf. Low 2000); mathematically, she finds that Pueblo Bonito is one of only two Chaco great houses (with Pueblo Alto) in which the calculated mean or center point was in its plaza (Metcalf 1997:285). Discussion about Pueblo Bonito's plaza focuses mostly on the timing of enclosure and the numbers of people who were thereby included, and changes in the number who could be accommodated within the walled precinct. Whether or not the open area southeast of the original roomblock constituted the equivalent of a "plaza" (e.g., Cooper 1995; Lekson 1986), by the mid-eleventh century, in Lekson's Stage II, walls (and banks of rooms within them) defined a more formal plaza space, "joining its [east and west] extremes into a compact whole" (Judd 1964:93; cf. Cooper 1995:160, 183; Lekson 1986:132, 134). These walls were subsequently razed (Lekson 1986:134). Plaza enclosure is certainly not an event unique to Pueblo Bonito, although among Chacoan great houses it appears to have occurred there first (e.g., Cooper 1995:273, 275; Lekson 1986).

In the course of excavation along these early plaza-bounding structures, Judd encountered an intriguing, *later* feature within the plaza, an enigmatic "low wall" about which I have found few remarks (see Figure 7.2). What makes the wall intriguing is precisely its ambiguity with respect to site layout and to its potential for shaping communal social gatherings, especially their degree of inclusiveness.

Judd's description relates that

> the last recognizable East Court surface, the surface upon which the bordering court walls were built [was that] upon which a lone wall crosses from east to west. The original height and purpose of this cross-wall remain unknown, but it was late in point of time and it had meaning for the Late Bonitians. It stood 18 inches high and 16 inches wide where we found it, abutting the exterior of Room 165, and apparently had replaced an earlier one on a surface 3 feet lower.
>
> [At] 6 feet 7 inches short of [later-built room] 149, a vertical break, straight as a door jamb, occurred in that cross-wall. The next 3½ feet consisted of coarser stonework as though a deliberate fill-in and the remaining 3 feet, on a foundation 11 inches below the surface, had been reduced to court level as though for an open passageway (1964: 113–114).

Although the wall appears on master plans of the site (e.g., Figure 7.2 here, from Lekson 1986, a schematized rendering showing no west-end gap), it receives little attention in print and is not included in maps of individual construction stages. I would guess that the stratigraphic and chronometric ambiguity of this puzzling construction (and that of multiple others) is what precludes age assignment. From Judd's Figure 5, the wall appears to share the same alignment azimuth of the western half of the final southern wall—that is, the angle Sofaer (1997, Chapter 9, this volume; cf. Farmer 2003) sees as acknowledging equinox sunrise—as well as perhaps of some of the "subfloor walls and foundations" Judd unearthed beneath the southern part of the west court. An earlier wall paralleled this one, scarcely more than two feet to the south, and was underlain, in turn, by sections of a razed and buried warren of rooms that may have included a predecessor to the north-south spine wall, but without the latter's precise solar

alignment. With erection on the final plaza floor, it seems most likely that, by the time the wall was built, the ponderosa pine was no longer alive (cf. Stein, Suiter, and Ford 1997:144–145; Windes 2003:23). But as I read the circumstantial evidence and interpolate uneasily from Judd's Figures 4 and 5 to Lekson's Stages II and III (his Figures 4.20 [b] and [c]), I venture to speculate that construction of the earlier east-west wall—along, perhaps, with the putative predecessor to the north-south spine wall—could correspond to the time of Stage III, which Lekson assigns to 1050–1060 (Lekson 1986:134) or to a transitional time between II and III (notionally, sometime around 1050, or perhaps slightly earlier; cf. Windes 2003:22). According to Dean and Windes's assessment (as reported by Stein, Suiter, and Ford 1997:145), the ponderosa pine likely expired sometime between 1020 and 1059. Perhaps, but only perhaps, the razed north-south wall was an initial attempt to replace the wooden gnomon. Or, at least as plausibly, perhaps "replacement" of the emphatic sort in the Stage VII wall wasn't yet socially necessary to reinforce enactment of Pueblo Bonito's "middle place" role.

I draw two principal points from the foregoing, admittedly quite speculative, reconstructions. The first is that, while frustratingly ambiguous evidence from razed construction precludes confident interpretations as to their place in space, time, and meaning at Pueblo Bonito, it doesn't mean that they weren't originally significant to social understanding. We need to resist reifying appropriately cautious absence of *inference* as original absence of *importance*. The second point concerns implications from the ambiguous east-west wall: although neither its significance nor its original form is known, its mere existence suggests we might consider finer division of the ostensibly open, accessible east court within Pueblo Bonito civic space. Built on the final plaza surface, the wall would have been visible in some form to late residents. If originally low, it plausibly channeled movement at least subtly. If higher than the wall that is currently preserved, its channeling role would have been more emphatic, and together with what I understand was a single, narrow pueblo entry, between rooms 137 and 140, the enigmatic wall might have rendered the southeast sector the least accessible plaza space.

Rather than extending discussion of plaza space, I want to focus briefly on other places that might be deemed public or civic or communal ritual space. Aside from ritual sanctity of homes (e.g., citing Eliade and others: Bustard 1996:57–58; Stein and Lekson 1992:94), and the increasingly debated nature of kivas, characteristics of at least three other architecturally defined spaces invite consideration here. One is the pair of earthen platforms south of the enclosure wall (Lekson, Chapter 2, this volume); the second is a series of "shrines" affixed to the exterior of the pueblo, and the third, the burial rooms described earlier, in Room 33 and its north-sector neighbors. The brief discussion that follows treats them, as well as interments in various sectors of the building, with respect to social practices associated with ritual—especially, again, to implications of secrecy and exclusion as compared with openness and inclusion.

The earth mounds at Pueblo Bonito have stirred vigorous discussion. Drawing on Judd and Windes, Lekson (1986:144) dates the initial soil accumulation between 1050 and 1075, with construction of bounding walls "in Stage VI, or later (1075–1105)." Stein and Lekson (1992) consider the result and the process of their creation to be key components of the "ritual landscape" at Pueblo Bonito. Indeed, they find the "mound [with or without stone facing] and its structured relationships with other architectural elements to be manifest . . . at the scale of the household, at the scale of the ritual landscape that provides the focus for the community, and at the scale of the Chaco complex" (1992:97; cf. Windes, Chapter 3, this volume). Based on the wider range of earth-mound forms beyond the Pueblo Bonito instance, Stein and Lekson remark that the earthen masses are obviously not defensive. In each case, the mound

> does, however, provide a tangible barrier between the great house and the great beyond, and arguably functions as a conceptual boundary delineating sacred space. Because of this inferred function, we refer to this feature as the *nazha*, a Navajo term meaning to spiritually surround (Stein and Lekson 1992:96).

Fowler and Stein identify earth mounds and perimeter berms as important defining elements of eleventh-century great house layouts extending beyond Pueblo Bonito and Chaco Canyon, layouts whose histories of planning and internal change mirrored "evolution of the architecture of the Chaco complex" (1992:113).

Wills (2001), however, takes issue with inferring, in the mounds, the intentional, ritual creation of sacred architecture, based on his reexamination of evidence from the mounds at Pueblo Bonito (Judd 1964:212–222, Figure 24, and 1981) and Pueblo Alto. Although he suggests that the mounds "would have offered excellent though limited locations for public oratory, and in modern pueblos the trash middens are considered 'sacred' locations in certain social contexts," he maintains that their identification as "an architectural metaphor for Chacoan society" remains unfounded (2001:447–448).

Although I find Wills's critique compelling in many of its specifics, the larger geometries with which the Pueblo Bonito mounds—in their final, walled form—articulate compel me to consider that these already established features could well have been incorporated into an emerging larger whole. That is, by the late eleventh century cosmographic expression at Pueblo Bonito had become architecturally quite emphatic. If I read the evidence correctly, the cardinal spine wall together with pronounced internal symmetries and complementarities of the pueblo around the cardinal axis are coeval with a different azimuth projected beyond the building from the east wall of Rooms 149–152 and great Kiva A, extending between the earth mounds and across the canyon to Casa Rinconada (Stein and Lekson 1992: Figure 8-9; Stein, Suiter, and Ford 1997: Figures 9.5 and 9.7; cf. Judd 1964: Figure 5). The *perception* of this azimuth as a line of sight would have been limited within the limits of the building perhaps (judging, for example, from Figure 7.5) to people atop the northernmost perimeter rooms (especially 207 and 208), or the roof of Kiva A, or even the southernmost roomblock adjoining Kiva B. Still, what appears to be the precision of the alignment seems unlikely to be coincidence in a period of emphatic choreography for public hierophany within the pueblo, and the earth mounds—and especially the corridor between them—seem plausible framing for a processional route connecting with an important southerly destination (or origin point) for intra-canyon pageantry and devotional activities (cf. Fritz 1978, 1987; Stein et al., Chapter 8, this volume).

Expressing the larger picture more concisely, I would suggest that as the numbers of pilgrims and other visitors grew in the eleventh century—whether they brought turquoise, timber, pottery, chert, or simply themselves—perhaps the need for more explicit expression of the importance of their destination grew as well. Insofar as an individual visitor's presence might not have lasted through an entire daily cycle, the complementary manifestation of solar and celestial hierophanies identifying Pueblo Bonito's standing as "middle place" might well have expanded in importance.

I turn now to symmetry and complementarity in another sense, captured in Windes's statement that "The latest room masonry is to be found in Rooms 28B, 55, and 57, and in the unusual 'shrine' structures built at the site's southeastern corner (Judd 1964:173, 176). All of these rooms lie close together in the site's north-central area in front of the very earliest architecture, where a number of very late vessels were found" (Windes 2003:28; cf. Stein, Suiter, and Ford 1997:138). Reference to the "very late vessels" points to such rooms as 28, 32, and 33. Windes goes on to assert the likelihood "that the late vessels were additions to earlier caches or perhaps the earlier materials were scavenged or curated. Either way, the late vessels suggest the perpetuation of ritual, although it might not have been temporally or culturally continuous" (Windes 2003:30).

The "shrines," on the other hand, consist of a "sub-surface cylinder" (Pepper's Room 190), a series of box-like constructions abutting Room 176 (Judd 1964:175–176), as well as what appears to be similar construction abutting Room 142, the southeast "corner" of the portion of the final pueblo wall with the solar alignment (see Figure 7.2). Writing of those "boxes" adjoining Room 176, Judd says that they "seem absolutely purposeless except as shrines. Apparently added one at a time, their floor levels vary and their stonework differs. As we found them they were without lateral openings or evidence of roofing; each was filled with clean wind-borne sand" (1964:176). I would note an additional series of smaller "boxes" affixed to the northeast section of the perimeter wall of Rooms 186 and 187 and discovered by Judd during investigation of the Northeast Foundation Complex (Judd 1964:146). They appear only on his Figure 11 (and his Plate 42), and the one complete receptacle had dimensions of "45 inches by an average of 19; inside, 27 by 12. It was floored by a single sandstone slab laid [and] ceiled 15 inches above with slab-covered small poles the ends of which had been inserted into the ruin wall." He makes no functional inference and indicates that the box contained "only a handful of miscellaneous deer and small mammal bones, two Old Bonitian black-on-white sherds, and an ironstone concretion" (Judd 1964:146). This would have been near the road cited as passing by the north side of the building. I suggest, then, that all of these boxes may have been shrines for offerings, perhaps from pilgrims on their arrival at or their departure from the pueblo. Although Judd's description gives no hint as to what the offerings in the smaller boxes were, I believe nonetheless that the idea merits consideration.

By extension, the earlier and later "boxes" seem plausibly considered as complements to earlier and later practices in the northern-sector rooms, perhaps appropriately placed in the opposing intercardinal spatial sector. In the complex ritual center that was Pueblo Bonito, there surely were multiple and different kinds of observances (e.g., Toll 2001), available to and participated in by varied ranges of people. Some occurred in hidden places (e.g., Rooms 33, 32, 28) whereas others (e.g., perhaps at the external boxes) would have been witnessed and/or participated in by a much wider group, at one time or across time. These practices doubtless changed, at least somewhat, over the centuries. But as Windes indicates, there were clearly threads of continuity as well, even in the presence of temporal and cultural disjunctions. Different groups may have been responsible for, or subscribed to, different devotional practices, and perhaps distinctions I've suggested here relate to different social groups often cited (see above) as having control of particular areas of the building. But however hidden or secret, *the practices and the beliefs* underlying them must have been *shared* (e.g., A. Joyce 2000), and in that sense, as much "publicly" acknowledged as they were "privately" enacted. Had they not been shared, the threads of

193

ritual continuity would not have held. Nor would the social memory I have inferred for the building, as a whole, have endured.

CONCLUDING THOUGHTS

In the preceding pages, I have put forward some ideas about social aspects of architectural stasis and change in Pueblo Bonito. The remarks were offered as footnotes, a category of comment that I take to be subsidiary to main texts. Footnotes afford opportunity for support or minor disagreement with ideas presented in central narratives, but they do not claim to supplant the narratives.

The range of what is *not* addressed in this collection of footnotes is necessarily far broader than what is, and from my outsider's view, there is much exciting room for extended discussion of social implications of Pueblo Bonito's architectural evidence. Let me cite just three examples.

I have omitted consideration in any depth of political organization and leadership at Chaco, although these are clearly critical matters, under prominent, closely argued, and *continuing* discussion. As many authors have demonstrated, political organization and leadership are materialized in architecture and space, and the range of new models and methods being invoked is quite provocative (e.g., Cameron and Toll 2001; Metcalf 1997; Neitzel 2003, Chapter 5, this volume; Wills 2000).

Likewise omitted here are more specific phenomena such as any correlation between road construction and changes within the pueblo. These surely had important social implications, as hinted, if in passing, by Cooper's (1995:278) remarks: "It is puzzling that at the time that more people were being brought into the Chacoan system, spaces that could accommodate larger numbers were being encroached by construction and made harder to access from the outside." I offered one possibility earlier, about growth in numbers of visitors, but it is only one alternative and the subject merits closer consideration (see Lekson, Chapter 2, this volume; Stein et al., Chapter 8, this volume).

A third omission here is an area ripe for further consideration, even if much of that will remain controlled speculation. I refer to the puzzling array of razed constructions within the heart of the building (a few of them touched on earlier) and, most dramatically, in the "Northeast Foundation Complex," a term Windes emphatically rejects (personal communication, 2002), based on his own excavations there. Label aside, what were these constructions? Why were they not completed? Or if completed in some sense, why were they destroyed? Such abandonment and even destruction is certainly common in the world, but the causes are not always the same, and the occurrences always beg explanation.

I found two principal views on the "Northeast Foundation Complex," in particular: that it was a "grandiose" expansion, scrapped before completion, after investing considerable effort (e.g., Cooper 1995:183; Judd 1964:153–154; Lekson 1986:136–137), and that it was a 1:1 *model* for construction, evidence for problem-solving analogic design (Lekson 1981; Stein and Lekson 1992:92). Cooper's comments indirectly suggest a possible third avenue of interpretation. What she infers specifically is that "The ambitious, contradictory and soon-abandoned Northeast Foundation of Pueblo Bonito Stage V is the single best argument against centralized decision-making, although it may have represented an attempt to do so" (Cooper 1995:279). That statement made me wonder whether the intricate, partially completed (Lekson 1986:136; Windes, personal communication, 2002), and now exceedingly enigmatic constructions might register the effects of factionalism. That is, within what is recognized, more often than not, as having been a *corporate* leadership organization (e.g., Cameron and Toll 2001; Metcalf 1997; Wills 2000), there was perhaps expanded space for disagreement. And although Chaco society is also recognized increasingly as distinct from modern Pueblo organization, it might not be amiss to recall the dramatically documented Orayvi factional dispute (Titiev 1944), and its expression in architecture within that pueblo (Cameron 1999). Of course, the Orayvi experience does not equate with events in Pueblo Bonito's history, but its consideration might be instructive.

It is an understatement to acknowledge that Pueblo Bonito is and remains a complicated place, with an equally complicated and intricate life history. The footnotes I have offered here are simply that, footnotes to a life history that many people

194

have been writing. I look forward to reading whole new chapters, by those and other authors, as the biography expands.

ACKNOWLEDGMENTS

I am grateful to Steve Lekson for the invitation to participate in the on-site gathering at Chaco Canyon in October 2000, and in this volume. I thank the many Chaco and Southwesternist scholars who welcomed me so cordially into their midst, sharing generously of their insights—not to mention detailed tours of Pueblo Bonito and other Chaco buildings, unpublished maps and manuscripts, and other truly invaluable bibliographic advice. In particular, I single out Taft Blackhorse, Patty Crown, Dabney Ford, Steve Lekson, Joan Mathien, Ben Nelson, Bob Preucel, John Schelberg, Anna Sofaer, Phil Tuwaletstiwa, Chip Wills, Tom Windes, and John Stein (who, among other things, drove all the way back from Gallup, after the close of the formal conference, to help lead a special guided tour of Pueblo Bonito!). Chelsea Blackmore contributed important help at crucial points, especially with the illustrations. And as always, I am deeply grateful to Tom Patterson, for encouragement and critical readings of the manuscript as it unfolded (as well as for understanding when I unfolded maps and other documents over ever-larger expanses of horizontal surfaces in our house).

REFERENCES CITED

Akins, Nancy J., and John D. Schelberg
1984 Evidence for Organizational Complexity as Seen from the Mortuary Practices at Chaco Canyon. In *Recent Research on Chaco Prehistory*, edited by W. James Judge and John D. Schelberg, pp. 89–102. Reports of the Chaco Center 8. National Park Service, Albuquerque.

Ashmore, Wendy
1989 Construction and Cosmology: Politics and Ideology in Lowland Maya Settlement Patterns. In *Word and Image in Maya Culture*, edited by William Hanks and Don S. Rice, pp. 272–286. University of Utah Press, Salt Lake City.
1991 Site-Planning Principles and Concepts of Directionality among the Ancient Maya. *Latin American Antiquity* 2:199–226.
2005 The Idea of a Maya Town. In *Structure and Meaning in Human Settlement*, edited by Tony Atkin and Joseph Rykwert, pp. 35–54. University of Pennsylvania Museum Publications, Philadelphia.

Aveni, Anthony F.
2001 *Skywatchers*. University of Texas Press, Austin.

Barrett, John C.
1999 The Mythical Landscapes of the British Iron Age. In *Archaeologies of Landscape: Contemporary Perspectives*, edited by Wendy Ashmore and A. Barnard Knapp, pp. 253–265. Blackwell, Oxford, UK.

Basso, Keith H.
1996 *Wisdom Sits in Places: Landscape and Language among the Western Apache*. University of New Mexico Press, Albuquerque.

Bradley, Richard
1987 Time Regained—The Creation of Continuity. *Journal of the British Archaeological Association* 140:1–17.
1993 *Altering the Earth: The Origins of Monuments in Britain and Continental Europe*. Monograph Series, No. 8. Society of Antiquaries of Scotland, Edinburgh.

Bustard, Wendy J.
1996 *Space as Place: Small and Great House Spatial Organization in Chaco Canyon, New Mexico, A.D. 1000–1150*. Ph.D. dissertation, University of New Mexico. University Microfilms, Ann Arbor.

Cameron, Catherine M.
1999 *Hopi Dwellings: Architecture at Orayvi*. University of Arizona Press, Tucson.

Cameron, Catherine M., and H. Wolcott Toll
2001 Deciphering the Organization of Production in Chaco Canyon. *American Antiquity* 66:5–13.

Cooper, Laurel Martine
1995 *Space Syntax Analysis of Chacoan Great Houses*. Ph.D. dissertation, University of Arizona. University Microfilms, Ann Arbor.

Crown, Patricia L., and W. James Judge
1990 Synthesis and Conclusions. In *Chaco and Hohokam: Prehistoric Regional Systems in the American Southwest*, edited by Patricia L. Crown and W. James Judge, pp. 293–308. School of American Research Press, Santa Fe.

Doxtater, Dennis
1991 Reflections on the Anasazi Cosmos. In *Social Space: Human Spatial Behavior in Dwellings and Settlements*, edited by Ole Grøn, Ericka Engelstad, and Inge Lindblom, pp. 155–184. Odense University, Odense, Denmark.

Durand, S. R.
1992 *Architectural Change and Chaco Prehistory*. Ph.D. dissertation, University of Washington. University Microfilms, Ann Arbor.

Eliade, Mircea
1959 *The Sacred and the Profane: The Nature of Religion*, translated by Willard R. Trask. Harcourt Brace, San Diego.

English, Nathan B., Julio L. Betancourt, Jeffrey S. Dean, and Jay Quade
2001   Strontium Isotopes Reveal Distant Sources of Architectural Timber in Chaco Canyon, New Mexico. *Proceedings of the National Academy of Sciences* 98:11891–11896.

Farmer, James D.
2003   Astronomy and Ritual in Chaco Canyon. In *Pueblo Bonito's Centennial: New Approaches to Big Site Archaeology in Chaco Canyon*, edited by Jill E. Neitzel, pp. 61–71. Smithsonian Institution Press, Washington DC.

Fowler, Andrew P., and John R. Stein
1992   The Anasazi Great Houses in Space, Time, and Paradigm. In *Anasazi Regional Organization and the Chaco System*, edited by David E. Doyel, pp. 101–122. Anthropological Papers 5. Maxwell Museum of Anthropology, University of New Mexico, Albuquerque.

Freidel, David, Linda Schele, and Joy Parker
1993   *Maya Cosmos: Three Thousand Years on the Shaman's Path*. William Morrow, New York.

Fritz, John M.
1978   Paleopsychology Today: Ideational Systems and Adaptation in Prehistory. In *Social Archeology: Beyond Subsistence and Dating*, edited by Charles L. Redman, Mary Jane Berman, Edward V. Curtin, William T. Langhorne, Jr., Nina M. Versaggi, and Jeffery C. Wanser, pp. 37–59. Academic Press, New York.
1987   Chaco Canyon and Vijayanagara: Proposing Spatial Meaning in Two Societies. In *Mirror and Metaphor: Material and Social Constructions of Reality*, edited by Donald W. Ingersoll, Jr., and Gordon Bronitsky, pp. 313–349. University Press of America, Lanham, MD.

Gillespie, Susan D.
1991   Ballgames and Boundaries. In *The Mesoamerican Ballgame*, edited by Vernon L. Scarborough and David R. Wilcox, pp. 317–345. University of Arizona Press, Tucson.
2000   Maya "Nested Houses": The Ritual Construction of Place. In *Beyond Kinship: Social and Material Reproduction in House Societies*, edited by Rosemary A. Joyce and Susan D. Gillespie, pp. 135–160. University of Pennsylvania Press, Philadelphia.

Hall, Edward T.
1966   *The Hidden Dimension*. Anchor/Doubleday, Garden City, New York.

Hall, Robert L.
1997   *An Archaeology of the Soul: North American Indian Belief and Ritual*. University of Illinois Press, Urbana.

Hillier, Bill, and Julienne Hanson
1984   *The Social Logic of Space*. Cambridge University Press, Cambridge.

Joyce, Arthur A.
2000   The Founding of Monte Albán: Sacred Propositions and Social Practices. In *Agency in Archaeology*, edited by Marcia-Anne Dobres and John Robb, pp. 71–91. Routledge, London.

Joyce, Rosemary A.
2000   Heirlooms and Houses: Materiality and Social Memory. In *Beyond Kinship: Social and Material Reproduction in House Societies*, edited by Rosemary A. Joyce and Susan D. Gillespie, pp. 189–212. University of Pennsylvania Press, Philadelphia.

Judd, Neil M.
1964   *The Architecture of Pueblo Bonito*. Smithsonian Miscellaneous Collections 147(1). Washington, DC.
1981   *The Material Culture of Pueblo Bonito*. Reprints in Anthropology 23. J&L Reprint, Lincoln NE. (Originally published in 1954 as Smithsonian Miscellaneous Collections 124)

Judge, W. James
1984   New Light on Chaco Canyon. In *New Light on Chaco Canyon*, edited by David Grant Noble, pp. 1–12. School of American Research Press, Santa Fe.
1989   Chaco Canyon–San Juan Basin. In *Dynamics of Southwest Prehistory*, edited by Linda S. Cordell and George J. Gumerman, pp. 209–261. Smithsonian Institution, Washington, DC.

Lekson, Stephen H.
1981   Cognitive Frameworks and Chacoan Architecture. *New Mexico Journal of Science* 21(1):27–36.
1986   *Great Pueblo Architecture of Chaco Canyon*, reprint ed. University of New Mexico Press, Albuquerque. (Originally published in 1984, National Park Service, Albuquerque)
1989   Kivas? In *The Architecture of Social Integration in Prehistoric Pueblos*, edited by William D. Lipe and Michelle Hegmon, pp. 161–167. Occasional Paper 1. Crow Canyon Archaeological Center, Cortez, CO.
1999   *Chaco Meridian: Centers of Political Power in the Ancient Southwest*. Altamira Press, Walnut Creek, CA.

Low, Setha M.
2000   *On the Plaza: The Politics of Public Space and Culture*. University of Texas Press, Austin.

Marshall, Michael P.
1997   The Chacoan Roads: A Cosmological Interpretation. In *Anasazi Architecture and American Design*, edited by Baker H. Morrow and V. B. Price, pp. 62–74. University of New Mexico Press, Albuquerque.

Mathien, Frances Joan
1997   Ornaments of the Chaco Anasazi. In *Ceramics, Lithics, and Ornaments of Chaco Canyon: Analyses of Artifacts from the Chaco Canyon*

196

Wendy Ashmore

Project, 1971–1978, Vol. I: Ceramics, edited by Frances Joan Mathien, pp. 1119–1220. Publications in Archeology 18G, Chaco Canyon Series. National Park Service, Santa Fe.

2001 The Organization of Turquoise Production and Consumption by the Prehistoric Chacoans. *American Antiquity* 66:103–118.

Metcalf, Mary Patricia
1997 *Civic Spaces: Architectural Expressions of Political Organization in the Prehistoric Northern Southwest, A.D. 1000–1300.* Ph.D. dissertation, University of Virginia. University Microfilms, Ann Arbor.

Neitzel, Jill E.
2003 The Organization, Function, and Population of Pueblo Bonito. In *Pueblo Bonito's Centennial: New Approaches to Big Site Archaeology in Chaco Canyon*, edited by Jill E. Neitzel, pp. 143–149. Smithsonian Institution Press, Washington, DC.

Nelson, Nels C.
1996 Notes on Pueblo Bonito. In *Pueblo Bonito*, by George Pepper, reprint ed., pp. 381–390. University of New Mexico Press, Albuquerque. (Originally published in 1920 as Anthropological Papers of the American Museum of Natural History 27, New York)

Ortiz, Alfonso
1969 *The Tewa World: Space, Time, Being, and Becoming in a Pueblo Society.* University of Chicago Press, Chicago.

Ortiz, Simon J.
1994 What We See: A Perspective on Chaco Canyon and Pueblo Ancestry. In *Chaco Canyon: A Center and Its World*, by Mary Peck, Stephen H. Lekson, John R. Stein, and Simon J. Ortiz, pp. 65–72. Museum of New Mexico Press, Santa Fe.

Pepper, George H.
1909 The Exploration of a Burial-Room in Pueblo Bonito, New Mexico. In *Putnam Anniversary Volume: Anthropological Essays Presented to Frederic Ward Putnam in Honor of His Seventieth Birthday*, by Franz Boas et al., pp. 196–252. G. E. Stechert, New York.

1996 *Pueblo Bonito*, reprint ed. University of New Mexico Press, Albuquerque. (Originally published in 1920 as Anthropological Papers of the American Museum of Natural History 27. New York.)

Redman, Charles L.
1990 The Comparative Context of Social Complexity. In *Chaco and Hohokam: Prehistoric Regional Systems in the American Southwest*, edited by Patricia L. Crown and W. James Judge, pp. 277–292. School of American Research Press, Santa Fe.

Renfrew, Colin
2001a From Social to Cognitive Archaeology: An Interview with Colin Renfrew. *Journal of Social Archaeology* 1:13–34.

2001b Production and Consumption in a Sacred Economy: The Material Correlates of High Devotional Expression at Chaco Canyon. *American Antiquity* 66:14–25.

Richards, Colin
1990 The Late Neolithic House in Orkney. In *The Social Archaeology of Houses*, edited by Ross Samson, pp. 111–124. Edinburgh University Press, Edinburgh.

Robin, Cynthia
1999 Towards an Archaeology of Everyday Life: Maya Farmers of Chan Nòohol and Dos Chombitos Cik'in, Belize. Unpublished Ph.D. dissertation, Department of Anthropology, University of Pennsylvania.

2002 Outside of Houses: The Practices of Everyday Life at Chan Nòohol, Belize. *Journal of Social Archaeology* 2:245–268.

Scully, Vincent
1989 *Pueblo: Mountain, Village, Dance*, second ed. University of Chicago Press. Chicago.

Snead, James E., and Robert W. Preucel
1999 The Ideology of Settlement: Ancestral Keres Landscapes in the Northern Rio Grande. In *Archaeologies of Landscape: Contemporary Perspectives*, edited by Wendy Ashmore and A. Bernard Knapp, pp. 169–197. Blackwell, Oxford.

Sofaer, Anna
1997 The Primary Architecture of the Chacoan Culture. In *Anasazi Architecture and American Design*, edited by Baker H. Morrow and V. B. Price, pp. 88–132. University of New Mexico Press, Albuquerque.

Sofaer, Anna, Michael P. Marshall, and Rolf M. Sinclair
1989 The Great North Road: A Cosmographic Expression of the Chaco Culture in New Mexico. In *World Archaeoastronomy*, edited by Anthony F. Aveni, pp. 365–376. Cambridge University Press, Cambridge.

Stein, John R., and Stephen H. Lekson
1992 Anasazi Ritual Landscapes. In *Anasazi Regional Organization and the Chaco System*, edited by David E. Doyel, pp. 87–100. Anthropological Papers No. 5, Maxwell Museum of Anthropology, Albuquerque.

Stein, John R., Judith E. Suiter, and Dabney Ford
1997 High Noon in Old Bonito: Sun, Shadow, and the Geometry of the Chaco Complex. In *Anasazi Architecture and American Design*, edited by Baker H. Morrow and V. B. Price, pp. 133–148. University of New Mexico Press, Albuquerque.

Stuart, David E.

1997   Power and Efficiency in Eastern Anasazi Architecture. In *Anasazi Architecture and American Design*, edited by Baker H. Morrow and V. B. Price, pp. 36–52. University of New Mexico Press, Albuquerque.

Thomas, Julian

1993   The Politics of Vision and the Archaeologies of Landscape. In *Landscape: Politics and Perspectives*, edited by Barbara Bender, pp. 19–48. Berg, Oxford.

Titiev, Mischa

1944   *Old Oraibi: A Study of the Hopi Indians of Third Mesa*. Papers of the Peabody of Museum of Archaeology and Ethnology 22 (1). Harvard University, Cambridge.

Toll, Wolcott H.

2001   Making and Breaking Pots in the Chaco World. *American Antiquity* 66:56–78.

Townsend, Richard F.

1986   Artists Reconstruction of Pueblo Bonito. In *Mysteries of the Ancient Americas: The New World before Columbus*. Reader's Digest, Pleasantville, NY.

1992   Landscape and Symbol. In *The Ancient Americas: Art from Sacred Landscapes*, edited by Richard F. Townsend, pp. 29–47. Art Institute of Chicago and Prestel Verlag, Chicago and Munich.

Tringham, Ruth

1994   Engendered Places in Prehistory. *Gender, Place, and Culture* 1:169–203.

Urton, Gary F.

1981   *At the Crossroads of the Earth and the Sky*. University of Texas Press, Austin.

Vivian, R. Gwinn

1990   *The Chacoan Prehistory of the San Juan Basin*. Academic Press, New York.

Vogt, Evon Z.

1992   The Persistence of Tradition in Zinacantan. In *The Ancient Americas: Art from Sacred Landscapes*, edited by Richard F. Townsend, pp. 61–69. Art Institute of Chicago and Prestel Verlag, Chicago and Munich.

Wills, W. H.

2000   Political Leadership and the Construction of Chacoan Great Houses, AD 1020–1140. In *Alternative Leadership Strategies in the Prehispanic Southwest*, edited by Barbara J. Mills, pp. 19–44. University of Arizona Press, Tucson.

2001   Ritual and Mound Formation during the Bonito Phase in Chaco Canyon. *American Antiquity* 66:433–451.

Windes, Thomas C.

2003   This Old House: Construction and Abandonment at Pueblo Bonito. In *Pueblo Bonito's Centennial: New Approaches to Big Site Archaeology in Chaco Canyon*, edited by Jill E. Neitzel,, pp. 14–32. Smithsonian Institution Press, Washington, DC.

Windes, Thomas C., and Dabney Ford

1992   The Nature of the Early Bonito Phase. In *Anasazi Regional Organization and the Chaco System*, edited by David E. Doyel, pp. 75–85. Anthropological Papers 5. Maxwell Museum of Anthropology, Albuquerque.

1996   The Chaco Wood Project: The Chronometric Reappraisal of Pueblo Bonito. *American Antiquity* 61:295–310.

Windes, Thomas C., and Peter J. McKenna

2001   Going Against the Grain: Wood Production in Chacoan Society. *American Antiquity* 66:119–140.

Zeilik, Michael

1989   Keeping the Sacred and Planting Calendar: Archaeoastronomy in the Pueblo Southwest. In *World Archaeoastronomy*, edited by Anthony F. Aveni, pp. 143–166. Cambridge University Press, Cambridge.

Wendy Ashmore

8

Revisiting Downtown Chaco

John Stein

Richard Friedman

Taft Blackhorse

Richard Loose

IN THIS CHAPTER we construct a digital three-dimensional model of "downtown" Chaco Canyon as it may have appeared at 1130, the approximate date that great house construction ceased.[1] Our reconstructions are based on empirical evidence gathered from detailed field surveys, photogrammetric analysis, and remote sensing analysis. Much can be learned about the physical form of a "ruin" by taking careful measurements to model the terrain precisely, map the location of cultural features, identify the context of cultural features in a larger framework, and map/model the form and structure of surface anomalies. The buildings in Chaco Canyon, which now lay in ruin, have traditionally been viewed by archaeologist and layman alike as containers that must be opened up, or excavated, to analyze the clues to the past that are hidden within. In the haste to uncover these clues, the three-dimensional form or shape of the structure and its relationship to other features in the area have been largely ignored.

Presented here are the results of detailed analyses of the physical forms of the containers themselves, and their relationship to other cultural and natural features in Chaco Canyon. No excavations were done for this analysis, but excavation reports and/or records were used where available. One does not

need to look inside a container to see, measure, and describe its external manifestation, or its relationships with other containers, cultural features, and natural features. However, a good working knowledge and understanding of geology, geomorphological processes, large-scale mapping, and coordinate systems is a must for an exercise of this nature.

A primary rationale for the creation of a digital map of the Chaco Canyon landscape is resource management, and accordingly, our model is based on real-world coordinates. To visualize and build a reconstruction of this scale and complexity requires collecting and evaluating information from a multitude of diverse sources, and inevitably, this body of information will not be in full agreement. In contrast with textual reporting, where ambiguity in and conflict between information sources can be presented and debated independently, graphic reporting requires a researcher to be decisive about how tall a building may have stood or if a feature should be excluded from the model because it is arguably not of the correct time period. Numerous competing narratives are latent in the database that underlies a digital reconstruction, and a seemingly endless number of alternate but credible scenarios have to be evaluated in the course of building the model.

We had long been aware that only a fraction of the spatial data required to build this model was available from archival sources and that a detailed archaeological inventory, land survey, and program of aerial image acquisition and interpretation would be the unavoidable consequence of our commitment. Creating an internally consistent, high-resolution spatial database referenced to real-world coordinates anchors the model firmly to geographic reality and accurately portrays the fundamental spatial relationships among the primary features of the built environment, the terrestrial landscape, and the movements of the heavenly bodies.

Reconstructing a complex built environment from archaeological data is a complicated, time-consuming (expensive), and inherently risky endeavor. Most archaeologists (wisely) fear to tread the twisted paths of field observation, extrapolation, informed conjecture, and graphic commitment necessary for the illustration of an individual structure of the built environment. Southwestern archaeologists, for the most part, have happily delegated the responsibility of architectural reconstruction to artists in the employ of *National Geographic* or *Reader's Digest*.

Popular images of precolumbian Southwestern architecture can be traced to the overactive imaginations of artists and exhibit specialists. Models and images of landscapes convey very powerful, but often inconsistent and inaccurate, messages. Our reconstruction has been in process off and on for more than three decades and yet it remains incomplete in many significant areas of interest. To bring the reconstruction to its present state of completeness required (in archaeological parlance) that we resurvey the core area of the Chaco complex. We were also obliged to acquire new aerial photography and digital imagery; perform subsurface remote sensing in select locations; review and acquire more than a century of original notes, maps, and photographs; and perhaps most important, consult with Navajo *hataałii* ("singers," chanters, ceremonial practitioners). Our reconstruction could not have been completed without recourse to contemporary spatial data and remote sensing technologies.

As regards the study of precolumbian buildings, we discovered that architects and archaeologists have interests that are complementary but not necessarily mutually intelligible. Kievit (1998:103) found data collected by archaeologists to be of limited use in reconstructing and understanding the built environment in Chaco Canyon.

Because archaeology relies largely on a process of extrapolation and inference, we find it curious that this enthusiasm for accuracy in reconstructing the nature of the whole from a few fragments has not been routinely applied to architecture. The reconstruction of any past process, event, or building from fragmentary data is necessarily conjectural; however, of all the artifacts of past human behavior, architecture most resembles language in that it communicates multiple levels of meaning through ordered relationships of form and space (Alexander et al. 1977; Broadbent 1973, 1980; Hillier and Hanson 1984; Hillier et al. 1978; Leach 1983; McGuire and Schiffer 1983; Rappaport 1982, 1988; Stein and Lekson 1992; White 1975). Certain levels of meaning conveyed by architecture are universal; characteristics that communicate nonverbally with the user/builder often communicate the same message to the outsider as well. Higher, "symbolic" levels of meaning evoke emotional response and are nonlexical or nondiscursive in nature (Doxtater 1984; Washburn and Crowe 1988).

Our reconstructions are based on detailed, spatially accurate observations of the landscape and structures at Chaco, but in fairness to the achievements of Chacoan architecture, we go beyond the "raw data." We extrapolate and (to a degree) conjecture, much as did Tatiana Proskouriakoff (1946) in her classic reconstructions of Maya architecture. To err on the side of misplaced caution does no service to Chaco, nor would allowing an overactive imagination to run rampant. (A strict reading of the evidence, for example, would require us to assume that no building at Chaco was ever finished, because no intact exterior roofs survive.) Clearly, many forms and elements in the Chacoan architectural canon no longer exist (materially) in modern or historic Native architectures. There was more to Chaco than meets the eye, and more things under the Chaco sun than were dreamt of in Mindeleff's (1891) "A Study of Pueblo Architecture." Our reconstructions, however, are constrained by what is known about the architectural traditions of North America and Mexico in the tenth through fourteenth centuries, an era when

200

Native societies may have been more richly inter-connected and more regionally aware than many archaeologists of the twenty-first century are.

Navajo tradition about Chaco, its region, and its history enlightens and adds another level of detail and contextual meaning to much of our work.[2] *Hataałii* know Chaco Canyon as Jish chaago (The Place Of The Sacred Bundle) and respect it as a place of dark power and spiritual danger. Navajo ceremonial history makes reference to specific structures, spaces, features, and locales in downtown Chaco as well as related features of the built and natural environment of the greater region (Fishler 1953; Goddard 1933; Haile 1981; Matthews 1994; O'Bryan 1956; Reichard 1944; Simpson 1960:37–38; Van Valkenburgh 1941; Wheelwright 1946; Wyman 1957). Navajo tradition describes the reign of Nihwiilbiih (The Gambler), a sorcerer who came from far to the south. Nihwiilbiih seized the power of the portal at Tse-biinaholts'a Yałti (described here as "the Amphitheater"), enslaved the peoples living in the region, and focused the Chaco complex on the portal. Patterning in architecture and material culture suggests that The Gambler's reach encompassed approximately 80,000 square miles of the southern Colorado Plateau and endured for approximately eight centuries (500–1300). We speculate that the ancestors of many of the contemporary tribes (representing multiple ethnic and language groups) were participants (either willing or unwilling) in The Gambler's empire.

But the remains at Chaco are not prehistoric in the sense of being "before history": the memory of Chaco continues to be preserved in the oral history and ceremonial repertoire of most if not all of the indigenous societies in the region today. Certain clans of the Diné (the present-day Navajo) claim a direct and continuous association with Chaco dating from times before the arrival of The Gambler. Information about what happened at Chaco continues to be curated in the content of specific ceremonial repertoires closely controlled by *hataałii*. This information is tied in with celestial cycles and cosmology (Blackhorse et al. 2003; Williams et al. 2006). Navajo peoples, residing on the Chacoan landscape, retain specific historical details embedded in features and structures of that landscape (Begay 2004), much as Keith Basso (1996) describes

in his study of Apache landscapes, *Wisdom Sits in Places*.

Although we emphasize Navajo traditions in our interpretations, our intent is not to denigrate or ignore other contemporary Native groups' knowledge, traditional history, or involvement in the history of Chaco Canyon. Like the Diné, those peoples have rich and vivid oral histories detailing activities and events specific to Chaco Canyon. Many studies of Chaco foreground Pueblo traditions and histories. Here, however, we emphasize the traditions and histories of the Diné. Navajo traditions provide rich resources for Chaco history, and we believe that these resources have been unduly overlooked in archaeological attempts to understand Chaco Canyon.

To the reader not familiar with the pitfalls inherent in reconciling the content of traditional histories with "scientific evidence," we offer a few discouraging words. Traditional histories are characteristically cosmological in nature and function to preserve high-level information necessary to understand and interact properly with the forces of the universe. To prevent loss and possible misuse (resulting in harm), the information content of these histories is encrypted in a variety of ways. It is an understatement to say that the content of these narratives is complex and abstract; they may even seem nonsensical if interpreted literally from the vantage point of a foreign ideology. On the other hand, the narratives do reference actual people, events, and places in a drama that unfolds on a real landscape—in this case, the landscape of the Four Corners region.

Intellectual traditions that rely on memorization and oral recitation maintain rigid requirements for accuracy. The opposite of Western science, these traditions rely heavily on iconography, poetics, narratives, and ritual drama to compress and synthesize information that carries multiple levels of meaning, and trained ceremonialists choose which level of meaning to interpret based on the circumstances at hand. We are talking about intellectual traditions of societies whose ceremonialism is the umbrella beneath which ecological, economic, social, and political relations occur. Ceremonialism relates humans to each other and to the non-human beings and forces of nature around them. The accumulated knowledge of generations is stored and related largely through ritual dramas and related activities.

Ceremonialism is the framework on which people organize their knowledge of natural and cultural history to interpret what they find in the world. To begin to understand the importance of narratives in these intellectual traditions, one must first consider what it is like to live every moment within an overarching framework of ceremonialism.

The images and explanation we present herein are derived primarily from examination of the present landscape in downtown Chaco. We were able to identify and document significant, but previously overlooked, components of the primary architecture, including great mounds; "pyramids"; massive, veneered platforms; a vast outdoor amphitheater; altars; roads; and causeways. In addition, we have begun to question the validity of conventional interpretation for categories of features, such as "small houses" and agricultural "fields." Newly recognized features, and reinterpretations of known structures, suggest a very different Chaco than a community of small and great houses, agricultural fields, and canals.

RECONSTRUCTING THE BUILT ENVIRONMENT

We have worked diligently to build a landscape model of central Chaco Canyon based on accurate, real-world coordinates (Plate 8.1; plates begin following page 264). Building this model required integrating coordinate (map), image, and elevation data within an interoperable geospatial information technology environment. This landscape model is the indispensable base for our reconstruction.[3] Our primary source of information for both the natural and cultural domains is the present surface. We traversed the study area many times in the course of establishing registration points and collecting the location data on ground coordinates needed to rectify the stereo aerial photography. We then retraced our steps to acquire firsthand map data of all visible architectural remains, from precolumbian to contemporary.

Plate 8.2 shows the footprint of the primary structures that would have comprised downtown Chaco in the early twelfth century. Because our mapping effort is extensive in scale, and our time limited, intensity (translate: detail) is localized; overall, our survey at the stage presented herein is thorough but not necessarily comprehensive. For example, we were unable to capture at least two classes of architectural/material remains in sufficient detail to serve as a basis for reconstruction. Ephemeral stone and sherd scatters on the canyon floor between Kin Kletso and 29SJ834 and 835 suggest the possibility of numerous temporary structures. Documenting these scatters would require a considerable time investment, even with the use of contemporary mapping technologies. Another area that begged for additional effort is the base of the cliff and the vertical surface of the cliff face from Pueblo Bonito to the end of the Chetro Ketl Rincon. Behind Chetro Ketl especially, open, ramada-like structures with very high roofs appear to have been built against and anchored to the cliff face.

Much of the precolumbian architecture within downtown Chaco has been excavated and left open to the elements. Many structures serve as exhibits and are routinely maintained and repaired. These ruins are highly visible and easily mapped; however, the exposed fabric is not always original and the complete footprint is rarely exposed to view. In the interest of accuracy, we consulted published and unpublished accounts of investigations at Chaco, including primary field notes for several of the major sites (Judd 1959a, 1964; Lekson 1985; McKenna and Truell 1986; Pepper 1920; Vivian and Mathews 1965).[4] In some instances we were able to fill in architectural detail using aerial photogrammetry. In other instances (for example, at Chetro Ketl), where portions of the structure had not been excavated, or had been excavated but not reported, or had been obscured by the process and by-products of excavation, it was necessary to return to the site and carefully remap these areas.

Pueblo Bonito is the largest, most complex structure in downtown Chaco. Reconstruction of Pueblo Bonito and analysis of the chronology of its construction were conducted as a separate project (Stein et al. 2003). Because this earlier model was also built using real-world coordinates, we were able to integrate the structure data directly onto the new terrain model.

The identification and documentation of the Chaco "linescape" (alignments) as well as related, large-scale but low-visibility landscape architecture depended on analysis of aerial photography and detailed, on-the-ground mapping. Published maps were consulted (e.g., Loose and Lyons 1976;

Obenauf 1980; Stein and Lekson 1992; Vivian 1983a, 1983b; Windes 1987), but because of the inherent complexity of the subject matter, the very large scale at which these features are manifest, piecemeal reporting, guesswork, and a variety of other accuracy issues, we illustrate only those features that we could confidently identify on the ground, from aerial photography, or preferably from both (Plate 8.3). Therefore, the configuration of alignments we show is internally consistent but not necessarily comprehensive. We make no claim that all alignments and landscape architecture in the study area have been identified.

Not all alignments were created equal. With some exceptions, all "roads" are linear, formalized sections of longer alignments, but not all formalized aspects of alignments are roads. The outward form of the Chaco complex appears to be dictated by an underlying web of alignments—a *linescape*. This web may be likened to the initial, lightly drawn lines of a construction drawing that are partially inked over in the completed work. In downtown Chaco, the underlying pattern of alignments was only partially formalized by "road" construction. A majority of alignments appear to have served as the connecting threads between a variety of celestial, natural terrestrial, and built forms but were not formalized by etching into the earth's surface. Alignments follow a complex and as yet poorly understood logic that from the perspective of Western thought is largely counterintuitive. The emphasis on addressing celestial phenomena (e.g., Marshall 1997; Sofaer and Sinclair 1987; Sofaer et al. 1982) and the consistent use of bifold rotational symmetry to wed opposites and structure the movement of architectural forms through time/space (Doxtater 1984; Fritz 1978; Stein et al. 1997, 2003; Washburn and Crowe 1988) enable the elucidation of alignments with some degree of confidence.

In addition to their uncompromising linearity, an often-cited characteristic of Chacoan roads is a uniform width of 9 m (e.g., Stein 1983; for a recent discussion see Vivian 1997). This is based largely on the study of the North Road and the fan of roads that converge on Pueblo Alto from the north. Once inside the Chaco complex, the few broad, extra-canyon avenues are joined by narrower, avenue-like features ranging from 3 to 6 m in width as well as a host of alignments formalized only by feature placement, scrub lines (temporarily devegetated areas), or perishable monuments.

The "roads" converging on Pueblo Alto are among the most formalized of the Chaco alignments. They are also located in a context where they have been well preserved. Many—and perhaps most—of the Chaco alignments were minimally formalized, located in environments where they are poorly preserved, have been obscured by later human activity (primarily in the nineteenth and twentieth centuries), or a combination thereof.

The majority of the Chaco alignments were apparently never more than narrow lines cleared of vegetation and/or marked by widely spaced perishable monuments (i.e., poles). Nevertheless, because of the sheer number of lines, their length (to the horizon), uncompromising linearity, and etched signature, the linescape was likely to have been the most visible and impressive aspect of the Chaco built environment.

The alignments shown in our reconstruction are all based on tangible evidence derived from aerial photography, terrestrial photography, and ground documentation. Many alignments were visible as linear features on multiple images but lacked a ground signature. Conversely, road architecture such as short swales, ramps, gates, and curbing in the vicinity of primary structures clearly visible from the ground perspective was not always visible in aerial photography. In the interest of objectivity, we documented these short road segments and associated features as we encountered them, paying close attention to the morphology of the swale and the orientation of features. In this way we were able to delay judgment on the destination of these alignments until we had assembled a comprehensive map. Our reward for not trying to second-guess the orientation of the alignments was the emergence of a pattern that did not in fact fit our expectations. When viewing the array of alignments, keep in mind that these features were never intended to be straightforward, simple pathways linking one building with the next.

FEATURE DESCRIPTIONS

Following are descriptions of select features and categories of features that appear in our reconstruction of downtown Chaco. Most of the features

203

are easily recognized as architecture; however, important locations may also be unmodified natural features, natural features modified to resemble built features, and even built features constructed to resemble natural features.

Pine Tree at Pueblo Bonito

During the National Geographic Society's excavation of Pueblo Bonito in the mid 1920s, the stump of a ponderosa pine tree was discovered in the West Plaza of Pueblo Bonito (Judd 1954: Plate 2; Stein et al. 1997: Figure 9.1). Judd (1954:3) interpreted the stump as evidence of a living tree. Dean and Windes (in Stein et al. 1997:144–145) reexamined the stump (JPB-99) and concluded that the tree was a ponderosa pine with a trunk diameter of about 52 cm. It had begun its life no later than AD 732 and died between 1020 and 1050. Thus the tree was approximately a century old at the time of the first documented construction at Old Pueblo Bonito and would have died prior to or coincident with the initiation of Stage III construction (Stein et al. 2003:49–50). There seems little reason to doubt that the tree was a significant aspect of the architecture of Pueblo Bonito; it was a node in the internal geometry of the building and may have functioned as a "World Tree" (Stein et al. 1997). If the tree had grown in situ as Judd surmised, it might also have played a role in the selection of the Pueblo Bonito site. An alternative scenario is that the tree was harvested elsewhere with the root ball intact and emplaced in the West Plaza coincident with the initiation of Stage III construction. However the pine came to be located in the West Court, by the mid twelfth century it was no longer a living tree, and if it remained standing, it was as a pole. Although the height of such a pole is guesswork, according to the Western Wood Products Association (1995) an average ponderosa pine with a similar diameter grown under favorable conditions could be 75 feet in height.

Threatening Rock

The significance of Threatening Rock has long been a subject of speculation (Judd 1959b, 1964; Lister and Lister 1981:51, 76, 120, 121, 124, 126; Marshall 2003; Stein et al. 2003; Vivian and Hilpert 2002:239). The enormous rock (Figure 8.1) towered over Pueblo Bonito until 1941, when it fell and crushed the northeastern portion of the building. In Richard Wetherill's time the rock was known as the "elephant." Judd (1938, 1959b) referred to the rock as the "braced-up-cliff," one translation for the Navajo name for Pueblo Bonito. The builders of Pueblo Bonito constructed a massive wall beneath the rock (Figure 8.1a), which is commonly interpreted as a futile attempt to postpone the inevitable fall. (This feature is discussed below.)

The traditional Navajo name for Threatening Rock and Pueblo Bonito, Tse bii yah nii aha (pronounced "say bih yah nee ah-ha"), does not translate well into English but implies several levels of connection, partly physical and partly esoteric, between the building and the rock. Lt. James H. Simpson first uses the name "Pueblo Bonito" in his 1849 journal of a military reconnaissance of the region (Simpson 1960). Guides for the expedition, presumably Hosta of Jemez Pueblo or Carraval of San Ysidro, supplied the name. In the Spanish language, Pueblo Bonito means "beautiful village." Today, the name seems appropriately romantic; however, it is doubtful that this ruin in the remote and hostile (both in the military and the environmental sense) region of Chaco Canyon was widely known to the Spanish community of New Mexico at that time or that it was considered "beautiful." It seems more likely that "Pueblo Bonito," like "Canyon de Chelly," is an example of transliteration.

Spanish was the lingua franca of the time. Minimally the translation of the traditional name would have progressed from Navajo to Spanish to English. This is further complicated by Tse bii yah nii aha being a sacred name for perhaps the most spiritually powerful place in Navajo Country; as such it would have been dangerous for some even to utter the name. As is the case today, this type of information would have been tightly controlled by hataałii and would not have been common knowledge. We suggest the possibility that Navajo informants, through translators such as Hosta, referred to the area using the generic term tse' biniit'a, which translates as "along or up-against the rock." A well-known example of a similar transliteration is Tse Bonito, a contemporary town in New Mexico. The Navajo name for that place is Tse Biniit'a, but in its Navajo/Spanish form it is locally translated as

FIGURE 8.1A. Historic view of Tse bii yah nii aha, Threatening Rock, showing "retaining wall." (Photograph by Mindeleff, courtesy of Smithsonian Institution, National Anthropological Archive NPC 02881.02, SPC 013844.02 Album 1, BAE 4362)

"Pretty Rock." Because the Spanish referred to contemporary settlements as well as ancient ruins as "pueblos," it seems probable that the terms Pueblo and Biniit'a (Bonito) were combined at this time.

The Navajo name for Tse Bii yah nii aha makes no distinction between the towering rock and the building beneath it; the unique, shrinelike shape of Pueblo Bonito and its juxtaposition to Threatening Rock suggest a purposeful connection. Unlike the ponderosa pine, however, there is no question that the natural form preceded the building beneath it. Many aspects of the built environment reinforce the idea that Threatening Rock was an important consideration in locating Pueblo Bonito (see Marshall 2003). We reject the idea that Pueblo Bonito's builders engaged in an unsystematic and ultimately futile effort to brace Threatening Rock. The "retaining wall" was a complex structure formed from

massive amounts of adobe and stone that was faced with fine masonry. The structure formed a filled and paved platform with a level surface that extended well beyond Threatening Rock to the west and east. The eastern extension of this platform is known as Hillside Ruin (Stein et al. 2003). Like the South Mounds/platforms, the space between the outside wall of Pueblo Bonito and the retaining wall of the platform accommodates a formalized avenue that traversed the long axis of Chaco Canyon. Plate 8.3 illustrates this alignment as well as a near cardinal alignment that links Threatening Rock with Pueblo Bonito, Wetherill's Dam (described below), and Casa Rinconada.

Caves

Several naturally formed shallow caves eroded into the cliff face are clearly visible from most locations

FIGURE 8.1B. Oblique aerial photograph of Pueblo Bonito by Charles Lindberg, 1929. (Courtesy of Museum of New Mexico, MNM 130198, SAR 59008)

in downtown Chaco. Two of these caves are of interest here. The first is located in the cliff face east of Lizard House Arroyo and faces west across the Chetro Ketl Field. The second is due west of the first, facing east from high in the cliff face at the mouth of South Gap. The cave overlooking Lizard House Arroyo is alluded to in Navajo ceremonial history as the hole for a golflike game ('*alkal*) The Gambler forced his captives to play in order to enslave them. The cave in South Gap is the terminus of an especially elaborate set of formalized roads and platforms.

Tsebiinaholts'a Yałti (The Amphitheater)

A natural arc in the cliff face between Pueblo Bonito and Chetro Ketl (Figures 8.2a and 8.2b) is known by Navajo *hataałii* as Tsebiinaholts'a Yałti ("say bih nah holts ah yal tee," loosely translated as Concavity In Bedrock That Speaks). This alcove

is the point of origin of the Chihwojoolyee (Datura ceremony), and it is still visited by the *hataałii* who practice this ceremony. Tsebiinaholts'a Yałti is the origin place of the tones that give power to contemporary Navajo chants, and also of the concepts of *taal* (chant) and *ta'a'l* (ceremonial pathway). Tsebiinaholts'a Yałti is a portal to the dimension of the deities and was recognized as such in the times before the arrival of Nihwiilbiih (The Gambler). Upon learning the location of this portal, Nihwiilbiih, already a great sorcerer, seized it and accessed its power (Blackhorse et al. 2002).

The alcove of Tsebiinaholts'a Yałti opens to the south and is 152 m across. The curvature of the natural arc, if projected, forms a circle 340 m in diameter that perfectly encompasses the area bounded by the Northeast Foundation complex/Hillside Ruin at Pueblo Bonito, the Talus Unit at Chetro Ketl, and the northern edge of the present Chaco Wash (Plate 8.4). Given the lack of tangible evidence of a formal enclosure, the projected circle is admittedly a matter of speculation; however, it is clearly a delineated space that is level, and conspicuously devoid of features and material culture. We interpret this conspicuous void in the architecture of downtown Chaco to be an outdoor performance area.

The Tsebiinaholts'a Yałti alcove was considerably modified. Centered in the natural arc is a smaller, inner alcove that was created by the removal of up to 2 m of the cliff face in an area 60 m across and 3 m high. Around 360 m³ (about 58 dump truck loads) of material was removed from the inner alcove (Loose 2001:7). A set of three cliff cavities is centered in the back wall of the alcove (see description below), and an apparent altar is associated with a panel of petroglyphs (29SJ1931) at the eastern edge of the alcove.

We conducted an acoustical study of Tsebiinaholts'a Yałti (Loose 2001, 2002). The curved surfaces are toric with a horizontal radius of curvature of 170 m and a vertical radius of curvature of 46 m; the cliff wall is more steeply curved vertically than horizontally. Experiments with sound included the broadcast of continuous audio frequency tones and sine wave sweeps aimed at the center of the radius of curvature from various locations, including the Casa Rinconada Mound (see description below). Quantifiable results were

206

FIGURE 8.2A. Tsebiinaholts'a Yałti, showing the inner alcove, altar, and cliff cavities.

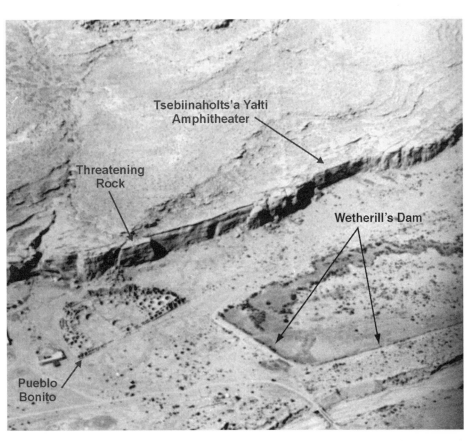

FIGURE 8.2B. 1929 Lindberg photo showing Tsebiinaholts'a Yałti. (Courtesy of Museum of New Mexico, MNM 130226, SAR 59018)

Revisiting Downtown Chaco

captured by analysis of recordings from locations along the central axis of the arc, also including the Casa Rinconada Mound. Tsebiinaholts'a Yałti has a "line" rather than a "spot" focus, and a single echo. Under certain conditions this echo will form a "virtual sound image" analogous to the visual image seen in a mirror; the sound seems to originate from the other side of the cliff wall. Experiencing the behavior of the tones firsthand was an unforgettable experience. The canyon floor was filled with sound, and at certain frequencies there was a sensation of being "bathed" in sound as standing waves of sound formed along the axis of the amphitheater.

Tsebiinaholts'a Yałti exhibits acoustical properties comparable to those of the great European cathedrals and concert halls (Loose 2001). The optimum range of decay of the sound signal (reverberation) necessary for enhancing the acoustical signal is 0.5 to 3 seconds; the reverberation times in the Chaco Amphitheater ranged from 1.3 to 2 seconds. Cathedrals and concert halls are essentially musical instruments, and each exhibits unique properties and special effects. Musical compositions written for performance in a specific theater or cathedral might have to be "adapted" if they were to be performed elsewhere. A certain "volume threshold" is required to stimulate many of the special sound effects of a large theater. The optimum performance of a structure the size of Tsebiinaholts'a Yałti would require the coordinated efforts of a large number of people.

Tsebiinaholts'a Yałti is the geometric center of the Chaco complex and as such is arguably the most important space in the Chaco world. Sets of alignments connecting Pueblo Alto with Tsin Kletzin and Peñasco Blanco with Una Vida and Kin Nahasbas intersect in Tsebiinaholts'a Yałti. Of particular interest is the intersection at the center of the Tsebiinaholts'a Yałti void of two defining axes of the Chaco complex: the north-south axis between Pueblo Alto and Tsin Kletzin, which is heavily formalized (it becomes the principal alignment of the North Chaco Road) and a line that can be drawn between the fifth-century great kivas at Peñasco Blanco and Shabik'eshchee Village. At first glance this latter connection seems improbable: the azimuth of the line lies midway between winter solstice sunrise and the lunar minor standstill, it

exceeds 14 km in length, and the two structures are not intervisible. After further consideration, however, it is apparent that this line is threaded through Chaco Canyon as if it were the eye of a needle, passing through the space between Pueblo Bonito and Threatening Rock. Although it was built six centuries later, the flattened portion of the north wall of Pueblo Bonito accommodates this alignment. The Shabik'eshchee–Peñasco Blanco alignment suggests that the significance of Tse bii yah nii aha and Tsebiinaholts'a Yałti and the primary configuration of the Chaco complex were well established half a millennium before construction began at Pueblo Bonito in the early ninth century.

Cliff Cavities

Between fifteen and twenty holes were pecked and drilled into the cliff face between Kin Kletso and Chetro Ketl. These are the "Cliff Cavities" described by Julian (1933) and Keur (1933). Because of Dorothy Keur's interest in these features, they are popularly known as "DoDo holes" after Dorothy's nickname (Dabney Ford, personal communication 2003). The holes range from about 30 to 60 cm in diameter and may extend several meters into the cliff face. The height of the holes on the cliff face varies considerably, but they are commonly located 1–3 m above grade.

Four of the cliff cavities are associated with Hillside Ruin and the Amphitheater; three occupy the quarter and half (center) positions in the back wall of Tsebiinaholts'a Yałti (see Figure 8.2a), and one is situated on the western end of Hillside Ruin (Figure 8.3). The westernmost of the three holes at Tsebiinaholts'a Yałti is the largest of the known cliff cavities; it lies on the primary north-south axis between Pueblo Alto and Tsin Kletzin and widens into a cave large enough to accommodate several persons.

We believe that the cliff cavities are examples of alignment formalization, functioning as benchmarks and receptacles for offerings. The configuration of the cavities suggests that the alignments were envisioned as entering and/or exiting the cliff face at these locations.

Another interesting aspect of the cliff face in the Amphitheater and Hillside vicinity is the presence of numerous deeply scoured, then scored areas that we interpret as the systematic removal of glyphs. At

FIGURE 8.3. Photo of cliff cavity at west end of Hillside Ruin that shows evidence of an iconoclastic event.

Hillside in particular, a line of scoured areas suggesting an underlying script is centered on the cliff cavity.

Earthen and Platform Architecture

In Chaco Canyon, the study of solid/earthen forms as architecture results largely from interest in features interpreted to be dams, ditches, roads, or road-related structures such as ramps (Cameron 2002; Kincaid 1983; Nials et al. 1987; Vivian 1983a). Unlike the landscape in downtown Chaco, many extra-canyon great houses and their associated landscapes remain uncompromised by large-scale excavation and development. Experience with these less-extensive but better-preserved landscapes has expanded our knowledge of earthen architectural vocabularies and the rules that organize them. Armed with this knowledge we have returned to Chaco Canyon with an expanded set of expectations (e.g., Cameron 2002; Fowler and Stein 1992; Kintigh et al. 1996; Lekson 1984; Marshall et al. 1979; Nials 1983a; Nials, Stein, and Roney 1987;

Roney 1992; Ruppé et al. 2001; Stein 1987; Stein and Fowler 1996; Stein and Lekson 1992; Stein and Levine 1983; Stein and McKenna 1988; Stein and Roney 1987; Thompson et al. 1997).

Earthen and landscape architecture in Chaco Canyon is at least as old as the first settlements at Peñasco Blanco and Shabik'eshchee Village in the fifth century. In these pithouse villages the living space was literally carved into the earth. It is possible, if not probable, that the formalization of the Chaco linescape was concurrent with these early settlements. By 1130, the time of our reconstruction, the formalization of the Chaco core was essentially if not actually complete, and it was a complex, layered composition that was primarily earthen.

CHETRO KETL FIELD

The Chetro Ketl field was first observed by Gordon Vivian and Charlie Steen during a flight over Chaco Canyon (Vivian and Mathews 1965:12) and was interpreted as the signature of successive fields on the alluvial fan. This interpretation is consistent

209

Revisiting Downtown Chaco

with a generalized view of precolumbian agriculture shared by many Southwestern archaeologists, and it remains the prevailing explanation for this feature (Loose and Lyons 1976; Vivian 1990; Vivian and Hilpert 2002). After expending a great deal of time, energy, and technology on this feature, we suggest that it may more likely have been a playing field, and less likely an agricultural field.

The "Chetro Ketl field" (Figure 8.4, Plate 8.5) is a rectangular area of the canyon floor located 220 m up-canyon from Chetro Ketl. The area is defined on the north and west by adobe berms 7 m in width and 5 to 20 cm in present height above ground surface. Lesser berms 20–30 cm in width are truncated at the ground surface but are well defined as bright grayish white in contrast to the dark brown of the silty infill surface. These lesser berms form a grid network encompassing a rectangle measuring 140 by 122 m. The size of the grid cells varies, but not greatly. There are approximately 30 cells, and

a representative cell is 14 by 20 m in internal dimensions. The gridded area appears to have been constructed by means of removal of 50+ cm of overburden to expose a compact substrate that was then partially leveled. The eastern edge of the excavated area is delineated by the face of the cut into the original ground surface. The grid network only partially fills the rectangular footprint. A mounded area in the northeast quarter may conceal an architectural feature, and much of the remainder of this quarter of the feature was apparently never gridded. Additional wide, low berms similar to those that bound the rectangular "field" area add significantly to the scale and complexity of the architecture of the feature. The longest of these "berms" is 436 m in length and passes through the south half of the grid on an azimuth of 292°. Loose and Lyons (1976) describe this as a summer solstice sunset alignment adjusted for the near horizon of the canyon edge. Anna Sofaer

FIGURE 8.4. Aerial photograph of Chetro Ketl Field showing differences in vegetation. (Photography by EnerQuest Systems flown June 2000)

Stein, Friedman, Blackhorse, and Loose

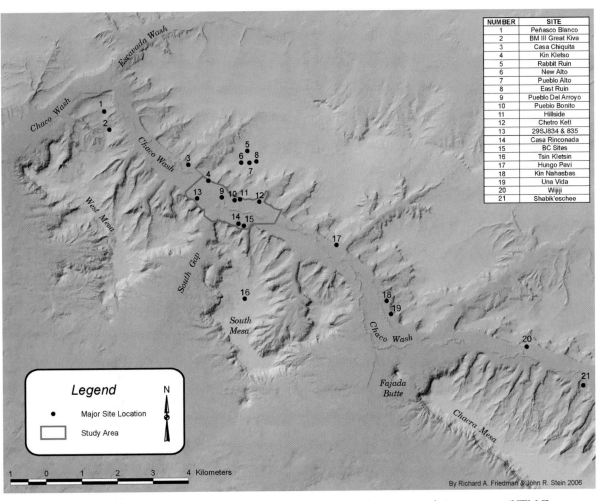

NUMBER	SITE
1	Peñasco Blanco
2	BM III Great Kiva
3	Casa Chiquita
4	Kin Kletso
5	Rabbit Ruin
6	New Alto
7	Pueblo Alto
8	East Ruin
9	Pueblo Del Arroyo
10	Pueblo Bonito
11	Hillside
12	Chetro Ketl
13	29SJ834 & 835
14	Casa Rinconada
15	BC Sites
16	Tsin Kletsin
17	Hungo Pavi
18	Kin Nahasbas
19	Una Vida
20	Wijiji
21	Shabik'eschee

Legend

N

• Major Site Location

▭ Study Area

1 0 1 2 3 4 Kilometers

By Richard A. Friedman & John R. Stein 2006

PLATE 8.1. Chaco Canyon digital elevation model showing major sites and primary study/survey area. (UTM Zone 13, NAD 1983)

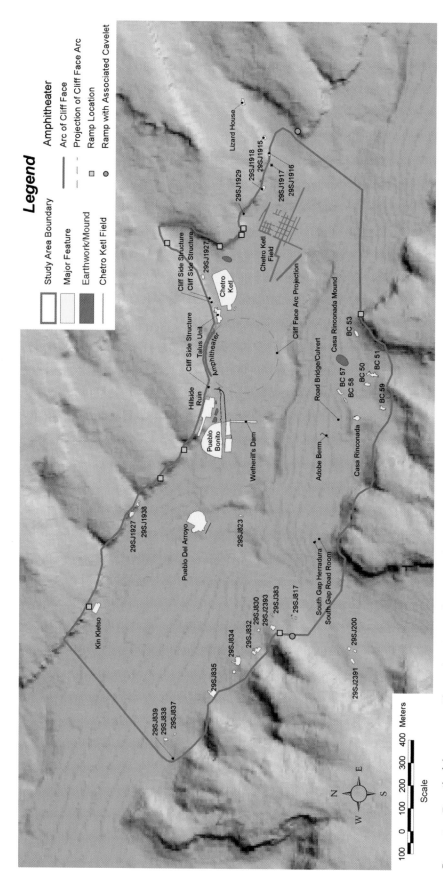

Legend

Amphitheater

— Arc of Cliff Face

– – – Projection of Cliff Face Arc

▢ Ramp Location

● Ramp with Associated Cavelet

▢ Study Area Boundary

▢ Major Feature

▓ Earthwork/Mound

— Chetro Ketl Field

Lizard House

29SJ1929
29SJ1918
29SJ1915
29SJ1917
29SJ1916

Chetro Ketl Field

Cliff Side Structure
Cliff Side Structure

29SJ1927

Chetro Ketl

Cliff Side Structure
Talus Unit

Amphitheater

Cliff Face Arc Projection

Hillside Ruin

Casa Rinconada Mound
BC 53

Pueblo Bonito

BC 57
BC 50
BC 51
BC 58

Road Bridge/Culvert

BC 59

Wetherill's Dam

Casa Rinconada

Adobe Berm

29SJ1927
29SJ1938

Pueblo Del Arroyo

29SJ823

South Gap Herradura
South Gap Road Room

Kin Kletso

29SJ834
29SJ832
29SJ830
29SJ2393
29SJ383
29SJ817

29SJ835

29SJ2391
29SJ200

29SJ839
29SJ838
29SJ837

N
W   E
S

Scale

100 0   100 200 300 400 Meters

PLATE 8.2. Detail of downtown Chaco showing architectural footprints. (UTM Zone 13, NAD 1983)

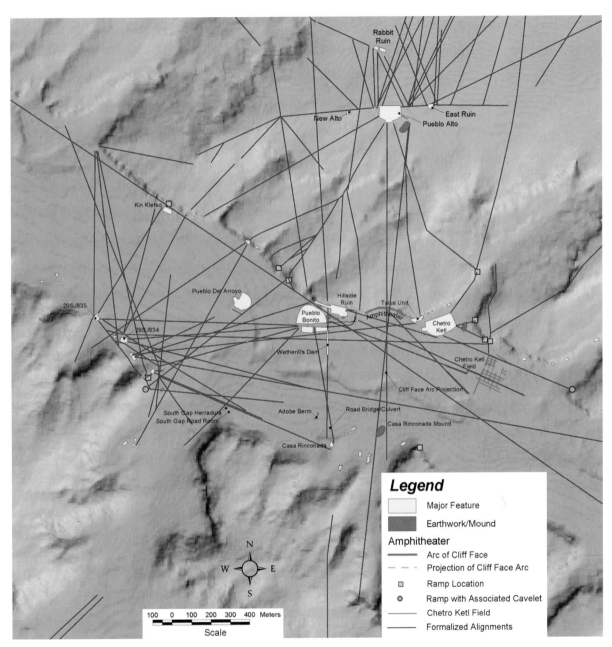

Legend

| | Major Feature |
| | Earthwork/Mound |

Amphitheater
——— Arc of Cliff Face
– – – Projection of Cliff Face Arc
□ Ramp Location
◯ Ramp with Associated Cavelet
——— Chetro Ketl Field
——— Formalized Alignments

Rabbit Ruin

New Alto

East Ruin
Pueblo Alto

Kin Kletso

Pueblo Del Arroyo

29SJ835

29SJ834

Hillside Ruin

Talus Unit

Pueblo Bonito

Amphitheater

Chetro Ketl

Chetro Ketl Field

Wetherill's Dam

Cliff Face Arc Projection

South Gap Herradura
South Gap Road Room

Adobe Berm

Road Bridge/Culvert

Casa Rinconada Mound

Casa Rinconada

N
W   E
S

100 0 100 200 300 400 Meters

Scale

PLATE 8.3. Formalized alignments identified in downtown Chaco. (UTM Zone 13, NAD 1983)

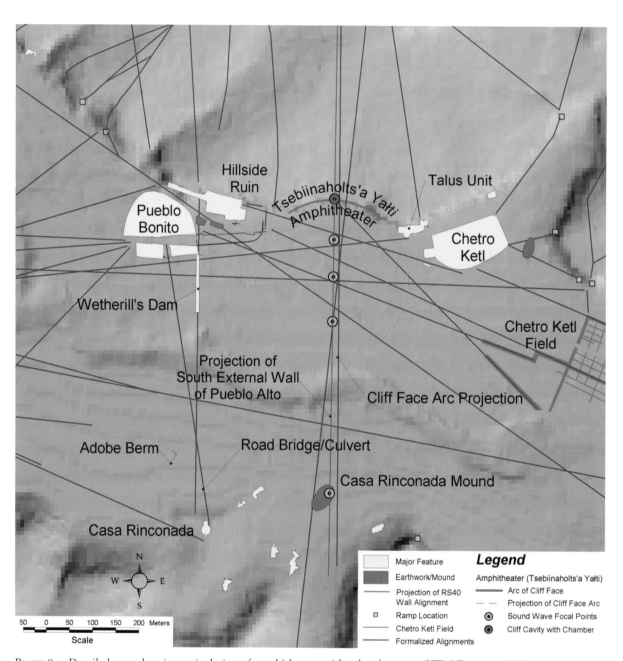

Pueblo Bonito

Hillside Ruin

Tsebiinaholts'a Yałti Amphitheater

Talus Unit

Chetro Ketl

Wetherill's Dam

Chetro Ketl Field

Projection of South External Wall of Pueblo Alto

Cliff Face Arc Projection

Adobe Berm

Road Bridge/Culvert

Casa Rinconada Mound

Casa Rinconada

N
W   E
S

50   0   50   100   150   200 Meters

Scale

Major Feature

Earthwork/Mound

Projection of RS40 Wall Alignment

Ramp Location

Chetro Ketl Field

Formalized Alignments

Legend

Amphitheater (Tsebiinaholts'a Yałti)

Arc of Cliff Face

Projection of Cliff Face Arc

Sound Wave Focal Points

Cliff Cavity with Chamber

PLATE 8.4. Detailed map showing articulation of amphitheater with other features. (UTM Zone 13, NAD 1983)

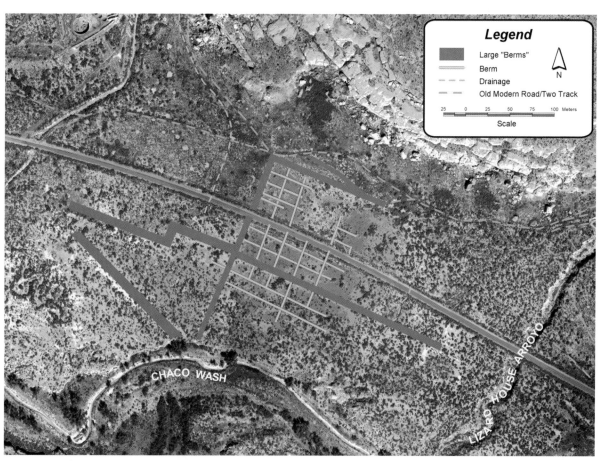

PLATE 8.5. Map of Chetro Ketl Field created from aerial photo interpretation and ground survey. (UTM Zone 13, NAD 1983)

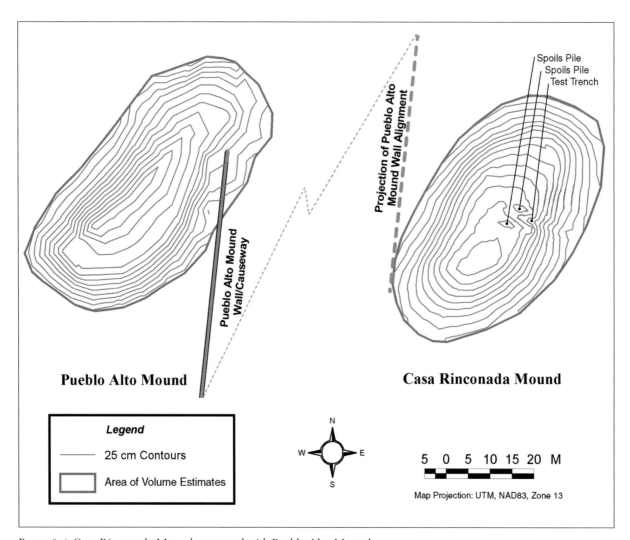

Plate 8.6. Casa Rinconada Mound compared with Pueblo Alto Mound.

PLATE 8.7. View of Hillside Ruin showing ramps and causeway (Wetherill's Dam).

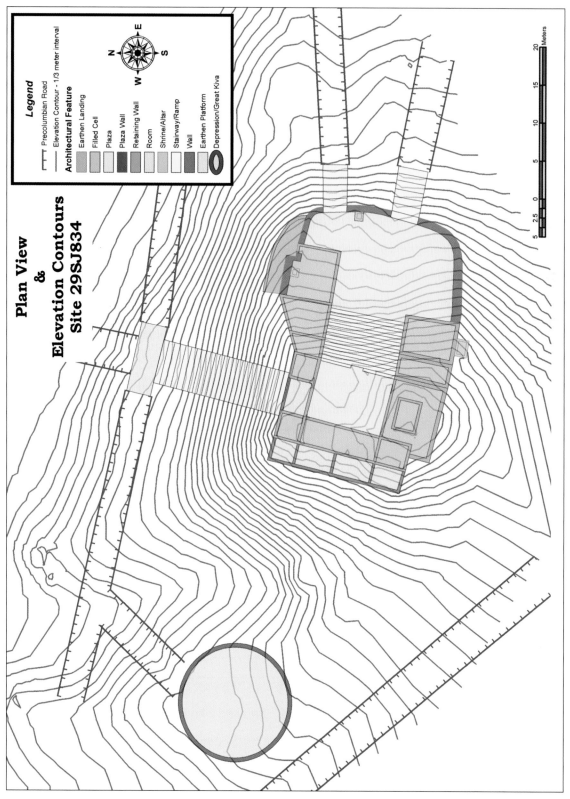

Plan View & Elevation Contours Site 29SJ834

Meters

PLATE 8.8A. Planimetric view of 29SJ834. Developing an accurate, spatially referenced planimetric map, and detailing open and filled cells is the first step in 3D model preparation. (UTM Zone 13, NAD 1983)

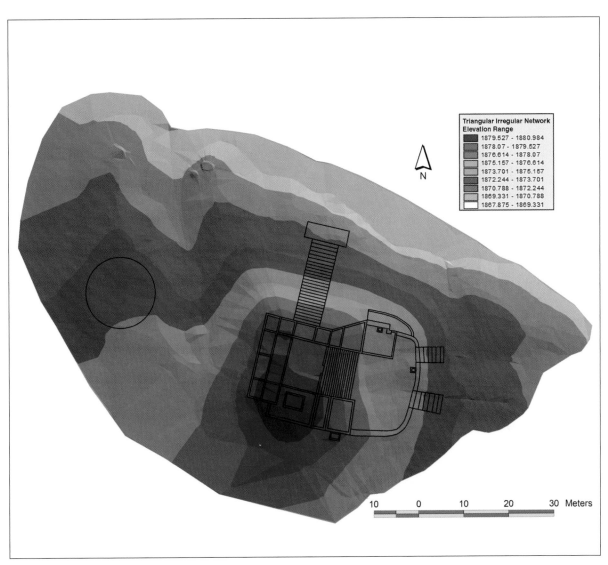

Triangular Irregular Network
Elevation Range
■ 1879.527 - 1880.984
■ 1878.07 - 1879.527
■ 1876.614 - 1878.07
■ 1875.157 - 1876.614
■ 1873.701 - 1875.157
■ 1872.244 - 1873.701
■ 1870.788 - 1872.244
■ 1869.331 - 1870.788
□ 1867.875 - 1869.331

N

10   0   10   20   30 Meters

PLATE 8.8B. A hill-shaded elevation model, or Triangular Irregular Network (TIN), is used as an aid in 3D modeling and room/cell classification. A structure is classified as open or filled based on the presence/absence of standing masonry, the extent of associated rubble, and the general profile from the walls to the center of the room. Structures that have a convex profile (greater elevation in the center than at the walls) and little or no associated wall rubble are classified as filled cells. Structures that have a concave profile and/or standing masonry are classified as rooms.

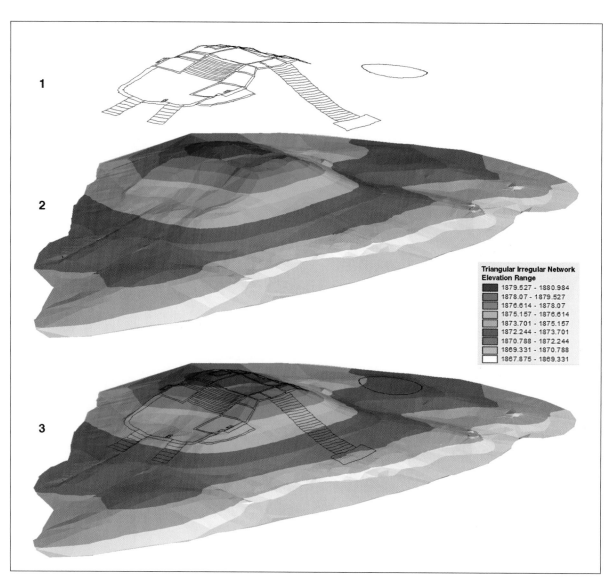

1

2

3

Triangular Irregular Network
Elevation Range
1879.527 - 1880.984
1878.07 - 1879.527
1876.614 - 1878.07
1875.157 - 1876.614
1873.701 - 1875.157
1872.244 - 1873.701
1870.788 - 1872.244
1869.331 - 1870.788
1867.875 - 1869.331

PLATE 8.8C. Computer visualization tools aid in the 3D reconstruction process. (1) 3D view of site planimetric map,
(2) 3D view of elevation model, (3) 3D view of planimetric
map draped over elevation model.

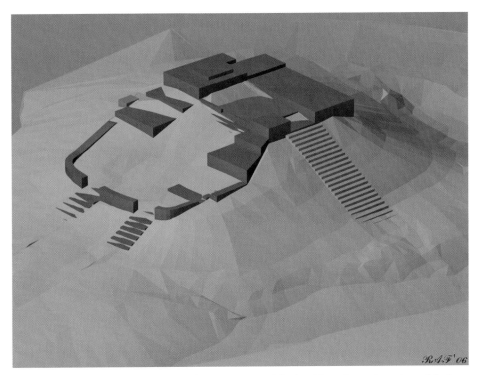

PLATE 8.8D. 3D perspective view of the massing model of 29SJ834 in conjunction with the digital elevation model of the site as it appears today. This type of information is used to ensure that the massing model accurately reflects what the site may have looked like before its currently reduced state.

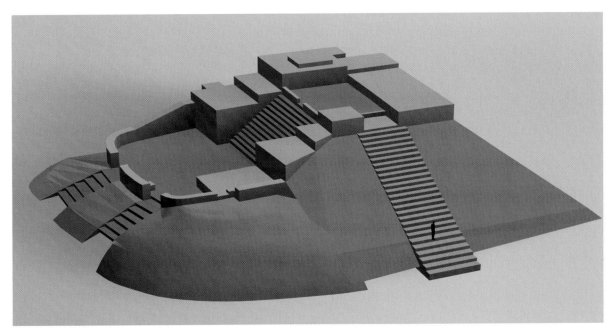

PLATE 8.8E. Perspective view from the northeast of the final massing model for 29SJ834. The large stairway from the lower plaza to the upper plaza was inferred based on the minimal amount of erosion evident along the east edge of the upper plaza, the extensive earthen mass that currently exists between the upper and lower plazas, and the need for a mode of travel between the upper and lower plazas. The six-foot-tall figure near the base of the north stairway was placed there to give the viewer a sense of scale.

PLATE 8.8F. The massing model of 29SJ834 placed onto a digital terrain: perspective view from the northeast. This type of illustration allows researchers to visualize what 29SJ834, associated archaeological features, and the surrounding terrain may have looked like approximately 800 years ago.

PLATE 8.8G. The massing model of 29SJ834 placed onto a digital terrain: perspective view from the north.

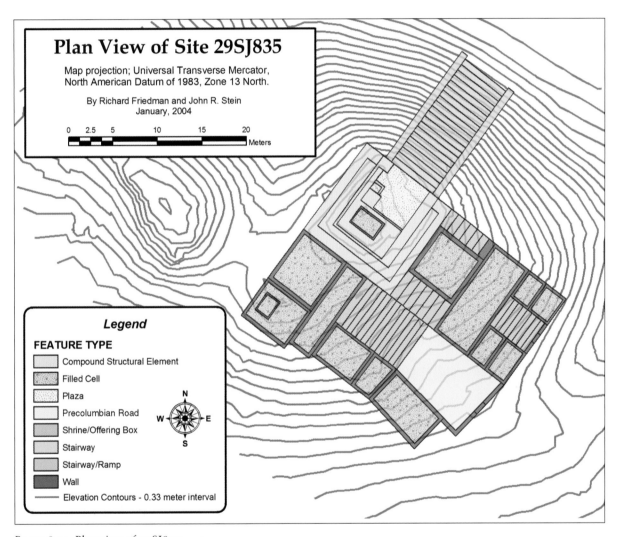

PLATE 8.9A. Plan view of 29SJ835.

PLATE 8.9B. Perspective view of the final massing model for 29SJ835 integrated into the digital terrain model. The view is from the north-northeast.

PLATE 8.9C. Perspective view of the final massing model for 29SJ835 integrated into the digital terrain model. The view is from the east.

PLATE 8.10. 3D perspective view from the southwest of Pueblo Bonito (on the left), Chetro Ketl (on the right), and the Amphitheater (in the center) and the surrounding architectonic landscape as it may have looked approximately 800 years ago.

PLATE 8.11. 3D perspective view from the southeast of several BC sites (in the bottom half of the image), Casa Rinconada (circular structure on the left half and way up the image), Pueblo Bonito (upper right), and Pueblo Del Arroyo (upper center).

PLATE 8.12. 3D perspective view of 29SJ834, 29SJ835, and the surrounding architectonic landscape as it may have looked approximately 800 years ago.

(personal communication, 2004) notes that the azimuth is also consistent with the position of the moon at the minor standstill. On the ground this alignment/berm articulates with the wide ramp on the east end of the Hillside Ruin platform. A similar berm angles from the Chaco Wash on an orientation addressing the center of the Amphitheater.

In 1974 the National Park Service excavated a series of trenches into the "field" (Loose and Lyons 1976). Loose and Lyons (1976:139, 141) describe the berms as earthen levees composed of sand interfingered with lenses of clay. Clay lenses 5–20 cm in thickness and at a depth of 40 to 50 cm mark what they interpret as the "old field surface." A massive, compact sandy clay layer extended to the bottom of the trenches, which ranged from 60 cm to 1 m below the laminated clay layer. Loose and Lyons (1976: Figure 5) illustrate three distinct episodes of levee construction with the final levee truncated at the present surface. Clay lenses can be seen covering the levees from top to bottom without substantial variation in thickness. The uniformity in the thickness of the clay layers suggests either that the entire area including the levees was completely submerged by a clay-charged slurry and then allowed to stand unagitated until it evaporated or alternatively that the levees were purposely surfaced with a clay plaster.

From the beginnings of archaeological investigation in Chaco Canyon, evidence of farming or the lack thereof has been a hot-button topic. Successful Navajo fields in the area show that agriculture is possible, but overall the conditions in the canyon appear to be unfavorable for any sustained, large-scale effort (Benson et al. 2003, 2006). Canyon soils generally, and particularly the sediments within the Chetro Ketl field, are clay- and salt-saturated. Judd (1964:230–231) and Love (1980:343–345) note that fine-grained, clay-rich sediments such as those in the Chetro Ketl field are poorly suited to agriculture because they are practically impermeable and laden with black alkali. Loose and Lyons (1976:144, 147, 151) point out that the Chetro Ketl field is quantitatively and qualitatively different from any other Chaco Canyon features tentatively identified as fields, with the possible exception of the fragment of a grid pattern west of Casa Rinconada.[5] Based on evidence of extensive land leveling, wall/berm intersections

consistently within 1% of 90°, and an axial orientation very near the summer solstice sunset position, Loose and Lyons (1976:151) concluded that the "field" had been designed and engineered. Other explanations have been offered. Tom Windes and Peter McKenna (personal communication 2002) speculate that it may represent mixing or settling pits for obtaining the tons of clay adobe needed for construction of the great houses. Dave Love (1980:345) suggests that the grids would be more useful for raising frogs or freshwater shrimp than for growing corn. Stein and Fowler (1996: 118) speculated that the "field" might be the adobe and sand equivalent of the Northeast Foundation Complex at Pueblo Bonito. Finally, Navajo ceremonial history describes the area of the Chetro Ketl field as a playing field where The Gambler would engage challengers in a golf-like game focused on the cave (described above) on the east side of Lizard House Wash.

An additional aspect of the "field" that requires clarification is the date of its construction and use. Loose and Lyons (1976:143–144) report an archaeomagnetic date of 1250 for three samples from the clay layer on the surface of the "field" (described in Nichols 1975). This date, derived from unburned sediments by an experimental technique, can be used to argue that the feature is precolumbian, but we doubt that it is sufficiently precise for finer chronological placement. The ceramic assemblage associated with the "field" and the articulation of the "field" with the primary architecture of the canyon suggest a construction date no later than 1130.

Our investigation of the Chetro Ketl field is not yet complete; however, our findings to date argue against the hypothesized functions of agriculture, hod pits, or building foundations; we concede that the frog pond idea may have some merit. The larger "berms" contain the gridded area of the feature, but they are also formalized segments of longer alignments. The berms extend beyond the gridded area of the field, and at least one appears to be superimposed on the grid. These berms also functioned as elevated roads or causeways. Based on our current knowledge of the Chetro Ketl field and its environs, the explanation offered by Navajo ceremonial history that it was a performance area seems most likely.

Casa Rinconada Mound

The Casa Rinconada Mound is an elongated, rounded feature 62 m long, 35 m wide, and 3 m in height (Plate 8.6). Our estimate for the volume of the mound is 2,111 m³ (340 dump truck loads). The Casa Rinconada Mound has long puzzled archaeologists (Nials et al. 1987:15). In the oral history of canyon archaeology, the mound is suspect first because it is eerily unnatural and second because it is not obviously cultural; there is no evidence of architecture or material culture on its surface. The mound is so devoid of the telltale evidence of occupation or use that it was not assigned a site number in the Chaco inventory survey (Hayes 1981).

As shown in Plate 8.6, the Casa Rinconada Mound and the Pueblo Alto Mound are virtually identical in size, shape, and orientation. These two mounds are also connected by the principal north-south axis of the Chaco Complex, and they are juxtaposed on this axis in a symmetrical, bifold rotation relationship. Bifold rotation is a common organizational element of Chacoan architecture.

The Casa Rinconada Mound has been trenched by archaeologists, but no records of the excavation(s) have been found. A short section of trench cut into the east side of the mound remains open, however, and our examination revealed that it is sterile of cultural material. A sandstone boulder with angular edges is exposed in the trench, but it is not a bedrock outcrop. The mound appears to be composed wholly of mixed natural materials that were excavated elsewhere and deposited at this location. A large number of spalls with exposed caliche deposits litters the mound surface, indicating that they have been removed from a deeper substrate and overturned (see Nials 1983b:6-39). A further indication that the mound is not bedrock is its stratigraphic location relative to the wall of the nearby South Mesa. Were this a natural feature, it would have a dark, carbonaceous shale core. Exposures in the test trench, however, indicate that the core of the mound is composed of unconsolidated alluvial material.

The virtual absence of cultural material on and in the Casa Rinconada Mound as well as its lack of proximity to a great house are unique among the known mounds in Chaco Canyon. The other great mounds that have been identified in the canyon are clearly associated with great houses, and their surfaces are characteristically littered with potsherds and other cultural detritus. Great mounds, both in and beyond the canyon, are largely composed of fill, construction waste, and cultural debris (Cameron 2002; Fowler and Stein 1992; Kincaid 1983; Marshall et al. 1979; Nials et al. 1987; Stein and Lekson 1992), and archaeologists have traditionally interpreted them as monumental "trash piles" indicating the presence of a large population over a long period of time. But test excavation of the Pueblo Alto Mound (Windes 1987) and repeated excavation of the mounds at Pueblo Bonito (Judd 1964) demonstrated that these masses were produced purposefully and rapidly (Windes 1987, but also see Wills 2001).

The mass of the Rinconada Mound is approximately three times the volume of the Casa Rinconada great kiva. We speculate that the fill from the excavation of the great kiva comprises the core of the mound.

Hillside Ruin

Hillside Ruin is constructed against the cliff face behind and east of the standing envelope of Pueblo Bonito. The building is reduced to a mass of adobe and sandstone rubble with no standing walls, and it exhibits an unusual signature for monumental structures in Chaco Canyon. Judd (1964:146–147) trenched up to and exposed sections of the perimeter wall of Hillside Ruin and partially excavated a kiva in the courtyard. He noted that Hillside Ruin was constructed on adobe foundations which overlay the extensive "foundation complex" east of Pueblo Bonito. Based on this apparent superimposition, the use of masonry similar but arguably inferior to the last style in use at Pueblo Bonito, and the presence of "late" ceramics, Judd determined that Hillside Ruin was a small "pueblo" postdating and unrelated to Pueblo Bonito. His explanation for the scarcity of material culture and the unusual character of the adobe and rubble mix that covered the mound was that Hillside was a short-lived settlement robbed of useable masonry following its abandonment. Judd was apparently disappointed with what was found (or was not found) at Hillside Ruin; he made no attempt to map the building, and he omitted it from his otherwise comprehensive maps.

Although Hillside Ruin is one of the most massive structures in downtown Chaco, the rounded contours of the rubble mound are overshadowed by the standing architecture of Pueblo Bonito. Judd's interpretation of the building (with variations) went unchallenged for many years (e.g., Stein and Fowler 1996; Vivian and Hilpert 2002:123). During a recent effort to reconstruct the architectural history of Pueblo Bonito (Stein et al. 2003), it was necessary to revisit Hillside Ruin and map the structure in as much detail as possible. This was accomplished over a period of several years and many field visits in different light, vegetation, temperature, and moisture conditions. After much deliberation, we concluded that Hillside Ruin is the eastern extension of the platform constructed at the base of Threatening Rock (see Figure 8.1a).

In mass, form, and elevation, the Threatening Rock–Hillside Platform resembles the South Mounds/platforms at Pueblo Bonito; they are raised, level, paved surfaces composed of fill contained by massive, well-finished masonry retaining walls. The Hillside Platform clearly articulates with several formalized avenues and alignments (Plate 8.7) which access the surface of the platform by means of masonry stairways and wide (presumably paved) ramps. Features resembling altars are located at the intersection of the stairway/ramp and the upper level of the platform. The Hillside Platform addresses a broad avenue that passes behind Pueblo Bonito and connects Peñasco Blanco with Kin Nahasbas. Masonry used in the construction of the retaining walls and features at Hillside Ruin is the McElmo style of the early to mid twelfth century (see Lekson 1984:23–24 for discussion of McElmo-style masonry). "McElmo" masonry in Chaco Canyon is characterized by shaped blocks of the friable yellow sandstone of the canyon walls and talus slopes. The visual contrast between the yellow, McElmo-period masonry of the Hillside Platform and the dark brown slabs in the retaining wall of the earlier, western end of the "Threatening Rock" platform must have been striking. We suggest that contrast was an intentional and meaningful aspect of Chaco architectural design (Fowler and Stein 1992).

Although the McElmo style of masonry was assembled with the same care and precision as the earlier styles, an unfortunate characteristic of the style, especially in Chaco Canyon where the source materials are exceptionally soft and friable, is its poor resistance to the elements. We attribute the unusual texture of the Hillside rubble mound to the extreme weathering of the masonry containment of what is otherwise an essentially adobe and rubble-filled structure. Also, the environs of the Hillside Platform have been extensively disturbed by archaeological excavation, the fall of Threatening Rock, staging activities for the clean-up of the Threatening Rock debris field, and the construction, use, and later removal of an NPS water tank and waterline. Although the area east of Pueblo Bonito and south of Hillside Ruin has been extensively and perhaps completely disturbed, three earthen mounds located in this area appear to be in situ features. Our determination that these are intact mounds is based on examination of photographs taken before and during the excavation of the Northeast Foundation Complex. The scale, placement, and signature of these mounds resemble those of the earthworks characteristically associated with extra-canyon community great houses (Cameron 2002; Fowler and Stein 1992; Nials et al. 1987; Stein and Lekson 1992). Likewise, the massing of Hillside Ruin would result in a structure that, when approached from the south, would resemble a community-type great house.

WETHERILL'S DAM

The feature known as Wetherill's Dam (Judd 1954:1) is a substantial earthen berm 9 m wide and 1.60 m high that originates at the southeast corner of the East Mound at Pueblo Bonito and extends due south for approximately 125 m (see Figure 8.2b, Plates 8.2, 8.4, and 8.7). Upon reaching the north cutbank of the Chaco Wash the berm turns eastward and parallels the cutbank for several hundred meters. Levine (1989) suggests that Richard Wetherill constructed the dam in 1902 to satisfy the terms of his homestead application. The northern end of the dam and a ditch originating in the Chetro Ketl Rincon is shown on a map prepared on November 30, 1906, by William Strover of the General Land Office. A photograph taken in 1897, however, shows an existing berm/vegetation anomaly in the location of the north-south section of the "dam," but no evidence of the east-west berm (Figure 8.5). Ground observation of the dam

FIGURE 8.5. 1897 photo showing linear alignment now known as Wetherill's Dam. (Lister and Lister 1981: Figure 20)

revealed clear differences in the composition of the north-south and east-west berms, indicating that Richard Wetherill embellished an existing precolumbian feature to create the north-south arm of the dam and constructed the east-west berm in its entirety. The dam was intended to capture runoff from the Chetro Ketl Rincon.

The cardinal orientation of the north-south arm of Wetherill's Dam and its articulation with Casa Rinconada, the southeast corner of the South Mounds at Pueblo Bonito, the southeast corner of Pueblo Bonito's envelope, and the center of Threatening Rock reinforce our interpretation of the feature as a formalized precolumbian alignment. It is likely that the dam originally resembled the larger berms described at Chetro Ketl Field, and it too may have functioned as an elevated road surface.

SHAPED HILLS, STEPPED MOUNDS, PYRAMIDS

We documented two massive structures (29SJ834 and 835) on the south side of Chaco Canyon and west of South Gap that we interpret to be stepped mounds/truncated pyramids. More specifically, we interpret these structures to be natural hills that have been purposefully shaped and embellished to create elevated, leveled surfaces on pyramid-shaped

mounds. Our documentation process and reconstruction of these structures is illustrated in Plates 8.8 and 8.9 (see also Friedman and Stein 2002). The massing of 29SJ834 in particular invokes the image of a large, but as yet unexcavated, great house. The importance of the place is announced literally (at least it was in 1972 when the senior author first viewed it) by a thick blanket of high-quality ceramic pieces; shell, shale, and turquoise beads; shell ornaments; and well-crafted miniature arrowheads. A remnant of McElmo-style core-and-veneer wall still protrudes prominently from the crest of the mound. 29SJ834 and 835 figure prominently but anonymously in the archaeological thinking about Chaco Canyon; these are Gladwin's (1945) Hosta Butte phase "Knoll Pueblos." Surface evidence suggests repeated episodes of shallow "testing," and we presume that these efforts were abandoned once it was determined that the associated artifacts were concentrated on the surface of an essentially sterile substrate. Repeated attacks despite consistently negative results are not unheard of in Chaco Canyon archaeology; Judd describes repeated trenching of the South Mounds at Pueblo Bonito with the same undesirable results. We also visited these ruins many times over the years, expecting with each visit that we would find and ultimately document unexcavated great houses. But each visit ended in confusion and disappointment; the size, shape, and composition of the rubble was all wrong, and there wasn't enough of it to account for the exaggerated massing of these structures.

Following our reconstruction of Pueblo Bonito and Hillside Ruin (Stein et al. 2003) and a similar ongoing effort to document and reconstruct the extensive precolumbian landscape of Cemetery Ridge at Newcomb, New Mexico (Friedman et al. 2003), we were better prepared to interpret such structures as 29SJ834 and 835. At Pueblo Bonito and Hillside Ruin Judd (1964) had documented the extensive use of adobe for pavement, abutments, and buttressing. But the adobe component of Chaco architecture has historically been overshadowed by a consuming fascination with the masonry remains. Adobe features are common in Chaco Canyon and can be identified in weathered surface remains. In the process of (figuratively) dismantling and reconstructing Pueblo Bonito and

214

Hillside Ruin (Stein et al. 2003) it became apparent that the great houses were, by design, complex in the vertical plane, and that this complexity was largely achieved by the removal and/or emplacement of massive amounts of fill. For example, the surfaces of the courts at Pueblo Bonito were raised as much as 2 m by the purposeful addition of fill material. Further, the masonry envelope identified with great house architecture was used to create "filled" as well as conventional interior spaces. The Threatening Rock–Hillside Platform and the South Mounds at Pueblo Bonito are examples of massive, filled constructions contained by adobe buttressing and conventional core-and-veneer masonry walls.

An alternative strategy for creating a solid/filled architectural mass is to sculpt and treat an existing natural feature. We first became aware of this technique at Cemetery Ridge, where extensive leveling and paving as well as large-scale shaping and armoring of natural surfaces were made obvious by the contrast between the unsorted cobble substrate and the color, texture, and homogeneity of massive amounts of adobe introduced to the mesa top. Other examples of shaping and embellishing of already impressive natural features can be found at Bis sa'ani (Breternitz et al. 1982), Pierre's Ruin (Stein and Levine 1983), Nataanii Bikin, and Big House (Fowler and Stein 1992).

Interpreting such structures as 29SJ834 and 835 is difficult because they were shaped and finished using soft, impermanent materials such as adobe, unconsolidated fill, and friable sandstones. Perishable materials used for log-and-stake steps or pole construction would have rotted away hundreds of years ago. The once crisp and hard-edged lines of these shaped mounds must now be interpolated largely through attention to contour. The character of surface treatment and the mass and form of structural embellishment must be deduced from the distribution and telltale differences in color and texture of the remaining materials. At 29SJ834 and 835 there is no mistaking the fact that the natural shape of the underlying hills was modified into uniformly sloped, flat surfaces intersecting at straight, hard edges. The masonry rubble covering the slopes varies from chunks to slabs to largish blocks.

29SJ834 is a massive, steep-sided structure, so we should not be surprised that the surface detail has either been washed away or obscured by once-higher material moving downslope. The signatures of ramps/stairways are at once obvious and subtle. The "ramps" must have been stepped, using either solid stone blocks or log or stone risers backed by fill, and possibly surfaced with adobe or slabs. The surface treatment of the slopes is also guesswork. Our guesses include horizontally stepped block, slab shingles, slab mosaic set in adobe, and a rough-textured stucco of rubble and adobe.

At the base of 29SJ834 we identified a large, circular, great kiva–like structure reminiscent of the "dance plazas" documented at many community great houses of the post Chaco period. From the surface signature, we concluded that the structure was excavated to a depth of approximately 2.5 m below grade and may have supported an above-grade superstructure of poles and brush.

Southwestern archaeology conventionally portrays ruined structures in plan view. The rectangular cells in plan view appear to be rooms, and rooms are assumed to be residential. The plans of 29SJ834 and 835 incorporate rectangular cells of core-and-veneer, McElmo-style masonry, and not surprisingly, these cells have historically been interpreted as conventional habitation rooms. Upon close examination, however, the walls appear to have been relatively low, and the resulting shallow cells were filled to create a stable, elevated surface/platform at the crest of the modified hill. Filling a masonry envelope is a common means of creating a level, elevated surface. A similar situation has been demonstrated in Classic period platform mounds in the Hohokam area, where structural cells were once interpreted as pueblo rooms but are now understood as a technological development in earthen, solid-core architecture (Lekson, personal communication 2003). Filling a lattice of cells constructed expressly for pyramid construction is also documented in Central and South America (Clancy 1994:91).

We found no evidence to suggest that "kivas" were incorporated into the architecture of 29SJ834 and 835, but we did identify massing at the highest elevations of the mounds that we interpret as altars. The architectural caps on these mounds may have served as foundations for temporary structures. Such is the case on temple mounds throughout the New World.

215

29SJ834 and 835 each address two or more features in the larger landscape (Plate 8.3). In both cases the ramp down the north slope addresses Kin Kletso. 29SJ834 is the western terminus of the alignment of the front wall of the east court at Pueblo Bonito, and 29SJ835 is the western terminus of the alignment of the front wall of the west court at Pueblo Bonito (an equinox alignment). The configuration of one route dividing into two, or two routes converging into one as they ascend to a platform or shrine, is a common characteristic of Chaco roads.

We expended a considerable amount of time and effort collecting detailed spatial information at 29SJ834 and 835, but we acknowledge that they are difficult sites to read and that some details of the architecture are open to question. The reconstruction process makes no allowances for ambiguity; the stairways, for example, are either there or they are not. We anticipate quibbles over details, but we are confident that these two structures are natural hills purposefully sculpted to be truncated pyramids.

Stepped mounds and truncated pyramids are common architectural forms in the precolumbian New World, including North America (Morgan 1980:xxix). Further, the architectural tradition of mounds, avenues, and massive earthwork enclosures oriented with respect to celestial bodies and constructed utilizing proportional geometric principles was already ancient in 800 when construction began at Pueblo Bonito.

Conclusions

Assembling our reconstruction of the Chaco core (Plates 8.10–8.12) required intensive survey (in both an archaeological and a cadastral sense) of the floor of Chaco Canyon from Lizard House Arroyo to Casa Chiquita; acquisition of archival and current aerial photography as well as resistivity and magnetic subsurface imagery for selected targets; review of publications, original notes, photographs, and maps; transfer of the relevant spatial information into the digital medium; and rectifying this information to real-world coordinates. The rectified images and maps, as layers of compatible spatial data, were stored and manipulated within a Geographic Information System.

A very real and difficult aspect of representing the landscape as it might have appeared in 1130 was the identification, documentation, and subsequent removal (in the digital sense) of the numerous features and modifications to the landscape that date from the late nineteenth century to the present. We found that a century of small-scale settlement, large-scale archaeology, and National Park Service development has obliterated or significantly altered much of the original cultural landscape, but we were also surprised and pleased to discover that sections of precolumbian alignments are preserved and still traceable in the undisturbed portions of the canyon floor.

Equally important, collecting the information in the way that we did—with newly available technologies and other lines of evidence such as traditional histories—enabled us to identify previously unrecognized classes of features, the recognition of which is critical to understanding what was going on at Chaco. Because we are a tribal program, our data collection and interpretive methodologies are in keeping with the policy of the Navajo Nation Historic Preservation Department. Intrusive data collection (testing, excavation, artifact collection) is not an option except in salvage situations. We "mined" the archives rather than the canyon itself.

The images of our reconstruction, as presented herein, are digitally rendered coordinate data. In our visualization of the precolumbian built environment in downtown Chaco we emphasize the accurate portrayal of the plan, the massing of structural forms, and the spatial relationships that integrate them. In short, we documented downtown Chaco as it would have been envisioned and experienced by the architects, builders, and users—that is, as a single architectural composition.

Based on Navajo ceremonial narratives, long hours of on-the-ground documentation, the results of an acoustics study, and the fact that the amphitheater occupies the geometric center of the Chaco complex, we are confident that the apparently empty space bounded by Pueblo Bonito and Chetro Ketl is an outdoor performance area (Plate 8.10).

We found the linescape that underlies and structures the Chaco complex to be much more intensive, much larger, much more sophisticated, and much older than previously thought. The "roads," by virtue of the investment in their construction,

216

are the most visible manifestations of the linescape, but they are segments of much longer, but less formalized, alignments. We believe that the origin of the linescape is at least as early as the fifth century, when the construction of the Shabik'eshchee and Peñasco Blanco great kivas marked the meets and bounds of the future Chaco complex. We view the architecture of the Chaco complex as in-fill and progressive elaboration of the linescape.

The Gambler is credited as the architect of the Chaco complex in the oral histories and ceremonial narratives of most (and perhaps all) of the Four Corners tribes (Gabriel 1996). There are a number of versions of the Gambler narrative; the content of the story is largely metaphorical, and we have no doubt that important events and individuals are conflated. Having said that, we believe that The Gambler was a real individual or, more probably, individuals.

The linescape, as formalized by The Gambler, is a four-dimensional construct in that it is structured by astronomical cycles and therefore incorporates time in its design. In its entirety it is a shamantic construct and therefore does not fit neatly within our preconceived notions of function.

Our survey data (Plates 8.2 and 8.3) have some important implications. The sites that we re-recorded have neither agricultural nor domestic residential functions. Like other structures in the core, they commonly employ massive adobe or masonry walls. The newly identified features also have no domestic functions. All the architectural features that we recorded are extensions of the rigid plan established and delineated by the linescape. Major structures of the core formerly described as pueblos, such as Hillside and 29SJ834 and 835, are elevated platforms of earthen fill. A significant amount of the architecture of the core shows evidence of extensive leveling, paving, removal, and placement of massive amounts of fill. This purposeful use of the earthen medium explains the "empty rooms" and the scarcity of artifacts. It also reinforces our contention that excavation is neither the only nor the most effective way of obtaining information about Chaco.

NOTES

1. All dates in this chapter are AD. The reconstruction presented here is based on information gathered from the 1990s to the present by staff, research partners, and consultants of the Navajo Nation Historic Preservation Department's Chaco Protection Sites Program (CPSP). Approximately half of the Protection Sites identified in the "Chaco Outlier" legislation are located on Navajo Nation lands. In 1992, Congress authorized funding specifically for the management of the Navajo Chaco Protection Sites, and the Navajo Nation selected the National Park Service to administer those funds by means of a cooperative agreement.

The CPSP is responsible for the identification, documentation, protection, and management of precolumbian remains of the Chaco period within approximately 17.5 million acres surrounding Chaco Culture National Historical Park. Accordingly, the Program has emphasized the application of GIS, GPS, and remote sensing technologies to capture, study, and document the tangible remains of some very large and extensively developed precolumbian landscapes. Identification and documentation of the tangible remains is only a first step in the interpretation of the landscape and ultimately understanding its meaning and significance to our constituents, the Navajo people.

2. We are grateful to Dr. Klara Kelley, a long-time colleague and an expert on Navajo ceremonial history and landscape, for contributing substantially to this discussion concerning use of oral history. For recent discussions of various intellectual traditions (e.g., oral history, history, and science) and interpretation of the archaeological record, see Anyon et al. 1997; Watkins 2000; Whiteley 2002.

The portions of this chapter concerning The Gambler and other specific Navajo traditions are based on information collected by Taft Blackhorse, a native Navajo speaker with access to esoteric information.

3. Many advances have been made in remote sensing, survey methodology, and spatial data base technology since the work of the Remote Sensing Center in the mid 1970s. These include affordable computer systems, Geographic Information System (GIS) software, Global Positioning Systems (GPS), Laser Detection and Ranging (LIDAR), and Multispectral Imaging Systems.

Perhaps the most significant aspect of these new technologies is the ability to collect, store, and analyze data in a digital environment. The collection of new stereo aerial imagery, GPS positional data, and the integration of archival image and point data into the digital environment has facilitated the production of a comprehensive set of data layers rectified to real-world coordinates.

These data can be experienced as an analog landscape. Using GPS technology, features identified from images can be located on the ground. This alone would be a tremendous advantage to large-scale landscape studies in which subtle features such as precolumbian "roads" can be identified on an image but are all but invisible from the ground perspective. The layering of rectified images becomes even more interesting and useful when they are merged. Layering conventional stereo aerial images taken years apart, or layering multispectral or geophysical data onto conventional aerial photography, results in a hybrid landscape in which spatial relationships are held constant. For example, merging of images taken in different seasons or under different light conditions will enhance the subtle trace of an alignment that was not visible on either of the two images individually. Using terrain models generated from LIDAR or conventional imagery through photogrammetric techniques, landscapes can also be illuminated from a point source that could not occur naturally.

For the documentation of "roads" and other large-scale but subtle landscape features we relied primarily on aerial imagery, such as the 1934 1:48000 Fairchild aerials, 1:3000 and 1:6000 images captured in 1973 by Koogle and Poole Engineering, 1991 multispectral and conventional 1:3000 imagery captured by NASA in 1996, LIDAR and conventional imagery at a scale of 1:3000 captured by EnerQuest in 2000, and 1:12000 conventional black-and-white stereo aerial imagery captured by Thomas R. Mann and Associates in 2001. Information from the aerial imagery was supplemented by subsurface imagery acquired by means of a resistance and magnetometer survey at the Northeast Foundation Complex, the Amphitheater, and the Chetro Ketl field.

Our reconstruction is an entirely digital representation of real-world coordinates within a rigid geospatial grid (Friedman 2000). Initial massing of architectural forms was generated in a GIS environment and was then exported to a commercial 3D modeling software designed for this application. This allowed us to make modifications to the models and model features that would not have been possible with the GIS software. Ultimately, the digital elevation models (DEMs), three-dimensional models, and auxiliary GIS data for features such as the roads were imported into a Photorealistic Terrain Modeling, Visualization, Rendering, and Animation Software which enables the retention of real-world coordinates and spatial relationships.

Canyon-Wide Terrain Model

A terrain model of Chaco Canyon was generated from 1:12000 black-and-white stereo pairs flown in 2001 by Thomas R. Mann and Associates. The model area is 14.3 km long by 2.4 km wide and encompasses approximately 13.3 square miles. The model is centered on Chaco Canyon and encompasses an area extending from the cliffs west of the confluence of the Chaco and Escavada washes to approximately one-quarter mile east of Gallo Canyon. Terrain data were derived from autocorrelation of stereo pairs extracting a digital terrain (mass points) model. Georeferencing for the stereo aerial photography was accomplished with centimeter-accuracy GPS. From the terrain model a 1 m DEM was generated that had a vertical accuracy of approximately 2 m. This DEM was in turn used in combination with the stereo aerial photography to generate orthophotos of the canyon at 0.5 m resolution. These custom data products are a significant improvement in detail over available USGS data with a resolution of 10 m. The 3D visualizations in this chapter could not have been created using standard USGS products.

Study Area Terrain Model

The project is focused on an area 3.3 km east to west by 1.14 km north to south, encompassing approximately 1.6 square miles of the floor of Chaco Canyon from the cliff face east of Lizard House Arroyo, west to Casa Chiquita, and a few hundred meters south into South Gap. This is the area often called "downtown Chaco."

Within the project area, the canyon-wide terrain model was modified to reflect increased localized accuracy in the areas of Pueblo Bonito, the Casa Rinconada Mound, and 29SJ834 and 29SJ835 on the south side of Chaco Canyon, west of the mouth of South Gap. In the area of Pueblo Bonito, localized accuracy was refined to about 0.3 m using GPS with centimeter-level accuracy to collect information from the present surface and a 1 ft contour map of the area (Quackenbush 1934). The 1934 map was also useful because it was annotated and it identified the boundaries of features of historical or archaeological interest that are no longer extant, such as Threatening Rock. Localized accuracies at the other locations were more restricted and relied on acquisition of point and breakline data collected by means of GPS with centimeter-level accuracy.

Major modifications of the terrain model for the study area included the removal of historical features such as bridges, culverts, roads, facilities, and parking lots. Areas of known recent erosion were restored to near-original elevations. Note that in our reconstruction, the Chaco Wash is incised. Our reasoning on this issue is that if the wash wasn't incised during precolumbian times, the water table would have been significantly higher. A higher water table would have flooded pit-structures such as those exposed in the arroyo wall (described in Judd 1924) and any below-grade structures in the courts of Pueblo Bonito or Pueblo del Arroyo.

Mapping was done with a two- or three-man crew using pin flags to mark features, corners, or wall segments that were then located with the GPS receiver. To obtain centimeter-level accuracy, a base station was set up at benchmark H068 south of Pueblo Bonito. H068 is a geodetic reference point for the State of New Mexico High Accuracy Reference Network (HARN).

4. We examined documents at the National Anthropological Archives and the National Museum of the American Indian (Smithsonian Institution, Suitland, Maryland) as well as at Chaco Canyon and Aztec Ruins National Monument.

5. An area of the canyon floor below Casa Rinconada has been compared to the Chetro Ketl Field (Loose and Lyons 1976; Vivian 2000) based on similarities in the color and texture of the surface and a hint of a grid pattern. In our investigation of the area between the great kiva and the existing park service road (see Plate 8.3) we found one L-shaped adobe berm equivalent in mass to the interior divisions in the Chetro Ketl field. The clay content is greater within the area defined as a possible "field" than in the surrounding area, but the "Rinconada Field" is not as saturated with clay as the Chetro Ketl field. The feature illustrated by Vivian (2000:6) as well as several scattered rock concentrations are located within the "Rinconada Field" area. We mapped these locations and found that the feature illustrated by Vivian is a culvert on the avenue connecting Pueblo Bonito with Casa Rinconada (Plate 8.3).

References Cited

Alexander, Christopher, Sara Ishikawa, and Murray Silverstein
1977   *A Pattern Language.* Oxford University Press, New York.

Anyon, Roger, T. J. Ferguson, Loretta Jackson, Lillie Lane, and Phillip Vicente
1997   Native American Oral Traditions and Archaeology: Issues of Structure, Relevance, and Respect. In *Native Americans and Archaeologists: Stepping Stones to Common Ground*, edited by Nina Swidler, Kurt E. Dongoske, Roger Anyon, and Alan S. Downer, pp. 77–87. AltaMira Press, Walnut Creek, CA.

Basso, Keith
1996   *Wisdom Sits in Places.* University of New Mexico Press, Albuquerque.

Begay, Richard M.
2004   Tsé Bíyah 'Anii'áhí: Chaco Canyon and Its Place in Navajo History. In *In Search of Chaco: New Approaches to an Archaeological Enigma*, edited by David Grant Noble, pp. 54–60. School of American Research Press, Santa Fe.

Benson, L., L. Cordell, K. Vincent, H. Taylor, G. L. Farmer, and K. Futa
2003   Ancient Maize from Chacoan Great Houses: Where Was It Grown? *Proceedings of the National Academy of Sciences (USA)* 100:13111–13115.
2006   The Agricultural Productivity of Chaco Canyon and the Source(s) of Pre-Hispanic Maize Found in Pueblo Bonito. In *Histories of Maize*, edited by John Stoller, Robert Tykot, and Bruce Benz, pp. 289–314. Academic Press, San Diego.

Blackhorse, Taft, John R. Stein, June-el Piper, and Jay S. Williams
2002   Navajo Oral History of a Precolumbian Amphitheater in Chaco Canyon, New Mexico. Paper prepared for the session on Ancient Acoustics at the First Pan American/Iberian Meeting on Acoustics, December 4, Cancun, Mexico. Published online in the *Journal of the Acoustical Society of America* 112(5):2285. <http://asa.aip.org/jasa.html>

Blackhorse, Taft, Jay S. Williams, and June-el Piper
2003   *Iikááh* and Monuments of Regional and Celestial Landscapes. Paper presented at the session of "Monuments, Landscapes, and Cultural Memory" at the Fifth World Archaeological Congress, June, Washington, DC. Submitted for publication.

Breternitz, Cory Dale, David E. Doyel, and Michael P. Marshall, eds.
1982   *Bis sa'ani: A Late Bonito Phase Community on Escavada Wash, Northwest New Mexico.* Papers in Anthropology 14. Navajo Nation Archaeology Department, Window Rock, AZ.

Broadbent, Geoffrey
1973   *Design in Architecture: Architecture and the Human Sciences.* John Wiley and Sons, New York.
1980   Building Design as an Iconic Sign System. In *Signs, Symbols and Architecture*, edited by G. Broadbent, Richard Bunt, and Charles Jencks, pp. 311–332. John Wiley and Sons, New York.

Cameron, Catherine M.
2002   Sacred Earthen Architecture in the Northern Southwest: The Bluff Great House Berm. *American Antiquity* 67:677–695.

Clancy, Flora

1994   *Pyramids*. Smithsonian Institution Press, Washington, D.C., and St. Remy's, Montreal.

Doxtater, Dennis

1984   Spatial Opposition in Nondiscursive Expression: Architecture as Ritual Process. *Canadian Journal of Anthropology* 4(1):1–17.

Fishler, Stanley A.

1953   *In the Beginning: A Navaho Creation.* University of Utah Anthropological Paper 13. University of Utah Press, Salt Lake City.

Fowler, Andrew P., and John R. Stein

1992   The Anasazi Great House in Space, Time, and Paradigm. In *Anasazi Regional Organization and the Chaco System*, edited by David E. Doyel, pp. 101–122. Anthropological Papers 5. Maxwell Museum of Anthropology, University of New Mexico, Albuquerque.

Friedman, Richard A.

2000   Geospatial Technologies Create New Windows to the Past at Chaco Culture National Historical Park. Paper presented at ESRI International Users Conference, San Diego. <http://gis.esri.com/library/userconf/procoo/professional/abstracts/a561.htm>

Friedman, Richard A., and John R. Stein

2002   Native American Ruins in 3D. *Geospatial Solutions* (May):28–29.

Friedman, Richard A., John R. Stein, and Taft Blackhorse Jr.

2003   A Study of a Pre-Columbian Irrigation System at Newcomb, New Mexico. ESRI Journal of GIS in Archaeology I. <http://www.esri.com/library/journals/archaeology>

Fritz, John M.

1978   Palaeopsychology Today: Ideational Systems and Human Adaptation in Prehistory. In *Social Archaeology: Beyond Subsistence and Dating*, edited by C. Redman, pp. 39–59. Academic Press, New York.

Gabriel, Kathryn

1991   *Roads to Center Place: A Cultural Atlas of Chaco Canyon and the Anasazi.* Johnson Books, Boulder.

1996   *Gambler Way: Indian Gaming in Mythology, History, and Archaeology in North America.* Johnson Books, Boulder.

Gladwin, Harold Sterling

1945   *The Chaco Branch: Excavations at White Mound and in the Red Mesa Valley.* Medallion Papers 33. Gila Pueblo, Globe, AZ.

Goddard, Pliny Earle

1933   *Navajo Texts.* Anthropological Papers of the American Museum of Natural History 34(1). New York.

Haile, Berard

1981   *The Upward Moving and Emergence Way: The Gishin Biye' Version.* University of Nebraska Press, Lincoln.

Hayes, Alden C.

1981   A Survey of Chaco Canyon Archaeology. In *Archaeological Surveys of Chaco Canyon, New Mexico*, edited by A. C. Hayes, D. M. Brugge, and W. J. Judge, pp. 1–68. Chaco Canyon Studies, Publications in Archaeology 18A. National Park Service, Albuquerque.

Hillier, Bill, and Julie E. Hanson

1984   *The Social Logic of Space.* Cambridge University Press, Cambridge.

Hillier, B., A. Leaman, P. Stansall, and M. Bedford

1978   Space Syntax. In *Social Organization and Settlement: Contributions from Anthropology, Archaeology, and Geography*, edited by D. Green, C. Hasselgrove, and M. Spriggs, pp. 343–381. BAR International Series (suppl) 47(2). Oxford.

Judd, Neil M.

1938   Navajo Name for Chaco Rock. *Southwestern Monuments Monthly Reports* (September). Coolidge, AZ.

1954   *The Material Culture of Pueblo Bonito.* Smithsonian Miscellaneous Collections 124(1). Washington, DC.

1959a *Pueblo del Arroyo, Chaco Canyon, New Mexico.* Smithsonian Miscellaneous Collections 138(1). Washington, DC.

1959b The Braced-up Cliff at Pueblo Bonito. In *Smithsonian Institution Annual Report for 1958*, pp. 501–511. Washington, DC.

1964   *The Architecture of Pueblo Bonito.* Smithsonian Miscellaneous Collections 147(1). Washington, DC.

Julian, Hurst R.

1933   A Short History of the Events That Led to the Discovery of the Cliff Cavities. In Papers of Neil M. Judd, Box 1, Interior Department, Chaco Canyon National Monument, Correspondence relating to Braced-up-Cliff, on file, Smithsonian Institution, National Anthropological Archives, Smithsonian Museum Support Center, Suitland, Maryland.

Keur, Dorothy L.

1933   Weekly Reports July 8–August 5, 1933. On file, Chaco Culture National Historical Park.

Kievit, Karen A.

1998   *Seeing and Reading Chaco Architecture at AD 1100.* Ph.D. dissertation, Department of Anthropology, University of Colorado, Boulder.

Kincaid, Chris, ed.

1983   *Chaco Roads Project Phase I: A Reappraisal of Prehistoric Roads in the San Juan Basin.* Bureau of Land Management, Santa Fe and Albuquerque.

Kintigh, Keith, W. Todd L. Howell, and Andrew I. Duff

1996   Post Chacoan Social Integration at the Hinkson Site, New Mexico. *Kiva* 61:257–274.

Leach, Edmund R.

1983   The Gatekeepers of Heaven: Anthropological Aspects of Grandiose Architecture. *Journal of Anthropological Research* 39:243–263.

Lekson, Stephen H.

1984   *Great Pueblo Architecture of Chaco Canyon, New Mexico.* Chaco Canyon Studies, Publications in Archaeology 18B. National Park Service, Albuquerque.

1985   The Architecture of Talus Unit, Chaco Canyon, New Mexico. In *Prehistory and History of the Southwest: Collected Papers in Honor of Alden C. Hayes*, edited by Nancy Fox, pp. 43–59. Papers of the Archaeological Society of New Mexico 11. Albuquerque.

1999   *Chaco Meridian: Centers of Political Power in the Ancient Southwest.* Altamira Press, Walnut Creek, CA.

Levine, Frances

1989   Homestead in Ruins: Richard Wetherill's Homestead in Chaco Canyon. In *From Chaco to Chaco: Papers in Honor of Robert H. Lister and Florence C. Lister*, edited by Meliha S. Duran and David T. Kirkpatrick, pp. 45–58. Archaeological Society of New Mexico Papers 15.

Lister, Robert H., and Florence C. Lister

1981   *Chaco Canyon: Archaeology and Archaeologists.* University of New Mexico Press, Albuquerque.

Loose, Richard W.

2001   A Report on Tse Biinaholtsa'a Yałti (Curved Rock That Speaks): An Open-Air Public Performance Theater at Chaco Canyon, New Mexico. Ms. on file, Chaco Culture National Historical Park.

2002   Computer Analysis of Sound Recordings from Two Anasazi Sites in Northwestern New Mexico. Paper prepared for the session on Ancient Acoustics at the First Pan American/Iberian Meeting on Acoustics, December 4, Cancun, Mexico. Published online in the *Journal of the Acoustical Society of America* 112(5):2285. <http://asa.aip.org/jasa.html>

Loose, Richard W., and Thomas R. Lyons

1976   The Chetro Ketl Field: A Planned Water Control System in Chaco Canyon. In *Remote Sensing Experiments in Cultural Resource Studies: Non-Destructive Methods of Archaeological Exploration, Survey and Analysis*, assembled by T. R. Lyons, pp. 133–156. Report of the Chaco Center No. 1. National Park Service, University of New Mexico, Albuquerque.

Love, David W.

1980   *Quaternary Geology of Chaco Canyon, Northwestern New Mexico.* Ph.D. dissertation, University of New Mexico, Albuquerque

Marshall, Anne L.

2003   The Siting of Pueblo Bonito. In *Pueblo Bonito: Center of the Chacoan World*, edited by Jill E. Neitzel, pp. 10–13. Smithsonian Institution Press, Washington, DC.

Marshall, Michael P.

1997   The Chacoan Roads: A Cosmological Interpretation. In *Anasazi Architecture and American Design*, edited by Baker H. Morrow and V. B. Price, pp. 62–74. University of New Mexico Press, Albuquerque.

Marshall, Michael P., John R. Stein, Richard W. Loose, and Judith E. Novotny

1979   *Anasazi Communities of the San Juan Basin.* Public Service Company of New Mexico, Albuquerque, and New Mexico Historic Preservation Division, Santa Fe.

Matthews, Washington

1994   *Navajo Legends.* University of Utah Press, Salt Lake City. (Originally published in 1897)

McGuire, Randall H., and Michael B. Schiffer

1983   A Theory of Architectural Design. *Journal of Anthropological Archaeology* 2:277–303.

McKenna, Peter J., and Marcia L. Truell

1986   *Small Site Architecture of Chaco Canyon, New Mexico.* Chaco Canyon Studies, Publications in Archaeology 18D. National Park Service, Santa Fe.

Mindeleff, V.

1891   A Study of Pueblo Architecture: Tusayan and Cibola. *Eighth Annual Report of the Bureau of American Ethnology*, pp. 3–228. Washington, DC.

Morgan, William N.

1980   *Prehistoric Architecture in the Eastern United States.* MIT Press, Cambridge.

Nials, Fred L.

1983a   Factors Affecting the Visibility of Roads. In *Chaco Roads Project Phase I: A Reappraisal of Prehistoric Roads in the San Juan Basin*, edited by Chris Kincaid, pp. 5-1 to 5-25. Bureau of Land Management, Santa Fe and Albuquerque.

1983b   Physical Characteristics of Chacoan Roads. In *Chaco Roads Project Phase I: A Reappraisal of Prehistoric Roads in the San Juan Basin*, edited by Chris Kincaid, pp. 6-1 to 6-50. Bureau of Land Management, Santa Fe and Albuquerque.

Nials, Fred, John Stein, and John Roney

1987   *Chacoan Roads in the Southern Periphery: Results of Phase II of the BLM Chaco Roads Project.* BLM Cultural Resource Series No. 1. Bureau of Land Management, Santa Fe and Albuquerque.

Nichols, Ron

1975   Archaeomagnetic Dating of Sediments in Chaco Canyon National Monument. Unpublished M.A. thesis, University of Oklahoma, Norman.

Obenauf, Margaret S.

1980   A History of Research on the Chacoan Roadway System. In *Cultural Resources and Remote Sensing*, edited by Thomas R. Lyons and Frances

Joan Mathien, pp. 123–167. National Park Service, Washington, DC.

O'Bryan, Aileen

1956 *The Diné: Origin Myths of the Navaho Indians.* Bureau of American Ethnology Bulletin 163. Government Printing Office, Washington, DC.

Pepper, George H.

1920 *Pueblo Bonito.* Anthropological Papers 27. American Museum of Natural History, New York.

Pinkley, F.

1938 The Saga of Threatening Rock. *Southwestern Monuments Monthly Reports* (April). Coolidge, AZ.

Proskouriakoff, Tatiana

1946 *An Album of Maya Architecture.* Carnegie Institution of Washington, Washington, DC.

Quackenbush, A. D.

1934 NM/CHAC-4940 (Map). National Park Service, Chaco Canyon National Monument. On file, Chaco Culture National Historical Park.

Rappaport, Amos

1982 *The Meaning of the Built Environment: A Nonverbal Communication Approach.* Sage Publications, Beverly Hills.

1988 Levels of Meaning in the Built Environment. In *Cross-Cultural Perspectives in Nonverbal Communication*, edited by Fernando Poyatos, pp. 317–336. Hogrefe and Huber, Toronto.

Reichard, Gladys

1944 *The Story of the Navajo Hail Chant.* J. J. Augustin, New York. On file, Museum of Northern Arizona Research Library, Flagstaff.

Roney, John R.

1992 Prehistoric Roads and Regional Integration in the Chacoan System. In *Anasazi Regional Organization and the Chaco System*, edited by David E. Doyel, pp. 123–131. Maxwell Museum Papers in Anthropology No. 5. University of New Mexico, Albuquerque.

Ruppé, Patricia, Richard Friedman, and John R. Stein

2001 Eighth-Century "Chaco Roads" on the Eastern Chuska Slope. Paper presented at the 66th Annual Meeting of the Society for American Archaeology, April 18–22, New Orleans.

Simpson, Lt. James H.

1960 *Navaho Expedition. Journal of a Military Reconnaissance from Santa Fe, New Mexico to the Navaho Country Made in 1849.* Edited and annotated by Frank McNitt. University of Oklahoma Press, Norman.

Sofaer, Anna, and Rolf M. Sinclair

1987 Astronomical Marking at Three Sites on Fajada Butte. In *Astronomy and Ceremony in the Prehistoric Southwest*, edited by J. Carlson and W. J. Judge, pp. 43–70. Papers of the Maxwell Museum of Anthropology, No. 2. University of New Mexico, Albuquerque.

Sofaer, Anna, Rolf M. Sinclair, and Leroy E. Doggett

1982 Lunar Markings on Fajada Butte, Chaco Canyon, New Mexico. In *World Archaeoastronomy: Selected Papers from the 2nd Oxford International Conference on Archaeoastronomy, Held at Merida, Yucatan, Mexico, 13–17 January 1986*, edited by Anthony F. Aveni, pp. 169–181. Cambridge University Press, Cambridge.

Stein, John R.

1983 Road Corridor Descriptions. In *Chaco Roads Project Phase I: A Reappraisal of Prehistoric Roads in the San Juan Basin*, edited by Chris Kincaid, pp. 8-1 to 8-15. Bureau of Land Management, Santa Fe and Albuquerque.

1987 Architecture and Landscape. In *An Archaeological Reconnaissance of West-Central New Mexico: The Anasazi Monuments Project*, by Andrew P. Fowler, John R. Stein, and Roger Anyon, pp. 71–103. On file, New Mexico Historic Preservation Division, Santa Fe.

Stein, John R., and Andrew P. Fowler

1996 Looking beyond Chaco in the San Juan Basin and Its Peripheries. In *The Prehistoric Pueblo World, AD 1150–1350*, edited by Michael A. Adler, pp. 114–130. University of Arizona Press, Tucson.

Stein, John R., and Stephen H. Lekson

1992 Anasazi Ritual Landscapes. In *Anasazi Regional Organization and the Chaco System*, edited by David E. Doyel, pp. 87–100. Anthropological Papers No. 5. Maxwell Museum of Anthropology, University of New Mexico, Albuquerque.

Stein, John R., and Daisy F. Levine

1983 Appendix C: Documentation of Selected Sites Recorded during the Chaco Roads Project. In *Chaco Roads Project Phase I: A Reappraisal of Prehistoric Roads in the San Juan Basin*, edited by Chris Kincaid, pp. C-1 to C-64. Bureau of Land Management, Santa Fe and Albuquerque.

Stein, John R., and Peter J. McKenna

1988 An Archaeological Reconnaissance at Aztec Ruins National Monument. Ms. on file, Aztec Ruins National Monument.

Stein, John R., and John R. Roney

1987 An Inventory of Sites Significant to the Study of Chacoan Roads in the Southern San Juan Basin. In *Chacoan Roads in the Southern Periphery: Results of Phase II of the BLM Chaco Roads Project*, by Fred Nials, John Stein, and John Roney, pp. 142–210. Bureau of Land Management, Albuquerque.

Stein, John R., Dabney Ford, and Richard Friedman

2003 Reconstructing Pueblo Bonito. In *Pueblo Bonito: Center of the Chacoan World*, edited by Jill E. Neitzel, pp. 33–60. Smithsonian Institution Press, Washington DC.

222

Stein, John R., Judith E. Suiter, and Dabney Ford
1997   High Noon in Old Bonito: Sun, Shadow and the Geometry of the Chaco Complex. In *Anasazi Architecture and American Design*, edited by Baker H. Morrow and V. B. Price, pp. 133–148. University of New Mexico Press, Albuquerque.

Thompson, Ian, Mark Varien, and Susan Kenzle, with Rina Swentzell
1997   Prehistoric Architecture with Unknown Function. In *Anasazi Architecture and American Design*, edited by Baker H. Morrow and V. B. Price, pp. 149–158. University of New Mexico Press, Albuquerque.

Van Valkenburgh, Richard F.
1941   Dine Bikeyah. Ms. prepared for the U.S. Indian Service, Navajo Agency, Window Rock, AZ.

Vivian, Gordon, and Tom W. Mathews
1965   *Kin Kletso: A Pueblo III Community in Chaco Canyon, New Mexico.* Southwest Parks and Monuments Association, Globe, AZ.

Vivian, R. Gwinn
1983a Identifying and Interpreting Chacoan Roads: An Historical Perspective. In *Chaco Roads Project Phase I: A Reappraisal of Prehistoric Roads in the San Juan Basin*, edited by Chris Kincaid, pp. 3-1 to 3-18. Bureau of Land Management, Santa Fe and Albuquerque.
1983b Discovery and Description: Chaco Field Studies from 1963 to 1980. In *Chaco Roads Project Phase I: A Reappraisal of Prehistoric Roads in the San Juan Basin*, edited by Chris Kincaid, pp. A-1 to A-33. Bureau of Land Management, Santa Fe and Albuquerque.
1990   *The Chacoan Prehistory of the San Juan Basin.* Academic Press, San Diego.
1997   Chacoan Roads: Morphology. *Kiva* 63:7–34.
2000   Economy and Ecology. In *Ancient Chaco's New History*, assembled by Stephen H. Lekson, pp. 5–7. Archaeology Southwest 14(1). Center for Desert Archaeology, Tucson.

Vivian, R. Gwinn, and Bruce Hilpert
2002   *The Chaco Handbook: An Encyclopedic Guide.* University of Utah Press, Salt Lake City.

Washburn, Dorothy K., and D. W. Crowe
1988   *Symmetries of Culture: Theory and Practice of Plane Pattern Analysis.* University of Washington Press, Seattle.

Watkins, Joe
2000   *Indigenous Archaeology: American Indian Values and Scientific Practice.* AltaMira Press, Walnut Creek, CA.

Western Wood Products Association
1995   Pine Species Facts <http://www.wwpa.org/ ppine. htm>.

Wheelwright, Mary C.
1946   *Hail Chant and Water Chant.* Navajo Religion Series 2. Museum of Navajo Ceremonial Art, Santa Fe.

White, Edward T.
1975   *Concept Sourcebook: A Vocabulary of Architectural Forms.* Architectural Media, Tucson.

Whiteley, Peter M.
2002   Archaeology and Oral Tradition: The Scientific Importance of Dialogue. *American Antiquity* 67:405–413.

Williams, J. S., T. J. Blackhorse, J. R. Stein, and R. Friedman
2006   Iikááh: Chaco Sacred Schematics. In *Religion in the Prehispanic Southwest*, edited by Christine S. VanPool, Todd L. VanPool, and David A. Phillips Jr., pp. 103–114. Altamira Press, Walnut Creek, CA.

Wills, W. H.
2001   Mound Formation and Ritual during the Bonito Phase in Chaco Canyon. *American Antiquity* 66:433–452.

Windes, T. C.
1987   *Investigations at the Pueblo Alto Complex, Chaco Canyon, New Mexico, 1975–1979.* Chaco Canyon Studies, Publications in Archaeology 18F. National Park Service, Santa Fe.

Wyman, Leland C.
1957   *Beautyway, a Navaho Ceremonial.* Bollingen Series, Princeton University Press, Princeton.

9

The Primary Architecture
of the Chacoan Culture

A Cosmological Expression

Anna Sofaer

STUDIES BY THE SOLSTICE PROJECT indicate that the major buildings of the ancient Chacoan culture of New Mexico contain solar and lunar cosmology in three separate articulations: their orientations, internal geometry, and geographic interrelationships were developed in relationship to the cycles of the sun and moon.

From approximately 900 to 1130, the Chacoan society, a prehistoric Pueblo culture, constructed numerous multistoried buildings and extensive roads throughout the eighty thousand square kilometers of the arid San Juan Basin of northwestern New Mexico (Cordell 1984; Lekson et al. 1988; Marshall et al. 1979; Vivian 1990) (Figure 9.1). Evidence suggests that expressions of the Chacoan culture extended over a region two to four times the size of the San Juan Basin (Fowler and Stein 1992; Lekson et al. 1988). Chaco Canyon, where most of the largest buildings were constructed, was the center of the culture (Figures 9.2 and 9.3). The canyon is located close to the center of the high desert of the San Juan Basin.

Twelve of the fourteen major Chacoan buildings are oriented to the midpoints and extremes of the solar and lunar cycles (Sofaer, Sinclair, and Donahue 1991). The eleven rectangular major Chacoan buildings have internal geometry that corresponds to the relationship of the solar and lunar cycles (Sofaer, Sinclair, and Donahue 1991). Most of the major buildings also appear to be organized in a

solar-and-lunar regional pattern that is symmetrically ordered about Chaco Canyon's central complex of large ceremonial buildings (Sofaer, Sinclair, and Williams 1987). These findings suggest a cosmological purpose motivating and directing the construction and the orientation, internal geometry, and interrelationships of the primary Chacoan architecture.

This essay presents a synthesis of the results of several studies by the Solstice Project between 1984 and 1997 and hypotheses about the conceptual and symbolic meaning of the Chacoan astronomical achievements. For certain details of Solstice Project studies, the reader is referred to several earlier published papers.[1]

BACKGROUND

The Chacoan buildings were of a huge scale and "spectacular appearance" (Neitzel 1989). The buildings typically had large public plazas and elaborate "architectural earthworks" that formed road entries (Stein and McKenna 1988). The major Chacoan buildings, the subject of the Solstice Project's studies (Figures 9.3 and 9.4), are noted in particular for their massive core veneer masonry. They were up to four stories high and contained as many as seven hundred rooms, as well as numerous kivas, including great kivas, the large ceremonial chambers of prehistoric Pueblo culture (Lekson

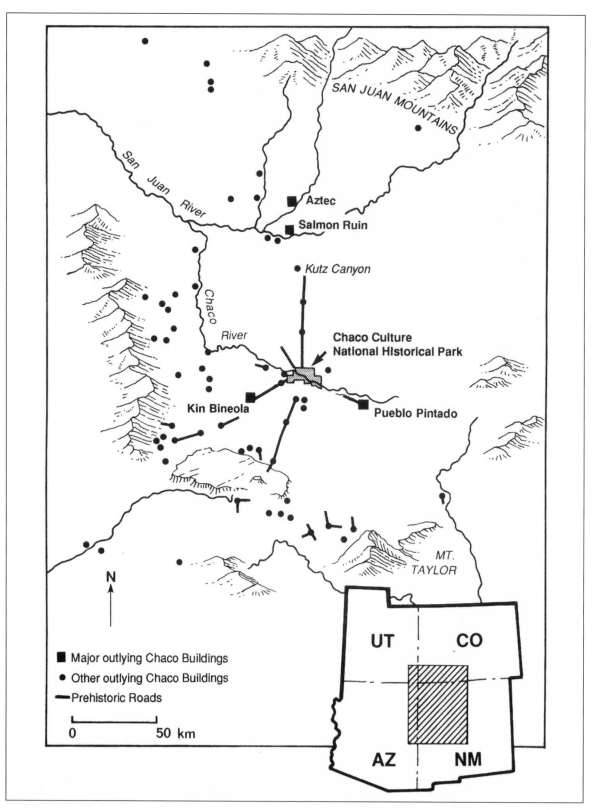

FIGURE 9.1. The San Juan Basin and adjoining region, showing the buildings and roads of the Chacoan culture. The inset shows the relation of this region to the present-day states. (Suzanne Samuels, By Design Graphics; © 1995 by The Solstice Project)

226

Anna Sofaer

FIGURE 9.2. Aerial view of central area of Chaco Canyon, looking north. The photograph shows three major buildings: Pueblo Bonito (left), Pueblo Alto (above center), and Chetro Ketl (right). Casa Rinconada (bottom center) and New Alto are also shown. (Photograph by Adriel Heisey, © 1995 by Adriel Heisey)

1984; Marshall et al. 1979; Powers, Gillespie, and Lekson 1983).

The construction of the major Chacoan buildings employed enormous quantities of stone and wood. For example, 215,000 timbers—transported from distances of more than 80 km—were used in the canyon in the major buildings alone (Lekson et al. 1988). The orderly, gridlike layout of the buildings suggests that extensive planning and engineering were involved in their construction (Lekson 1984; Lekson et al. 1988).

No clear topographic or utilitarian explanations have been developed for the orientations of the Chacoan buildings. The buildings stand free of the cliffs, and their specific orientations are not significantly constrained by local topography.[2]

227

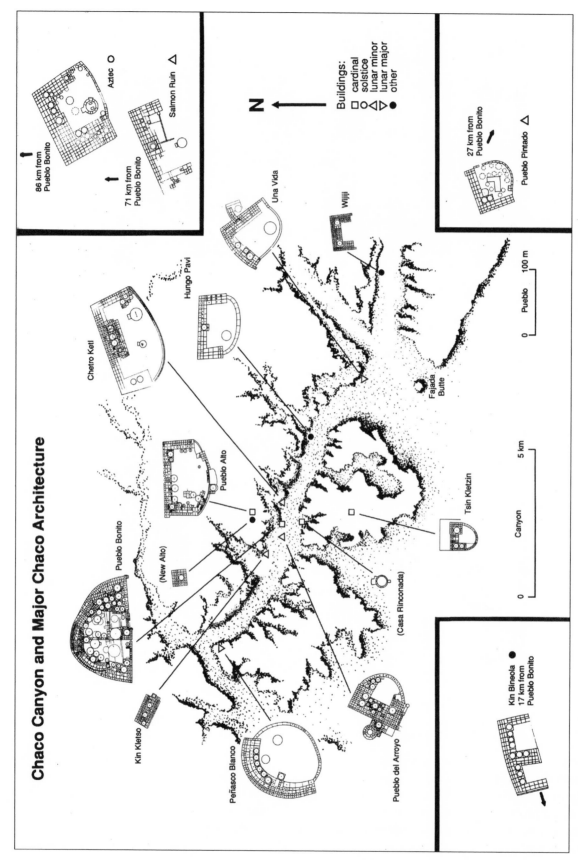

Chaco Canyon and Major Chaco Architecture

Buildings:
□ cardinal
○ solstice
◁ lunar minor
▷ lunar major
● other

N

Aztec ○

Salmon Ruin △

86 km from Pueblo Bonito

71 km from Pueblo Bonito

Una Vida

Wijiji

Hungo Pavi

Chetro Ketl

Fajada Butte

Pueblo Alto

Tsin Kletzin

(New Alto)

Pueblo Bonito

(Casa Rinconada)

Kin Kletso

Peñasco Blanco

Pueblo del Arroyo

0   Canyon   5 km

0   Pueblo   100 m

Pueblo Pintado △

27 km from Pueblo Bonito

Kin Bineola ●

17 km from Pueblo Bonito

FIGURE 9.3. Chaco Canyon, showing the locations and ground plans of ten major buildings (and two minor buildings). Four outlying major buildings are also shown. The astronomical orientations of the buildings are indicated. (Fabian Schmid, Davis, Inc.; and Suzanne Samuels, By Design Graphics; © 1995 by The Solstice Project)

FIGURE 9.4. Aerial photographs of two major buildings in Chaco Canyon, Pueblo Bonito (upper) and Pueblo del Arroyo (lower) with ground plans of these buildings. (Photographs by Koogle and Pouls for the National Park Service; graphics by Suzanne Samuels, By Design Graphics; © 1993 by The Solstice Project)

Although the need to optimize solar heating may have influenced the general orientations of the buildings, it probably did not restrict their orientations to specific azimuths. Similarly, environmental factors, such as access to water, appear not to have dominated or constrained the Chacoans' choice of specific locations for their buildings.[3]

The Chacoans also constructed more than two hundred kilometers of roads. The roads were of great width (averaging 9 m wide), and they were

229

developed, with unusual linearity, over distances of up to fifty kilometers. Their construction required extensive surveying and engineering (Kincaid 1983). Investigations show that certain of the roads were clearly overbuilt if they were intended to serve purely utilitarian purposes (Lekson 1991; Roney 1992; Sofaer, Marshall, and Sinclair 1989; Stein 1989),[4] and that they may have been constructed as cosmographic expressions (Marshall 1997; Sofaer, Marshall, and Sinclair 1989).

Scholars have puzzled for decades over why the Chacoan culture flourished in the center of the desolate environment of the San Juan Basin. Earlier models proposed that Chaco Canyon was a political and economic center where the Chacoans administered a widespread trade and redistribution system (Judge 1989; Sebastian 1992). Recent archaeological investigations show that major buildings in Chaco Canyon were not built or used primarily for household occupation (Lekson et al. 1988). This evidence, along with the dearth of burials found in the canyon, suggests that, even at the peak of the Chacoan development, there was a low resident population. (Estimates of this population range from 1,500 to 2,700 [Lekson 1991; Windes 1987].) Evidence of periodic, large-scale breakage of vessels at key central buildings indicates, however, that Chaco Canyon may have served as a center for seasonal ceremonial visitations by great numbers of residents of the outlying communities (Judge 1984; Toll 1991).

Many aspects of the Chacoan culture—such as the transport of thousands of beams and pots—have struck archaeologists as having a "decided aura of inefficiency" (Toll 1991). Other findings—such as "intentionally destroyed items in the trash mounds," "plastered-over exquisite masonry," and strings of beads "sealed into niches" in a central great kiva—indicate esoteric uses of Chacoan constructions. It has been suggested that, in the "absence of any evidence that there is either a natural or societal resource to which Chaco could control access by virtue of its location" (Toll 1991), Chaco Canyon was the center of exchange of information and knowledge (Sebastian 1991). Two other archaeologists suggest that Chaco Canyon was a "central archive for esoteric knowledge, such as maintenance of the region's ceremonial calendar" (Crown and Judge 1991).

Scholars have commented extensively on the impractical and enigmatic aspects of Chacoan buildings, describing them as "overbuilt and overembellished" and proposing that they were built primarily for public image and ritual expression (Lekson et al. 1988; Stein and Lekson 1992). Some observers have thought that the Chacoan buildings were developed as expressions of the Chacoans' "concepts of the cosmos" (Stein and Lekson 1992) and that their placement and design may have been determined in part by "Chacoan cosmography" (Marshall and Doyel 1981). One report proposes that "Chaco and its hinterland are related by a canon of shared design concepts" and that the Chacoan architecture is a "common ideational bond" across a "broad geographic space" (Stein and Lekson 1992). That report suggests that the architectural characteristics of Pueblo Bonito, one of the two largest and most central buildings of the Chacoan system, are rigorously repeated throughout the Chaco region. Thus, important clues to the symbology and ideology of the Chacoan culture may be embedded in its central and primary architecture and expressed in the relationship of this architecture to primary buildings in the outlying region.

Numerous parallels to the Chacoan expressions of cosmology appear in the astronomically and geometrically ordered constructions of Mesoamerica—a region with which the Chacoans are known to have had cultural associations (Aveni 1980; Broda 1993). Moreover, traditions of the descendants of the prehistoric Pueblo people, who live today in New Mexico and Arizona, also suggest parallels to the Chacoan cosmology and give us insight into the general cosmological concepts of the Chacoan culture.

Previous Work

Solstice Project studies, begun in 1978, documented astronomical markings at three petroglyph sites on Fajada Butte, a natural promontory at the south entrance of Chaco Canyon (Figure 9.3). Near the top of the butte, three rock slabs collimate light so that markings of shadow and light on two spiral petroglyphs indicate the summer and winter solstices, the equinoxes, and the extreme positions of the moon, that is, the lunar major and minor standstills (Sofaer, Zinser, and Sinclair 1979; Sofaer, Sinclair, and Doggett 1982; Sinclair et al. 1987). At two other sites on the butte, shadow and light patterns on five petroglyphs indicate solar noon and the solstices and equinoxes (Sofaer and Sinclair 1987).

A 1989 Solstice Project study showed astronomical significance in the Chacoans' construction of the Great North Road (Sofaer, Marshall, and Sinclair 1989). This 9-m-wide, engineered road extends from Chaco Canyon north 50 km to a badlands site, Kutz Canyon (Figure 9.1). The purpose of the road appears to have been to articulate the north-south axis and to connect the canyon's central ceremonial complex with distinctive topographic features in the north.

Prior to the Solstice Project studies of the Chacoan constructions, others had reported cardinal orientations in the primary walls and the great kiva of Pueblo Bonito, a major building located in the central complex of Chaco Canyon, and in Casa Rinconada, an isolated great kiva (Williamson et al. 1975, 1977). Researchers have also shown that certain features in Pueblo Bonito and Casa Rinconada may be oriented to the solstices (Reyman 1976; Williamson et al. 1977; Zeilik 1984).[5]

Certain early research also highlighted astronomically related geometry and symmetry in the Chacoan architecture. One scholar describes "geometrical/astronomical patterns" in the extensive cardinal organization of Casa Rinconada (Williamson 1984). His report notes that these patterns were derived from the symmetry of the solar cycle, rather than from the observation of astronomical events from this building. Similarly, other research describes a symmetric, cardinal patterning in the geographic relationships of several central buildings, and it further suggests that other major buildings—outside of the center and out of sight of the center—were organized in symmetric relationships to the cardinal axes of the center (Fritz 1978).

These previous findings led the Solstice Project to examine and analyze the orientations, internal geometry, and interrelationships of the major Chacoan buildings for possible astronomical significance. The Solstice Project's study regarded as important both orientations to visible astronomical events and expressions of astronomically related geometry. In the following analysis, the Solstice Project considers the orientations of the major Chacoan buildings, and of their interbuilding relationships, to astronomical events on both the sensible and the visible horizons.[6]

SOLAR AND LUNAR ORIENTATIONS OF THE MAJOR CHACOAN BUILDINGS

The Solstice Project asked if the fourteen major buildings were oriented to the sun and moon at the extremes and mid-positions of their cycles—in other words, the meridian passage, the solstices and the equinoxes, and the lunar major and minor standstills. The rising and setting azimuths for these astronomical events at the latitude of Chaco Canyon are given in Figure 9.5. (The angles of the solstices, equinoxes, and lunar standstills are expressed as single values taken east and west of north as positive to the east of north and negative to the west of north.)

In the clear skies of the high desert environment of the San Juan Basin, the Chacoans had nearly continuous opportunity to view the sun and the moon, to observe the progression of their cycles, and to see the changes in their relationships to the surrounding landscape and in patterns of shadow and light.

The sun: The yearly cycle of the sun is evident by its excursions to the extreme positions: rising in the northeast at the summer solstice and in the southeast at the winter solstice; setting in the northwest at the summer solstice and in the southwest at the winter solstice. At equinox, in the middle of these excursions, it rises and sets east and west. At solar noon, in the middle of its daily excursion, the sun is on the meridian—in other words, aligned with the north-south axis.

The cardinal directions (0°, 90°) are regarded in this paper as having the solar associations of equinox and meridian passage.[7] In a location surrounded by significantly elevated topography, however, the equinox sun can also be observed on the visible horizon in sunrise and sunset azimuths that are not the cardinal east-west axis of the sensible horizon.

The moon: The moon's standstill cycle is longer (18.6 years) and more complex than the sun's cycle, but its rhythms and patterns also can be observed in its shifting positions on the horizon, as

The Primary Architecture of the Chacoan Culture

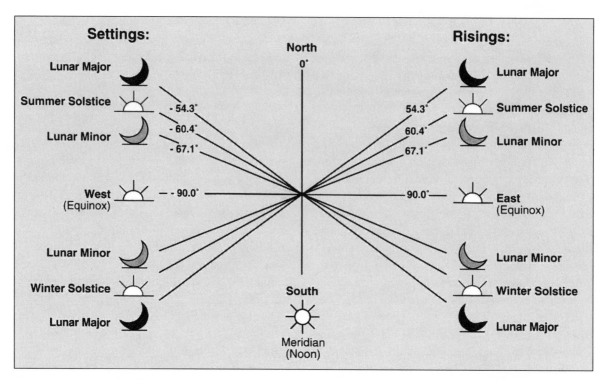

FIGURE 9.5. Azimuths of the rising and setting of the sun and moon at the extremes and mid-positions of their cycles, at the latitude (36° north) of Chaco Canyon. The meridian passage of the sun is also indicated. The lunar extremes are the northern and southern limits of rising or setting at the major and minor standstills. (Fabian Schmid, Davis, Inc.; and Suzanne Samuels, By Design Graphics; © 1995 by The Solstice Project)

well as in its relationship to the sun (see also Aveni 1980: Chapter 3). In its excursions each month it shifts from rising roughly in the northeast to rising roughly in the southeast and from setting roughly in the northwest to setting roughly in the southwest, but a closer look reveals that the envelope of these excursions expands and contracts through the 18.6-year standstill cycle. In the year of the major standstill, this envelope is at its maximum width, and at the latitude of Chaco, the moon rises and sets approximately 6.1° north and south of the positions of the rising and setting solstice suns. These positions are the farthest to the northeast and northwest and southeast and southwest that the moon ever reaches. In the year of the minor standstill, nine to ten years later, the envelope is at its minimum width, and the moon rises and sets approximately 6.7° within the envelope of the rising and setting solstice suns.

The progression of the sun and the moon in their cycles can also be quite accurately observed in their changing heights at meridian passage and in the accompanying shifts in shadow patterns.

A number of factors, such as parallax and atmospheric refraction, can shift and broaden the range of azimuth where the risings and settings of the solstice suns and the standstill moons appear on the horizon. In addition, judgments in determining a solar or lunar event introduce uncertainties. These judgments involve determining which portion of the object to sight on and what time to sight it in its rising or setting, as well as identifying the exact time of a solstice or a standstill. Calculations for the latitude and environment of the Chaco region show the standard deviation developed from these sighting conditions and uncertainties: 0.5° in locating a solstice event; 0.5° in locating the minor standstill; and 0.7° in locating the major standstill (Sinclair and Sofaer 1993; see also Hawkins 1973:287–288).

The Solstice Project surveyed the orientations of the fourteen largest buildings of the Chaco cultural region as ranked by room count (Powers, Gillespie, and Lekson 1983) (Figures 9.1 and 9.3, Table 9.1). The group comprises twelve rectangular and two crescent-shaped buildings that contained 115 to 695

232

Anna Sofaer

TABLE 9.1. Sizes and Orientations of Major Chacoan Buildings (Positive azimuths are east of north; negative azimuths are west of north.)

Building	Number of Rooms	Area (m²)	Length of Principal Wall or Axis (m)	Orientations of:		
				Princ. Wall or Axis	Perp.	Diagonals
Pueblo Bonito	695	18,530	65	0.21° 0.14°	-89.79° ± 0.14°	
Chetro Ketl	580	23,395	140	69.60° ± 0.50°	-20.40° ± 0.50°	-86.4°
Aztec	405	15,030	120	62.47° ± 0.33°	-27.53° ± 0.33°	86.6° 37.2° -81.4° 24.8°
Pueblo del Arroyo	290	8,990	80	24.79° ± 0.25°	-65.21° ± 0.25°	-1.6° 49.9°
Kin Bineola	230	8,225	110	78.7° ± 3.2°	-11.3° ± 3.2°	-77.6° 54.2°
Peñasco Blanco	215	15,010	100	36.8° ± 1.3°	-53.2° ± 1.3°	
Wijiji	190	2,535	53	83.48° ± 0.15°	-6.52° ± 0.15°	-62.0° 49.2°
Salmon Ruin	175	8,320	130	65.75° ± 0.15°	-24.75° ± 0.15°	88.4° 43.3°
Una Vida	160	8,750	80	-35.18° ± 0.15°	54.82° ± 0.15°	
Hungo Pavi	150	8,025	90	-85.24° ±0.15°	4.76° ±0.15°	-61.4° 70.7°
Pueblo Pintado	135	5,935	70	69.90° ±0.15°	-20.10° ± 0.15°	31.4°
Kin Kletso	135	2,640	42	-65.82° ± 0.64°	24.18° ± 0.64°	87.38° -38.09°
Pueblo Alto	130	8,260	110	88.9° ±1.3°	-1.1° ± 1.3°	-68.6° 64.8°
Tsin Kletzin	115	3,552	40	89° ± 2°	-1° ± 2°	-66° 51°

© 1994 Solstice Project

Note: Number of rooms and area from Powers et al. 1983: Table 41.

rooms and were one to four stories high (Powers, Gillespie, and Lekson 1983). Ten buildings are located in the canyon, and four are located outside the canyon.

The buildings in the survey represent the Chacoans' most elaborate architecture. They include all of the large buildings in the canyon and the only outlying buildings that share the massive scale and impressive formality of the large buildings in the canyon (Lekson 1991; Roney 1992).[8]

All of the buildings in the Solstice Project's studies were developed between the late 800s and 1120s (Lekson 1984; Marshall et al. 1979; Powers, Gillespie, and Lekson 1983). Although the earlier buildings were modified and whole new buildings were constructed within this period, all the buildings that the Solstice Project surveyed were in use and most were being extensively worked on in the last and most intensive phase of Chacoan construction, from 1075 to about 1115 (Lekson 1984).

233

Six teams, working with the Solstice Project between 1984 and 1989, surveyed the orientations of most of the exterior walls of the twelve rectangular buildings. (The teams did not survey three short exterior walls of the rectangular buildings because the walls were too deteriorated.) The Solstice Project also surveyed the long back wall and the exterior corners of Peñasco Blanco, as well as the two halves of the exterior south wall and the primary interior wall of Pueblo Bonito, which approximately divides the plaza. In addition, the Solstice Project surveyed the dimensions of most of the exterior walls of the fourteen buildings. The teams established references at the sites by orienting to the sun, Venus, Sirius, or Polaris, or by tying to first- and second-order survey control stations.

Most of the walls are quite straight and in good condition at ground level and can be located within a few centimeters. Ten to thirty points were established along the walls and were measured in relation to the established references. These values were averaged to calculate the orientations of the walls. The Solstice Project was able to estimate based on multiple surveys of several walls that most of its measurements are accurate to within 0.25° of the orientation of the original walls. (Table 9.1 indicates where the survey was less accurate.)

The survey defined the orientations of the twelve rectangular buildings as either the direction of the longest wall (termed here the "principal" wall) or the perpendicular to this wall.[9] In all but one of the rectangular buildings, this perpendicular represents the "facing" direction of the building, the direction that crosses the large plaza. With respect to the crescent-shaped buildings, the orientation of Pueblo Bonito is defined as the primary interior wall that approximately divides the plaza and the perpendicular to that wall, which corresponds closely in its orientation to that of a major exterior wall.[10] The orientation of Peñasco Blanco is defined by its symmetry as the line between the ends of the crescent and the perpendicular to this line (Figure 9.6).

The results of the survey show that the orientations of eleven of the fourteen major buildings are associated with one of the four solar or lunar azimuths on the sensible horizon (Tables 9.1 and 9.2, and Figure 9.6).[11] Three buildings (Pueblo Bonito, Pueblo Alto, and Tsin Kletzin) are associated with the cardinal directions (meridian and equinox). One building (Aztec) is associated with the solstice azimuth. Five buildings (Chetro Ketl, Kin Kletso, Pueblo del Arroyo, Pueblo Pintado, and Salmon Ruin) are associated with the lunar minor standstill azimuth (Figure 9.7), and two buildings (Peñasco Blanco and Una Vida) are associated with the lunar major standstill.[12]

The orientations of the eleven major buildings that are associated with solar and lunar azimuths fall within 0.2° and 2.8° of the astronomical azimuths on the sensible horizon. Of these eleven, nine fall within 0.2° and 2.1° of the astronomical azimuths. The remaining two buildings, Chetro Ketl and Pueblo Pintado, are oriented respectively within 2.5° and 2.8° of the azimuth of the lunar minor standstill. (The wider differences in the orientations of these latter buildings from the lunar minor standstill are in the direction away from the solstice azimuth, which reinforces the conclusion that these buildings are associated with the moon rather than the sun.)

A number of factors (together or separately) could account for the divergence of the actual orientations of the major Chacoan buildings from the astronomical azimuths. These may include small errors in observation, surveying, and construction and a desire by the Chacoans to integrate into their astronomically oriented architecture symbolic relationships to significant topographic features and/or other major Chacoan buildings. (See for example the discussion in this essay of the solar-lunar regional pattern among the major Chacoan buildings.)[13]

The Solstice Project found that the eleven buildings that are oriented to astronomical events on the sensible horizon are also oriented to the same events on the visible horizon. The reason for this is that the topography introduces no significant variable in the observation of the rising or the setting astronomical events from these buildings. The divergence of the orientations of these buildings from the azimuths of astronomical events in one direction on the visible horizon (0.5° to 2.5°) is approximately the same as the divergence described above of their orientations from the azimuths of the same astronomical events on the sensible horizon.[14] The differences between the orientations to the sensible and those to the visible horizon are so small as to not clearly indicate to which of these horizons the architects of Chaco oriented their

Anna Sofaer

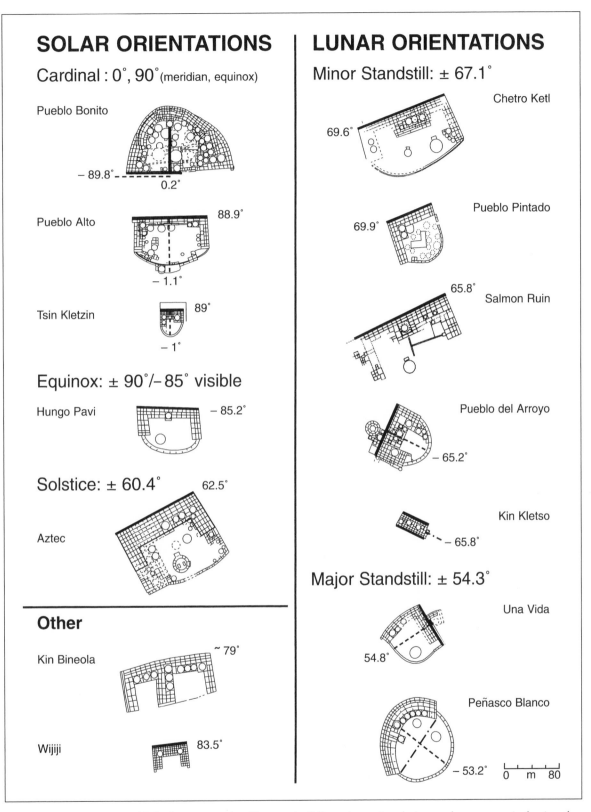

FIGURE 9.6. Orientations of the fourteen major Chacoan buildings shown in relation to the astronomical azimuths on the sensible horizon. For one building, Hungo Pavi, the orientation to the equinox sunrise on the visible horizon also is indicated. (Suzanne Samuels, By Design Graphics; © 1995 by The Solstice Project)

The Primary Architecture of the Chacoan Culture

TABLE 9.2. Orientations of Major Chacoan Buildings (Positive azimuths are east of north; negative azimuths are west of north.

	Principal Wall or Axis	Perpendicular	
Pueblo Bonito	0.2°	-89.8°	} 0°, 90° Cardinal (meridian, equinox)
Pueblo Alto	88.9°	-1.1°	
Tsin Kletzin	89.0°	-1.0°	
Hungo Pavi	-85.2°		} -85° Equinox/visible
Aztec	62.5°		} 60.4° Solstice
Peñasco Blanco		-53.2°	} 54.3° Lunar Major Standstill
Una Vida		54.8°	
Pueblo del Arroyo		-65.2°	}
Kin Kletso	-65.8°		}
Salmon Ruin	65.8°		} 67.1° Lunar Minor Standstill
Chetro Ketl	69.6°		}
Pueblo Pintado	69.9°		}
Wijiji	83.5°		
Kin Bineola	~ 79.0°		

© Solstice Project 1995

buildings. The Solstice Project finds no evidence that the Chacoans were interested in making such a distinction in the case of eleven buildings.

Hungo Pavi, the twelfth building, appears to be oriented too far (4.8°) from the equinox rising or setting sun on the sensible horizon to qualify as an orientation associated with the solar azimuths on that horizon. It is, however, oriented to within one degree of the visible equinox sunrise.[15] Because of the topography, there is no corresponding visibility from Hungo Pavi to the equinox setting sun.

With respect to Wijiji and Kin Bineola, there appear to be no solar or lunar events associated with either the sensible or the visible horizon.[16] To conclude, orientation to the extremes and mid-positions of the solar and lunar cycles apparently played a significant role in the construction of the primary Chacoan architecture. No utilitarian reasons appear to explain the astronomic orientations of twelve of the fourteen major buildings.

Other researchers of prehistoric puebloan buildings report solar and lunar orientations and associations. At Hovenweep, in southern Utah, the orientations and locations of portholes of certain tower-like structures appear to be related to the

solar cycle (Williamson 1984). Chimney Rock, an outlying Chacoan building in southern Colorado, appears to have been situated for its view of the major northern standstill moon rising between natural stone pillars, "chimney rocks" (Malville and Putnam 1989; Malville et al. 1991). The relationship of this building to the lunar major standstill moon is underscored by the close correspondence of the tree-ring dates of its timbers with the occurrences of the lunar major standstill (1075 and 1094) at the peak of the Chacoan civilization. These findings in the outlying region of the Chacoan culture, as well as earlier findings of solar and lunar light markings in Chaco Canyon, support the phenomenon of solar and lunar orientations in the primary Chacoan buildings.

SOLAR-LUNAR GEOMETRY INTERNAL TO THE MAJOR CHACOAN BUILDINGS

The Solstice Project's survey of the eleven rectangular major Chacoan buildings found strictly repeated internal diagonal angles and a correspondence between these angles and astronomy. The internal angles formed by the two diagonals and the long back walls of the rectangular buildings cluster in two groups (Figure 9.8A): sixteen angles in nine buildings are between 23° and 28°;[17] and six angles in four buildings are between 34° and 39°. (One of the buildings, Aztec, was constructed first as a rectangular building with shorter side walls [Aztec I] that were extended in a later building stage [Aztec II] [Ahlstrom 1985]. It is of interest that when the side walls of Aztec I were extended to form Aztec II, the builders shifted from one preferred angle to the other.)

At the latitude of Chaco, the angles between the lunar standstill azimuths on the sensible horizon and the east-west cardinal axis are 22.9° and 35.7°, respectively (Figure 9.8B). The correspondence between these angles of the solar-lunar relationships and the internal diagonal angles is intriguing. It suggests that the Chacoans may have favored these particular angles in order to incorporate a geometry of the sun and moon in the internal organization of the buildings.[18]

In addition, three rectangular buildings (Pueblo Alto, Salmon Ruin, and Pueblo del Arroyo) are oriented on the sensible and visible horizons along one or both of their diagonals, as well as on their principal walls or perpendiculars, to the lunar minor standstill azimuth and to one of the cardinals (Table 9.1). The Chacoans may have intended the two phenomena—internal geometry and external orientation—to be so integrated that these three rectangular buildings would have both solar and lunar orientation.

A similar solar-lunar geometry appears to have guided the design of all of the major Chacoan buildings (Sofaer 1994).[19] Furthermore, as with the three rectangular buildings discussed above, it appears that certain other of the major buildings also contain both solar and lunar orientations.

SOLAR-LUNAR REGIONAL PATTERN BETWEEN THE MAJOR CHACOAN BUILDINGS

Having seen that the Chacoans oriented and internally proportioned their major buildings in relationship to astronomy, the Solstice Project asked if the geographical relationships between the major buildings likewise expressed astronomical significance.

One scholar observed that four key central buildings are organized in a cardinal pattern (Fritz 1978).

FIGURE 9.7. The moonrise seen through two doorways of Pueblo del Arroyo on April 10, 1990, when the moon rose at −67.5° on the visible horizon, close to the 67.1° azimuth of the lunar minor standstill. Although we do not know whether an exterior wall, which is now deteriorated, blocked this view, the photograph illustrates the framing of the minor standstill moon by other exterior doorways and it conveys the perpendicular direction of the building toward the minor standstill moon (see Figure 9.6). (Photograph by Crawford MacCallum, © 1990 by The Solstice Project)

The line between Pueblo Alto and Tsin Kletzin is north-south; the line between Pueblo Bonito and Chetro Ketl is east-west. This work also showed that these cardinal interrelationships of four central buildings involved a symmetric patterning. The north-south line between Pueblo Alto and Tsin Kletzin evenly divides the east-west line between Pueblo Bonito and Chetro Ketl.

The Solstice Project found, in addition, that three of the four buildings involved in these cardinal interbuilding relationships are cardinal in their individual building orientations (Table 9.3; Figures 9.2, 9.9, and 9.10).[20] These findings suggest that the Chacoans coordinated the orientations and locations of several central buildings to form astronomical interbuilding relationships. The Project

237

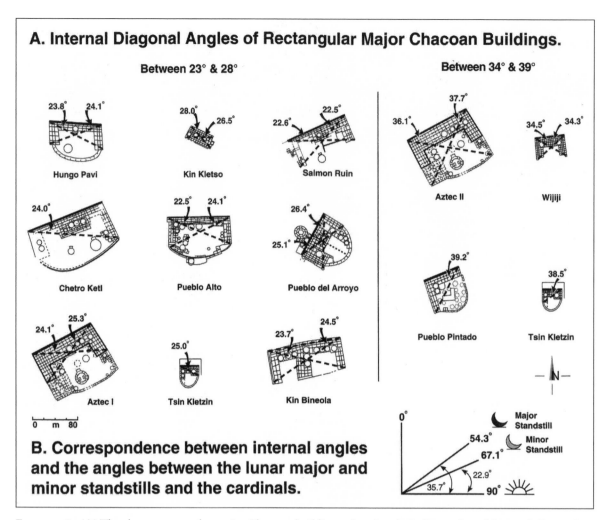

A. Internal Diagonal Angles of Rectangular Major Chacoan Buildings.

Between 23° & 28°

Between 34° & 39°

Hungo Pavi — 23.8°, 24.1°

Kin Kletso — 28.0°, 26.5°

Salmon Ruin — 22.6°, 22.5°

Chetro Ketl — 24.0°

Pueblo Alto — 22.5°, 24.1°

Pueblo del Arroyo — 26.4°, 25.1°

Aztec II — 36.1°, 37.7°

Wijiji — 34.5°, 34.3°

Pueblo Pintado — 39.2°

Tsin Kletzin — 38.5°

Aztec I — 24.1°, 25.3°

Tsin Kletzin — 25.0°

Kin Bineola — 23.7°, 24.5°

0 m 80

— N —

B. Correspondence between internal angles and the angles between the lunar major and minor standstills and the cardinals.

0°
54.3° Major Standstill
67.1° Minor Standstill
35.7° 22.9° 90°

FIGURE 9.8. (A) The eleven rectangular major Chacoan buildings, showing their diagonals and internal diagonal angles. (Two building phases at Aztec are shown.) (B) The correspondence of these angles to the angles between the lunar standstill azimuths and the cardinal directions. (Suzanne Samuels, By Design Graphics; © 1995 by The Solstice Project)

then asked if there were other such relationships between the major buildings.

As Table 9.3 and Figures 9.9 and 9.11 show, numerous bearings between thirteen of the fourteen major buildings align with the azimuths of the solar and lunar phenomena associated with the individual buildings.[21] Only one major building, Salmon Ruin, is not related in this manner to another building. In questioning the extent to which these astronomical interbuilding relationships were intentionally developed by the Chacoans, the Solstice Project examined the pattern formed by them. In a manner similar to the central cardinal patterning, the bearings between the lunar-oriented buildings and other buildings appear to form lunar-based

relationships that are symmetric about the north-south axis of the central complex (Figure 9.11).

The two isolated and remote outlying buildings, Pueblo Pintado and Kin Bineola, 27 km and 18 km, respectively, from the canyon center, are located on lines from the central complex that correspond to the bearings of the lunar minor standstill. As in the cardinal patterning, these lunar-based interbuilding relationships are underscored by the fact that they involve buildings that also are oriented individually to the lunar standstills (for one example see Figure 9.12a). Specifically, Chetro Ketl, Pueblo del Arroyo, and Kin Kletso—the three buildings in the central complex that are oriented to the lunar minor standstill—also are related to Pueblo

TABLE 9.3. Astronomical Bearings between Astronomically Oriented Buildings (Positive azimuths are east of north; negative azimuths are west of north)

Astronomically Oriented Buildings	Astronomical Bearings to Other Buildings			
	Buildings	Azimuth (degrees)	Differences between astronomical azimuth and interbuilding bearings (degrees)	Distance (km)
Cardinal Buildings associated azimuths 90°/0° Pueblo Bonito	Chetro Ketl	-88.7	-1.3	0.72
	Aztec	-2.2	2.2	86.3
Pueblo Alto	Tsin Kletzin	0.6	-0.6	3.7
	Aztec	-2.5	2.5	86.0
Hungo Pavi	- -	- -	- -	- -
Tsin Kletzin	Pueblo Alto	0.6	-0.6	3.7
	Aztec	-2.3	2.3	89.0
Solstice Building associated azimuth ±60.4° Aztec	- -	- -	- -	- -
Lunar Minor Buildings associated azimuth ±67.1° Chetro Ketl	Kin Bineola	69.3	-2.2	17.1
	Pueblo Pintado	-69.9	2.8	27.2
	Kin Kletso	-69.9	2.8	1.5
Pueblo del Arroyo	Hungo Pavi	-69.3	2.2	3.4
	Kin Bineola	67.8	-0.7	16.2
	Wijiji	-65.9	-1.2	8.4
Salmon Ruin	- -	- -	- -	- -
Pueblo Pintado	Chetro Ketl	-69.9	2.8	27.2
	Pueblo Bonito	-70.3	3.2	27.9
	Peñasco Blanco	-68.6	1.5	32.1
	Pueblo Alto	-68.0	0.9	27.8
	Kin Kletso	-69.9	2.8	28.7
Kin Kletso	Chetro Ketl	-69.9	2.8	1.5
	Pueblo Pintado	-69.9	2.8	28.7
	Wijiji	-64.5	-2.6	9.0
	Pueblo Alto	65.8	-1.3	1.3
	Kin Bineola	65.9	-1.2	16.0
	Hungo Pavi	-65.2	-1.9	4.0
Lunar Major Buildings associated azimuth ±54.3° Peñasco Blanco	Pueblo Bonito	-55.9	1.6	4.2
	Pueblo del Arroyo	-55.8	1.5	4.1
	Una Vida	-56.7	2.4	9.8
	Kin Bineola	55.0	0.7	14.3
Una Vida	Chetro Ketl	-51.3	-3.0	4.8
	Pueblo Bonito	-55.8	1.5	5.4
	Peñasco Blanco	-56.7	2.4	9.8
	Pueblo del Arroyo	-55.8	3.0	5.7
	Kin Kletso	-55.8	1.4	6.3

© Solstice Project 1995

Pintado and Kin Bineola on bearings oriented to the lunar minor standstill. It is of interest that Pueblo Pintado also is oriented to the lunar minor standstill (Figures 9.11 and 9.12a).[22] In addition, two major buildings, Wijiji and Hungo Pavi, located outside of the central complex but within the canyon, also are on the bearing from the central complex to Pueblo Pintado and to the lunar minor standstill (Figure 9.11).[23]

The relationship of the central complex to Pueblo Pintado (southeast of the canyon) is to the rising of the southern minor standstill moon; the relationship of the central canyon complex to Kin Bineola (southwest of the canyon) is to the setting of this same moon. Thus the north-south axis of the central complex is the axis of symmetry of this moon's rising, meridian passage, and setting, as well as the axis of the ceremonial center and of the

239

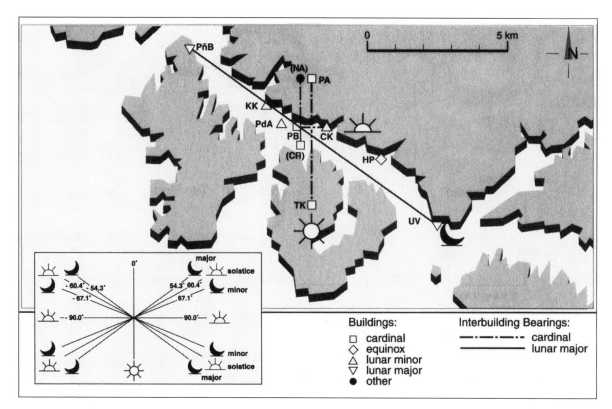

FIGURE 9.9. The locations and orientations of the buildings in Chaco Canyon. The diagram shows the bearings between buildings that correlate with the orientations of individual buildings to the cardinal directions and to the lunar major standstill azimuths. (Fabian Schmid, Davis, Inc.; © 1995 by The Solstice Project)

relationships of these significant outlying structures to that center.

It is of further note that Pueblo Pintado and Kin Bineola are regarded as having particularly significant relationships with the buildings in the canyon. One archaeologist reports that these two buildings are more like the canyon buildings than they are like other outlying buildings, and he suggests, because of their positions to the southeast and southwest of the canyon, that they could be viewed as the "gateway communities" (Michael P. Marshall, personal communication 1990).

This lunar-based symmetrical patterning about the north-south axis of the central ceremonial complex also is expressed in the relationships of the lunar major–oriented buildings, Una Vida and Peñasco Blanco, to that complex (Figure 9.9). Without knowing the astronomical associations of these buildings, other scholars had observed the symmetrical relationship of Una Vida and Peñasco Blanco to the north-south axis, as described above, between two major buildings in the central complex, Pueblo

Alto and Tsin Kletzin; and one of these scholars described this relationship as, along with the cardinal relationships of the central complex, "establishing the fundamental symmetry of the core development of Chaco Canyon" (Fritz 1978; Stein and Lekson 1992).

From the central complex, bearings to the major standstill moon are also the bearings to Una Vida and Peñasco Blanco, the only major Chacoan buildings that are oriented to the lunar major standstill (Figure 9.12b). This correspondence of the interbuilding relationships with the individual building orientations is again what is found with the cardinal and lunar minor relationships of the major buildings. Here it also is striking that the two buildings are equidistant from the north-south axis of the central complex. It is of further interest that the bearing from Peñasco Blanco to Kin Bineola also corresponds with the bearing to the lunar major standstill (Figure 9.11).[24] Una Vida, Peñasco Blanco, and Kin Bineola, along with Pueblo Bonito, share the earliest dates among the major

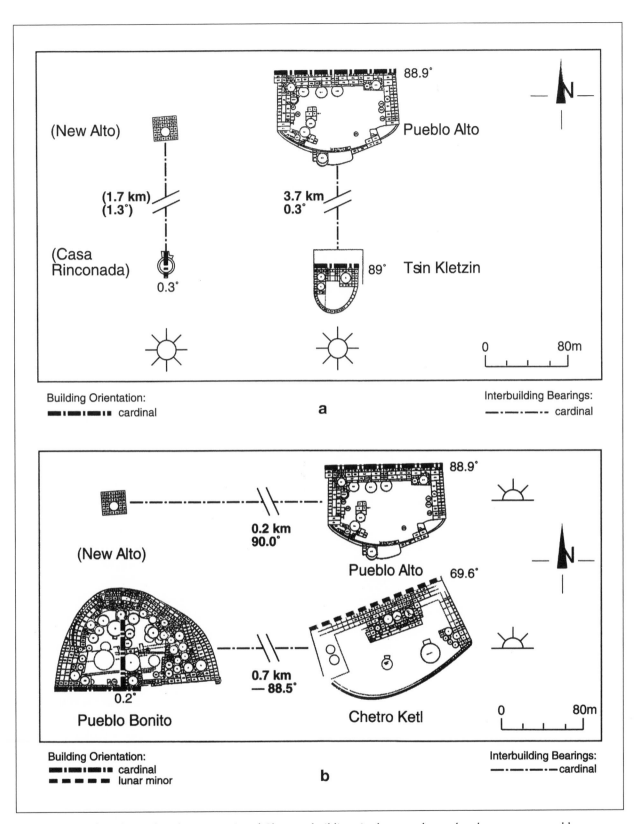

FIGURE 9.10. The relationships between pairs of Chacoan buildings in the central complex that are connected by astronomical bearings: (a) north-south connections, and (b) east-west connections. (Fabian Schmid, Davis, Inc.; © 1995 by The Solstice Project)

241

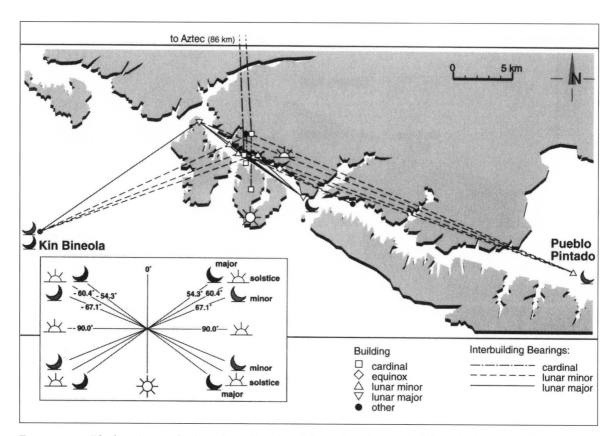

FIGURE 9.11. The locations and orientations of twelve of the major Chacoan buildings, including Kin Bineola and Pueblo Pintado outside the canyon. The diagram shows bearings between buildings that correlate with the orientation of the individual buildings to the cardinal directions and the lunar major and minor standstill azimuths. (Fabian Schmid, Davis, Inc.; © 1995 by The Solstice Project)

Chacoan buildings (Lekson 1984; Marshall et al. 1979).

Thus, from the central complex of Chaco Canyon, in the year of the major standstill moon, there was a relationship to that moon, as it rose farthest south in its full cycle, that also incorporated a relationship to Una Vida; and, in that same year, as the moon made its excursion to setting farthest north in its full cycle, it was on a bearing from the central complex that incorporated a relationship with Peñasco Blanco. Furthermore, in that year, the southern major standstill moon that rose on the bearing from Peñasco Blanco to Una Vida and the central complex would set on the bearing from Peñasco Blanco to the outlying major building, Kin Bineola. This phenomenon may have been intended to draw Kin Bineola into a lunar major relationship with Peñasco Blanco and with Peñasco Blanco's lunar major connection with Una Vida and the central canyon complex.[25]

At the other end of the lunar standstill cycle, nine to ten years later, in the year of the minor standstill moon, two outlying buildings, Kin Bineola and Pueblo Pintado, would be drawn into relationship with the central complex by their locations on bearings from the central complex that are to the rising and setting of the southern minor standstill moon.

Finally, in the face of the evidence that the Chacoans oriented and proportioned their major buildings in relationship to the solar and lunar cycles—and also interrelated their cardinally oriented buildings in a cardinal and symmetrical pattern—it is difficult to dismiss as coincidental the lunar-based interbuilding relationships, which are based on the same principles.[26] The recurring correlation of the interbuilding lines with the astronomical phenomena associated with the individual Chacoan buildings, and the centrally and symmetrically organized design of these lines, suggest that

242

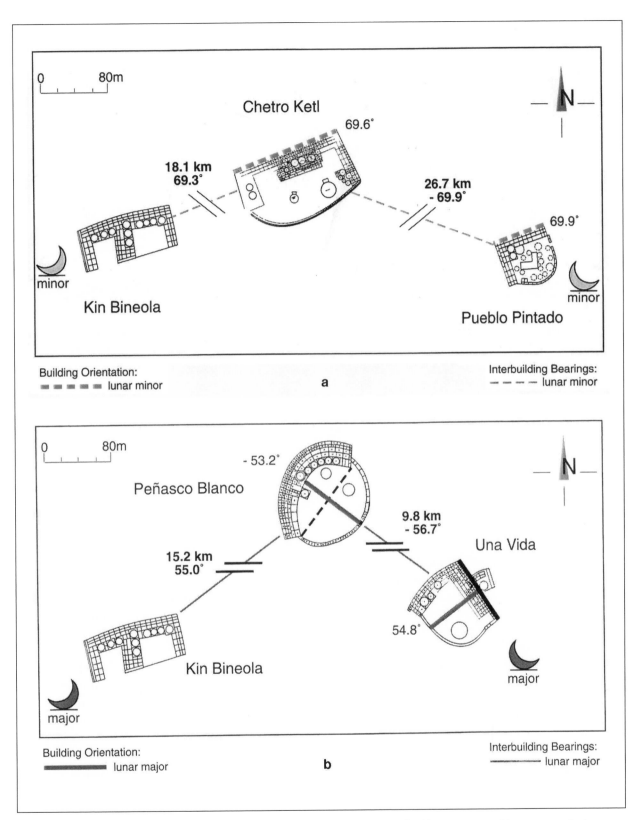

FIGURE 9.12. The relationships between two groups of three major Chacoan buildings connected by astronomical bearings aligned to (a) the lunar minor standstill and (b) the lunar major standstill. (Fabian Schmid, Davis, Inc.; © 1995 by The Solstice Project)

The Primary Architecture of the Chacoan Culture

the Chacoan culture coordinated the locations and orientations of many of its major buildings to form an interbuilding regional pattern that commemorates and integrates the cycles of the sun and the moon.[27]

Most of the buildings related by astronomical interbuilding lines are not intervisible. In general, this is because the canyon and other topographic features block the views between the buildings, especially those related over long distances. Thus the astronomical interbuilding lines could not have been, in general, used for astronomical observations or predictions.[28] It is of interest that the Chacoan roads, which are typified by their rigorous straight course, frequently appear to ignore topographic obstacles and connect sites that are great distances apart and are not intervisible.

CONSIDERATION OF THE EVOLUTION OF ASTRONOMICAL EXPRESSION IN CHACOAN ARCHITECTURE

The evidence of a conscious effort by the Chacoans to orient and interrelate their buildings on astronomical bearings raises a number of questions for further study. Were the building locations selected because they fell on astronomical bearings from other buildings? Were the interbuilding bearings developed from a plan? Were some buildings originally located for reasons other than astronomy and later drawn into the astronomical regional pattern?

It will probably never be known how great a role astronomy played in the decisions regarding the placement of the Chacoan buildings. Nor does it appear possible to know the extent of planning that preceded the development of the astronomical expressions in Chacoan architecture.[29] The data presently available on the chronology of the construction of the major buildings, however, do provide some insight into the history of the development of astronomical orientations and interrelationships among the major Chacoan buildings.

These data show that astronomical orientation appears to have played a part in Chacoan architecture from the earliest to the latest phases of its construction. Pueblo Bonito's north-south axis was incorporated in a major interior wall in the building's earliest design in the late 800s (Stein, Suiter, and Ford 1997), and this north-south axis was

extended and elaborated in the construction of the primary interior wall during the building's last phase of construction, in the late 1090s. The cardinal orientations of Pueblo Alto and Tsin Kletzin were developed in the early 1000s and the early 1100s, respectively. The lunar orientations were developed from the mid 900s (in Una Vida) through the early 1100s (in Kin Kletso).

Available data on the evolution of individual buildings show that, for most of the fourteen major buildings, the walls that are revealed today—and that were the subject of this study—are the original walls of these buildings, or that they follow closely the orientation of the buildings' prior walls. These data indicate that the orientation of two of the fourteen buildings changed significantly from one building phase to another.

It is also of interest that three of the four buildings in which the earliest dates were found among the fourteen major buildings (Peñasco Blanco, Una Vida, and Kin Bineola) are involved in the lunar major standstill interbuilding bearings. (Curiously, Peñasco Blanco is one of the two buildings that shifted from an earlier orientation [of −67°, in 900–915] to a later orientation [of −53.2° in 1050–1065].)

With further dating information it may be possible to know more of the evolution of astronomical expression in the Chacoan buildings. Such information could also shed light on the intriguing possibility that there may be, as there was found to be at Chimney Rock, correlations between the building phases of the major Chacoan buildings and the astronomical cycles (Malville and Putnam 1989).

SPECULATIONS ON THE CHACOANS' EXPERIENCE

Many of the major buildings appear to incorporate interesting views and experiences of the sun and moon at the extremes and mid-positions of their cycles. For example, each day at meridian passage of the sun, the mid-wall which approximately divides the massive structure of Pueblo Bonito casts no shadow. Similarly, the middle of the sun's yearly passage is marked at Pueblo Bonito as the equinox sun is seen rising and setting closely in line with the western half of its south wall. Thus, the middle of the sun's daily and yearly journeys are visibly in

Anna Sofaer

alignment with the major features of this building, which is at the middle of the Chacoan world.[30]

From many of the other major buildings, the sun and moon at the extreme positions of their cycles would be seen rising and/or setting along the long back walls or across the plazas at angles perpendicular to the back walls. In buildings oriented in their facing directions to the lunar standstill azimuths, the rising or setting moon, near its extremes, would be framed strikingly by the doorways (Figure 9.7).

Also visually compelling would have been the view from Peñasco Blanco of the moon rising at the major standstill position. This building is located 5.4 km northwest of Pueblo Bonito near the top of West Mesa. From it, one would view the southern major standstill moon rising in line with the mid-axis of the building's crescent, and also on a bearing to Pueblo Bonito and to the central complex of the canyon. The bearing would appear to continue through the valley of the canyon to the rising moon on the horizon. This event marked the time when the moon rises farthest south in its full cycle, once every eighteen to nineteen years.

This dramatic view of the major standstill moonrise also embodied astronomical and symmetrical relationships to nonvisible objects. Out of sight, but on the alignment between the viewer at Peñasco Blanco and the rising moon, is Una Vida, the one other of the Chacoan buildings that is oriented to the major standstill moon. Some viewers would likely have known of this nonvisible building's position on the bearing from Peñasco Blanco to the major rising moon, and they may also have known of Una Vida's and Peñasco Blanco's symmetrical relationship with the north-south axis of the central complex—in other words, that the two buildings are located the same distance from the north-south axis. Seeing the southern major standstill moon set over the mesa rise behind Peñasco Blanco would have conveyed to some Chacoans that as it set, out of view, on the sensible horizon it was on a bearing with Kin Bineola, out of view, 14.3 km to the southwest. Thus the experience of viewing the moon rising and setting at its southern major standstill from Peñasco Blanco would have involved seeing certain visible—and knowing certain nonvisible—aspects of the building's relationships with astronomy and with other major Chacoan buildings.

In the sculptured topography of the southern Rockies, at a location 150 km north of Chaco, the Chacoans witnessed a spectacular view of the moonrise at its major standstill. From their building situated high on an outcrop at Chimney Rock, once every eighteen to nineteen years, the Chacoans watched the moon rise between two nearby massive stone pillars.

Thus, while certain aspects of Chacoan architecture embed relationships on astronomical bearings to nonvisible objects, others appear to have been designed and/or located to frame, or to align to, bold displays of astronomy. Furthermore, some Chacoan astronomical expressions are on bearings that ignore topographic features, while others use topography dramatically to reinforce the visual effects of the architectural alignments to the sun and moon.

CONCLUDING DISCUSSION

Peoples throughout history and throughout the world have sought the synchronization and integration of the solar and lunar cycles. For example, in times and places not so remote from Chaco, the Mayas of Mesoamerica recognized the 19-year metonic cycle—the relationship of the phase cycles of the moon to the solar cycle—and noted elaborately, in the Dresden Codex, the pattern of lunar eclipses (Aveni 1980).[31] The Hopi, a Pueblo people living today in Arizona, are known to have synchronized the cycles of the sun and moon over a two-to-three-year period in the scheduling of their ceremonial cycle (McCluskey 1977). At Zuni Pueblo in northwestern New Mexico, the joining of Father Sun and Mother Moon is sought constantly in the timing of ceremonies (Tedlock 1983).

Each of the Chacoan expressions of solar and lunar cosmology contains within it this integration of the sun and the moon. For example, at the three-slab site on Fajada Butte, the sunlight in a dagger-like form penetrates the center of the large spiral at summer solstice near midday, the highest part its cycle (Sofaer, Zinser, and Sinclair 1979); and, as though in complement to this, the moon's shadow crosses the spiral center at the lowest point of its cycle, the minor standstill (Sofaer, Sinclair, and Doggett 1982). In the same way, the outer edges of the spiral are marked by the sun in light patterns at

245

winter solstice, and the moon's shadow at its maximum extreme is tangent to the left edge.

This integration of the sun and the moon is in the three expressions of solar-lunar cosmology in Chacoan architecture. Five major buildings commemorate the solar cycle: three in their cardinal orientations, one in its equinox orientation, and one in its solstice orientation. Seven of the other nine major buildings commemorate the lunar standstills: five the minor standstill, and two the major standstill. And the overall patterning of the buildings joins the two sets of lunar-oriented buildings into relationship with the cardinal-solar center in a symmetrically organized design. The geometry of the rectangular buildings again expresses the joining of sun and moon; the internal angles related to the cardinal and lunar azimuths bring a consciousness of each of these cycles into the layout of the buildings.

Commemoration of these recurring cycles appears to have been a primary purpose of the Chaco phenomenon. Many people must have been involved over generations in the planning, development, and maintenance of the massive Chacoan constructions. The work may have been accomplished in relatively short periods of time (Lekson 1984) and perhaps in episodes timed to the sun and moon. This activity would have unified the Chacoan society with the recurring rhythms of the sun and moon in their movements about that central ceremonial place, Chaco Canyon.[32]

There are many parallels to the cosmological patterning of the Chacoan culture in the architectural developments of the Mesoamerican cultures. These developments occurred in the region to the south of Chaco, for several centuries before, during, and after Chaco's florescence.

It is observed that "the coordination of space and time in the Mesoamerican cosmology found its expression in the orientations of pyramids and architectural complexes" (Broda 1982) and in the relationships of these complexes to outlying topography and buildings (Broda 1993). Ceremonies related to the dead and timed to the astronomical cycles occurred in Mesoamerican centers (Broda 1982). In central structures of the ceremonial complexes, light markings commemorated the zenith passage of the sun (Aveni 1980). Certain of the ceremonial centers were organized on axes close to the cardinal directions (Aveni 1980; Broda 1982). It is stated that cosmological expression in Mesoamerica "reached an astonishing degree of elaboration and perfection," and that its role was "to create an enduring system of order encompassing human society as well as the universe" (Broda 1993). A Mesoamerican archaeoastronomer comments that "a principle of cosmic harmony pervaded all of existence in Mesoamerican thought" (Aveni 1980).

The parallels between Mesoamerica and Chaco illustrate that the Chacoan and Mesoamerican peoples shared common cultural concerns. In addition, the several objects of Mesoamerican origin that were found in Chacoan buildings indicate that the Chacoans had some contact with Mesoamerica through trade.

In the complex cosmologies of the historic Pueblo peoples, descendants of the Chaocans, there is a rich interplay of the sun and moon.[33] Time and space are integrated in the marking of directions that order the ceremonial structures and dances, and in the timing of ceremonies to the cycle of the sun and the phases of the moon. The sun and the moon are related to birth, life, and death.[34] Commemoration of their cycles occurs on some ceremonial occasions in shadow-and-light patterns. For instance, sunlight or moonlight striking ceremonial objects or walls of ceremonial buildings may mark the solstices, as well as the meridian passage of the solstice sun and the full moon, and time the beginning and ending of rituals.

In many Pueblo traditions, the people emerged in the north from the worlds below and traveled to the south in search of the sacred middle place. The joining of the cardinal and solstice directions with the nadir and the zenith frequently defines, in Pueblo ceremony and myth, that sacred middle place. It is a center around which the recurring solar and lunar cycles revolve. Chaco Canyon may have been such a center place and a place of mediation and transition between these cycles and between the worlds of the living and the dead (F. Eggan, personal communication 1990).[35]

For the Chacoans, some ceremonies commemorating the sun and the moon must have been conducted in relatively private settings, while others would have been conducted in public and monumental settings. A site such as the three-slab site would have been visited probably by no more than two or three individuals, who were no doubt highly initiated, specialized, and prepared for witnessing the light markings.[36] By contrast, the buildings would have been visited by thousands of people participating in ceremony.

The solar and lunar cosmology encoded in the Chacoans' massive architecture—through the buildings' orientations, internal geometry, and geographic relationships—unified the Chacoan people with each other and with the cosmos. This order is complex and stretches across vast reaches of the sky, the desert, and time. It is to be held in the mind's eye, the one that sees into and beyond natural phenomena to a sacred order. The Chacoans transformed an arid empty space into a reach of the mind.

Acknowledgments

The generous help and disciplined work of many individuals made possible the research presented here. We are particularly indebted to Rolf M. Sinclair (National Science Foundation) for his help in the rigorous collection and reduction of large amounts of data, for his thoughtful analysis of naked-eye astronomical observations, and for his help in organizing numerous and complicated surveying trips. We most especially appreciate his dedication to pursuing the truth through thousands of hours of discussion and analysis of the Chacoan material.

We wish to express a special thanks to John Stein (Navajo Nation) for sharing with us, over fifteen years, his many insights to the nonmaterial side of the Chaco phenomenon. To our knowledge, John was the first scholar to speak of Chacoan architecture as "a metaphoric language" and to express the view that the Chacoan roads were built for purposes other than utilitarian functions. He early on saw geometric complexity in the individual buildings and their interrelationships.

Phillip Johnson Tuwaletstiwa (the Hopi Tribe), the late Fred Eggan (Santa Fe), and Jay Miller (Chicago) helped us move from the confines of an engineering and surveying perspective to think of the rich and complex dualities of Pueblo cosmology and their analogies with the Chacoan developments. The late Alfonso Ortiz (University of New Mexico), when first viewing our material on the patterning of Chacoan roads and major buildings, observed that these complex constructions were developed as though they were to be seen from above.

Tuwaletstiwa was also responsible for initiating the surveys that form the basis of our studies. Most of the surveys were carried out by Richard Cohen (National Geodetic Survey), assisted by Tuwaletstiwa, and supplemented by William Stone (National Geodetic Survey). Other surveys were conducted by Robert and Helen Hughes and E. C. Saxton (Sandia National Laboratories); C. Donald Encinias and William Kuntz, with the cooperation of Basil Pouls (Koogle and Pouls Engineering, Inc.); James Crowl and associates (Rio Grande Surveying Service); Scott Andrae (La Plata, NM), assisted by Dabney Ford (National Park Service) and Reid Williams (Rensselaer Polytechnic Institute); and William Mahnke (Farmington, NM).

Michael Marshall (Cibola Research Consultants) shared with us his comprehensive knowledge of Chacoan archaeology, and his keen insights into the Chacoans' use of topography. Stephen Lekson's (University of Colorado) extensive knowledge of the major buildings in Chaco Canyon was invaluable to us. We also benefited from many helpful discussions regarding Chacoan archaeology with John Roney (Bureau of Land Management), Dabney Ford, and Thomas Windes (National Park Service). LeRoy Doggett (U.S. Naval Observatory), Bradley Schaefer (Goddard Space Flight Center), and the late Gerald Hawkins (Washington, DC) assisted with a number of points concerning the naked-eye astronomical observations. Crawford MacCallum (University of New Mexico) photographed the moonrise under unusual lighting conditions.

We thank J. McKim Malville (University of Colorado) for a number of interesting discussions and a tour of several northern prehistoric puebloan building complexes, where he has identified astronomical building orientations and interbuilding relationships, and Murray Gell-Mann (Santa Fe Institute) for joining us for a tour of several major Chacoan buildings and contributing stimulating and encouraging comments on our early analysis of possible astronomical significance in the Chacoan architecture.

William Byler (Washington, DC) once more gave us extremely generous and thoughtful assistance in editing the final manuscript that was published in Morrow and Price's 1997 edited volume by the University of New Mexico Press. The graphics were prepared by Suzanne Samuels (By Design Graphics) and by Fabian Schmid with the cooperation of Davis, Inc. (Washington, DC).

The fieldwork in Chaco Canyon was done with the helpful cooperation of former superintendents, Thomas

Vaughan and Larry Belli, with the thoughtful guidance of National Park Service archaeologist Dabney Ford, and with the generous assistance of many other staff members of Chaco Culture National Historical Park.

NOTES

1. For convenience the reader can find most of these papers on the Solstice Project's website: www.solstice project.org.

2. The long back walls of five of the ten major buildings located in Chaco Canyon are somewhat parallel to local segments of the north canyon wall. Since there are innumerable locations along this canyon wall where significantly different orientations occur and where these buildings could have been placed, this approximate parallel relationship does not appear to have been a constraint on the orientations of these five buildings.

3. In the literature of Chacoan studies, we find one suggestion of a utilitarian reason for the location of the major buildings, and it applies to only one building. Specifically, it has been suggested that Tsin Kletzin was placed to optimize the direct sight lines to six other buildings (Lekson 1984:231). A suggestion by Judge (1989) that three major buildings "functioned primarily as storage sites to accompany resource pooling and redistribution within the drainage systems they 'controlled'" locates them only generally.

4. For an example of a nonutilitarian Chacoan road, see Dabney Ford's finding of a road connecting the canyon floor with the three-slab site on Fajada Butte (Ford 1993).

5. In addition, the relationship of Pueblo Bonito's design to the solar cycle appears to be symbolically represented in a petroglyph on Fajada Butte in Chaco Canyon. (Sofaer and Sinclair 1989:499; Sofaer 2006).

6. "Sensible horizon" describes the circle bounding that part of the earth's surface if no irregularities or obstructions are present. "Visible horizon" describes the horizon that is actually seen, taking obstructions, if any, into account.

7. It would seem unlikely that the Chacoans, who incorporated cardinal orientations in their architecture, and who also marked the equinoxes and meridian passage in light markings, did not associate the north-south axis with the sun's meridian passage and the east-west axis with the sun's rising and setting positions at equinox.

8. See also Lekson 1991: "Using intrinsic criteria, one could argue that only the Big Four (Salmon Ruin, Aztec, Pueblo Pintado, and Kin Bineola) . . . were identical to Pueblo Bonito and Chetro Ketl." Eventually, the Solstice Project will also study the "medium-size" (Powers et al. 1983) and the more remote Chacoan buildings for possible astronomical significance.

9. In most cases the longest wall is obvious. For the orientation of Pueblo Pintado, values were taken for the longer of the two walls and the perpendicular to it. For Kin Kletso, the orientations of the two long walls of equal length, which differed in orientation by only 0.8°, were averaged. Kin Bineola's principal wall is not a straight wall, but three sections, which vary by several degrees. The sections were averaged in the value given here, and the error quoted (±3°) reflects the differences in the sections.

10. The Solstice Project notes that other scholars have described the cardinal orientation of Pueblo Bonito by the direction of this primary interior wall and the direction of the western half of the south wall (Williamson et al. 1975, 1977). The eastern half of the south wall, which is not perpendicular to the primary interior wall and is oriented to 85.4°, is a curious departure from these perpendicular relationships.

11. The orientation of Hungo Pavi as reported here corrects an error in an earlier paper (Sofaer, Sinclair, and Donahue 1991). The orientations of nine other major Chacoan buildings are also reported here with slightly different values than those reported in the earlier paper. These changes are the result of certain refinements in a further reduction of the Solstice Project's survey data. The changes, unlike in the case of Hungo Pavi, are so slight (from 0.1° to 0.7°) that they do not affect the conclusions.

12. It is of interest that a unique and extensive construction of the Chacoan culture, the Chetro Ketl "field," which is a grid of low walls covering more than twice the land area of the largest Chacoan building, appears also to be oriented to the azimuth of the lunar minor standstill. This construction was reported to have an orientation of −67° (Loose and Lyons 1977). It should be further noted that the Solstice Project's survey found that the orientation of the perpendicular of Kin Klizhin, a tower kiva located 10 km from Chaco Canyon, is −65°, an azimuth also close to the azimuth of the lunar minor standstill.

13. In certain of the Solstice Project's earlier studies of Chacoan constructions, an emphasis was given to substantiating claims of accurate alignments. The author

believes that this focus sometimes blinded us in our search for the significance of the orientations and relationships developed by this prehistoric and traditional society, to whom symbolic incorporation of astronomical relationships would have been at least as important as the expression of optimal accuracy. In addition, in several instances, the Project's studies have shown that alignments (such as the north orientation of the Great North Road) are adjusted off of precise astronomical direction in order to incorporate other symbolic relationships (Sofaer, Marshall, and Sinclair 1989).

14. The preliminary results of the Solstice Project's study of elevated horizons that are near certain of the major buildings show that from eight of these eleven buildings both the rising and setting astronomical events occur within 1° to 3° of the building orientations.

15. The preliminary results of the Solstice Project's current study show that none of the other thirteen buildings is oriented, as Hungo Pavi is, to an astronomical event on only the visible and not the sensible horizon.

16. The Solstice Project finds that the orientation of Wijiji, which is approximately 6.5° off of the cardinal directions, is also close to the orientation of New Alto, Aztec East, and the east and north walls of the great kiva of Pueblo Bonito, as well as the orientation of several interbuilding relationships. Although there is no obvious astronomical reason for the selection of this azimuth for building orientations and interrelationships, its repetition indicates that it may have been significant to the Chacoans. In addition, at Wijiji at winter solstice the sun is seen rising in a crevice on the horizon (Malville 2005:75). The Solstice Project survey shows that the alignment from Wijiji to this event is also the diagonal of the building. Other instances of astronomical orientation of the diagonals of the buildings are discussed in the next section of this chapter.

17. Because of the deterioration of one of its short walls, Chetro Ketl has only one measurable diagonal angle.

18. The Chacoans may have had additional reasons to consistently choose angles of approximately 23° and 36°. It has been suggested that these angles were also used by a Mesoamerican culture (Clancy 1994; Harrison 1994).

It is of interest that only at locations close to the latitude of Chaco Canyon (i.e., 36°) do the angles of 23° and 36° correspond with the relationships of the cardinal directions and the lunar major and minor standstill azimuths. In addition, at the latitude of 36° at solar noon on equinox day, the shadow of a stick or other vertical object cast on a flat surface forms a right angle triangle that has the internal angles of 36° and 54°. The correspondence of the internal angles of the major Chacoan buildings with angles apparently favored by a Mesoamerican culture, as well as with the angles evident in the solar and lunar astronomy that occurs only close to the latitude of Chaco, raises intriguing questions. It may be that Chaco Canyon was selected as the place, within the broader cultural region of Mesoamerica, where the relationships of the sun and the earth, and the sun and the moon, could be expressed in geometric relationships that were considered particularly significant.

Of further interest is one archaeologist's discussion of the location of Chaco Canyon and Casas Grandes, a postclassic Mesoamerican site, on the same meridian. He suggests that this correspondence may have been an intentional aspect of the locating of Casas Grandes (Lekson 1996). Casas Grandes is 630 km south of Chaco Canyon.

19. The Solstice Project's further study of the internal design of the major Chacoan buildings suggests that one of the solar-lunar angles found in the rectangular buildings, 36°, is also incorporated in the design of three other major buildings (Pueblo Bonito, Peñasco Blanco, and Una Vida) and that Kin Bineola's design (like Aztec I and II) incorporates 36° as well as 24°. In addition, in several of these buildings the solar-lunar geometry is combined with orientational relationships to both the sun and the moon (Sofaer 1994). It also is of interest that three great kivas in Chaco Canyon are organized in geometric patterns of near-perfect squares and circles. This further geometric study of Chacoan architecture will be presented in work that is in preparation by the Solstice Project.

20. The Solstice Project also found that cardinal interbuilding lines relate two minor buildings located in the central canyon to each other and to one of the major central buildings involved in the central cardinal patterning. The line between Casa Rinconada, the cardinally oriented great kiva, and New Alto aligns closely with the north-south axis of Casa Rinconada, and New Alto lies directly west of the cardinally oriented Pueblo Alto (Figures 9.2, 9.3, 9.9, and 9.10). An internal feature of Casa Rinconada appears to mark the kiva's north-south relationship with New Alto. The south stairway of Casa Rinconada is positioned slightly off the axis of symmetry of the kiva, and this stairway is also offset in the south doorway. The effect of the offset placement of this stairway is that from its center one

249

sees New Alto over the center of the north doorway on a bearing of 1.3°. (Although the construction of Casa Rinconada was completed before the construction of New Alto, it is possible that the position of the stairway within the south doorway of Casa Rinconada was modified at the time of New Alto's construction.)

Three long, low walls extending from Pueblo Alto (surveyed by the Solstice Project) are also cardinally oriented, and they appear to further elaborate the cardinal pattern of the central complex (Windes 1987).

21. The astronomical interbuilding bearings shown in Table 9.3 and in Figures 9.9 and 9.11 are defined as the bearings between two buildings that align (within 3°) with the rising or setting azimuths of the astronomical phenomena associated with one of the two buildings.

The Solstice Project identified the locations of the fourteen major buildings from the coordinates of the 7.5' topographic survey maps of the U.S. Geological Survey. The relative locations of certain of the central buildings were confirmed by direct surveying and by the use of existing aerial photography. The bearings of the interbuilding lines were taken from the estimated centers of the buildings. (The close relationship of two very large buildings, Pueblo Bonito and Chetro Ketl, introduced the only uncertainty. In this case, however, it was observed that each point in Chetro Ketl is due east of each point in Pueblo Bonito.) The relative locations of the buildings could be identified to within 15 m on the maps. The Solstice Project estimates that its measurements have a typical uncertainty in the bearing of an interbuilding line of 0° 12' at an average separation of 4.7 km for the ten buildings within the canyon, and much less uncertainty in the bearings of interbuilding lines extending outside the canyon.

22. The orientation of the perpendicular of Pueblo Pintado is to the azimuth that corresponds with a bearing to Salmon Ruin, 85 km from Pueblo Pintado; furthermore, the azimuth of the orientation of the perpendicular of Salmon Ruin also corresponds with this bearing. Perhaps these relationships were deliberately developed by the Chacoans to join two outlying major buildings that are oriented to the minor standstill moon on a bearing perpendicular to the azimuth of the minor standstill moon and to draw Salmon Ruin into connection with the central complex of Chaco Canyon, to which Pueblo Pintado is related by lunar minor standstill relationships (as is suggested elsewhere in this chapter).

23. It is of interest that the two other Chacoan constructions, the Chetro Ketl "field" and Kin Klizhin (a

tower kiva), that are oriented to the lunar minor standstill are also on the lunar minor standstill interbuilding bearings from the central complex to Kin Bineola and to Pueblo Pintado, respectively (see note 12).

24. The Solstice Project's preliminary investigations of several C-shaped, low-walled structures (Windes 1978) and three sets of cairns located in and near Chaco Canyon show that the bearings between these sites are oriented to the lunar major standstill. It is also of interest that several recent findings by others suggest astronomical relationships among sites within prehistoric pueblo building complexes, including one Chacoan building complex, in southwestern Colorado (Malville et al. 1991; Malville and Putnam 1989).

25. It is of interest that Ron Sutcliffe documented another interbuilding bearing: Peñasco Blanco to Casa Rinconada on the alignment to the rising of the southern major standstill moon, June 11, 2006.

26. Certain of the astronomical interbuilding relationships within the canyon, such as that between Una Vida and Peñasco Blanco, appear to correspond roughly with the topography of the canyon. While this correspondence suggests the possibility that the relationship between these buildings could have fallen into lunar alignment by coincidence, it does not explain the other interlocking aspects of these buildings, which suggest an intentional marking of the lunar major relationship between them. The relationships of the central complex to Pueblo Pintado and Kin Bineola on the lunar minor bearings are not affected by the canyon topography because these buildings are located beyond the canyon. The lunar minor relationships of the central complex to Hungo Pavi and Wijiji could have been affected in part by accommodation to the canyon topography. This would not discount the possibility that these relationships had lunar significance for the Chacoans.

27. Although the Solstice Project cannot be certain that all of the astronomical interbuilding bearings that are shown in Table 9.3 and Figure 9.11 were intentionally developed by the Chacoans, it seems important at this stage in our study to present all the interbuilding bearings that meet the criterion described above (see note 21).

One astronomical interbuilding bearing which has not been discussed in the text deserves particular note. Aztec, 86 km north of Pueblo Bonito, is located on a bearing from the central complex of Chaco that could have been regarded by the Chacoans as a continuation of the north-south axis of the central buildings and their interbuilding relationships (Table 9.3 and Figure 9.11). Certain analysis suggests that the north-south bearing between Chaco and Aztec had particular significance to the Chacoans. Aztec, itself a massive architectural complex, is regarded as an important late center of the Chacoan culture. An architectural study shows that Aztec appears to be "modeled on standards fixed in Pueblo Bonito" (Stein and McKenna 1988). An author of this latter study further notes that the core activity of the Chacoan culture moved in the late 1100s from Chaco Canyon to Aztec (Fowler and Stein 1992), and that this center maintained an active relationship with the canyon through the 1100s and 1200s (John Stein, personal communication 1996). Furthermore, another study suggests that a north-south alignment between Chaco Canyon and Casas Grandes, a Mesoamerican site 630 km south of Chaco, developed in the 1300s, extended the earlier north-south axis from Aztec through Chaco (Lekson 1996).

28. Preliminary results of the Project's study of elevated horizons in the views to astronomy from certain major buildings suggest that the orientations of most of the interbuilding bearings to astronomical events on the sensible horizon (as shown in Table 9.3) are within 3° of the same astronomical events on the visible horizon. Exceptions to this generality appear to be the interbuilding bearings from Pueblo del Arroyo and Peñasco Blanco to Kin Bineola, from Kin Kletso to Pueblo Alto, and from Chetro Ketl to Kin Kletso.

29. In regard to the techniques used for orienting and interrelating buildings on astronomical bearings, the Solstice Project's experiments have shown that the cardinal directions can be determined with shadow and light to within one quarter of a degree (Solstice Project, pre-published report 1988; see also Williamson 1984:144). Recordings of the shadows cast by a vertical object onto a flat surface during several hours of the sun's midday passage indicate the cardinal directions. If this were done at a site with flat horizons toward the lunar standstills, at the time of the lunar standstills on that same surface where the cardinal directions would be recorded, the azimuths of the rising and setting standstill moons could also be recorded. It is possible that the Chacoan architects and planners used such a recording of the solar-lunar azimuths for incorporating lunar orientations in their buildings and in the interrelationships of their buildings, instead of waiting for the recurrence of the lunar events on the local horizons. The wait for the recurrence of the lunar major standstill would be 18 to 19 years. The Solstice Project has also shown that interrelating the buildings which are not intervisible could have been done with quite simple intersite surveying techniques.

30. See note 5.

31. It has been suggested that the Mayas' interest in the lunar eclipse cycle may have involved knowledge of the lunar standstill cycle (Dearborn 1992). Floyd Lounsbury (personal communication 1982) expressed a similar opinion a number of years ago.

32. W. J. Judge and J. M. Malville speculate on Chaco as a center for lunar eclipse prediction (1993), and the Malvilles suggest that ceremonial pilgrimage to Chaco Canyon was scheduled to the solar and lunar cycles (Malville and Malville 1995).

33. For ethnographic reports on the cosmology of the historic Pueblo Indians, see Sofaer, Marshall, and Sinclair (1989); Sofaer and Sinclair (1987); Sofaer, Sinclair, and Doggett (1982); Sofaer, Zinser, and Sinclair (1979); and Williamson (1984).

34. M. C. Stevenson (1894:143): "The moon is father to the dead as the sun is father to the living."

35. Fred Eggan's studies of the Hopi "roads" suggested to him several parallels with the Chacoans' use of roads. Eggan noted that at Hopi the spirits of the dead emerge from the world below and travel on symbolic roads to visit with the living, and that the Great North Road of Chaco appears to have been built to join the ceremonial center symbolically with the direction north and with the world below (Fred Eggan, personal communication 1990).

36. Alfonso Ortiz, *The Sun Dagger* film (The Solstice Project 1982).

REFERENCES

Ahlstrom, Richard Van Ness
1985   *Interpretation of Archeological Tree-Ring Dates.* Ph.D. dissertation, University of Arizona, Tucson.
Aveni, Anthony F.
1980   *Skywatchers of Ancient Mexico.* University of Texas Press, Austin.
Broda, Johanna
1982   Astronomy, *Cosmovisión*, and Ideology in Prehispanic Mesoamerica. In *Ethnoastronomy and Archaeoastronomy in the American Tropics*, edited by Anthony F. Aveni and Gary Urton, pp. 81–110. Annals of the New York Academy of Sciences.
1993   Archaeoastronomical Knowledge, Calendrics, and Sacred Geography in Ancient Mesoamerica. In *Astronomies and Culture*, edited by C. Ruggles and N. Saunders, pp. 253–295. University Press of Colorado, Niwot.

251

Clancy, Flora S.

1994   Spatial Geometry and Logic in the Ancient Maya Mind. Part 1: Monuments. In *Seventh Palenque Round Table, 1989*, Merle Greene Robertson, gen. ed., Virginia M. Fields, vol. ed., pp. 237–242. Pre-Columbian Research Institute, San Francisco.

Cordell, Linda S.

1984   *Prehistory of the Southwest*. Academic Press, Orlando.

Crown, Patricia L., and W. James Judge, Jr.

1991   Synthesis and Conclusions. In *Chaco and Hohokam: Prehistoric Regional Systems in the American Southwest*, edited by Patricia L. Crown and W. James Judge, Jr., pp. 293–308. School of American Research Press, Santa Fe.

Dearborn, David D.

1992   To the Limits. *Archaeoastronomy and Ethnoastronomy News: Quarterly Bulletin of the Center for Archaeoastronomy* 3:1, 4.

Ford, Dabney

1993   The Spadefoot Toad Site: Investigations at 29SJ629. In *Marcia's Rincon and the Fajada Gap Pueblo II Community, Chaco Canyon, New Mexico*, edited by Thomas C. Windes, Vol. I, Appendix H. Reports of the Chaco Center 12. National Park Service, Albuquerque.

Fowler, Andrew P., and John Stein

1992   The Anasazi Great House in Time, Space, and Paradigm. In *Anasazi Regional Organization and the Chaco System*, edited by David E. Doyel, pp. 101–122. Maxwell Museum of Anthropology, Anthropological Papers 5. University of New Mexico, Albuquerque.

Fritz, John M.

1978   Paleopsychology Today: Ideational Systems and Human Adaptation in Prehistory. In *Social Archeology, Beyond Subsistence and Dating*, edited by Charles L. Redman et al., pp. 37–59. Academic Press, New York.

Harrison, Peter D.

1994   Spatial Geometry and Logic in the Ancient Mayan Mind. Part 2: Architecture. In *Seventh Palenque Round Table, 1989*, Merle Greene Robertson, gen. ed., Virginia M. Fields, vol. ed., pp. 243–252. Pre-Columbian Research Institute, San Francisco.

Hawkins, Gerald S.

1973   *Beyond Stonehenge*. Harper and Row, New York.

Judge, W. James, Jr.

1984   New Light on Chaco Canyon. In *New Light on Chaco Canyon*, edited by David G. Noble, pp. 1–12. School of American Research Press, Santa Fe.

1989   Chaco Canyon—San Juan Basin. In *Dynamics of Southwest Prehistory*, edited by Linda S. Cordell and George J. Gumerman, pp. 209–262. Smithsonian Institution Press, Washington, DC.

Judge, W. James, Jr., and J. McKim Malville

2004   Calendrical Knowledge and Ritual Power. In *Chimney Rock: The Ultimate Outlier*, edited by J. McKim Malville, pp. 151–163. Lexington Books, Lanham, MD.

Kincaid, Chris, editor

1983   *Chaco Roads Project Phase I: A Reappraisal of Prehistoric Roads in the San Juan Basin*. Bureau of Land Management, Albuquerque.

Lekson, Stephen H.

1984   *Great Pueblo Architecture of Chaco Canyon*. National Park Service, Albuquerque.

1991   Settlement Patterns and the Chacoan Region. In *Chaco and Hohokam: Prehistoric Regional Systems in the American Southwest*, edited by P. L. Crown and W. J. Judge, Jr., pp. 31–56. School of American Research Press, Santa Fe.

1996   Chaco and Casas. Paper presented at the 61st Annual Meeting of the Society for American Archeology.

Lekson, Stephen H., Thomas C. Windes, John R. Stein, and W. James Judge Jr.

1988   The Chaco Canyon Community. *Scientific American* (July):100–109.

Loose, Richard W., and Thomas R. Lyons

1977   The Chetro Ketl Field: A Planned Water Control System in Chaco Canyon. In *Remote Sensing Experiments in Cultural Resource Studies*, assembled by Thomas R. Lyons, pp. 133–156. Reports of the Chaco Center 1, National Park Service, Washington, DC.

McCluskey, Stephen C.

1977   The Astronomy of the Hopi Indians. *Journal for the History of Astronomy* 8:174–195.

Malville, J. McKim

2005   Ancient Space and Time in the Canyons. In *Canyon Spirits: Beauty and Power in the Ancestral Puebloan World*, essays by S. H. Lekson and J. M. Malville, photographs by J. L. Ninnemann, foreword by F. C. Lister, pp. 65–86, University of New Mexico Press, Albuquerque.

1993   Astronomy and Social Integration among the Anasazi. In *Proceedings of the Anasazi Symposium, 1991*, edited by Jack E. Smith and Art Hutchinson, pp. 155–166. Mesa Verde Museum Association.

Malville, J. McKim, and Nancy J. Malville

1995   Pilgrimage and Astronomy at Chaco Canyon, New Mexico. Paper presented at the National Seminar on Pilgrimage, Tourism, and Conservation of Cultural Heritage, January 21–23, Allahabad, India.

Malville, J. McKim, and Claudia Putnam

1989   *Prehistoric Astronomy in the Southwest*. Johnson Books, Boulder.

252

Anna Sofaer

Malville, J. McKim, Frank W. Eddy, and Carol Ambruster
1991   Moonrise at Chimney Rock. *Journal for the History of Astronomy* (Supplement 1b: *Archeoastronomy*) 16:S34–S50.

Marshall, Michael P.
1997   The Chacoan Roads—A Cosmological Interpretation. In *Anasazi Architecture and American Design*, edited by Baker H. Morrow and V. B. Price, pp. 62–74. University of New Mexico Press, Albuquerque.

Marshall, Michael P., and David E. Doyel
1981   An Interim Report on Bis sa'ni Pueblo, with Notes on the Chacoan Regional System. Ms. on file, Navajo Nation Cultural Resource Management Program, Window Rock, AZ.

Marshall, Michael P., John R. Stein, Richard W. Loose, and Judith E. Novotny
1979   *Anasazi Communities of the San Juan Basin.* Public Service Company of New Mexico, Albuquerque.

Morrow, Baker H., and V. B. Price, eds.
1997   *Anasazi Architecture and American Design.* University of New Mexico Press, Albuquerque.

Neitzel, Jill
1989   The Chacoan Regional System: Interpreting the Evidence for Sociopolitical Complexity. In *The Sociopolitical Structure of Prehistoric Southwestern Societies*, edited by Steadman Upham, Kent G. Lightfoot, and Roberta A. Jewett, pp. 509–556. Westview Press, Boulder.

Powers, Robert P., William B. Gillespie, and Stephen H. Lekson
1983   *The Outlier Survey: A Regional View of Settlement in the San Juan Basin.* National Park Service, Albuquerque.

Reyman, Jonathan E.
1976   Astronomy, Architecture, and Adaptation at Pueblo Bonito. *Science* 193:957–962.

Roney, John R.
1992   Prehistoric Roads and Regional Integration in the Chacoan System. In *Anasazi Regional Organization and the Chaco System*, edited by David E. Doyel, pp. 123–132. Maxwell Museum of Anthropology, Anthropological Papers 5. University of New Mexico, Albuquerque.

Sebastian, Lynne
1991   Sociopolitical Complexity and the Chaco System. In *Chaco and Hohokam: Prehistoric Regional Systems in the American Southwest*, edited by Patricia L. Crown and W. James Judge, Jr., pp. 107–134. School of American Research Press, Santa Fe.
1992   Chaco Canyon and the Anasazi Southwest: Changing Views of Sociopolitical Organization. In *Anasazi Regional Organization and the Chaco System*, edited by David E. Doyel, pp. 23–34. Maxwell Museum of Anthropology, Anthropological Papers 5. University of New Mexico, Albuquerque.

Sinclair, Rolf M., and Anna Sofaer
1993   A Method for Determining Limits on the Accuracy of Naked-Eye Locations of Astronomical Events. In *Archaeoastronomy in the 1990s*, edited by Clive Ruggles, pp. 178–184. Group D Publications, Loughborough, UK.

Sinclair, Rolf M., Anna Sofaer, John J. McCann, and John J. McCann, Jr.
1987   Marking of Lunar Major Standstill at the Three-Slab Site on Fajada Butte. *Bulletin of the American Astronomical Society* 19:1043.

Sofaer, Anna
1994   Chacoan Architecture: A Solar-Lunar Geometry. In *Time and Astronomy at the Meeting of Two Worlds*, edited by Stanislaw Iwaniszewski et al., pp. 265–278. Warsaw University, Poland.
1997   The Primary Architecture of the Chacoan Culture: A Cosmological Expression. In *Anasazi Architecture and American Design*, edited by Baker H. Morrow and V. B. Price, pp. 88–130. University of New Mexico Press, Albuquerque.
2006   Pueblo Bonito Petroglyph on Fajada Butte: Solar Aspects. In *Celestial Seasonings: Connotations of Rock Art, 1994 IRAC Proceedings*, Rock Art-World Heritage, edited by E. C. Krupp, pp. 397–402. American Rock Art Research Association, Phoenix.

Sofaer, Anna, and Rolf M. Sinclair
1987   Astronomical Markings at Three Sites on Fajada Butte. In *Astronomy and Ceremony in the Prehistoric Southwest*, edited by John Carlson and W. James Judge Jr., pp. 43–70. Maxwell Museum of Anthropology, Anthropological Papers No. 2. University of New Mexico, Albuquerque.
1989   An Interpretation of a Unique Petroglyph in Chaco Canyon, New Mexico. In *World Archaeoastronomy*, edited by Anthony F. Aveni, p. 499. Cambridge University Press, Cambridge.

Sofaer, Anna, Michael P. Marshall, and Rolf M. Sinclair
1989   The Great North Road: A Cosmographic Expression of the Chaco Culture of New Mexico. In *World Archaeoastronomy*, edited by Anthony F. Aveni, pp. 365–376. Cambridge University Press, Cambridge.

Sofaer, Anna, Rolf M. Sinclair, and LeRoy Doggett
1982   Lunar Markings on Fajada Butte, Chaco Canyon, New Mexico. In *Archaeoastronomy in the New World*, edited by Anthony F. Aveni, pp. 169–181. Cambridge University Press, Cambridge.

Sofaer, Anna, Rolf M. Sinclair, and Joey B. Donahue
1991   Solar and Lunar Orientations of the Major Architecture of the Chaco Culture of New Mexico. In *Colloquio Internazionale Archeologia e Astronomia*, edited by G. Romano and G. Traversari, pp. 137–150. Rivista di Archaeologia, Supplementi 9, edited by Giorgio Bretschneider. Rome, Italy.

253

Sofaer Anna, Rolf M. Sinclair, and Reid Williams

1987   A Regional Pattern in the Architecture of the Chaco Culture of New Mexico and its Astronomical Implications. *Bulletin of the American Astronomical Society* 19:1044.

Sofaer, Anna, Volker Zinser, and Rolf M. Sinclair

1979   A Unique Solar Marking Construct. *Science* 206:283–291.

Stein, John R.

1989   The Chaco Roads—Clues to an Ancient Riddle? *El Palacio* 94:4–16.

Stein, John R., and Stephen H. Lekson

1992   Anasazi Ritual Landscapes. In *Anasazi Regional Organization and the Chaco System*, edited by David E. Doyel, pp. 87–100. Maxwell Museum of Anthropology, Anthropological Papers 5. University of New Mexico, Albuquerque.

Stein, John R., and Peter J. McKenna

1988   *An Archaeological Reconnaissance of a Late Bonito Phase Occupation near Aztec Ruins National Monument.* National Park Service, Southwest Cultural Resource Center, Santa Fe.

Stein, John R., Judith E. Suiter, and Dabney Ford

1997   High Noon in Old Bonito: Sun, Shadow, and the Geometry of the Chaco Complex. In *Anasazi Architecture and American Design*, edited by Baker H. Morrow and V. B. Price, pp. 133–148. University of New Mexico Press, Albuquerque.

Stevenson, Mathilda Coxe

1894   The Sia. In *Eleventh Annual Report of the Bureau of Ethnology*. Smithsonian Institution, Washington, DC.

Tedlock, Barbara

1983   Zuni Sacred Theater. *American Indian Quarterly* 7:93–109.

Toll, Henry Walcott

1991   Material Distributions and Exchange in the Chaco System. In *Chaco and Hohokam: Prehistoric Regional Systems in the American Southwest*, edited by Patricia L. Crown and W. James Judge, Jr., pp. 77–108. School of American Research Press, Santa Fe.

Vivian, R. Gwinn

1990   *The Chacoan Prehistory of the San Juan Basin.* Academic Press, San Diego.

Williamson, Ray A.

1984   *Living the Sky.* Houghton Mifflin, Boston.

Williamson, Ray A., Howard J. Fisher, and Donnel O'Flynn

1977   Anasazi Solar Observatories. In *Native American Astronomy*, edited by Anthony F. Aveni, pp. 203–218. University of Texas Press, Austin.

Williamson, Ray A., Howard J. Fisher, Abigail F. Williamson, and Clarion Cochran

1975   The Astronomical Record in Chaco Canyon, New Mexico. In *Archaeoastronomy in Pre-Columbian America*, edited by Anthony F. Aveni, pp. 33–43. University of Texas Press, Austin.

Windes, Thomas C.

1978   *Stone Circles of Chaco Canyon, Northwestern New Mexico.* Reports of the Chaco Center No. 5, Division of Chaco Research, National Park Service, Albuquerque.

1987   *Investigations at the Pueblo Alto Complex, Chaco Canyon, New Mexico, 1975–1979.* Vol. 1: *Summary of Test and Excavations at the Pueblo Alto Community.* Publications in Archeology 18F. National Park Service, Santa Fe.

Zeilik, Michael

1984   Summer Solstice at Casa Rinconada: Calendar, Hierophany, or Nothing? *Archaeoastronomy* 7:76–81.

254

Wendy Ashmore
Department of Anthropology
University of California, Riverside
Riverside CA 92521-0418
wendy.ashmore@ucr.edu

Taft Blackhorse, Jr.
GreatHouse Environmental, LLC
PO Box 919
Fort Defiance, AZ 86504

Dra. Patricia Fournier
División de Posgrado
Escuela Nacional de Antropología e Historia
A.P. 86-098
México D.F. 14391, MEXICO
pat_fournier@yahoo.com

Rich Friedman
City of Farmington
GIS Division
Farmington, NM 87401
RFriedman@fmtn.org

Stephen H. Lekson
Curator of Anthropology
University Museum UCM 218
University of Colorado, Boulder
Boulder, CO 80309
Lekson@colorado.edu

Richard W. Loose
Organ Mountain Research
PO Box 278
Organ, New Mexico 88052
rloose@earthlink.net

Jill E. Neitzel
Assistant Professor
Department of Anthropology
University of Delaware
Newark, DE 19711

Anna Sofaer
Solstice Project
222 E Marcy St.
Santa Fe, NM 87501

John Stein
Navajo Nation Historic Preservation Department
Chaco Protection Sites Program
PO Box 4950
Window Rock, AZ 86515

Ruth M. Van Dyke
Assistant Professor
Department of Anthropology
Colorado College
14 E. Cache La Poudre St.
Colorado Springs, CO 80903

Thomas C. Windes
US National Park Service &
University of New Mexico
305 Richmond Dr. SE
Albuquerque, NM 87106
windes@unm.edu

INDEX

Numbers in italics indicate figures

adobe: and jacal structures in San
Juan Basin, 60–61; and walls of
early great houses, 52
Adler, Michael A., 118
agriculture, and Chetro Ketl field,
211. *See also* food and food processing
Akins, Nancy, 140, 141
Alta Vista (Mexico), 168, 169
American Museum of Natural History, 1, 129
amphitheater, between Chetro Ketl
and Pueblo Bonito, 206, 216
antechambers, of great kivas, 98,
101, 102, 104, 113, 115, 117
archaeology: and approaches to
room function, 13; and National
Park Service policy of preservation
at Pueblo Bonito, 142, 147; and
stratigraphy of mounds, 39. *See
also* burials; ceramics; middens
Archaeology of Chaco Canyon, The
(School of Advanced Research
Press 2006), 3–4
architecture. *See* earthen architecture;
great houses; great kivas; mounds;
kivas; pithouses and pitstructures;
platforms; plazas; remodeling;
rooms and roomblocks
artists, and popular images of precolumbian Southwestern architecture, 200
Ashmore, Wendy, 5
astronomical alignments: and ceremonial function of Pueblo Bonito,
135–36, 138, 143, 145–46, 187;
of Chetro Ketl field, 210–11; of
great kivas, 120; and location of
Pueblo Bonito, 186; and rear wall
of Chetro Ketl, 162, 163; Solstice
Project and analysis of in Chacoan
architecture, 225–47. *See also* cosmology; directional orientation
Aveni, Anthony E., 246
axis mundi, 183, 185. *See also* pine
tree
Aztec Ruins: and astronomical alignments, 233, 234, 235, 236, 237,
238, 250–51n27 and Chetro Ketl,
175n2; and great kivas, 117, 118;
and Great North Road, 175n2;
and Hubbard Triwall, 39, 40; and

room-wide platforms, 16; and
twelfth-century building forms, 38

balconies: and architectural form of
great houses, 10, 28; and rear wall
of Chetro Ketl, 164
Balcony House (Mesa Verde), 28
Basketmaker III period: and alignment of villages, 83; and
antecedents of great kiva, 94; and
linkages to past in Chacoan architecture, 120; and siting of great
houses, 144
Basso, Keith, 201
behavioral interpretations, of Pueblo
Bonito, 131–37. *See also* social
organization
benches: and features of round
rooms, 24, 26; and great kivas,
101, 104, 106, 113, 117
berms: and Chetro Ketl field, 210,
211; and Wetherill's Dam, 213–14
Bernardini, Wesley, 29, 146
Big Juniper House, 37
Bis sa'ani, 215
Blackhorse, Taft, 5, 217n2
Blinman, Eric, 55, 71, 81, 86
Bradfield, Wesley, 101
Bradley, Ronna J., 65, 66, 74, 86n1,
86n3
Broda, Johanna, 246
builder, architectural forms and role
of, 7, 9
building materials, and storage
rooms, 13, 14. *See also* adobe;
materials
burials: and ceremonial function of
Pueblo Bonito, 138–39, 140–41,
182, 183, 185; and mounds at
early great houses, 69
Burns, Barney Tillman, 49
Bustard, Wendy, 29, 144, 146, 182

calendric cycle, of community activity, 187–88
cannibalism, evidence for at Pueblo
Bonito, 138–39
Canyon de Chelly (Arizona), 146
cardinal alignments. *See* directional
orientation
Casa Abajo, 57, 66
Casa Chiquita, 37

Casa del Rio, 51, 57, 67–71, 84, 85
Casa Rinconada, 97: and astronomical alignments, 241, 249–50n20;
and great kivas, 112–14, 120, 183;
material requirements for construction of, 21; and mounds, 212;
possible "field" at, 219n5
Casas Grandes (Mexico), 249n18,
251n27
caves, in cliff face of downtown
Chaco, 205–206
Cedar Hill site, 55
ceiling, and features of round rooms,
25. *See also* roofs and roofing
Cemetery Ridge (New Mexico), 214,
215
ceramics: and architectural trends in
San Juan Basin, 52; and assemblages from Cibola tradition in
San Juan Basin, 45, 47; and evidence for migration at Pueblo Pintado, 81; and tri-walled structures
at Pueblo del Arroyo, 40
ceremonies: and chambers with
firepits, deflectors, and ventilators,
18; and cosmological expression in
Mesoamerica, 246; in great kivas,
118, 119; and role of Pueblo
Bonito as ceremonial center,
135–36, 137; and use of term *ceremonial center*, 147. *See also* ritual
Chaco Additions Survey, and great
kiva 29SJ2557, 116
Chaco Canyon. *See* astronomical
alignments; great houses; great
kivas; mounds; terrain model;
three-dimensional model
Chaco Culture National Historical
Park, 3
Chaco Halo: and contextual analysis
of Pueblo Bonito, 140; and great
kivas in outlier communities,
117
Chaco Project (1971–1986), 1, 3
Chaco Protection Sites Program
(CPSP), 3, 217n1
Chaco River, and San Juan Basin, 46,
70
Chaco Synthesis (1997–2004), 3–4
Chaco System, and origins of early
great houses, 48
Chacra Mesa, 97, 115–16

257

Chetro Ketl, 8, 9, *156*: and astronomical alignments, *233, 234, 235, 237, 238, 239, 241, 243*; changing faces of, 172–74; and Chetro Ketl field, 159, 209–11, 219, 248n12, 250n23; and colonnade, 14, 15, 166–70; and construction sequence, 32, 157–58, *160*; and Court Kiva, 27, 97, 101–102, 105–107, 165–66, 172, 173; description of, 155–57; eleventh-century building at, 33, 34, 35, 85; and firepits, 16; and great kivas, 20, 21, 97, 101–107, 165–66; history of research at, 157; and kiva features, 22, 23, 26, 165; and long, low walls, 41; and mealing bins, 18; and mounds, 38, 39; and plazas, 159–61, 164–65, 172, 174; and roads, 158–59, 170–71, 173–74; and room suites, 29–30; size and placement of rear rooms, 13, 14; and tower kiva, 21; and twelfth-century building, 37; ventilators and deflectors in rooms, 18; and viewscape, 158–72, 174–75n1–2
Chichen Itza (Yucatan), 168
chiefdoms, and interpretations of Chacoan social organization, 147
Chimney Rock (Colorado), 236, 244, 245
chronology. *See* dating
Chuska region: and immigration into interior San Juan Basin, 82; material culture and ties to Chaco Canyon, 81; roads between Chaco Canyon and, 67; and "sacred economy," 188
CKI and CKII great kivas (Chetro Ketl), 97, 101, 102–105
"clan kivas," 18, 20
cliff cavities, in cliff face between Kin Kletso and Chetro Ketl, 208–209
climate, and effect of freeze-and-thaw cycles on earthen architecture, 61
colonnade, at Chetro Ketl, 14, 15, 166–70
communications system, at Casa del Rio, 71. *See also* linescape; viewscape
Conant, Kenneth, 129
construction: schematic of for great houses, 8; sequence of at Chetro Ketl, 157–58, *160*. *See also* cost; labor; materials; remodeling
contextual analysis, of Pueblo Bonito, 137–41
Cooper, Laurel Martine, 182, 183, 194

copper, and ritual deposits at Pueblo Bonito, 139
cosmology: Chacoan expressions of solar and lunar, 245–47; importance of North in Chacoan, 83; parallels to Chacoan in Mesoamerica, 230, 246. *See also* ideology; symbolism
cost, of great kiva construction, 21. *See also* economy
Court Kiva (Chetro Ketl), 27, 97, 101–102, 105–107, 165–66, 172, 173
craft materials and production: evidence for at Casa del Rio, 70; and storage rooms, 13. *See also* ornament industry
Crown, Patricia L., 18–19, 120, 135, 144, 146, 172–73, 230

dating: of Chetro Ketl field, 211; of construction sequences at Chetro Ketl, 157; of great kivas in Chaco Canyon, 96; maps and reconstruction of Pueblo Bonito and, 127–31
Dean, Jeffrey S., 48, 191, 204
defense, and location of Pueblo Bonito, 138. *See also* violence
deflectors (fire screens): and function of rooms, 18, 23; and great kivas, 101, 102, 108, 113, 117
design and designers: architectural forms and role of, 7, 9; of Pueblo Bonito, 185–88
digital map, of Chaco Canyon landscape, 199–217
Di Peso, Charles C., 15, 166
directional orientation: and ceremonial function of Pueblo Bonito, 136, 138, 146, 187; of Chaco Amphitheater, 208; of early great houses, 57, 73; of great kivas, 117, 120; and importance of North in Chaco world, 183, 185; and relationships between major buildings of Chaco, 237–44; and siting of Pueblo Alto, 138; and solar cycle, 231; of Wetherill's Dam, 214. *See also* astronomical alignments; landscape; viewscape
Dolores River Valley, and early great houses, 58, 60–64
Doxtater, Dennis, 146, 185, 186
Doyel, David E., 117, 230
Dresden Codex, 245
dualism: concept of in Chacoan worldview, 95; and ideology of great kivas, 119, 120–21; and interpretation of Pueblo Bonito, 146. *See also* symbolism

Duckfoot site, 50
Durand, Stephen, 143, 146
Dutton Plateau, and orientation of early great houses, 73

earthen architecture, in Chaco Canyon, 209–16. *See also* mounds; plazas
East Community, 57, 58, 60, 84, 85
economy: and assumption of redistribution in analysis of Chacoan, 147; Chuska Valley and "sacred," 188. *See also* exchange networks; labor; materials; trade and trade goods; wealth
Eggan, Fred, 251n35
El Cuarenta (Mexico), 169
Eliade, Mircea, 185, 186, 187
environment: of interior San Juan Basin, 48–49; reconstruction of built at Chaco, 202–203. *See also* climate; landscape
Escalante Ruin, 37
exchange networks, and contact between Mesoamerica and Southwest, 169. *See also* trade and trade goods

Fajada Butte, and astronomical symbolism in petrogylphs, 206, 230–31, 245, 248n5
Fajada Gap, and great kiva, 97, 114–15
Fajada South Fork community, 81
Fajada Wash, and 29MC184 site, 53–55
Farmer, James, 136, 138
Ferdon, Edward, 166
firepits and fireboxes: in Chacoan round room, 23; and function of great house rooms, 16–18; and great kivas, 101, 102, 105, 113, 114, 117
floor vaults: and features of round rooms, 23–24, 26; and great kivas, 98, 102, 105, 106, 113, 117, 118
food and food processing: and storage rooms, 13; and surpluses at Casa del Rio, 70, 73
Ford, Dabney, 32, 131, 136, 149n1, 181, 182, 187, 188, 248n4
form, of Chacoan architecture, 7–42
Fort Wingate, 117, *118*
Fournier, Patricia, 5
Fowler, Andrew P., 50, 186–87, 192, 211
Friedman, Richard, 5, 142
Fritz, John M., 183, 186, 188, 240
"Fritz line," 175n2, 188
front row rooms, 11, 12

"gateway communities," Pueblo Pintado and Kin Bineola as, 240
gender. *See* sex ratios
Gillespie, William B., 109
Gladwin, Harold Sterling, 214
Great Bend site, 51, 57, 79–81
great houses: approaches to interpretation of, 5, 41; architecture of early period in interior San Juan Basin, 45–86; astronomical alignments of outlying, 236; and definition of architectural tradition at Chaco, 1, 41; and description of architectural forms, 7–42; monumentality of, 4. *See also* Aztec Ruins; Casa Rinconada; Chetro Ketl; Hungo Pavi; Kin Bineola; Kin Kletso; Peñasco Blanco; Pueblo Alto; Pueblo Bonito; Pueblo del Arroyo; Pueblo Pintado; Tsin Kletzin; Una Vida; Wijiji
great kivas: antecedents of, 94–95; and architectural forms, 20–21; as characteristic of Classic Bonito phase of Chacoan architecture, 93; and community-level decision-making and dispute resolution, 83–84; conversion of Chaco-type round room to, 27; description of classic Chacoan, 95–117; and elevated plaza at Chetro Ketl, 165–66; and Pueblo Bonito as ceremonial center, 135; and social organization, 117–22
Great North Road, 170, 174, 175n2, 203, 231, 251n35. *See also* roads and road networks
great pitstructure, 94
Great Pueblo Architecture of Chaco Canyon (Lekson 1984), 4, 5
Great West Road, 67, 71, 78
grid network, and Chetro Ketl field, 210

Hanson, Julienne, 181
Hataalii (Navajo singers), 200, 201, 204, 206
Hawley, Florence M., 52, 98, 101, 104, 105
Hayes, Alden C., 112, 166
health, and evidence of social hierarchy from burials at Pueblo Bonito, 140
Hewett, Edgar Lee, 5, 99, 101, 104, 109, 113, 155, 164, 165, 166, 172
Hillier, Bill, 181
Hillside Ruin (Pueblo Bonito), 145, 205, 208–209, 212–13, 217
Hogback community, 57, 81, 83

Hohokam, 167, 169, 215
Holsinger, S. J., 28, 40
Hopi, 141, 245, 251n35
Hosta Butte, early great houses and view of, 65, 66, 73, 77
House of the Giant Midden, 51, 57, 65–66
households: and estimated population of Pueblo Bonito, 137; numbers of in early great houses, 83, 86n2; ratio of kivas to numbers of, 19–20. *See also* residences
House of the Weaver, 78
Hovenweep (Utah), 236
Hudelson, Sam, 101
Hudson, Dee, 136, 143
human sacrifice, evidence for at Pueblo Bonito, 138–39
Hungo Pavi, 9: and astronomical alignments, 233, 235, 236, 238, 239, 248n11, 249n15, 250n26; dating of initial construction at, 32; and eleventh-century building, 34, 85; and great kivas, 20, 21, 97, 109, *111*; and Salmon Ruins, 175n2
Hyde Exploring Expedition, 128–29

ideology, role of great kivas in Chacoan, 119–22. *See also* cosmology; symbolism
incidental rooms, 17, 28
isolationist model, of interaction between Southwest and Mesoamerica, 167

Jackson, William H., 52, 128, 129
Judd, Neil M., 14, 15, 16, 17, 18, 21, 24, 25, 26, 27, 33, 36, 39, 52, 83, 96, 97–98, 99, 129, 132, 134–35, 136, 138, 140, 144, 148, 149n2, 172, 181, 187, 190–91, 193, 204, 211, 212, 213, 214
Judge, W. James, Jr., 230, 248n3, 251n32
Julian, Hurst R., 208

Kearns, Tim, 67
Kelley, Klara, 217n2
Kern, Edward & Richard, 128
Keur, John, 142, 208
"keyhole" plan, of small round rooms, 27, 28
Kiatuthlanna Black-on-white ceramics, and House of the Great Midden, 66
Kievet, Karen A., 142, 146, 171, 174n1, 200
Kim-me-ni-oli Wash, and Casa del Rio, 71, 72

Kin Bineola, 51, 57, 74, 75: and astronomical alignments, 233, 235, 236, 238, 239, 240, 242, 243, 248n9, 250n26; and descriptions of early great houses, 72–73; and midden deposits, 84, 85; twelfth-century construction at, 38
Kin Kletso, 9: and astronomical alignments, 234, 235, 236, 238, 239, 248n9; and firepits in rooms, 16; and Fritz line, 175n2; and tower kiva, 21; and twelfth-century building forms, 37, 38
Kin Klizhin, 21, 55, 248n12, 250n23
Kin Nahasbas, 57–58, 97, 107–109, *110*
Kintigh, Keith W., 121
Kin Ya'a, 21
Kiva A (Pueblo Bonito), 97, 99–101
Kiva G complex (Chetro Ketl), 165, 172, 173
Kiva Q (Pueblo Bonito), 97–99
kivas: and elevated plaza at Chetro Ketl, 165, 172; and Pueblo Bonito as ceremonial center, 135, 144–45; ritual renewals of, 172–73; and round rooms, 18–20; and terminology, 10, 18, 20. *See also* great kivas; tower kivas
Kiva 2C (Pueblo Bonito), 97
Knowles, Ralph L., 163
Kohler, Timothy A., 71

labor, and construction: of elevated plaza at Chetro Ketl, 165, 174; of great kivas, 21; of Pueblo Bonito, 136, 140; of roads, 41
La Ferrería (Mexico), 168–69
Lake Valley site, 51, 57, 71–72, 85
landscape: and digital map of Chaco Canyon, 199–217; integration of into design of Pueblo Bonito, 145; of interior San Juan Basin, 48–49; and modification of early great houses, 66–67, 82; and mounds as cultural features, 49–51; and roads at Chetro Ketl, 170; and selection of location for Pueblo Bonito, 186–87. *See also* directional orientation; linescape; viewscape
La Quemada (Mexico), 168
laser scan, of Pueblo Bonito, 142
Leinau, Alice, 101
Lekson, Stephen H., 5, 36, 52, 82, 83, 96, 98, 99, 101, 102, 109, 112, 130, 133, 141, 142, 144, 149n1, 166, 172, 173, 174, 182, 185, 187, 191, 192, 230, 248n8
Levine, Francis, 213

linescape, of Chaco complex, 202–203, 216–17
Lino Gray ceramics, 45, 47
Lister, Robert H., 166
Lizard House Arroyo, 206
Location of High Devotional Expression (LHDE), 147, 186, 188
Loose, Richard W., 5, 210–11
Lounsbury, Floyd, 251n31
Love, David W., 211
Lowry Ruins, 117, *118*
Luhrs, Dorothy, 107, 108
Lumpkins, William, 136
lunar alignments. *See* astronomical alignments
Lyons, Thomas R., 210–11

macaws/parrots, 15, 139
Malville, J. M., 251n32
manos, 70, 73. *See also* food and food processing
Marshall, Anne, 146
Marshall, Michael P., 65, 66, 71, 73, 74, 77, 86n1, 86n3, 114, 115, 138, 143, 144, 145, 146, 185, 230
materials, and requirements for construction of Pueblo Bonito, 136, 143. *See also* building materials
Mathews, Tom W., 36
Mathien, F. Joan, 1, 3, 107, 108, 144
Maya, 183, 185, 245, 251n31. *See also* Chichen Itza
McElmo phase, and great house construction in twelfth century, 36, 37, 213
McKenna, Peter J., 81, 188, 211
McPhee Pueblo, 61–63
mealing bins, and room function, 18
measurement systems, and Pueblo Bonito, 136, 143
Mesa Verde region, and archetype of Chacoan round room, 22
Mesoamerica: and interpretations of great house architecture, 41; models of influence on Chacoan architecture, 166–69; parallels to Chacoan cosmology in, 230, 246. *See also* Maya
metates, 70, 73
Metcalf, Mary Patricia, 135, 136, 183, 190
Mexico. *See* Mesoamerica
Michoacan (Mexico), 169
middens: estimated volumes of, 86–87n3; and Great Bend site, 80; and interpretation of mounds, 38–39; at Kin Bineola, 75. *See also* mounds

migrations: and ceramics at Pueblo Pintado, 81; into interior San Juan Basin in late 800s, 82
Miller, James Marshall, 26, 101
Mills, Barbara, 146
Mindeleff, V., 200
"moat," at Chetro Ketl, 161–62
modifications: and development of Chacoan round room, 26; in form and design of Chacoan building, 9. *See also* remodeling
monumentality, of Chacoan great houses, 4
Morris, Earl H., 21, 101
Morris, Neal, 61
mounds: and architectural forms, 38–39; at Casa del Rio, 67, 69, 70–72; at Casa Rinconada, 212; and early great houses, 85; as features on cultural landscape, 49–51; at Hillside Ruin, 213; at McPhee Pueblo, 63–64; at Pueblo Alto, 38, 39, 212; at Pueblo Bonito, 38, 39, 85, 145, 192–93, 212; shaped hills and pyramids, 214–16. *See also* middens
Museum of New Mexico, 101

Nataanii Bikin, 215
National Geographic Society, 129, 204
National Park Service, 1, 3, 4, 109, 113, 142, 144, 148, 211, 216
Navajo, and oral traditions about Chaco, 3, 200, 201, 204–208, 211, 216, 217
Neitzel, Jill E., 5
Nelson, Ben, 147, 166
New Alto, 9, 37, 120, 175n2, 241, 249n20
niches. *See* wall niches
Nihwiilbiih (The Gambler), 201, 206, 217
north. *See* directional orientation
Northeast Foundation Complex, 194, 213
Northwest Great Kiva (Peñasco Blanco), 97

"Old Bonito," and Chacoan design problems in early 1000s, 34
oral history and oral traditions: and cosmology in Pueblo ceremony and myth, 246; and Navajo narratives on Chaco, 201–202, 212, 217
ornaments: at Casa del Rio, 70, 72; at 29MC184 settlement, 55. *See also* trade and trade goods; turquoise
Ortman, Scott G., 62

past, references and linkages to in Chacoan architecture, 120, 144, 175n2. *See also* Basketmaker III period; pithouses and pitstructures; Pueblo I period
patios, and viewscape at Chetro Ketl, 171–72
Peckham, Stewart, 73, 79
Peñasco Blanco, 9: and astronomical alignments, 233, 234, 235, 236, 240, 242, 243, 244, 245, 250n26; and changes in settlement patterns, 84; earliest structures at, 52, 55–61; and earthen architecture, 209; and eleventh-century building, 35, 36; and great kivas, 20, 21, 97, 109, 112; and linescape of Chaco complex, 217; and mounds, 38, 39, 51, 85; and Pueblo I villages, 175n2; and tenth-century building, 31, 32
Pepper, George H., 14, 129, 130, 144, *180*
Peregrine, Peter, 141
permanence, of architectural forms, 9
petroglyphs, and astronomical markings, 206, 230–31, 245, 248n5
Pierre's Ruin, 215
pilasters, and features of round rooms, 24, 26
pine tree, incorporation of into design of Pueblo Bonito, 135, 144, 187, 204
Piper, June-el, 3
pithouses and pitstructures: and antecedents of kiva, 18, 19, 20, 94, 95, 107; and Pueblo Bonito as ceremonial center, 135, 144–45
planning: of Chacoan building, 7, 9; of Pueblo Bonito, 185–88; of 29SJ834 and 29SJ835 sites, 215
platforms: and earthen architecture in Chaco Canyon, 209–16; at Hillside Ruin, 213; in rear rooms, 13, 14, 15–16
Plaza Great Kiva (Hungo Pavi), 97, 112
plazas: and architectural form of great houses, 30–31; at Chetro Ketl, 159–61, 164–65, 172, 174; at Pueblo Bonito, 31, 160, 190–91
Plog, Stephen, 145
Pochteca model, of Mesoamerican influence on Southwest, 167
population: estimates of at peak of Chacoan development, 230; and immigration into interior San Juan Basin, 82; of Pueblo Bonito, 136–37, 141, 149n2; of villages in

Dolores Valley, 62. *See also* households; migration

Postlethwaite, W. W., 101

pottery. *See* ceramics

power, great houses as architectural expressions of, 174

proportions, of great house rooms, 12, *13*

Proskouriakoff, Tatiana, 200

proto-urban settlement, Pueblo Bonito as, 141

public space, and social interpretation of Pueblo Bonito, 190–94

Pueblo I period, and linkages to past in Chacoan architecture, 120, 144, 175n2

Pueblo Alto, 9: and astronomical alignments, 234, 235, 236, 237, 238, 239, 240, 241, 244, 249–50n20; contemporary standards in excavation of, 146; defense and location of, 138; earlier structure under, 87n5; eleventh-century building at, 33, 34; and great kivas, 21; as key site integrating Chaco with San Juan Basin, 86; and long, low walls, 41; and McElmo structures, 175n2; and mounds, 38, 39, 212; and roads, 203; and room proportions, *13*; and room suites, 29; and types of rooms, 14–15, 16

Pueblo Bonito, 9, *58*, *206*, 229: and astronomical alignments, 233, 234, 235, 236, 237, 239, 241, 244, 245, 248n5, 248n10, 250n27; and contextual analysis, 137–41; earliest structures at, 52, 55–61; eleventh-century building at, 33–34, 35, 36; and filled constructions, 215; and firepits in rooms, 16–17; and function of rooms, 15, 16–17, 18; and future research directions, 141–49; and great kivas, 20, 21, 96–101; and Hillside Ruin, 212; history of architectural studies at, 127; and incidental rooms, 28; and location of Casa Rinconada, 120–21; and long, low walls, 41; maps, reconstructions, and dates of, 127–31; and mealing bins, 18; and mounds, 38, 39, 85, 145, 192–93, 212; and pine tree, 135, 144, 187, 204; and plazas, 31, 160, 190–91; and Pueblo I villages, 175n2; reconstruction of and analysis of chronology, 202; repetition of architectural characteristics of through Chaco region, 230; and

room heights, 12; and room proportions, *13*; and room suites, 29–30; and round rooms, 19, 25–26; and settlement patterns, 84; size and placement of rear rooms, 13–14; and small round rooms, 27–28; social and behavioral interpretations of, 131–37, 179–95; and tenth-century building, 31, 32; and Threatening Rock, 137–38, 142, 204–205, 213; and twelfth-century building, 37; ventilators and deflectors in rooms, 18

Pueblo Bonito: Center of the Chacoan World (Neitzel 2003), 5

Pueblo del Arroyo, 9, 229: and astronomical alignments, 233, 234, 235, 236, 237, 238, 239; and balconies, 28; and eleventh-century building, 35, 36; and firepits, 16; and Fritz line, 175n2; and room heights, 12; and room proportions, *13*; and room suites, 29; and tri-walled structures, 39–40; and twelfth-century building, 36–37

Pueblo Pintado: and astronomical alignments, 233, 234, 235, 236, 238–39, 240, 243, 249n9, 250n22, 250n26; ceramics and evidence for migration at, 81; and Willow Canyon community, 75

pyramids, and earthen architecture in Chaco Canyon, 214–16

Rabbit Ruin, 37

rear rooms: and room-wide platforms, 13, 14, 15–16; size of, 11, 12; as storage rooms, 13

rear wall, of Chetro Ketl, 162–64, 172

rectangular rooms, and architectural forms of great houses, 10, *11*

Redman, Charles L., 186

Reiter, Paul D., 25, 93, 96, 98, 101, 105, 107, 113

religion: and conservatism of architecture, 119; and storage rooms, 13. *See also* ceremonies; ritual

remodeling: in form and design of Chacoan building, 9; of great kivas, 96, 103–104, 108; at McPhee Pueblo, 61; and ritual renewal of kivas, 173. *See also* modifications

Renfrew, Colin, 147, 188

residences: great houses as elite, 136, 173; interpretation of kivas as, 173. *See also* households

reuse, of Pueblo Bonito after abandonment, 145

Reyman, Jonathan E., 137, 144

Richert, Roland, 113

ritual: and cyclical actions in construction of Chacoan great houses, 188; and deposits at Pueblo Bonito, 139; interpretation of great houses as centers of, 85; and mounds at early great houses, 69, 71; and public space at Pueblo Bonito, 190; and ritual renewal of kivas, 172–73; role of great kivas in, 118–19. *See also* ceremonies

roads and road networks: and architectural forms, 40–41; and astronomical alignments, 229–30; and Casa del Rio, 71; and Chetro Ketl, 158–59, 170–71, 173–74; and Hopi, 251n35; and House of the Great Midden, 67; and linescape of Chaco complex, 202, 216–17, 218n3; and rear row additions to great houses, 14; and 29MC184 community, 54. *See also* Great North Road; Great West Road

Roberts, Frank H. H., Jr., 40, 94, 99

roofs and roofing: and features of round rooms, 24; of great kivas, 98, 101, 103–104, 107, 113, 117

rooms and roomblocks: and balconies, 10, 28; definition of in Chaco context, 9–10; and great kivas, 20–21; proportions of, 12; and round rooms, 18–28; size of, 10–12, 17; and suites, 29–30; and terraces, 10, 28–29; types of, 12–20

round rooms: and Chacoan room types, 21–27; and eleventh-century building forms, 34, 36; interpretation of as kivas, 18–20; non-Chacoan type of, 27–28

Ruppert, Karl, 39–40

Salmon Ruin: and astronomical alignments, 233, 234, 235, 236, 237, 238, 239, 250n22; and great kivas, 117, *118*; Great North Road and form of, 175n2

San Juan Basin, 46, 226: and early great houses outside Chaco core, 65–81; and great kivas in outlier communities, 117; landscape and environmental setting of, 48–49; increase in settlement in late Pueblo/early Pueblo II period, 94–95; new-style structures and site clustering in late 800s, 46–48; position of Chaco Canyon at center of, 138; Puebloan occupation from Basketmaker II through Pueblo III period, 45

rooms, 24; and great kivas, 101, 102, 113, 118; and rooms with firepits, 17–18

Walsh, Oscar B., *131*

warfare. *See* defense; violence

wealth, and great kivas, 21. *See also* economy

Wetherill, Richard, 204

Wetherill's Dam, 213–14

White Mound Black-on-white ceramics, 45, 47

Wijiji, *9*: and astronomical alignments, 233, 235, 236, 238, 239, 249n16, 250n26; and building

forms in eleventh century, 35, 36; and building forms in twelfth century, 37; and Chacra Mesa, 115–16; and great kivas, 97

Williamson, Ray A., 231

Willow Canyon site, *57*, 73–79

Wills, W. H., 5, 18–19, 69, 120, 135, 144, 145, 146, 172–73, 187–88, 192

Wilshusen, Richard H., 55, 62, 65, 81, 83, 84, 86, 118

Wilson, C. Dean, 81, 83

Windes, Thomas, 5, 14, 32, 39, 94, 95, 107, 108, 112, 114, 115,

130–31, 135, 136, 137, 144, 149n1, 163, 173, 181, 182, 188, 191, 193, 194, 204, 211

wings, addition of in eleventh-century building, 34

Wiseman, Regge N., 49

Woods, Janet, 101

world-systems model, 167

"World Tree," 204. *See also* pine tree

Yellow Jacket Ruin, 20, 173

Zeilik, Michael, 187

Zuni, 22, 121, 141, 245